Eve and the Ne\

Anna Wheeler 1785–?

Emma Martin 1812–51

Robert Owen 1771—1858

Fanny Wright 1795–1852

EVE AND
THE NEW JERUSALEM

SOCIALISM AND FEMINISM
IN THE NINETEENTH CENTURY

BARBARA TAYLOR

Harvard University Press
Cambridge, Massachusetts
1993

The portraits of Anna Wheeler and Emma Martin on the
frontispiece, and the facsimile of Catherine Barmby's
tract "The Demand for the Emancipation of Woman,"
are reproduced by kind permission of the Goldsmiths'
Library, University of London.

First Harvard University Press paperback edition, 1993

Library of Congress Cataloging-in-Publication Data

Taylor, Barbara, 1950–
    Eve and the New Jerusalem: socialism and feminism
    in the nineteenth century / Barbara Taylor.
        p. cm.
    Originally published: London : Virago Press, 1983.
    Includes bibliographical references and index.
    ISBN 0-674-27023-1
    1. Feminism – History – 19th century. 2. Women and
    socialism – History – 19th century. 3. Owen, Robert,
    1771-1858. 4. Collective settlements – History –
    19th century. 5. Utopian socialism – History –
    19th century. I. Title.

HQ1206.T33 1993   92-31980
305.42'09'034–dc20   CIP

CONTENTS

FOR GEORGE, TILLIE, AND LISE TAYLOR,
WITH LOVE

ACKNOWLEDGEMENTS

This book took many years to write – years in which its arguments were presented to dozens of feminist meetings, conferences and workshop discussions, in both Britain and America. Women in the London Feminist History Group heard the story of the Owenites in regular installments over the years, as did students who attended my adult education courses in women's history. One group of women spent twenty-four evenings in 1976 discussing the early Socialist feminists (shivering in the basement of the Essex Road Women's Centre) and I am particularly grateful to them. The critical support and encouragement I received on all these occasions kept the project alive. My biggest debt, then, is to the contemporary women's movement which has created so many platforms for feminist historical scholarship, and has given women like myself the confidence and motivation to speak from them.

The Canada Council for Research into the Social Sciences and Humanities funded the first four years of my research; thereafter the University of London Extra-Mural Department, the Workers Educational Association, and Bulmershe College of Higher Education (along with some discreet parental assistance) provided me with the income to finish it.

Eileen Yeo's wisdom, kindness and own brand of vigorous utopianism sustained me through the writing of the thesis (for the University of Sussex) on which the book is based. Trevor Evans has lived with the Owenites for almost as long as I have, and I thank him for his loving patience and support. Jane Caplan, Rosalind Coward, Leonore Davidoff, Catherine Hall, John F.C. Harrison, Michael Ignatieff, Cora Kaplan, Maureen Mackintosh, Jean McCrindle, Anne Phillips, Ellen Ross, Sheila Rowbotham,

Gareth Stedman Jones, Judith Walkowitz, and Stephen Yeo read and commented on parts or the whole of the manuscript, and I am deeply grateful for their good advice and warm fellowship. Ursula Owen and Ruthie Petrie made the editorial and publication processes a source of real pleasure for me. Librarians in the Goldsmiths' Collection at the University of London library carted heavy volumes of *The New Moral World* up and down many miles of stairs, and I thank them for it – particularly Miss Whitelegge. Finally, my friend and co-worker, Sally Alexander, has read most of what I've written for the last seven years, helped me disentangle my thoughts all along the way, given me whisky and encouragement when I needed it most, and taught me a good deal of what I know about being an historian, a teacher, and a sister.

INTRODUCTION

You look forward, as I do, to a state of society very different from that which now exists, in which the effort of all is to outwit, supplant and snatch from each other; where interest is systematically opposed to duty; where the so-called system of morals is little more than a mass of hypocrisy preached by knaves but unpractised by them, to keep their slaves, male as well as female, in blind uninquiring obedience; and where the whole motley fabric is kept together by fear and blood. You look forward to a better state of society, where the principle of benevolence shall supersede that of fear; where restless and anxious individual competition shall give place to mutual co-operation and joint possession; where individuals, in large numbers male and female, forming voluntary associations, shall become a mutual guarantee to each other for the supply of all useful wants . . . where perfect freedom of opinion and perfect equality will reign amongst the co-operators; and where the children of all will be equally educated and provided for by the whole . . . This scheme of social arrangements is the only one which will completely and for ever ensure the perfect equality and entire reciprocity of happiness between women and men.

(William Thompson to Anna Wheeler, 1825)

Political visions are fragile. They appear – and are lost again. Ideas formulated in one generation are frequently forgotten, or repressed, by the next; goals which seemed necessary and realistic to progressive thinkers of one era are shelved as visionary and utopian by their successors. Aspirations which find voice in certain periods of radical endeavour are stifled, or even wholly silenced, in others. The history of all progressive movements is littered with such half-remembered hopes, with dreams that have failed.

The socialist tradition, as it extends from the early nineteenth century to the present day, has been heavily marked by breaks, retreats, forgettings like these. Far from following a steady path of theoretical and strategical progress, socialist development has been characterized by ruptures so fundamental that they have often thrown into question not merely the means required to achieve common ends, but the ends themselves. The boundaries surrounding the socialist project have widened and narrowed as the ambitions shaping them have broadened or diminished.

No aspect of socialist tradition more clearly reveals this uneven, fractured history than its relationship to feminism.* Women have always played an important part in socialist organizations, but only at particular points have the independent aspirations of women – their aspirations to overturn their status as the 'second sex' – found a central place within socialist strategy. The Woman Question has moved in and out of socialist politics, leaving in its wake a host of unmet demands and unresolved questions – questions not only about present and potential relations between the sexes, but about the nature of the socialist enterprise itself.

Socialism emerged, in the early decades of the nineteenth century, as a humanist ideal of universal emancipation – the ideal of a communal society free of every inequality, including sexual inequality. 'The degree of emancipation of women is the natural measure of general emancipation,' Charles Fourier, one of the first French socialists, wrote;[1] and it was this commitment to female freedom as part of the wider struggle for human liberation which characterized this entire generation of socialist activists – from the followers of Fourier, Saint Simon and Cabet in France, to the American Fourierites and Transcendentalists, to the movement inspired by the Welsh factory-owner, Robert Owen, whose dream of a New Moral World of class and sex equality captured the imaginations of thousands of British

* The term 'feminism', it should be noted, was a late nineteenth century creation. (According to the *Oxford English Dictionary*, 'feminism' in the sense of 'the advocacy of the claims and rights of women' was not employed in England before 1895.) So its use in this book is an anachronism, justifiable on the grounds that for at least a century prior to the entry of the actual word into popular political discourse there existed the ideology which it described – a distinct and identifiable body of ideas and aspirations commonly known as 'the rights of women', the 'condition of women' question, the 'emancipation of women' and so on.

women and men for nearly a quarter century. This book is a study of the Owenite socialists, and their version of the early socialist-feminist ideal. It is an examination of how a vision – the vision of women's emancipation as an integral feature of a general social emancipation – arose, became part of the ideological armoury of a popular social movement, and inspired attempts to construct a new sexual culture in a society riven with sex- and class-based conflicts. It is also an exploration of the failure of that vision, and the significance of that failure for feminist socialist politics today.

The story of the Owenite movement has been persistently over-shadowed by the larger-than-life figure of its founder. Robert Owen (1771–1858) was the son of a Welsh saddler.[2] Born at a moment when the British industrial economy was rising on the tide of entrepreneurial enterprise, Owen rose with it, becoming (in his early twenties) manager of a Manchester cotton spinning company and eventually part-owner and manager of the huge New Lanark cotton mill near Glasgow. Such success stories were of course not uncommon at the opening of the mechanical age. But even among his fellow commercial pioneers Owen stood out as an exceptionally efficient and innovative capitalist – particularly when it came to managing what he described as the 'human capital' of the New Lanark workforce. Scottish workers (or so Owen claimed) were a notoriously feckless, undisciplined lot; but within a few years of Owen's takeover of the mill, there had been established a programme of work incentives and welfare measures (including model housing, health facilities and free schooling for the entire factory population) which transformed New Lanark into a triumph of social engineering – and one of the most profitable enterprises in the country. By the end of the Napoleonic Wars this display of (in Harriet Martineau's words) 'remarkable ability . . . in the conduct of the machinery of living'[3] had made Owen one of the most influential and respected industrialists in Europe, whose experiments in labour management attracted the attention of aspiring businessmen everywhere.

Yet it was precisely at this point that Owen took that startling detour which eventually set him on a wholly different path. The seeds of the change had already been sown in New Lanark, where success as a social administrator gradually bred in him (so he later recalled) the ambition not to be 'a mere manager of cotton mills' but 'to change the condition of the people':

> I saw all the steps in practice by which the change could be made
> . . . that if [the population of the world] were treated, trained,
> educated, employed, and placed, in accordance with the most plain
> dictates of common sense, crimes would terminate, the miseries of
> humanity would cease, wealth and wisdom would be universal . . .

With this, he had 'passed the rubicon': 'I should never cease my efforts to forward this change as long as life and health would admit.'[4]

Within a few years this resolution had transformed philanthropic Mr Owen of New Lanark into a fierce opponent of capitalism and full-time promoter of a new social order based on classless, co-operative communities. By 1824 he had given up commercial life entirely, travelling to America to try out his community schemes there and eventually returning to Britain to find himself at the head of a growing socialist movement. 'I had taken a most active part and a prominent lead in preparing the public mind for an entire change of system . . .'[5]

From this point onwards the story of Owen becomes the story of Owenism. As early as 1820 his publications had begun to attract a few adherents, mostly in the London radical intelligentsia. During his absence in America this small band of acolytes swelled into a national network of co-operative trading and manufacturing associations, all organized along collectivist lines and all working to accumulate sufficient funds for the establishment of Communities of Mutual Association. This early 'enthusiastic' phase of co-operative activity was succeeded by the militant trade union struggles of 1833–34, which in turn culminated in the establishment and demise of the first great attempt at a 'general union of the working classes', the Grand National Consolidated Trades Union. The collapse of the Consolidated Union in the summer of 1834 was followed by a brief period in which all Owenite activity ground to a near-halt; but then the phoenix of a new organization – the Association of All Classes of All Nations (AACAN) – rose from the ashes of general unionism to inaugurate a final decade of intense propagandistic and organizational activity. At the height of its strength in 1839–42 the AACAN (which soon became known as the Rational Society, or simply as Socialism*) had members in all parts of the country, and an influence which extended far beyond its formal membership, particularly in working-class districts. There was, as one newspaper noted during a high-point of AACAN recruitment, 'scarcely a town of any magnitude' in Britain without its Socialist contingent, busy preparing itself and its audiences for the New World to come.[6]

This is not to suggest (as some contemporary reports did) that Owenism was in any sense representative of working-class opinion, even radical working-class opinion, in the 1830s and 40s. At the peak of its popularity, early Socialism still remained a minority creed, drawing the bulk of its supporters from what Engels described as the 'most educated and solid elements' of the labouring population,[7] along with a substantial number of disaffected petit bourgeois intellectuals. These men and women were, and knew themselves to be, an iconoclastic vanguard whose views tended to be well in advance of even the most progressive-minded of their contemporaries. This was particularly true of their economic theories, their heterodox religious doctrines, and – above all – in their sexual politics, where the Owenite commitment to collectivized family life and female equality set them apart not only from their conservative opponents but also from most other radical movements of the period (including Chartism). It was, in the words of another sexual egalitarian, John Stuart Mill, 'to the signal honour' of the early Socialists 'that they assign [to women] equal rights, in all respects, with those of the hitherto dominant sex' at a time when most Britons were hostile or indifferent to women's plight; and for this, he suggested, they 'had entitled themselves to the grateful remembrance of future generations . . .'[8]

One hundred and fifty years later, however, it is precisely this aspect of Owenism – its theoretical and practical commitment to women's liberation – which is least remembered, least acknowledged, not only by academic historians but within the collective

* The term 'Socialist' was not widely used until the late 1830s, although it was first employed as early as 1827. In Britain, prior to 1850, it referred exclusively to the Owenites. In this book, I use the terms 'Owenite' and 'Socialist' (capitalized, since Socialist was then a formal, specific designation) interchangeably.

memory of the Left itself. Few studies of the movement mention it; almost none devote any serious attention to it.[9] Such forgettings are of course not uncommon in matters relating to women; the historical ear, at least until recently, has been tuned almost exclusively to the male voice. But the silence surrounding early socialist feminism reveals more than just the usual bland androcentricism of professional historians (including many radical historians). It is a symptomatic silence – one which reflects not ignorance or indifference but the character of the socialist tradition itself, as it has developed over the last century and a half.

To Robert Owen and his followers, particularly his feminist followers, socialism represented a struggle to achieve 'perfect equality and perfect freedom' at every level of social existence; a struggle which extended beyond the economic and political reforms necessary to create a classless society into the emotional and cultural transformations necessary to construct a sexual democracy. It was a style of radicalism which, as Engels noted critically, sought 'to emancipate all humanity at once' rather than 'a particular class to begin with',[10] and furthered this aim through a wholesale assault on all relations of dominance and subordination, including the 'tyrannical supremacy' of men over women. 'Whatever affects the condition of one sex, must, I conceive, affect the condition of the other,' one Owenite woman wrote in 1839:

> But a woman has been the slave of a slave . . . What is the result of [this]? . . . To create, by such arrangements, individual interest, till brothers and sisters, husbands and wives, look on each other with jealousy . . . to set up one half of the poor people against the other half, to subdue them and make them quiet . . .
>
> But . . . 'changes of no ordinary kind are at hand'. I perceive now that through the circulation of truth we are progressing towards the mansion of happiness, which, when gained, will . . . give emancipation to every human being from one end of the earth to the other . . . my tears flow when I compare this scene of confusion and opposition to that tranquil state of existence . . .[11]

Strategically, the success of such hopes was seen to depend on the power of 'benevolent reason' and practical co-operation to overwhelm the force of 'ignorant self-interest' and economic competition. The natural harmony of human needs would be realized through the peaceful suppression and replacement of all disharmonious ideas and institutions (including marriage and the family). It was this enthusiastic faith in the revolutionary potential of propaganda and example which led Marx and Engels, almost at the point of the movement's collapse, to condemn Owenism as 'Utopian'. The 'fantastic' dreams of the early socialists were 'foredoomed' to failure, they argued in *The Communist Manifesto* (and later, in Engels' case, in *Socialism: Utopian and Scientific*) because they were based merely on an optimism of the will rather than a 'scientific' assessment of the historical balance of class forces. The role of class antagonisms and class militancy in the transition to socialism was ignored: 'Historical action is to yield to their personal inventive action, historically created conditions of emancipation to fantastic ones, and the gradual, spontaneous organization of the proletariat to an organization of society specially contrived by these inventors.'[12] Nonetheless, if the Owenites' *strategy* was thus fatally flawed, their *aspirations* were still to be admired, particularly their proposals for socialized industry, decentralized government and – notably – 'the abolition of the family' and 'bourgeois marriage' which to Marx and Engels (as to the Owenites) represented little more than the legalized prostitution of women. Such doctrines provided 'most valuable materials for the enlightenment of the working class' they conceded.[13]

The concession was by no means a minor one. Yet over the years it has been largely forgotten, and what has remained in its stead is an increasingly rigid distinction between 'primitive' idealist Utopianism and the Scientific politics of proletarian communism – a distinction which acquired increased popularity after 1880 as organized (male) labour emerged as a key protagonist in the arena of national and international politics. The accelerating contest between capital and labour became the central axis on which all socialist strategies (non-Marxist as well as Marxist) turned, with every other struggle subordinated to that 'world-historical' battle.[14] The Owenite call for a multi-faceted offensive against all forms of social hierarchy, including sexual hierarchy, disappeared – to be replaced with a dogmatic insistence on the primacy of class-based issues, a demand for sexual unity in the face of a common class enemy, and a vague promise of improved status for women 'after the revolution'. This contraction of strategical imperatives was accompanied by a narrowing of theoretical alternatives as well. In place of the programme for a transformed personal and cultural existence which had been so central to pre-1850 socialism there gradually emerged, in all too many organizations, what William Morris condemned as a 'utilitarian sham Socialism' divested of any genuinely libertarian aims;[15] or what his twentieth century disciple, E.P. Thompson, has characterized as

> the whole problem of the subordination of the imaginative utopian faculties within the later Marxist tradition; its lack of a moral self-consciousness or even a vocabulary of desire, its inability to project any images of the future or even its tendency to fall back in lieu of these upon the utilitarian's earthly paradise – the maximisation of economic growth.[16]

The consequences of this development for feminism and feminists are still being felt in socialist organizations today. As the utopian imagination faded, so also did the commitment to a new sexual order. As the older schemes for emancipating 'all humanity at once' were displaced by the economic struggles of a single class, so issues central to that earlier dream – marriage, reproduction, family life – were transformed from political questions into 'merely private' ones, while women who persisted in pressing such issues were frequently condemned as bourgeois 'women's rightsers'.[17] Organized feminism was increasingly viewed not as an essential component of the socialist struggle, but as a dis-unifying, diversionary force, with no inherent connection to the socialist tradition.[18] And thus the present disowns the past, severing connections and suppressing ambitions once so vital to those who forged them.

Of course not all feminists *were* socialists – either in the Owenites' day or after. Owenite feminism emerged from a tradition of democratic sexual radicalism (the 'Rights of Woman') which travelled its own trajectory during the first half of the nineteenth century, eventually laying some of the ideological foundations for the Victorian women's movement. This tradition was itself a highly complex, fragmented one whose history is as yet almost wholly unexplored. The few studies which do exist tend to be thin and descriptive, and crippled by the same assumption which dominates most present-day socialist thinking on feminism: that struggles involving women's status and women's freedom are somehow less revolutionary in their implications than those based on class. This assumption is conveyed partly through the orthodox representation of pre-suffrage feminism as a movement composed solely of respectable middle-class ladies seeking merely to gain for themselves prerogatives which their menfolk enjoyed, rather than challenging the entire system of sex- and class-based prerogative itself; partly through the exclusion or marginalization of socialist feminism from most textbook accounts (which usually begin with the 'Rights of Woman' debate of the 1790s and then leap over a half century into the Victorian movement, with the period of Owenite activism unmentioned).[19] The image thus conveyed is of a politics far less challenging and subversive than its contemporaries believed it to be, and also far more homogeneous than current research reveals it to have been.[20] Like socialism, feminism also has been an arena for competing aspirations and ideals; a terrain on which ideological conflicts were fought which are only beginning to be understood. This book is part of that beginning.

The present must always condescend to the past, and from our vantage point there is much in the thinking of the pre-Marxian socialists which seems theoretically naive and strategically implausible. As a stage in the development of socialism, Owenism did indeed occupy (as Marx and Engels claimed) an era of political innocence, an Eden of socialist hope before the bitter apple of class warfare had fully matured. The miserable story of the movement's collapse, in a welter of class-based conflicts and recriminations, is evidence enough that the Fall was inevitable.[21] But to view Owenism solely in this light is to forget that it also expressed aspirations which did not disappear with the movement itself – aspirations which still must be met before some of us, at least, are prepared to declare that our battle is won.

But forgotten connections may be recalled and restored; visions revitalized. Today the movement of women is once again a crucial component in radical politics, particularly socialist politics. Our presence there, however, is a problematic, disturbing one, since we bring to the socialist struggle a sense of our own needs and demands – much more powerful and confident than a century ago – which simply cannot be contained within the restrictive boundaries of most left-wing thought and practice.[22] We, and those who ally themselves with us, are the Utopians of today; and in the end the case for our cause – for feminist socialism – must become the case for Utopianism itself, for a style of socialist endeavour which aims to transform the whole order of social life and in so doing transforms relations between the sexes. This was the Owenites' endeavour in which, hampered by their own difficulties and those of their times, they failed. We must not.

I

THE RIGHTS OF WOMAN:
A RADICAL INHERITANCE

'These may be termed Utopian dreams . . .'
(Mary Wollstonecraft, *A Vindication of the Rights of Woman*)

The ideological roots of Socialist feminism lay in the popular democratic tradition of the late eighteenth century, and in particular in the radical egalitarianism of the 1790s. Occasional voices had been raised on behalf of women's rights throughout the century, but it was only in that final, turbulent decade of revolution and counter-revolution that these cohered into a distinct political position. The woman responsible for this development was the feminist democrat, Mary Wollstonecraft, whose *Vindication of the Rights of Woman*, published in 1792, first pushed the demand for female emancipation directly into the mainstream of British political life. There it created a whirlpool of excitement and controversy which lasted for decades, and was still swirling around the early Owenites when they began to produce their own feminist writings, a quarter century later.

THE EGALITARIAN VISION

Hearing Mary Wollstonecraft through the pages of her *A Vindication* today, we usually imagine her speaking alone – an isolated shout of defiance with scarcely an echo of support around her. But a closer scrutiny of the intellectual and political milieu in which she moved reveals that this was far from the case. Throughout the late eighteenth century a steady stream of writing on women's position had flowed from the pens of the progressive literati: teachers in Dissenting academies, parliamentary

1

reformers, radical novelists, journalists, poets. Coteries of such dissident intellectuals were to be found in most large towns across Britain in the 1780s and 1790s, forming a network of petit bourgeois radicalism which extended into virtually all the political causes of the day. Mary's own London circle at this time encompassed the elite of this enlightened intelligentsia, many of whom shared her feminist views. Both her husband, William Godwin, and her close friend, Thomas Holcroft, attempted to enlist public support for Mary's ideas, as did another friend and political associate, Thomas Paine. Mary's female acquaintances included well-known 'bluestockings' like Anna Barbauld and Mary Hays, who also wrote essays on the position of women. 'Have you read that wonderful book, *The Rights of Woman*?' the radical poetess, Anna Seward, wrote to a friend shortly after its publication.[1]

Sceptics in religion, democrats in politics, reformers, visionaries, romantics – these men and women represented a style of social dissidence bold in its assumptions, universalist in its claims. '*Had we a place to stand upon, we might raise the world*,' Paine quoted Archimedes at the opening of the second part of his *Rights of Man*;[2] and for himself and most of his 'Jacobin'* associates, including Mary Wollstonecraft, revolutionary France seemed to be that place. 'The french revolution,' Mary wrote enthusiastically in 1793, 'is a strong proof how far things will govern men, when simple principles begin to act with one powerful spring against the complicated wheels of ignorance.'[3] The 'simple principles' which she had in mind were those which had inspired an entire generation of French and English radicals: the natural right of every individual to political and social self-determination; the evils of autocratic government, hereditary privilege, and unearned wealth; the perfectibility of human nature and human institutions; and – above all else – *egalité* as the foundation for a new morality within human relations. 'Virtue can only flourish among equals . . .'[4] 'My opinion, indeed, respecting the rights and duties of woman seem to flow

* The term 'Jacobin' was used in Britain to refer to anyone who supported the democratic principles of the French Revolution. Most British Jacobins, however, were not supporters of the Jacobin party in France itself (both Paine and Wollstonecraft gave their allegiance to the Jacobins' Girondist opposition).

naturally from these simple principles,' she explained at the beginning of the *Vindication*.[5]

The principles were, of course, far older than Mary's version of them; nor had she been the first to extend them to women. From the seventeenth century on, liberal advocates of constitutional government had argued that the power of men within families, like that of kings within nations, should be exercised only with the consent of the ruled.[6] The very idea of citizenship – of the self-determining individual as the legitimate source of political and social authority – undermined the ground on which masculine despotism, like absolute monarchy, had once stood firm. The *Vindication* opens with a letter to the French minister Talleyrand protesting the decision of the Convention in Paris to deny political rights to the revolutionary *citoyennes*: 'Consider, sir . . . if the abstract rights of man will bear discussion and explanation, those of women, by a parity of reasoning, will not shrink from the same test, though a different opinion prevails in this country . . .'

> Consider . . . whether, when men contend for their freedom, and to be allowed to judge for themselves respecting their own happiness, be it not inconsistent and unjust to subjugate women, even though you firmly believe that you are acting in the manner best calculated to promote their happiness? Who made man the exclusive judge, if woman partake with him of the gift of reason?
>
> In this style argue tyrants of every denomination, from the weak king to the weak father of a family; they are all eager to crush reason, yet always assert that they usurp its throne only to be useful. Do you not act a similar part when you *force* all women, by denying them civil and political rights, to remain immured in their families groping in the dark? for surely, sir, you will not assert that a duty can be binding which is not founded on reason? . . . unless women comprehend their duty, unless their morals be fixed on the same immutable principle as those of man, no authority can make them discharge it in a virtuous manner. They may be convenient slaves, but slavery will have its constant effect, degrading the master and the abject dependant . . .[7]

'Let there then be no coercion *established* in society,' she concluded further on, 'and the common law of gravity prevailing, the sexes will fall into their proper places . . .' – truly a classic affirmation of *laissez-faire* philosophy.[8]

Underlying this libertarian optimism was a critique of

3

conventional womanhood which emphasized its wholly 'artificial' character. In present-day society, Wollstonecraft admitted, women *were* inferior, but this inferiority was not, as was usually claimed, a result of mental or physical deficiencies, but the product of a male-defined social order which consigned women to a stultifying, crippling way of life. Doomed from infancy onward to be treated as personal slaves, women acquired slave-like characteristics, including servility, cunning, and the 'infantile imbecility' which in women was praised as 'sensibility'. 'It is time to effect a revolution in female manners – time to restore to them their lost dignity – and make them, as a part of the human species, labour by reforming themselves to reform the world.'[9]

This portrait of debased and degraded femininity was based, at least in part, on Mary's own experiences of petit bourgeois womanhood. As the daughter of a failed gentleman-farmer (himself the son of a textile manufacturer), Mary was born into a class whose public and private aspirations had been transformed by the rise of the industrial economy. Whereas in preceding centuries women of her background – wives and daughters of farmers, tradesmen, small merchants, manufacturers – had generally been employed as subsidiary partners in the family-based enterprises of their husbands or fathers, by the late eighteenth century all this had changed. A revolution in the scale and character of commercial operations had led to the replacement of family labour (particularly female family labour) by waged employees, while at the same time the expansion of personal wealth had encouraged *nouveau-riche* men to view their homes, and the women within them, as display cases for their affluence.[10] Women who had once made an essential contribution to family economies became idle, decorative accessories to their husbands, expected to do nothing but supervise servants and fill male leisure hours with gentle chatter and sexual pleasure: 'the toys of man,' in Wollstonecraft's bitter phrase, who 'must jingle in his ears whenever, dismissing reason, he chooses to be amused.'[11] Thus robbed of all serious social or economic functions, such women deteriorated, Mary claimed, into 'mere parasites' who lacked any sense of themselves as rational, self-determining beings. 'Confined . . . in cages like the feathered race, they have nothing to do but to plume themselves, and stalk with mock

4

majesty from perch to perch. It is true they are provided with food and raiment, for which they neither toil nor spin; but health, liberty and virtue are given in exchange.'[12] In a revealing analogy, she compared these degraded women of the 'middle ranks' with those arch-parasites, the British aristocracy, and contrasted both to bourgeois men, in whom 'business, extensive plans, excursive flights of ambition' had bred a fine sense of 'practical virtue':

> Abilities and virtues are absolutely necessary to raise men from the middle rank into notice, and the natural consequence is notorious – the middle rank contains most virtue and abilities. Men have thus, in one station at least, an opportunity of exerting themselves with dignity, and of rising by the exertions which will really improve a rational creature; but the whole female sex are . . . in the same condition as the rich, for they are born . . . with certain sexual privileges; and whilst they are gratuitously granted them, few will ever think of works of supererogation to obtain the esteem of a small number of superior people.[13]

If the model for genteel femininity was the life of the idle rich, the model for feminine freedom, it seems, was the life of the self-made businessman.

The *Vindication* is usually described as the founding text of modern bourgeois feminism, and quotations like these go far to corroborate that assessment. And yet the interpretation is not adequate. Both in terms of content and context, Wollstonecraft's contribution to feminist thought occupied a more radical ground than this. At a political level, her writings represented a high point of democratic radicalism in its revolutionary phase: an extended manifesto linking the emancipation of women to the social and political liberation of 'the people' as a whole. Tinkering with minor reforms didn't really interest Mary very much; like her mentor, Rousseau, she stood for the overthrow of the 'pestiferous purple' and all those who sheltered under it, believing that only then could the new world, 'the more perfect Age', begin to emerge. 'A new spirit has gone forth, to organize the body politic . . . Reason has, at last, shown her captivating face and it will be impossible for the dark hand of despotism again to obscure the radiance . . .'[14]

Like Rousseau also, Mary envisioned this new age as a time of perfect harmony between the aspirations of the individual and the collective needs of humanity as a whole – a harmony to be achieved through rational education and genuine social equality. The scope of the project took her right to the limit of the bourgeois-democratic outlook and occasionally a little way past it. At several points in her writings on economic developments, for example, she inveighed against the new 'aristocracy of commerce' emerging across Western Europe and America through whose industrial enterprises 'whole knots of men are turned into machines' and human needs sacrificed to the drive for profit.[15] 'England and America owe their liberty to commerce which created a new species of power to undermine the feudal system,' she writes prophetically in 1796. 'But let them beware of the consequences; the tyranny of wealth is still more galling than that of rank.'[16] That was a barrier to *liberté* which not even enlightened reason, it seemed, would be able to topple. Mary herself could do little more than gesture towards these new class divisions, but her willingness to do so signalled a heightened sophistication of social analysis which could be seen in her later writings on women as well. In her unfinished novel, *Maria or the Wrongs of Woman* (1798), she described the trials of a working-class girl whose seducer was not the usual dastardly blue-blood of Gothic fiction, but the Methodist owner of the slop-shop where she was employed. This girl, Jemima, was portrayed neither as passive victim nor saucy slut (the stock characterizations of proletarian women found in most middle-class writings of the period), but as a proud, intelligent girl whose sufferings, when set alongside those of the wealthy heroine, showed, in the author's words, 'the wrongs of different classes of women, equally oppressive, though, from the difference of education, necessarily various.'[17]

The same impulse which carried Mary to this point also led her to draw a comparison between the political subalternity of women and that of the male working class: an important augury of arguments to come.[18] Mary was the sort of democrat who was constantly running up against the limits of a merely bourgeois-democratic perspective, continually veering between the narrow class assumptions on which so much of the radical tradition was based and her own, far more subversive, sense of alternative social possibilities. At one point she even sketched out a proposal for a communalist society of small peasant-producers which could be established, she suggested ingenuously, simply by expropriating all the large estates in Britain and redistributing the land across the entire population.[19] Poverty would disappear, centralized government would no longer be required, and all forms of social hierarchy would vanish. A new age of absolute equality would dawn. 'These may be termed Utopian dreams . . .'

Utopian the idea may have been, but it was also highly characteristic – of both the woman and her time. The dialogue between reformist premises and utopian aspirations which can be heard so clearly in Mary's work was in fact, as Franco Venturi has shown, one key feature of late eighteenth century progressivism as a whole, 'polarizing the minds and spirits' of radical intellectuals all across Europe.[20] In Britain, the utopian side of this dialogue was most fully articulated not by Mary herself, but by two of her male contemporaries: Thomas Spence, a working-class pamphleteer, and Mary's own husband, William Godwin. Both were leading Jacobins who between them drew some of the crucial blueprints on which later Owenite schemes were based.

Godwin, a *soi-disant* philosopher and literary hack, was the most influential male theorist of British Jacobinism after Paine. In 1793 (four years before his wedding to Mary) he published his famous *Enquiry into Political Justice*, a formidable tome which managed to distill into one heady brew all the most grandiose aspirations of the Enlightenment – and then project them forward into a plan for a world communist order. Equality and the liberty of the individual were Godwin's central preoccupations: the only way the two could be achieved (and rendered compatible), he argued, was through the elimination of private property (which bred inequality) and the annihilation of government (which even in its benevolent aspects was a direct constraint on individual freedom). Both must be replaced by a world-wide system of small communities, economically maintained by small-scale, producer-run farms and workshops, and governed by local democratic councils.[21] Similar schemes were put forward by Spence, who throughout the 1790s bombarded the British population (particularly its 'Labouring Part') with little tracts and newspapers urging it to abandon acquisitive ways and establish an agrarian communist utopia (for which he modestly suggested the name 'Spensonia'). 'O hearken, ye besotted sons of men. By this one bold resolve your chains are eternally broken, and your enemies annihilated . . . and the whole earth shall at last be happy and live like brethren.'[22]

Both Godwin and Spence's proposals were genuinely innovative in many respects – but they also derived many of their emphases (and much of their force) from the oldest tradition of western utopianism – Christianity, and in particular Christian communitarianism. The vision of a perfect, and perfectly harmonious, community of equals had been a persistent sub-theme within Christian thought for centuries, from Thomas More's *Utopia* to the communist Digger communities of the mid-seventeenth century, through to eighteenth century utopian sects like the Shakers.[23] In every case, the aim of such groups or individuals had been to concretize a vision of social perfectibility which had at its centre the promise not only of spiritual regeneration but also of earthly self-fulfilment. Crucially (as we shall see in a later chapter), this was a promise extended to women as well as men. Women's status relative to men, particularly within marriage, had been a persistent preoccupation of virtually all utopian visionaries prior to Spence and Godwin – and it re-appeared very clearly in their writings as well. In Spensonia, Spence claimed, all women, married or single, would participate in the communal land economy on the same basis as men, and enjoy the same political rights (although the domestic responsibilities of married women would prevent them from actually sitting on government councils). Divorce would be allowed, and a woman's marital status would in all respects (except apparently the domestic workload) be equal to that of her husband.[24] Godwin's plans were less sharply defined than this, but his general intentions were clear: under ideal conditions, he argued in one of the most famous and controversial chapters of *Political Justice*, formal marriage could be abandoned in favour of sexual liaisons based solely on mutual desire and affection.[25] The co-residential family unit could be eliminated and a new style of domestic existence, based on communal arrangements, instituted in its stead. 'Pantisocracy', as this plan became known, deeply influenced Owen's later thinking on sexual relations.[26] It was also the inspiration of an entire generation of young Romantics, including a little band of poets (Coleridge, Southey, and Lovell) who in 1794 set off to initiate the Pantisocratic future on the banks of the Susquehanna River in America. All three young enthusiasts were disciples of Wollstonecraft as well as her husband, and plans for the New Life included an equal role for women in education and government, and an end to female responsibility for housework. 'Let the married Women do only what is convenient and customary for pregnant Women or nurses – ' Coleridge wrote cheerily, 'Let the husbands do *all* the rest – and what will that all be – ? Washing with a Machine and cleaning the House. One Hour's addition to our daily labour – and Pantisocracy in its most perfect sense is practicable.'[27]

Hopes like these, inspired by the same ideals as the *Vindication*, yet carrying its utopian message far beyond the point where Wollstonecraft had been willing to go, provided imaginative foundations on which Owenite feminism could later develop. But there was a second way in which the *Vindication* contributed to the radicalization of feminism in the post-Revolution period. As with any political document, the meaning of Wollstonecraft's book lay not only within its own pages, but in its fate as a text in the hands of the reading public. And in the case of the *Vindication*, that fate was inextricably tangled up with the bitter political struggles of the day.

FEMINISM AND COUNTER-REVOLUTION

The *Vindication* was published in 1792, the same year that the French Republic was proclaimed; the second part of Paine's *Rights of Man* reached the bookstalls; and the first working-class reform organizations in Britain were founded. It had been in print for less than a year when the French Jacobins killed a King and took power in the National Convention. In the months when it was being reviewed, the British government was preparing for a war on two fronts: with its revolutionary neighbour over the Channel, and with its own home-grown radical opposition, which by 1793 had swelled to include working people in towns and cities all over the country. 'A very general spirit of combination exists amongst all sorts of labourers and artisans, who are in a state of disaffection . . .' ran a typical report from one frightened magistrate at the time.[28] Faced with what was generally believed to be an internal revolutionary threat, landed aristocracy and industrial bourgeoisie buried their own differences long enough to unleash a series of Acts drastically restricting rights of assembly, publication, and free speech; they also encouraged a nationwide heresy hunt in which known Jacobins and their sympathizers were hounded and victimized. Over two thousand anti-Jacobin vigilante squads were formed, backed by factory-owners, landlords, local magistracy and churchmen.[29] 'I cannot give you an idea of the violence with which every friend of liberty is persecuted in this country,' the reformer Priestley wrote to a friend in 1793, two years after his own home had been burned down by 'Church and King' mobs.[30]

Faced with repression on one side and the new plebian militancy on the other, bourgeois revolutionism buckled. The boldest were either silenced or scattered; radical Dissenting academies were closed or neutralized; persecuted Jacobins, like Priestley, began to emigrate; Paine was forced to flee to France under the threat of imprisonment if he returned to England. Many others who had once willingly pushed open new doors to *liberté*, now, witnessing the growth of a working-class democratic movement, tried to bang them shut again. A sharp polarization of political attitudes occurred, in which uncompromising democrats were abandoned by their former friends, as egalitarian ideals once safely mooted within the classrooms and salons of genteel iconoclasts suddenly revealed themselves as dangerously subversive. Within a decade Price, Priestley, Wollstonecraft and Paine were all dead or in exile; Godwin had been consigned to intellectual oblivion; and a new style of middle-class reformer had emerged, his back firmly turned on the revolutionary optimism of the preceding era. 'A single mistake in extending equality too far may overthrow the social order and dissolve the bonds of society,' Jeremy Bentham warned in 1802:

> Equality might require such a distribution of property as would be incompatible with security . . . Equality ought not to be favoured, except when it does not injuriously affect security, nor disappoint expectations aroused by the law itself, nor disturb a distribution already settled and determined . . .[31]

That was a very long way from the barricades of *egalité*.

The political identity of the Rights of Women was established in these years of counter-revolutionary panic. Having first come into the public eye as the author of an impassioned defence of the French Revolution, Wollstonecraft already had a reputation as an insurrectionist, the English equivalent of 'the revolutionary harpies of France, sprung from night and hell . . .'[32] 'The female advocates of Democracy in this country, though they have had no opportunity of imitating the French ladies, in their atrocious acts of cruelty; have yet assumed a stern severity in the contemplation of those savage excesses . . .' ran one anti-Wollstonecraft tract titled *The Unsex'd Females*.[33] The publication of the *Vindication* in the same year as Paine's book only served to strengthen the existing connection. Viewed through the smoke of the Bastille, Wollstonecraft loomed like a blood-stained Amazon, the high priestess of 'loose-tongued Liberty', whose much-publicized love affairs also helped to convince the public that she wanted to extend libertarian principles into the bedroom as well as into government – a doctrine which 'if received, must overturn the basis of every civilized state'.[34] Respectable bluestockings, even her friend Anna Barbauld, hastened to repudiate such notions; some spoke in praise of Burke and damned the *Vindication*.[35] Feminism was pushed outside the pale of genteel opinion, which closed and hardened against it. By 1798 even a liberal-minded women's journal was 'relieved to report' that

> the champions of female equality, who were as inimical to the happiness and interest of the sex, as those who preached up the doctrine of liberty and equality to the men, are no longer regarded as sincere and politic friends . . .[36]

Of course some middle-class feminists remained, just as the democratic movement as a whole retained a thin, but influential layer of well-to-do Jacobins. In most towns there could be found a few like-minded men and women – young professionals, Unitarian intellectuals and the like – who continued to meet to exchange ideas and work for parliamentary reform alongside the artisans who made up the real backbone of British Jacobinism. One of the organizers of the radical London Corresponding

Society took a political tour of these towns in the mid-1790s, and there met several women democrats of this sort, including the wife of a Chatham doctor who praised Mary's book and gave him a little lesson in feminist politics: 'A *female* legislature, Sir, would never have passed those horrid Convention Bills, or abrogated the dear prerogative of speech':

> There was nothing, she thought, to which women were not competent; and she strongly censured our sex, for first depriving them of every source of intelligence, and then reproaching them for their levity and indiscretion! She had truth and reason on her side; I, therefore, heartily concurred in the justice of her remarks.[37]

But if Jacobin democrats were happy to applaud such sentiments, few of this lady's well-bred neighbours would. The effect of such hostility was to tighten the connection between feminism and the 'ultra-reformers', the most intransigent wing of the democratic movement, from which many Owenites later emerged. And it was women like this Chatham feminist who later became one important source of support for Owenite feminist ideas.

Counter-revolutionary panic had led to a political polarization in which feminists found themselves increasingly identified with the 'left' (as it was already becoming known) of the political spectrum. But panic alone – even one as intense and widespread as that generated by the French Revolution – cannot fully explain the major shift in ideological stance which occurred in these years. Anxiety must find expression in a language capable of situating and resolving it before it becomes translated into a new world-view. In the years after the Revolution the language in which a large section of the British upper and middle classes found that reassurance was religious enthusiasm. 'The awakening of the labouring classes, after the first shocks of the French Revolution, made the upper classes tremble,' Lady Shelley wrote in her diary at the time. 'Every man felt the necessity for putting his house in order . . .'[38] For many, this spiritual re-ordering led straight into the revivalist Church. Forming a growing band of Evangelicals, they called for a revolution in 'manners and morals' which would simultaneously improve the dissipated upper orders and subdue the lower. Jacobinism, a 'moral malady', could only be cured by a stiff dose of 'vital religion' – a 'practical Christianity' in which godliness, clean living and patriotism were inseparably joined, any neglect of one automatically implying negligence of the others. Or as one convert to the crusade put it:

> The true Christian will never be a leveller; will never listen to French politics, or to French philosophy. He who worships God in spirit and in truth will love the government and laws which protect him without asking by whom they are administered. But let it not be imagined that such characters will abound among the lower classes while the higher by their Sunday parties, excursions, and amusements, and vanities; by their neglect of public worship and their families show that they feel not themselves what perhaps they talk of, or recommend for the poor.[39]

Classes which had been pulled apart by social and political tensions were to draw together again in the arms of Christ and the British constitution. Irresponsible high life and insubordinate low would both be swept away, and in their stead would emerge the model Christian – industrious, sober, pious, narrow. All ranks having been thus reformed, rank itself would be ensured. 'Moderating the insolence of power, Christianity renders the inequalities of the social state less galling to the lower orders, whom she also instructs, in their turn, to be diligent, humble, patient . . .'[40] and so on. Where the Holy Word alone proved inadequate to the task, however, God's shepherds were also prepared to use sturdier rods on the plebian flock. The Society for the Suppression of Vice was an Evangelical body instituted by the leading Saint, William Wilberforce, which busied itself spying on, harassing, and prosecuting vendors of radical literature, as well as pestering blasphemers of a less political bent – Sabbath-breakers and so on. Leading Evangelicals placed themselves at the service of the anti-Jacobin campaign, producing thousands of tracts in which democratic views were pronounced not only seditious, but blasphemous. ' "What is *the new Rights of Man*?" one village yokel inquired of another in Hannah More's most popular tract, *Village Politics*, 'Jack: "Battle, murder, and sudden death." Tom: "What is it to be an *enlightened people*?" Jack: "To put out the light of the gospel, confound right and wrong, and grope about in pitch darkness." '[41]

In addition to their role as a vanguard of political con-servatism, these revivalists also played a key part in the

formation of Victorian sexual attitudes. The intense sentimentalization of the home which reached its peak in the mid-century had
its beginnings in their promotion of a 'domestic religion' centred
around the 'moral influence' of the wife and mother. All attempts
to extend women's role outside the family were condemned as a
threat not only to the balance of sexual power inside the
household, but also to the balance of moral forces within the
nation as a whole. The language was apocalyptic. 'If our women
lose their domestic virtues, all the charities will be dissolved, for
which our country is a name so dear,' a friend wrote to Hannah
More after reading her views on Female Duty; 'The men will be
profligate, the public will be betrayed, and whatever has blessed
or distinguished the English nation on the Continent will
disappear.'[42]

To sexual conservatives like these, feminist ideas represented
not only a threat to masculine pride and feminine purity, but an
insult to God Himself. Like the lower orders, women were closest
to their Maker when they were servicing their natural superiors.
Any notions to the contrary, derived from 'deistical philosophers', were given short shrift: 'Whether marriage establishes
between the husband and wife a perfect equality of rights, or
conveys to the former a certain degree of superiority over the
latter is a point not left among Christians to be decided by
speculative arguments,' intoned the Reverend Thomas Gisborne,
one of Wilberforce's men:

> The intimation of the divine will, communicated to the first woman
> immediately after the fall . . . is corroborated by various injunctions
> delivered in the New Testament.. . .' Wives submit yourselves unto
> your husbands as unto the Lord . . .'[43]

All these moralists loathed Wollstonecraft, 'that hyena in
petticoats' as Walpole referred to her in a letter to Hannah More.
More herself was prepared to condemn Mary's book without
reading it: 'There is something fantastic and absurd in the very
title,' she wrote back to him, adding that in her view 'there is no
animal so much indebted to subordination for its good behaviour
as woman.'[44] As in most Evangelical writings, 'good behaviour'
here meant sexual propriety. One of the most common accusations levelled against Wollstonecraft by these saintly critics was

sexual promiscuity; the other, related one, was religious infidelity. 'A woman who has broken through all religious restraints, will commonly be found ripe for every species of licentious indecorum,' one reverend gentleman explained.[45] Freethinking, free living, free loving, unwomanly habits of all sorts: for another century the name of Wollstonecraft would call up these associations, linked together in the public mind by the religious conservatives of her day.

For feminism, the evangelicals completed what the counter-revolutionary panic of the 1790s had begun. Not that the new religious view of womanhood was without its contradictions; indeed, as we shall see in a later chapter, the claims raised on behalf of a 'regenerating' female mission could, and sometimes did, become the basis of a feminist offensive.[46] But in general the effect was to detach sexual egalitarianism from the new canons of middle-class respectability, thereby alienating many uncompromising egalitarians from moral and social conventions. This had a decisive effect on the ideological formation of Socialist feminist politics. By identifying women's rights with sexual libertarianism, infidelism and social revolution, the new conservatives actually helped to fuse these aspects of radical thought together in the minds of their feminist opponents. By insisting that sexual equality would inevitably lead to 'the overthrow of all existing social institutions', including the church, marriage and family life, they assisted in the creation of a brand of feminism which had precisely those goals. And by equating the protest of women with the 'levelling' aspirations of the radical working class, they helped to forge that alliance between sex and class goals which emerged, a quarter-century later, in the Owenite movement.

FROM JACOBIN UTOPIANISM TO UTOPIAN SOCIALISM

If, as I have argued, there existed an unresolved tension between utopianism and reformism within pre-Socialist radicalism, then the revolutionary years of the 1790s saw the utopian side of this dialogue in the ascendant. A spirit of fierce, world-regenerating optimism permeated all the Jacobin literature. Most of the prominent intellectuals who expressed this spirit were drawn from that particular sector of the educated lower middle class to which Wollstonecraft belonged. Yet in their struggles to fashion a new order in the teeth of the old, these men and women reached out past their class origins to articulate a language of universal human liberation: the language in which Wollstonecraft's feminism first found its voice.

But the Jacobin moment was short-lived. By the turn of the century, with the weight of counter-revolution settled on the country, bourgeois ideals had narrowed and hardened. Religious revivalism, with its sanctification of patriarchal and class authority, continued to tighten its grip over the middle class, while even among non-religious liberals, Jacobinical principles of natural rights and universal equality gave way to a businesslike reformism aimed at consolidating the power of middle-class men and suppressing the claims of all those outside their ranks, notably the working class and women. Thus, for example, in the 1790s many leading democrats – including Wollstonecraft – had supported female and working-class enfranchisement,[47] on the grounds that a sovereign People could only exercise their sovereignty through direct representation in the State. But by 1824 James Mill, one of the key figures in middle-class liberalism, was able to dismiss the claims of women and working-class men to the vote, on the grounds that their interests could be effectively represented by others who were better able to wield political power on their behalf: husbands and fathers, in the case of women, and 'the most wise and virtuous part of the community, the middle rank', in the case of the working class. His position was supported by most other middle-class reformers who dismissed older egalitarian ideals out of hand; and in fact the 1832 Reform Bill which they engineered deliberately excluded working men and all women from the expanded franchise.[48]

The result was to detach the egalitarian-utopian impulse from its ideological origins, and send it along other routes: routes which soon ran directly counter to mainstream liberalism. In the years following Wollstonecraft's death in 1797, those who still clung to a vision of universal emancipation became increasingly aware of the impossibility of realizing that vision in a society where, in Shelley's words, 'the harmony and happiness of man/

Yields to the wealth of nations', and 'gold is a living god . . .'[49] The seeds planted by left-wing Jacobinism steadily grew, as the half-formed fears of an 'aristocracy of Commerce' voiced by Wollstonecraft in 1795 hardened into open criticism of commercialism and self-interested individualism. Thus, whereas in the 1790s the young Robert Owen had been busy running the New Lanark mills and propounding advanced views on capitalist management techniques, by 1820 he was a committed communist, arguing for the abolition of capitalist enterprise and the establishment of social communities similar to those proposed by Godwin and Spence.[50] Other radicals, particularly feminist radicals, followed a similar trajectory. William Thompson and Anna Wheeler were both revolutionary democrats and feminists of a Wollstonecraftian hue who were converted to Owenism in the 1820s. In 1825, Thompson, in association with Wheeler, published a book, *Appeal of One-Half the Human Race*, which first spelled out the rudiments of a Socialist feminist position.[51] The book was written primarily to refute James Mill's arguments against female enfranchisement; but having done this, it then went on to provide a much broader critique of the bourgeois liberal assumptions on which Mill's case had been based. The competitive individualism which Mill espoused (and which reflected current social realities) was utterly incompatible with genuine democratic ambitions, it claimed – and particularly with Thompson and Wheeler's own ambition for equality between the sexes. 'The present arrangements of society, founded on individual competition . . . are absolutely irreconcilable with the equality . . . of women with men', for how could women achieve equality with men as long as child-bearing and family responsibilities prevented them from acquiring equal wealth? 'Even were all unequal legal and unequal moral restraints removed . . . in point of independence *arising from wealth* they [women] must, under the present system of social arrangements, remain inferior'.[52] Only the new mode of social organization proposed by Owen, based on 'mutual co-operation and joint possession', could provide the material preconditions for women's emancipation.[53]

Thus the utopian element which had always been present in radical-democratic thought broke away and took on a political life of its own, gathering up with it all those aspirations towards 'human things . . . perfected'[54] which the mainstream current of reformist thought had abandoned, including the aspiration for female freedom. The link between women's emancipation and a general social emancipation which had begun to be forged in the era of democratic revolution now took on a new shape, as a concrete strategy for the creation of a 'Social System' which had the liberation of women as one of its central objects.

II

WOMEN AND THE NEW SCIENCE OF SOCIETY

THE NEW SCIENCE OF SOCIETY

'Utopianism', the label which Marx and Engels attached to the Owenite strategy,[1] and which has stuck to it ever since, was one which the early Socialists themselves firmly rejected. As far as Owen and his disciples were concerned, their schemes were anything but visionary; indeed, the key feature which distinguished their plans from all the other world-reforming projects which had preceded them, they claimed, was the 'wholly scientific' foundation on which theirs were based. Or as Anna Wheeler wrote in 1833, 'I hold it as one of the things the most impossible, that *not* having examined the social laws, institutions, and customs which have governed past, and continue to regulate present society . . . we can be but very *lukewarm* advocates of a better system.'[2] And it was from this commitment to the systematic examination of social possibilities that Owenite theory developed. 'We have hitherto . . . conducted our affairs by chance. This has heaped error upon error, until it has literally overwhelmed us with confusion . . .' the Edinburgh Owenite, John Gray, wrote, 'It is quite time that this state of things had an end . . .'[3] For chance and error the Owenites would substitute system and science — the New Science of Society, or Social Science: 'the science which determines . . . happiness or misery . . . by circumstances over which each individual has hitherto had little controul [sic] . . .'[4]

This new Science was, first and foremost, a science of human nature, or what Owen himself described as 'the science of the influence of circumstances over the whole conduct, character, and proceedings of the human race'. 'The character of man,' he explained in a famous passage,

> is, without a single exception, always formed for him . . . by his predecessors; who give him . . . his ideas and habits, which are the powers that govern and direct his conduct. Man, therefore, never did, nor is it possible he ever can, form his own character.[5]

The theory of social determination of character had been a key theme of progressive thought for decades before Owen announced his discovery of it,[6] but it was in his own writings and those of his followers that its political implications were most forcibly hammered out. For if all individual thought and behaviour was governed by determinate social and ideological conditions, then 'any general character, from the best to the worst, from the most ignorant to the most enlightened, may be given to any community, even to the world at large, by the application of proper means . . .'[7] 'I am not at all surprised at the worthy magistrate calling my scheme Utopian,' Owen wrote in reply to one critic, 'if he imagines that I contemplate a change of the character of man in such a society as that we live in . . . We can only change human nature by changing the circumstances in which man lives, and this change we will make so complete, that man will become a totally different being.'[8]

The 'circumstances' which were blamed for mankind's current condition were all those which promoted 'the principle of individual interests' over the 'principles of union and mutual co-operation'.[9] Early on in his career Owen named the three primary sources of social disunity as religion, marriage, and private property: religion because it perpetuated 'ignorant superstitions' about the innate imperfections of the human character and fomented a 'sectarian spirit' within its adherents; marriage because it converted women into male property and established 'single-family interests' which eroded neighbourly feelings; and private property because it made individual wealth the basis of social power and transformed all human relationships into competitive contests for individual gain.[10] At the root of all three was self-love, the clamouring ego, Rousseau's *amour de soi* which, if encouraged at the expense of *amour commun*, rendered all of human existence a wasteland of lonely avarice and self-seeking individualism. The theme had long been a powerful one among social dissidents, but it was in early Socialism that it achieved its clearest and most forceful expression. 'The present system of competition,' as one Birmingham Owenite wrote,

> is founded upon the predominance of the selfish and animal prin-
> ciples of our nature; each is left to take care of himself, and if he
> cannot do that the world has no place for him. There is no co-
> operation for the good of all; each class, each family, each indivi-
> dual, has interests at variance with those of his neighbours . . .
> every sound moral feeling is vitiated, every dissocial impulse called
> into habitual activity . . .[11]

Each class, each family, each individual: it was this emphasis on the universal fragmentation and alienation engendered by modern commercial society which characterized Owenite sociology. Although there were certain elements in the Owenite analysis which anticipated Marxism – notably a nascent theory of class exploitation[12] – in general the sweep of the Owenite critique was much wider than that of Marxism, encompassing all forms of social oppression, whether experienced in the work-place, the marketplace, the school or the home.[13] Capitalism – the 'competitive system' – was viewed not merely as a class-based economic order, but as an arena of multiple divisions and antagonisms, each of them lived in the hearts and minds of women and men, as well as in their material circumstances. It was a system saturated with injustice, riddled with inequalities, in which each injustice and inequality served not only to disable those in the subordinate role, but also to unbind the social fabric as a whole. But as all were infected, so all must be cured; every antagonism must be neutralized, every inequality eliminated. Only then would self-love give way to 'social sentiment' and, in Anna Wheeler's words, 'it will become evident to our *enlarged* perceptions, that happiness for social beings is a thing reflected from one to the other, from all to one.'[14] Only then would the freedom of the individual represent the emancipation of humanity as a whole.

The echoes of the old revolutionary democratic ideal are easy to hear: *egalité* universalized across sex and class, stiffened by a critique of the material and ideological sources of social hierarchy. The dream of universal freedom leaped the boundaries

21

of individual interest to become, as in the earlier communitarian sects, a 'levelling' vision, for 'how can men love one another when their interests are at variance?'[15] Only the harmonizing of all human needs, through communal ownership and the transformation of the human character, would ensure a new mode of loving, co-operative existence. To Marx and Engels, such a strategy was manifestly utopian since, in the words of the *Communist Manifesto*, it appealed 'to society at large' instead of the revolutionary interests of the working class in particular[16]; but to the Owenities, it was a clear expression of their faith in the underlying generosity of the human spirit, however corrupting its current 'circumstances', and also a direct reflection of their commitment to the abolition of all oppressions – whether of sex, colour or class. Love, not power, was the emotional platform on which all human relations, particularly sexual relations, would be reconstructed. 'Arouse, awake!' the *Appeal* exhorted its female readers, 'Demand . . . with confidence and dignity your portion of the common rights of all . . . and make the most certain step towards the regeneration of degraded humanity, by opening a free course for justice and benevolence, by no colour, by no sex, to be restrained . . .'[17]

The presentation of such ideas in a widely accessible format was a major preoccupation of Owenite feminists. Most early Socialists were publicists and propagandists rather than theorists, and the bulk of their writings were aimed at popularizing the New Science of Society, not refining it. Between 1825 and 1845 many dozens of newspaper articles, tracts, and published lectures appeared, written by Owenites or Owenite sympathizers, on the position of women, and most of these were propaganda pieces whose force derived not from their analytical weight or originality, but from the urgent political purpose behind them. Yet the movement also produced several texts which deserve to be considered intellectual founding documents of Socialist feminism. One of these was Owen's extraordinary *Lectures on the Marriages of the Priesthood in the Old Immoral World* (1835), discussed at length in a later chapter; another was *Appeal of One-Half the Human Race* (hereafter the *Appeal*).*

* The *Appeal* was published under Thompson's name. In the 'Letter to Mrs Wheeler' which opens the book, however, Thompson described how its argu-

The *Appeal*, it has already been noted, was written in response to James Mill's remarks on female enfranchisement, and the larger part of it was therefore taken up with a detailed refutation of Mill's claim that the political interests of women were 'contained' in those of their fathers and husbands. How could the interests of the female sex be said to be coincident with those of the male, Thompson demanded, when in every facet of social and economic life, particularly in domestic life, 'men have . . . invested themselves with despotic power' which they exercise with complete disregard for the needs of the women under their command? Fathers bartered their daughters in marriage; husbands subjected their wives to arbitrary and often humiliating authority; educators ridiculed women's mental abilities while employers either refused them work or purchased their labour for a pittance; and in the political arena women's lack of independent representation deprived them of any legal redress for these grievances. The conclusion was obvious:

> All women, and particularly women living with men in marriage
> . . . having been reduced to a state of helplessness, slavery, and of
> consequent unequal enjoyments, pains, and privations . . . are
> *more in need* of political rights than any other portion of human
> beings . . .[18]

The tone of this passage, with its emphasis on 'enjoyments, pains and privations' was typical of the *Appeal* as a whole. Thompson and Anna Wheeler, like Mill, were enthusiastic advocates of the Benthamite principle that the sole measure of the value ('utility') of any social arrangement was the quantity of happiness ('pleasure') it produced. But whereas to Bentham, Mill and other orthodox Utilitarians, happiness was simply the free

---

ments were conceived and developed by both of them. He had hoped Anna Wheeler would eventually author the entire text herself, but she had lacked the 'leisure and resolution' to do so, and had therefore only written a 'few pages' of it, while he had completed the rest: 'I being your interpreter and scribe of your sentiments.' His emphasis on the book as their 'joint property' led me to consider accrediting it to both of them here. But I have not done so, partly to avoid bibliographic confusion but also because, in the end, responsibility for its authorship clearly lay with him. (My hesitation in making this decision is worth noting simply as a measure of how vexed the problem of assigning authorship – particularly in such male/female intellectual partnerships – can be.)

pursuit of individual self-interest, to Owenite intellectuals like Thompson and Wheeler it was a social good, achieved not in 'selfish competition' with others but in 'general co-operation' with them.[19] In existing society, the *Appeal* acknowledged, the search for happiness was indeed a self-seeking, divisive affair, particularly within sexual relations where male pleasure almost invariably entailed female pain. But under the 'system of Mutual Association' proposed by Owen, 'the equalization of knowledge, rights and wealth between the sexes' would produce 'an entire reciprocity of happiness' between them, and inaugurate a new era of sexual joy and freedom. 'O woman, from your auspicious hands may the new destiny of your species proceed! . . . for as your bondage has chained down man to the ignorance and vices of despotism, so will your liberation reward him with knowledge, with freedom, and with happiness . . .'[20]

THE MAKING OF WOMANHOOD

Why is it, William Thompson demanded in an article published in the *London Co-operative Magazine* in 1826, that the female of the human species was everywhere dominated by the male, whereas in many other animal species a more equitable arrangement prevailed? The answer, he believed, was to be found partly in women's physical weakness and 'the prolonged helplessness of the young of the human race', but to this natural inferiority were then added 'fictitious failings' which were 'the mere results of the vicious circumstances surrounding women'.[21] In a society organized around human needs, women's innate physical disabilities would be offset by 'social arrangements' devised to give them the maximum support; but in a society organized around individual wealth, such liabilities forced women into a slavish dependence on men, thereby breeding in them a sense of inferiority and helplessness which 'sinks to the lowest possible degree that nature will admit the intellectual and moral nature of woman . . .'.[22] Femininity, in other words, was not a natural fact but a social creation; or as Anna Wheeler wrote in reply to a woman who had argued that it was impossible for sexes so inherently dissimilar to share a common system of government:

> If the differences in the nature of man and woman be so widely
> marked . . . (a belief that men have always found it convenient to
> establish) then there is some harmony in universal nature lost . . .
> Yet I believe that the obvious difference which now exists between
> the habits and feelings of both sexes, to arise from the unnatural
> position of both.[23]

The idea that women's apparent inferiority was a product of 'vicious circumstances' rather than innate deficiences had been a key theme in feminist writings from the early eighteenth century on, but it was in Owenite feminism that the argument was most fully developed – partly due to the strategic importance which the Owenites attached to the question of 'character formation' in general, but also in response to their religious opposition, for whom the innate imperfections of humanity – and particularly the female half of humanity – were a favourite theme. 'We must get entirely clear of all the notions . . . of original sin . . . to leave room for the expansion of the human heart,' Mary Wollstonecraft had written in 1794,[24] and several decades later this still remained an essential task, especially for women. For after all, as one Evangelical lady reminded her sisters in 1843, who was the Original Sinner? 'One painful pre-eminence we cannot deny to be ours, for "the woman was the first in the transgression", and to this hour the doom pronounced upon her at the fall is found in operation all over the world.' 'We suppose,' this writer went on to muse,

> that the serpent saw in her the indications of comparative weakness
> . . . she showed herself pre-eminently a fool . . . with this sad proof
> of her extreme instability before us, we had better refrain from
> speculating on the subject of her supposed inequality [sic] with
> men . . .[25]

Nor was Eve's susceptibility to reptilian blandishments the only weakness which distinguished her from Adam. 'The Power who called the human race into being,' ran one influential tract on Women's Duty, 'has, with infinite wisdom, regarded, in the structure of the corporeal frame, the tasks which the different sexes were respectively destined to fulfill.'[26] The 'close and comprehensive' reasoning powers of the male were complemented by the 'sprightliness and vivacity' which women brought to the holy duties of matrimony, motherhood, and the close reading of the

Bible. Other pious pedants wrote flatteringly of a unique female 'sensibility' which conveniently equipped women to do what their husbands would really rather not: attend church, care for children, visit the poor, and so on. Wollstonecraft had already attacked this sort of literature – 'Why are girls told they resemble angels, but to sink them below women?'[27] – but now the Owenite feminists developed this protest into a full-scale assault on all notions of innate feminine inferiority, and elaborated a counter-position based on the assumption of individual perfectibility. 'The laws of mind appear to admit of a constant progression,' as one woman wrote to the Owenite newspaper, *The New Moral World*, 'and if women are capable of experience, who shall say they are not perfectible?'[28]

The most important 'laws of mind' were, of course, the laws of 'external influence'. The character of woman, as the organizers of one short-lived Owenite feminist association wrote, 'has been formed by circumstances, all in opposition to her nature' which have stifled her abilities and deformed her personality: 'it is therefore necessary that women should endeavour to surround each other with such circumstances as shall truly and fully develop the entire character, and secure to them those privileges that nature intended.'[29] In the long run, this could only be done through the establishment of social communities, but in the short run it required intensive educational programmes which would make women 'conscious of the power they possess to free themselves from existing errors' and teach them 'how they can best exert that power for the benefit of the whole human race.'[30] 'It is my conviction that the relative inferiority, superiority, or equality of one sex to the other, cannot be ascertained until each shall have received a rational education,' another woman wrote.[31]

But in addition to education and social environment, certain physical attributes were acknowledged to play a part in the shaping of the female character. Many Owenites liked to reinforce their arguments for human perfectibility with a range of physical evidence aimed at demonstrating innate mental and bodily potential; particularly the equal potential of the sexes. Their enthusiasm for this sort of evidence was matched only by their eclecticism. Physiology, anatomy, sensationalist psychology, phrenology, Lamarckian evolutionist theory . . .

26

'Nothing is more pleasing,' as William Thompson wrote in an article which used Lamarck's findings to support his own case for the beneficial genetic effects of female education, 'than to find grand moral truths supported . . . by facts drawn from . . . the physical sciences' – a remark which helps to explain the Owenite addiction to facts of all sorts.[32] A lecture delivered by Anna Wheeler in 1829 was typical. Having demonstrated women's moral capacity with historical and literary examples, and their muscular potential with evidence from non-European societies, she went on to cite phrenological studies which had shown that 'all existing differences' in male and female skull topology were a result of education and 'the very different circumstances' of the sexes. And as for the brain itself:

> All the researchers of anatomy have not been able to prove a difference in the brain of either. Both receive the same impressions, arrange and preserve ideas, form memory and imagination; judge, compare and analyse; nor can indeed any difference be pointed out, but, that the organs of woman are generally smaller, but equally fitted to the purposes for which they are intended.[33]

Phrenology was particularly popular among the feminists, since it apparently provided them with an objective measure of masculine and feminine psychological traits. 'That the affections are far stronger in woman than in man . . . the experience of every day appears to me to confirm,' ran one letter to Owen's newspaper, *The Crisis*, in 1834, for 'the phrenologists also have discovered, that in them the organs of adhesiveness . . . are more developed . . .' Nonsense! was the immediate response from a woman correspondent, 'adhesiveness is pretty near equal in both', but whereas men 'adhere' to money and power, 'woman adheres to the slavish prejudices taught her . . .' – a use of the theory which made up in ingenuity what it lacked in (pseudo-) scientific accuracy.[34] In the same year as this exchange occurred the Owenite press also reported the activities of a Scottish feminist called Mrs Hamilton, who in the course of a lecture in Paisley whipped out a large handkerchief and 'after folding it in the form of a brain',

> began to describe how . . . phrenologists had proved, and she herself would prove, that women's brains were capable of being

27

improved to a degree which would make them equal and even excel the men in all the better accomplishments of our common nature, and give them power to break the chains of the tyrant and the oppressor, and set them completely free. (Immense applause).[35]

Equally enthusiastic use was made of another important body of scientific evidence: ethnographic data on women's position in non-European societies, in particular the 'savage' societies where amateur anthropologists (travellers, explorers) claimed to have witnessed sexual customs very different from the 'civilized' norm. This sort of literature was enormously popular among the early Socialists, for the obvious reason: 'every book which describes the customs of savage nations . . . serves to show the *unlimited* ductility of human nature . . .'[36] The Owenite literature was liberally sprinkled with snippets of information on 'Marriage among the Turks', 'The Amazon Women of the Lost Islands', 'Women's Condition among the Primitive Peoples of the Geenkonki Delta' and so on – which in the feminists' hands became a sort of rough-and-ready anthropology of sex roles. Anna Wheeler's use of the genre was typical:

> In reply to the charge of bodily weakness in women, M. de Chateaubriand . . . brings a host of evidence, from travellers and naturalists, to prove that this . . . is nothing but a *civilized disease*, imposed no doubt on women, to shorten the duration of life, and to provide men with a rapid succession of youthful slaves . . . Savage tribes acknowledge it not . . . men everywhere choosing their occupation compel women to drudgery, while they themselves engage in the most pleasurable and profitable pursuits of life.[37]

Cross-cultural analysis of this sort also contributed to another strand in Owenite theory: the development of an evolutionist account of mankind's social development, in which improvement of women's position within the family was postulated as a primary index of humanity's progress 'from savagery to civilization'. This idea had first been mooted by a number of eighteenth century moral philosophers, interested in charting a connection between the decline of patriarchal power and the rise of economic individualism,[38] but by the early nineteenth century it had become a favourite argument for all feminists.[39] Within Owenite circles it was particularly popular due to the influence of the French Socialist, Charles Fourier, who at the beginning of the

28

century had advanced an elaborate theory of mankind's evolution through a series of historical stages, each characterized by a determinant pattern of conjugal relations. The 'progressive liberation' of women within marriage, which could be traced from one stage to another, he argued, was *the fundamental cause of all social progress*. '*Social progress and changes of period are brought about by virtue of the progress of women towards liberty, and social retrogression occurs as a result of a diminution in the liberty of women.*'[40] The fascinating cosmology on which this thesis was based (in which sexual passion was analysed as an unconscious psycho-dynamic underlying all historical change) received little attention among English Socialist feminists, but the argument itself was frequently echoed in their writings.* 'Women, however high or low in the scale of cultivation, hold the destinies of mankind,' Frances Wright wrote in 1829,[41] while in the *Appeal* Thompson suggested that 'a comparative sketch . . . of the state of married women in different countries' would show

---

* Charles Fourier (1772–1837) was the son of a wealthy merchant. He lost his inheritance in the Revolution and thereafter became a commercial traveller and sales clerk, viewing at first hand the development of merchant capitalism. He explained his views on the position of women and the need for communist re-organization in a series of books published between 1808 and 1836, through which he won a small number of followers, some of whom attempted to found Fourierite communities in the early 1830s. But he remained essentially an isolated visionary, whose ideas were often so far in advance of his day that they perplexed even his most devoted disciples. In England, Fourierism was promoted by Anna Wheeler's friend, Hugh Doherty, who published a short-lived newspaper, *The Morning Star*, which made no mention of Fourier's sexual cosmology or his views on erotic freedom, but confined itself to expounding a feminist position virtually identical to the Owenites' own. One article in the *Star* (13 January 1840) explained that

it is not so much political rights as *social freedom* which is necessary to remedy the evils complained of by the labouring population in particular and the female sex generally; and the only way to obtain social freedom is to possess industrial independence . . . Not all the wealth of the world, in that state of social freedom, would purchase for a Prince, the unwilling charms of a free maiden whose heart said no . . . It is as vain for women to expect freedom in the present state of social organization . . . as it is for the labouring multitude to expect ease and plenty from universal suffrage and annual parliaments.

Fourierism attracted a much larger following, including a feminist following, in America, where a number of communities were founded on Fourierite principles in the 1830s and 1840s.

29

that 'the happiness . . . of the whole of society, is in direct ratio to an approach of an equality . . . of rights and duties, between husbands and wives . . .'[42]

Like Fourier, many Owenites viewed this progress of women towards freedom as 'the victory of human nature over brutality', of brain over brawn, of feminine reason and gentleness over masculine intolerance and violence. Free women would be the bearers of a new moral culture. Fettered women, on the other hand, were mental and moral cripples who contaminated all those around them. So degraded were such women that they were even incapable of experiencing their condition as servitude; their self-contempt and servility reduced them 'to such impotence, that they either voluntarily spring forward to meet the yoke and *vow* themselves slaves, or submit in sullen apathy to their fate . . .'[43] But once loosed from these psychic chains, women's 'more refined sentiments and moral capabilities' (in Wheeler's words) would become the spiritual lever elevating society as a whole. Femininity itself, as Wheeler explained, would become a regenerating force:

> When I advocate the Rights of Women . . . I do it under the most perfect conviction, that I am also pleading the cause of man by showing the mighty influence Women hold over the happiness or misery of men themselves, according as they are instructed or ignorant . . . fettered or free . . . So true is it that though men make the law, it is women who mould the manners and morals of society; and according as they are enlightened or ignorant, do they spin the web of human destiny.[44]

This notion that women had a unique moral mission to perform was popular among all kinds of people in the early nineteenth century, anti-feminist as well as feminist. Its ideological function was highly ambiguous. In the hands of anti-feminists, it usually served merely to buttress sentimental dogmas of domestic womanhood ('the Angel in the house')[45], but even among feminists it led to a celebration of female specialness and moral superiority which jostled uneasily with arguments against the concept of an innate femininity. In Owenite feminist literature, the two ideas frequently appeared within the same piece of writing, thereby displaying an unresolved tension between the desire to minimize sexual difference and the need to re-assert it in women's favour. This tension was particularly acute within Socialist rhetoric, since the very qualities which were considered quintessentially female were also those which the Owenites wished to see generalized across the population: love, compassion, generosity, charity. A good woman, it was implied, was a born communist. The argument was irresistibly attractive to most Socialist feminists, yet it opened the flood-gates to all sorts of sentimental notions about feminine specialness which women like Wheeler wanted to shut out. Some attempted a compromise:

> Women . . . are often amiable, and more sensible to general benevolence, more alive to the sentiments that civilize society, than men. Yet are these only the fair defects . . . of a bad system of education and false refinement . . .[46]

The horns of this particular dilemma are ones on which feminists have always been caught. Minimizing distinctions between the sexes ('The mind has no sex,' Fanny Wright once wrote)[47] gave coherence to demands for egalitarian treatment, but at the expense of ignoring those aspects of women's existence which simply could not be lived in the male mode. But to admit the particularity of women's lives and needs appeared to undercut the egalitarian argument; hence the tendency to couch such claims in terms of feminine superiority. The dilemma could only be resolved, as some Owenites realized, by postulating the simultaneous transformation of *both* sexes – the critique of socially-defined femininity must become a critique of masculinity as well. Women must 'indignantly reject the boon of equality with such creatures as men now are . . . full of ignorance and vanity, priding [themselves] on a sexual superiority entirely independent of any merit . . .,'[48] and turn instead to a strategy which would allow new ways of being men and women together. After all, as Wheeler pointed out, masculine 'selfishness and stupidity' were no more natural than feminine servility. 'I have no antipathy to men, but only institutions', she explained in her 1829 lecture, 'my object is to deprecate that narrow, stupid policy which divides their interests and in so doing makes a pandemonium of our earth, by forcing its inhabitants to be in constant opposition to each other!'[49]

Between the sexes, as between classes, it was 'circumstances' and 'institutions' which bred antagonism, not an inevitable division of needs and interests. What were the 'institutions' which placed men and women 'in constant opposition to each other'?

First and foremost, they were marriage and family life. At times the Owenites investigated other areas of conflict between men and women, such as sexual competition in the labour market. But at the heart of their analysis was a systematic critique of what they called 'the marriage system', that is, patriarchal marriage and the nuclear family ('single-family arrangements'). It was as fathers and husbands that men oppressed women; it was as daughters, wives and mothers that women experienced their most direct subjugation. Sexual subordination was basically a family affair.

SEX SLAVERY

The inequities of marriage had been a major theme of feminist writers from the seventeenth century onward. 'If Absolute Sovereignty be not necessary in a State how comes it to be so in a Family?' Mary Astell had demanded in 1700,[50] and over ninety years later Mary Wollstonecraft was still trying to force the same point upon her readers: 'The *divine right* of husbands, like the divine right of kings, may, it is hoped, in this enlightened age, be contested without danger . . .'[51] Unfortunately her own career, and the vituperation heaped upon her by opponents, demonstrated all too clearly the dangers of arguing such a position, and when her friend Mary Hays published a tract in support of the views expressed in the *Vindication* she was subjected to similar criticism. 'An opinion thus preposterous and inimical to the monarchical constitution of matrimony is one of the last qualities, almost, any man would wish to find in his wife,' one popular ladies' journal pronounced.[52] The wave of counter-revolution which swept across Britain had carried with it lurid tales of domestic life in revolutionary France, and the scandal surrounding Wollstonecraft's own unhappy love life sealed the connection. 'It is supposed that the chains of Hymen would be among the first that would be broken . . . in case of a Revolution . . .' Thomas Spence remarked.[53] Demands for marital reform, like the rest of the feminist programme, became tarred with the brush of infidelism and Jacobinism, until it was only in the most radical circles that such issues received a sympathetic hearing. Between the early 1830s and the mid-1840s dozens of letters from women appeared in the Owenite press voicing complaints and demands which few other journals would have published. 'Who . . . shall settle the question of the "True social position and claims of women?" ' began one:

> Men have hitherto done it. How has it been done? They have dictated duties towards *themselves,* and, with general consent, have punished us severely when those duties have not been rigidly observed . . .

'Have any of the self-named reforming parties, so vociferous now in England for their own rights, given a single thought to, or shown any desire for . . . change in this *Helot* condition of their country women?' the letter went on to demand, 'Alas! not one, beyond . . . the equalizing theory put forth by the founder of the Rational System of Society, the inimitable Robert Owen . . .'[54]

In order to understand this tradition of protest, and its place within Owenism, we need to look briefly at the sexual ideology in which it arose.

The Owenites inherited a conjugal ideal which had been con-structed in deliberate opposition to the marriage conventions of aristocratic England. From the seventeenth century onward, middle-class ideologues had attacked the cynical property marriages of the upper classes and posed in their place 'unions of the affections', freely-contracted 'companionate marriages' held together by heart-strings rather than purse-strings. Sexual love, previously assumed to exist only outside marriage, was now to be confined within it; the corollary to fierce Puritan injunctions against adultery and pre-marital sex was the romanticization of marriage itself. 'This state, with the affection suitable to it, is the completest image of heaven we can receive in this life . . .' ran a typical bit of moral advice in the mid-eighteenth century.[55] At its most consistent, this code was interpreted not only as the victory of solid bourgeois virtue over blue-blooded decadence, but also as an elevation of female status: 'I don't take the state of matrimony to be designed . . . that the wife is to be used as an upper servant in the house . . .' Daniel Defoe wrote in a classic statement of companionate sexual philosophy, 'Love knows no superior or inferior, no imperious command on the one hand, no reluctant subjection on the other.'[56]

This was an ideology riddled with contradictions. While marriage was being eulogized as a loving partnership, laws were simultaneously being passed which deprived married women of all rights over their property and person. Romantic marriage was asserted against the *mariage de convenance*, yet (Christopher Hill tells us) 'in practice . . . property was still the main consideration', and pre-marital chastity largely a commercial proposition: 'expensive goods must not be shop-soiled . . .'[57] Fidelity within marriage was proclaimed as a central virtue, but in all but the most Puritan households this was chastity for the wife alone: 'Home is the eternal prison-house of the wife,' Thompson wrote, 'The husband paints it as the abode of calm bliss, but takes care to find, outside of doors . . . a species of bliss not quite so calm, but of a more varied and stimulating description.'[58] And above all, marriage was to be based upon the free choice of both individuals involved, a contract willingly entered. But here the rhetoric barely masked a reality of power and coercion. 'Each man yokes a woman to his establishment, and calls it a *contract*,' ran one of the finer polemical passages of the *Appeal*:

> Audacious falsehood! A contract! Where are any of the attributes of contracts, of equal and just contracts, to be found in this transaction? . . . Have women been consulted as to the terms of this pretended contract? . . . Men enacted, that is to say, *willed* the terms, let women like them or not: man to be the owner, master, and ruler of every thing, even to the minutest action, and most trifling article of property brought into the common stock by the woman; woman to be the moveable property, and ever-obedient servant, to the bidding of man.[59]

'All women are slaves . . .' Wollstonecraft's fictional heroine, Maria, had cried out in 1798,[60] and almost thirty years later Owenites like Wheeler and Thompson were delivering the same message: 'A domestic, a civil, a political slave, in the plain unsophisticated sense of the word – in no metaphorical sense – is every married woman.' Like all other feminists of the day, they drew an analogy between black slavery* and 'the condition of women in this so-called *civilized* nation' where a husband has command not only over his wife's labour and property, but her body as well: 'his involuntary breeding machine and household slave . . .'[61]

Looking at the legal situation of the married woman in 1825, it is not difficult to see the force of the slavery analogy. The statutory expression for her status was *femme couverte*: her legal identity was 'covered' by that of her husband, and she became, in the words of another Owenite, 'an invisible woman – a species of ghost, who haunts her husband, and only becomes half solidified when he is no more.'[62] Not only did she have no right to enter contracts or own any property (including her earnings), but she had no rights over her children, whose guardianship passed from her husband to his nearest male relative at his death. The double moral standard was also legally entrenched: an adulterous wife lost all rights to maintenance and was liable to be abandoned on the basis of a judicial separation; an adulterous husband suffered no penalty, could pursue a wife who left him on account of his infidelity and sue her harbourers, and if he abandoned her could be made to provide support only on the basis of a court order establishing her need. Divorce was available to those who had the thousand pounds necessary to get a Private Member's Bill passed in Parliament dissolving their union; otherwise it was legally impossible (no woman had ever won a divorce in this way, although a number of men had). Wife-beating was legal, so long as the stick was no thicker than the man's thumb. 'And yet this state of the civilized wife, worse than that of the female West Indian slave, is termed a state of equality, of identity of interest, of involving of interests with those of her husband, her master!'[63]

Faced with this contradiction between the ideology of love-

---

* The analogy with black slavery was of particular significance to early nineteenth century feminists because of the popular campaign for the abolition of the British slave trade being waged at the time. The campaign, which was led by the Evangelicals, involved large numbers of women who were, however, consigned to an auxiliary position and even banned from direct participation in the 1840 World Anti-Slavery Congress held in London. Inevitably, this led some female abolitionists to compare their own situation to those of the men and women they were trying to liberate; particularly since there already existed a large feminist literature (including the *Appeal*) which drew such comparisons.

marriage and the reality of institutionalized male dominance, feminists from the seventeenth century on re-affirmed the romantic ideal and demanded the reforms necessary to realize it: civil and legal rights, education, improved employment opportunities – in short, what one woman described as 'a complete revolution which shall place women of every rank above the necessity of contracting . . . mercenary marriages . . . Why should not women, like men, be permitted and encouraged to assume a social position which should allow them, – still like men, to decline marriage, until free choice, preference, exclusive affection, nay *love* . . . determined their fate in wedlock?'[64] The marital tie must be emotional, not economic; female dependency must be replaced by mutual independence and respect, and in Wollstonecraft's words, men must become content with 'rational fellowship instead of slavish obedience . . .'[65]

As inheritors of this tradition, the Owenites also stressed these egalitarian reforms – with one crucial difference. The only way finally to end property in women, they argued, was to end private property itself. It was certainly a more radical solution than Wollstonecraft had posed, yet there is a sense in which it was the logical outcome of the demands which she and other feminists had raised. For as the *Appeal* pointed out, if the question is – how can women achieve equality of status in a society where status and power derive from wealth? – the answer is that they cannot. 'In the race of individual competition for wealth, men have such fearful advantages over women, from superiority of strength and exertion uninterrupted by gestation, that they . . . maintain the lead in acquisition . . .' Under capitalism, natural disabilities translate into direct oppression. Even if all the demands Wollstonecraft had raised three decades earlier had been met, still the economic basis of sexual subordination would remain:

> Let knowledge be equally and impartially conveyed to both sexes, let civil and political rights be equal to both, let acquired property at the death of parents be equally distributed to male and female: still the inequality of powers in the race of individual competition for wealth, must have a continual tendency to keep the average acquisitions of women under those of men . . .[66]

Men and money: it was the combined power of both which kept women in a state of 'helpless bondage'. 'But in community, money will not be known, neither will the want of it be dreaded, for all that can minister to the comforts of life will be had in abundance', Frances Morrison, another Owenite feminist, explained in a later tract on the marriage question, 'There will be no marrying for convenience merely (a very cold word), but real affection inspired by real and known worth on both sides.'[67] The realization of the old bourgeois ideal entailed the dissolution of bourgeois society itself. Love-unions could only be made under communism. 'All motives are here taken away from men to practise injustice; all motives are here taken away from women to submit to injustice . . . Who wishes, man or woman, in these Communities to be esteemed or loved, must deserve to be esteemed or loved . . .'[68]

The elimination of personal dependence was the key to female emancipation. Once both women and men relied on the communal unit for their basic material needs, male domination would lose all economic foundation, while the new educational and cultural opportunities made available to women in the social communities would free them from the crippling sense of inferiority which distorted sexual relations in the Old Immoral World. Moreover, within the new communities all living arrangements would be fully collectivized, allowing housework ('domestic drudgery') to be transformed from a private service into a social activity, performed on a rotational basis with the 'most scientific' equipment available. Prior to the Owenites, only the Pantisocratic poets had questioned women's primary responsibility for household labour and child-rearing (Wollstonecraft did suggest that women should be allowed to engage in other activities in addition to domestic duties, but never as an alternative to them), but now the *Appeal* extended its analysis of sex-slavery to include the sexual division of labour itself. 'Isolated and stultified with their children, with their fire and food-preparing processes', women become prisoners of routinized trivia. The 'passive machines for producing [children]', they thereby become mentally passive, as their 'eternal association with mere childhood and childish toys' reduced them to a perpetual infancy of mind and ability. There was nothing of the mid-Victorian romanticization of domestic life here: the privatized household was an 'isolated breeding establishment', a 'den of ignorance and misery' whose survival was incompatible with further human development.[69] In the new communities it too would be swept away and a new regime of communalized home life established.

These changes were essential for women; they were also essential for the progress of humanity as a whole. For as long as women remained subject to men within the patriarchal family, a major source of social disunity was perpetuated. The 'uniform injustice . . . practised by man towards woman' in the family, Thompson wrote, 'confounds all notions of right and wrong . . .'

> Every family is a centre of absolute despotism, where of course intelligence and persuasion are quite superfluous to him who has only to command to be obeyed: from these centres, in the midst of which all mankind are now trained, spreads the contagion of selfishness and the love of domination through all human transactions . . . This great obstacle must be removed before any real advance can be made to human happiness: not even Co-operation, without it, would produce happiness or virtue.[70]

The ideological underpinnings of the competitive system, in other words, were habits of dominance and subordination formed within the most intimate areas of life. The enslavement of women by men deformed human character and strangled human potential to the point where social hierarchy became accepted as natural and inevitable. This theme was most pronounced in Wheeler and Thompson's writings, where it developed into a ferocious attack on the competitive, egoistic male, the 'monarch of the domestic circle' who, having been trained to mastery within the family, then took this self-seeking mode into public life as well: 'He has been rendered incapable of considering the effects of his action over all whose interest they may reach: he calculates their effects with reference to himself alone . . . which leads him in all his actions to substitute power for right . . .'[71] *Homo Economicus*, the atomized, competitive individual at the centre of bourgeois culture, was the product of a patriarchal system of psycho-sexual relations.

Constructing an alternative to this would require not merely the reform of the marital family, but its abolition. In practice, the Owenites campaigned at both levels: for immediate reforms in marriage outside the social communities, and communalized family life within them. In 1835 Owen published the most influential Owenite text on the marriage question, *Lectures on the Marriages of the Priesthood in the Old Immoral World*, in which he argued for civil marriage and cheap, easy divorce – both demands which were also being raised by certain liberal Nonconformists at the time. Since the mid-eighteenth century only weddings performed in the Established Church had been legally recognized, a situation which generated great resentment within the Dissenting churches, and Owen's polemics against 'marriages of the Priesthood' were in tune with a rising chorus of opinion favouring an end to this monopoly.[72] Similarly, divorce reform was acquiring supporters among some of the boldest bourgeois Radicals, although it was years before they won enough support to achieve the desired changes.[73] At one level, then, Owen's writings – and those of other Socialist propagandists who wrote on these issues – can be seen as part of a growing movement for the liberalization of marriage. But they also led in a far more radical direction, towards a repudiation of the entire system of 'single-family arrangements'.

In Owen's marriage lectures, as in the *Appeal*, the family is condemned as a key source of competitive ideology, as well as the main institution responsible for the transmission of private property. There is, however, an interesting difference of emphasis between Owen's argument and the one developed in the *Appeal*. For Owen, it is the existence of the bourgeois family unit – the little commonwealth which looks only to its own interests and ignores those of its neighbours – which is the real barrier to social reform, rather than the power of the husband/father within the family, which he acknowledged but did not emphasize. The 'artificial union of the sexes, as devised by the priesthood, requiring single-family arrangements, and generating single-family interests' was, Owen argued, the foundation of all social inequalities:

> The children within these dens of selfishness and hypocrisy are
> taught to consider their own individual family their own world, and
> that it is the duty and interest of all within this little orb to do
> whatever they can to promote the advantages of all the legitimate
> members of it. With these persons it is *my* house, *my* wife, *my*
> estate, *my* children, or *my* husband; *our* estate; and *our* children

39

. . . *our* house and property . . . No arrangement could be better calculated to produce division and disunion in society . . .[74]

This pronounced emphasis on the anti-social functions of the family, rather than its patriarchal character, can be traced back to the groups from whom Owen first derived his anti-familial views. These were the Christian-communist sects which he encountered in America, whose opposition to the nuclear family was based less on a desire to equalize women's status (although at least one of these sects, the Shakers, strongly advocated female equality) than on a desire to minimize all 'individualized' allegiances which might undermine the communal spirit.[75] 'The great problem of Socialism,' as one leading American communitarian expressed it, 'is whether the existence of the marital family is compatible with that of the universal family, which the term "Community" signifies.'[76] That they were not at all compatible was the lesson which Owen took from his first community experiment, at New Harmony in America, where group cohesion was singularly lacking, due, he eventually decided, to the wedded status of most of its residents. 'Families trained in the individual system . . . have not acquired those moral qualities . . . necessary to promote full confidence and harmony among all the members . . .' he concluded sadly.[77]

In general, it should be said, Owen was not much of a feminist; or at least he was certainly far less concerned with the question of women's emancipation than many of his followers. He admired Wollstonecraft and was always ready to concede the justice of women's demands,[78] but his own personal style was so paternalistic that it militated against any real appreciation of the issues involved. All his major pronouncements on social policy, such as *The Book of The New Moral World*, contained statements promising women an egalitarian future, but even these writings displayed none of the passionate indignation which was to be found in the propaganda of the women Socialists or in the works of men like Thompson. And his lectures on marriage, although sympathetic to the plight of wives, tended to take a more carefully balanced view of the miseries of conjugal existence. Within conventional marriage, he argues, *all* are made to suffer. For the husband, marriage means disillusionment and bitterness, for having 'been taught to consider his wife a being possessing powers and capacities altogether different than those which nature has given her' his rude awakening into the realities of domestic life (and, Owen hints, sexual unhappiness) sends him off 'by some of the various roads which preṣent themselves . . . to seduce men from their disagreeable homes.' He readily acknowledges, however, that even this unsatisfactory option of disengagement was not available to the wife. As the possession of her husband 'by religion and law' she must 'have no will of her own, no opinions, nor any feelings but in accordance with the will, perhaps a capricious one, of her lord and master'. There can be no doubt, Owen adds, that she is 'the more to be pitied of the two', for as her duties as a homemaker increase so does her husband's sexual interest in her decline, until in order to gain her way she is 'necessarily forced to become a weak, cunning, deceptious, inferior being . . .'

> The fault, however, is not her's; . . . or her husband; both are forced to become victims, through a wretchedly ignorant system . . . There can scarcely be any real confidence between parties thus most unnaturally tied to produce unnatural children, to be placed under the most unnatural circumstances, that they may be trained, like their parents, to become most artificial and unnatural characters.[79]

The key word here is obviously 'natural'. Natural/unnatural, instinctual/artificial, spontaneous/constrained: these polarities dominate all of Owen's writings on human relations. The ties of affectionate care which bind people to one another are a phenomenon of Nature; their confinement within the boundaries of 'single-family arrangements' is a result of artificial social organization. The sympathy which individuals feel for each others' needs is an inborn emotion; the narrowing of this sympathy to one's immediate household is a 'vile distortion of our finest feelings'. Above all, sexual love is a spontaneous expression of the most joyous and pleasurable of our instincts; its repression within conventional marriage is a desecration of the natural order, a violation of 'the most sacred laws of our nature'. Here Owen brought his doctrine of character formation into the service of a most uncompromising sexual libertarianism:

> Now as men and women have not been formed with power to create their own feelings, or to love or hate at their own pleasure, but are,

41

on the contrary, compelled to receive such feelings as the influence
of external objects produce in their organization, it is blasphemy, if
anything is blasphemy, against the laws of their nature, for man or
woman to make any promises or engagements relative to their
feelings of affection or hatred . . . for each other . . .

You, therefore, commit a crime, against the everlasting laws of
your nature when you say that you will 'love and cherish' what
your organization may compel you to dislike and to loath, even in a
few hours . . .[80]

Silly as this extreme necessitarian doctrine may sound (one
opponent described Owen's view of love as 'one portion of
organized matter . . . [being] propelled to seek some other
portion of matter')[81] it had the important effect of denying any
contractual basis for human relations. Social relationships
must flow from instinctive emotion and desire; contractual
relations – the injunctions of law, religion, property regulations – are an iron web of rules strangling and dividing people
from one another. The favourite metaphors for this process
tended to be watery ones: sexual love was a flood, current, tide,
which could not be dammed, channelled, bottled up . . .[82] The
analogy with a natural force was very important, since it
highlighted the idea that sexual response was an emotional event
beyond the control of human will (what the Owenites called,
rather unfortunately, the 'doctrine of moral non-responsibility').
'Before I admit . . . of chaining any two individuals of opposite
sexes together for life, I must have ample proof that they can
control and subdue their affections through the whole of their
lives, in opposition not only to their own nature, but in direct
contradiction to the immutable law of the mighty whole,' as the
Spencean tailor, George Petrie, wrote.[83] The laws of Nature were
not merely to be recognized but to be obeyed. Those who defied
them were heretics, blasphemers; and the arch apostates were the
clergy themselves, who defiled Nature in the name of the false
idols of Christianity. In 1817 Owen had denounced all religion as
'a mass of iniquitous error', and now in his marriage writings this
infidelism reached new rhetorical heights. 'The marriages of the
world,' Owen blasted away, 'are . . . a Satanic device of the
Priesthood to place and keep mankind within their slavish
superstitions . . .

42

And to make a colourful pretence for these marriages, the priests
and the rich and the powerful . . . have united to contrive an artificial conduct for the industrious and poor, and to call that conduct
by high-sounding names, and especially to *call it virtuous.*[84]

These 'marriages of the law and gospels' are a 'terrible sacrifice
of our most delightful and innocent joys'; they 'drive pure and
genuine chastity far from the abodes of men . . .':

Chastity is a feeling . . . mysteriously implanted in human nature,
and exists only between the sexes when in their intercourse they feel
sincere and genuine affection for each other; and this delightful
union of heart and mind the Priesthood never gave by their
unhallowed and grossly absurd ceremonies . . . What a sacrilege of
the best and finest sympathies of our nature! What ignorance of the
organization of man and woman! What horrid sacrifice of the
happiness of the human life![85]

This impassioned plea for sensuality was interwoven with an
assortment of fascinating sexual theories, including the popular
notion that celibacy caused 'mental derangement or severe bodily
disease' (particularly in women, who withered if unwatered, so to
speak), and another that children conceived in unhappy
marriages were invariably physically inferior. Marriage was
therefore responsible not only for adultery and prostitution (since
natural needs which remained unsatisfied in conjugal relations
must find their outlet somewhere) but also for the physical and
spiritual degeneration of the species. No community could
possibly be built on such a corrupt and unstable foundation: 'No
community has yet been begun which did not consist of married
couples. I have known from the first that no such practice could
succeed . . . Before a community . . . can take place, our minds
must be born again . . .' So 'in this new world', as in Heaven, 'to
free it from sin and the cause of sin, there will be no marriages of
the priest or giving in marriage.'[86]

Apart from anything else, this aspect of Owen's thought must
surely cast doubt on the common interpretation of him as an
essentially Tory thinker. There was much more of Blake than
Cobbett or Carlyle in these celebrations of spontaneous
sensuality, and a good deal of Rousseau in his nostalgia for an
'original condition' of 'innocence and simplicity'.[87] But above all,
there was the persistent echo of Shelley – and behind him,

43

William Godwin – whose intransigent opposition to compulsory monogamy influenced a whole generation of sexual radicals, particularly male radicals. 'How long ought the sexual connection to last?' ran the accompanying notes to *Queen Mab*, Shelley's lyrical rendering of Godwin's *Political Justice*:

> What law ought to specify the extent of the grievances which should limit its duration? a husband and wife ought to continue so long united as they love each other; any law which should bind them to cohabit for one moment after the decay of their affection would be a most intolerable tyranny . . .[88]

'Love withers under constraint . . .'; or in Godwin's own words, 'the institution of marriage is . . . a monopoly, and the worst of monopolies', for through marriage the instinctual flow of sexual affection is checked 'by despotic and artificial means', thereby fomenting deceit and hypocrisy.[89] Only when the new social order outlined in *Political Justice* had been established, Godwin had claimed, would these crippling restraints be removed; only then, in Shelley's words, would 'Nature's primal modesty' triumph over 'dull and selfish chastity/That virtue of the cheaply virtuous/Who pride themselves in senseless and frost':

> Then, that sweet bondage which is Freedom's self . . .
> Needed no fetters of tyrannic law:
> Those delicate and timid impulses
> In Nature's primal modesty arose.
> And with undoubted confidence disclosed
> The growing longings of its dawning love . . .[90]

To describe this as a 'free love' philosophy – whether in Godwin, Shelley, or Owen – would be very misleading, since the idea of free love implies a casualness in sexual matters which was utterly foreign to the thinking of these romantic moralists. For all of them, and particularly for Owen, 'Nature's chastity' was not merely one of life's little pleasures, but the central, defining feature of moral existence, the key to earthly Paradise, the ladder on which we fallen angels might rise again. 'The solution of this great question is a most important point in a better arrangement of society . . .' as another Socialist put it, '[for] the love of human kind at large finds its highest expression, and is, as it were, brought to a focus in the free and unthwarted union of individuals of different sexes . . .'[91] Original sin may have gone the way of other 'monkish superstitions' in the Owenite *weltanschaung*, but only to be replaced with crimes against 'the holy spirit within us', the 'divine' Law of Love.

Like the rejection of property marriage, this celebration of the liberated libido also emerged directly from contradictions within bourgeois sexual ideology. From the time when 'unions of the affections' had begun to be counterposed to 'mercenary marriages', the problem of just what was meant by 'affection' had proved a persistent bugbear to Puritan moralists, who would repress the erotic implications of the doctrine within their own sermonizing only to see it surface again and again within radical heretical circles. In the mid-seventeenth century it had been the 'ranting' sects who celebrated carnality as a holy duty; in the late eighteenth century the young Godwinians advocated erotic love as Nature's law; and now there appeared the Owenites – whose own sexual philosophy was developing at a time when a new wave of puritanical ideologues were promulgating a sexual code bleaker, perhaps, than any which had preceded it.[92] 'A true love marriage purifies the debased imagination,' ran a standard text of Evangelical homilies, '. . . it teaches, practically, how empty is carnal, how solid is spiritual delight . . .'[93] It was against this arid promise of godly joys that Owen and his followers affirmed the blessings of natural religion – the sacred pleasures of the flesh. 'And do the laws of morality forbid the enjoyment of pleasure?' one Owenite woman wrote, 'What! Has Nature given to us affections merely for our torment? Are we possessed of our senses, only to deceive and betray us? . . . Ah, no; surely not!'[94]

In the early 1830s this strand in Owenite thinking was strengthened by the temporary presence of another group of erotic libertarians in their midst, the French Saint-Simonians, who arrived to propagandize England with their own brand of Socialism in 1832.* Female equality and the substitution of 'moral marriage'

---

* Claude-Henri de Saint Simon (1760-1825) was an aristocrat who evolved a scheme for an industrial utopia based on a rigid hierarchy of labour. After his death the sect (which was largely middle-class, with many civil servants among its members) became increasingly less concerned with their founder's social theory and more with the propagation of their erotic philosophy, for which they were eventually prosecuted and imprisoned, for offences against public order and

(free unions) for legal marriage were key tenets of Saint Simonianism, and soon the visitors were touring the country (the women in their notorious bloomers) delivering lectures on these themes to radical audiences everywhere.[95] Anna Wheeler had spent some time in a Saint Simonian group in France in 1818, and now she acted as their *patronne* in London, introducing them to other Owenites and translating their feminist writings for Owen's newspaper, *The Crisis*.[96] In 1833 Owen lent the Saint-Simonian missionaries his London premises for twice-weekly lectures on marriage and the 'Rights of Women', which attracted large audiences of women.[97] 'The principles of both are the same,' a hostile observer wrote of the English and French Socialists at the time, 'open profligacy and plunder, and they are . . . addressed, in the first instance, to the weaker sex, upon whom they hope to make a fatal impression, as the serpent succeeded with Eve.' Educated females, the writer went on, would see at once how the proposed sexual reforms would deprive them of every vestige of maidenly purity and self-respect; nonetheless, 'some few fallen members of the sex have had the hardihood to applaud the new doctrine . . .'[98]

Support for 'moral marriages' was not universal in the Saint Simonian membership, however, and eventually the group split over the issue, with the 'extreme' wing going on to develop a quasi-mystical view of sexual relations which, as we shall see in a later chapter, influenced a number of Owenites.[99] The 'moderate' wing, which seceded, included several women who had become very uneasy about the implications of such doctrines for women's

---

morality. An interesting view of the Saint Simonian presence in England is provided by this report from a French woman (herself a Fourierite) visiting in London at the time:

> They have here an Italian Saint-Simonian, called Fontana, who has turned the heads of the Owenite ladies, and makes Mr Owen scowl, since he is not happy to have someone filch his dear disciples. I have sent many ladies to their sermons and all have become so-called Saint-Simonians – could this be love of the doctrine or the doctrine's advocate? I don't know, but I suspect that English women care more for beautiful bodies than beautiful ideas. (Gans, *Socialistes*, p. 112)

There is no other evidence to support this claim of mass conversions among the Owenite women.

sexual status, and this was an unease which soon appeared within the English Socialist ranks as well. Feminists, even Socialist feminists, frequently took a dimmer view of amorous relations than their male comrades. Compare, for example, Owen's perorations on 'natural love' with this letter from Anna Wheeler to *The Crisis* discussing the nature of heterosexual passion in women, and its effects on their social position:

> Woman's love . . . is a fearful thing, because it has fixed and per-
> petuated the degradation of her sex, and arrested the moral progress
> of man himself; why should he change his unjust, cruel, and
> insulting laws for woman, when he can . . . through woman's
> power of loving, command worship and adoration . . .? This
> intensity of woman's love I believe to be the fatal result of her
> vicious and slavish training, and . . . the symbol of her deep
> degradation, moral and social . . .[100]

Love in women, she went on to say, has 'been made a supersti-tion', a sort of pseudo-religion, which like any other religion has as its object of worship only the mystified projection of the believer's own desires, 'and the hangman's wife has just as much reverence for . . . *her master*, as any other gentle dame who piously concentrates all useless affections on *one*, however worthless and vicious he may be . . .'

> I would not attempt to *rationalize* love . . . [for] all experience
> shows it is dangerous to *tamper* with, – but I would *rationalize*
> human character, from whence all these sentiments emanate . . . by
> the invigorating influence of a co-operating reason.[101]

Reason over Passion: this, far more than sexual freedom, tended to be the dominant theme of most feminist writings, not only in this period but also in the preceding one. It was a wonder-ful irony, for example, that Shelley had claimed to derive his opposition to marriage from Wollstonecraft's writings, since nothing could have been further from his lyrical hymns to sensuality than her brusque remarks on 'the depravity of the appetite which brings the sexes together . . .' 'Nature must ever be the standard of taste,' she wrote, 'yet how grossly is nature insulted by the voluptuary' which renders women 'the slaves of casual lust'.[102] A similar puritanism was common among Owenite women, reflecting not only their anxiety about unwanted pregnancy or their resentment against men who treated them as sexual playthings, but also a deep-seated fear of their own sexual feelings, the 'silken fetters' of desire which bind women to their oppressors. Loving men, women become hostages to their own hearts, incapable even of willing their freedom – 'sentimental slaves', in Anna's words. Better, surely, to 'let . . . *reason* teach passion to submit to necessity' and 'let the dignified pursuit of virtue . . . raise the mind above those emotions which rather embitter than sweeten the cup of life . . .'[103]

But whatever the desired content of love between women and men – rational or erotic – every Owenite agreed that it could not flourish in a situation where women were economically dependent upon men. Love must be removed from the nexus of personal power before its transformative potential could be realized. Similarly, 'family affection' must be released from the constraining framework of the isolated, anti-social household in order that it might serve as the unifying basis of a new social order. Far from desiring to eliminate the emotional bonds forged in domestic life, the Owenites wished to see those bonds communalized. 'Single families with separate interests' as Owen wrote, must be eliminated in order that 'communities . . . with one interest . . . arranged as one family' might flourish;[104] or as one movement propagandist wrote in a later tract:

> At what number shall we stop in a family? Shall it be three, thirty, three hundred, or three thousand? . . . In the new circumstances contemplated by Social Reformers, the instinct of family would, for the first time in human history, become productive of individual felicity and public benefit.[105]

It was this project – the 'enlargement of home', as one sympathizer called it – which shaped all the Owenites' plans for the future, and their hopes of emancipating women. Let us turn then, from the Owenites' analysis of women's oppression to their major strategy for ending it.

WOMEN AND THE SOCIAL SYSTEM

Kinship, as anthropologists constantly remind us, is not a blood tie, but a system of categories which serves to locate and prescribe social relationships. The narrowing or widening of these categories, or their transfer from one group of individuals to another regardless of consanguinity, indicates the detachability of kin from any biological foundation. Whether certain individuals become kin – and thereby acquire the responsibilities and rights associated with kinship – depends on their place within a grid of social roles imposed on a population by those who dominate it.

The Owenites' model of social organization was based on the detachment of kinship ties from the nuclear family and their subsequent extension across the entire membership of a community. All the rational planning, the 'scientific arrangements' and so on, were ultimately to have their roots in this emotional soil. 'The new state no less than the old would owe its origin and strength to the permanence of these relations: the mother and infant, the parent and offspring . . .' a Mr Alger explained in an 1835 lecture whose theme was family love as the model for community life.

> The old state indeed pampers and corrupts these natural
> sympathies, the rational state will cherish and healthfully develop
> them . . . extend the hand of brotherhood to the whole human
> family, and present irresistible motives for the free expansion of all
> the diviner functions of our race.[106]

It would be, another wrote, as if 'one family had multiplied as to fill the earth' and was then 'by the stipulations of kindred . . . pledged to co-operation in the full extent . . .'[107]

It was this goal which ultimately determined the design of the proposed communities. According to most of the blueprints drawn up, the entire population would be housed in several large, connected buildings with individual bedrooms for the adults and dormitories for the children. Eating, working and socializing were all to be done in communal areas. Owen's favourite plan was an enclosed 'parallelogram' which would house two thousand (the number considered ideal for a viable community), with schools, libraries, gymnasia, theatres, museums, workshops and kitchens all arranged around an enormous open courtyard. Alternative proposals for communities built on the 'cottage system' (separate residences for each family) were raised occasionally, but these were sharply dismissed as a 'step backwards' into an 'individualised' way of life in which the spirit of commonweal would be undermined by familial selfishness.[108]

Moreover, as Thompson pointed out, to retain such living arrangements would mean that each woman would remain subject to her individual husband and loaded with her individualized housekeeping responsibilities: both aspects of Old World family existence which must be completely eliminated.[109]

The abolition of private housework, as we noted earlier, was a central concern of all Owenite community planners. Nine-tenths of women's time, Thompson calculated, was taken up with this 'unproductive and repulsive drudgery'.[110] An article in *The New Moral World* which argued that children should perform all this labour (a suggestion raised frequently in the movement) went on to make the sort of statistical calculations dear to the heart of every scientific Socialist:

> It would be a curious calculation to ascertain how many hours of women's time is taken up in going to market and laying-in the smallest purchaseable quantities of the necessities of life. There must be 500,000 families, who every year purchase a housekeeping and a washing book; this at 3s per annum, is £75,000, which would build a very tolerable community.[111]

The advantages of collectivization of this work were a favourite theme. 'Now let us look into the house of a working-man who has a young family, and we shall see his poor wife distracted with innumerable cares. She has to prepare food, to clean the apartments, to wash and mend the clothes, and to nurse or watch a set of squalling brats . . . Where then is the wonder, if when her husband comes home at the close of the day, he finds her body worn down, and her temper ruffled?' But, 'what could be done by union of means and co-operation of efforts . . .!':

> Mrs A. we will suppose, has the best convenience for cooking, and perhaps also is an adept in the culinary department of housewifery; –Mrs B. has the largest copper, and perhaps other apparatus for washing; –While Mrs C. has a spacious room, and is best qualified to take care of young children . . . let us suppose that, with a hearty disposition to aid each other, they were to consult together as to the best means of getting through the aggregate domestic work of the association . . . can it for a moment be doubted that . . . the labour would be wonderfully abridged?[112]

Thompson's own community plans included a 'mechanical laundry' and kitchens on 'scientific principles', while the London

Co-operative Society promised that in its community all adults would perform housework in rotation. Owenite enthusiasm for technological development spilled over into all sorts of plans for household labour-saving devices whose ingenuity was matched only by their Heath Robinson-like eccentricity: one particularly elaborate scheme, for example, included a piece of dinner-time hardware in which, at the touch of a spring, 'a chain descends from the ceiling and conveys the dish of ducks to another table.'[113]

Child-care and education were also to become the collective responsibility of the community. The priority given to the remodelling of human character in the Owenite strategy led to detailed discussions of how little Socialists might best be trained, in which Owen's own contribution included some of the most sensible passages he ever wrote. The 'love of knowledge', he explained in one article, was a natural characteristic of children who 'if left to their own impulses, fill the air with perpetual questionings. Every new thing being a mystery to them, their demands for information are co-extensive with novelty' which for these little ones is 'co-extensive with the universe . . .' The stifling of this curiosity in children through 'rotten prejudice' would be one of the first things to end under socialism: 'rational children [would not] be stinted, rebuked, dispirited . . . [but allowed] a continuous elastic spirit, ever inquiring and ever extending to others the fulness of its own aspirations . . .'[114]

Biological parents, Owen argued in the *Lectures*, were actually the worst-equipped to perform the child-rearing task, since their own selfish feelings towards their offspring perpetuated unsocial attitudes. Not surprisingly, this argument did not acquire much popularity, and he soon dropped it. Collective nurseries, however, continued to feature in every community proposal. Whether they were to be sexually integrated was not usually discussed, but Owen himself urged it:

> It does not appear to me becoming to make any distinction in the sexes during childhood and youth . . . It may readily be proved that one sex cannot be instructed at any age independently of the other – male and female are essential in the human character – and without the relative admixture of their sensations, or the due comparison of their impressions, only a partial approach to wisdom can be attained.[115]

51

Given this argument, one might expect male responsibility for child-care to be urged, but the only time this was suggested was in the *Appeal*, where it was argued that children ought to be given facilities for play and left pretty much to their own devices: 'a superintendent only would be wanting, man or woman as may be most convenient . . .'[116]

Essentially what all these schemes entailed was the collectivization of all *reproductive* labour in the communities. (Even the 'natural suffering' of childbirth would be 'modified and softened' by 'superior science' and communal care, one enthusiast argued, thus guaranteeing that all children would have 'organizations of the first order of human nature' – a typical piece of early eugenics.)[117] Support for this derived from a combination of feminism and time-efficiency calculations. 'To be more respected,' as Thompson had written, 'women must be more useful', and to be more useful was to be more productive. Numerous calculations of the ratio of productive to unproductive labour available to community-builders (unproductive labour defined as including capitalists, lawyers, priests, 'shopmen, clerks, household servants, workmen's wives . . .') had convinced the Owenites that redeployment of unproductive labour would be essential for economic self-sufficiency. 'The strength of women is quite adequate to perform more than half the employments, now pursued exclusively by men . . . the utility of mere strength being now to so great an extent superseded by mechanical and other scientific means . . .'[118] Since the workshops in the communities were to employ 'the most improved machinery that we can procure or fabricate', the female labour-time which was saved through collective housekeeping could be invested in automated manufactures. Thus the sexual division of labour would at least be modified, if not eliminated entirely.

In many proposals, the traditional sexual division of labour was replaced by another which reminds us of the familial basis of the model: a division of tasks and responsibilities by age. In his *Book of the New Moral World* Owen developed just such a scheme, which was then taken up in a multitude of tracts, speeches, and plays in which the Owenites elaborated their hopes. In 1838 Robert Cooper, a Manchester Socialist, published a tract in which he described the labours of the New World in detail, beginning with housework which, he suggested, should be performed by children of eleven years or younger. The 'production of wealth' would be the responsibility of those aged between twelve and twenty-one, while its 'preservation and distribution' would be performed by everyone aged twenty-two to twenty-five. The 'formation of the character of the rising generation' would be the responsibility of those aged twenty-five to thirty-five; at thirty-five community residents would shoulder the burden of government, which they would carry until middle age. At forty-five, however, they would be freed for artistic or intellectual pursuits, tours of other communities, and so on. At each stage women would perform exactly the same tasks as men. 'Our females are not considered by the males, as they are generally in the old world, as their inferiors . . . mere creatures made for their sexual pleasure and indulgence;' Cooper wrote, 'but . . . as their equals, confidential companions . . . in their moral and intellectual improvements and enjoyments . . .'[119]

In addition to all these schemes for re-organized labour, the communities were also to have their own marriage procedures. Rules devised by Owen stipulated that a couple desiring to wed would make their intention known three months before the ceremony, which then simply required the declaration of their union before the whole of the assembled community. Intent to divorce could be declared any time after twelve months of marriage, but then the couple would have to wait six months before the divorce itself, in order to leave open every possibility of reconciliation. All divorced couples would have the right to re-marry. 'Under these arrangements, we have no doubt, a much more virtuous and happy state of society will be enjoyed than any which has existed at any time in any part of the world.'[120] In the scheme which Thompson drew up, all young people over a certain age were to be given bedrooms of their own, which they would retain throughout adulthood regardless of their sexual liaisons. That such liaisons would develop he openly acknowledged, adding that to satisfy 'those who have been accustomed to associate morals with the letters forming certain words or certain arbitrary . . . ceremonies' the word 'marriage' would, if couples chose, be applied 'to all intercourse tending to happiness . . .' The right to sexual intercourse did not, however, automatically imply the right to reproduce:

> No unmarried member could add a child to the infants of the schools without the knowledge of the whole community, nor of course without being liable to the influence of the public opinion of the whole community.[121]

The viability of this last regulation depended on the exercise of what Thompson called 'individual prudence' or, less discreetly, 'individual measures to limit population' – that is, contraception. In his community blueprint, *Practical Directions for the Establishment of Communities*, Thompson blamed what he called the 'one-pillow' system of sexual relations (marriage) for the rising birth-rate. In flat contradiction to Malthus, who had argued that sexual equality in a communist society would be a demographic disaster, Thompson claimed that even in the new communities the 'pain, confinement, and anxiety' associated with childbirth would prevent 'rational women' from over-producing, particularly once methods of preventing conception had been made known to them.[122] Unfortunately, at least one of the methods he had in mind seems unlikely to have met the purpose: 'In the human species the gentle motion of mere walking immediately after intercourse, will prevent the completion of the process of conception,' a procedure which is 'simple, reconcilable with the utmost delicacy, and [demands] nothing but a mental effort from the partner whom a new birth would most inconvenience.'[123]

How widespread support for birth control was among the early Socialists is not known. Owen himself always argued that Malthusian prophecies of over-population were entirely false, and that in a 'rational system' of production and distribution, scarcity of resources would be unknown. But the accusation that he imported condoms into his New Lanark factory (where the workforce was largely female) was never denied, and certainly at least one leading Owenite – George Holyoake – believed it to be true.[124] At any rate, whatever Owen's own views on the matter, there can be no doubt whatsoever about those of his son: in 1830 Robert Dale Owen published his *Moral Physiology*, one of the most important early birth control tracts. Robert Dale was more of a Malthusian than his father, but this was secondary to his commitment to the liberation of sexual pleasure from the burdens of procreation. 'I found all my arguments on the position that the pleasure derived from this instinct, independent of and totally distinct from its ultimate object, the reproduction of our race, is good, proper, worth securing and enjoying';[125] or as the more blunt-spoken Richard Carlile put it in his own contraception tract, 'what a dreadful thing it is that . . . love cannot be enjoyed without conception . . .!'[126] In particular, both stressed, women should be able to express their own sexual needs without fear of pregnancy. Control over her reproductive capacity was a woman's absolute right, Robert Dale believed: 'Her feelings, her interests . . . should be *an imperative law*. She it is who bears the burden, and therefore with her also should the decision rest.'[127]

Making babies, making marriages, making love – for the Owenite feminists these were all integrated into the making of a new world. Only a complete transformation of family life and sexual attitudes would free women and only the new Social System would revolutionize personal relationships in this way. No half-way measures would do. This did not mean, however, that the Owenites were hostile to immediate feminist reforms. All legal, political and educational improvements which could be effected in women's position in the Old Immoral World were considered progressive, and actively encouraged, particularly by upper and middle-class feminists in the movement. Yet at the same time such reforms were generally viewed – in the words of the *Appeal* – as 'negative advances' which would 'remove all superfluous restraints' on women and thereby place them in a more competitive position relative to men, but could never entirely equalize their status.[128] Even the parliamentary vote, a cause dear to the hearts of many early Socialist feminists, was considered only a limited demand, for, in Catherine Barmby's words, 'if all the souls now living . . . were to legislate' in favour of female enfranchisement 'and not decidedly . . . oppose and put down . . . private properties [sic], the legislation . . . would be in vain . . .'[129] Only the 'positive advance' of co-operative communitarianism could finally free women; or in the words of one woman, writing to *The New Moral World* in 1841, 'nothing short of a total revolution in all present modes of acting and thinking among mankind, will be productive of the great change so loudly called for by [women's] miserable state;

> and there is certainly no system so . . . likely . . . as that proposed by the benevolent Owen, of community of property and equality of persons, in which all are *free and equal* . . . Indeed, I am confident that if women really understood the principles and practice of Socialism, there would not be one who would not become a devoted Socialist.[130]

Let us meet some of the women who did.

III

FEMINIST SOCIALISTS:
SOME PORTRAITS

Until the late 1820s, adherence to Owenite views was almost entirely confined to a small number of radical intellectuals. But in the 1830s and 1840s support for the New Science of Society mushroomed. 'Little knots of Socialists appeared in almost every part of the country,' one journalist on *The Whitehaven Herald* observed in 1842, describing how even in his own small city the Owenite presence had swelled from two or three individuals to a band of several hundred, 'of whom a considerable proportion were females . . .'[1] Women appear to have taken an active part in this development right across the country. In 1833 a visiting Saint Simonian reported seeing large numbers of women at all Owenite meetings, including several who were 'noted for their writings and lectures'. 'I have seldom seen faces so animated as theirs,' he wrote admiringly, 'They felt their equality with men . . .'[2] Seven years later, in 1840, hostile observers were commenting on the 'crowds' of women who regularly attended Owenite lectures and meetings around the country.[3] Similar reports persisted until the collapse of the movement in 1845.

The majority of these women, like the men in the Owenite movement, came from the upper working class, with a substantial minority from the lower middle class and a tiny number from wealthy backgrounds.[4] The women who joined Queenwood, a Hampshire Owenite community, were mostly the wives and daughters of skilled factory operatives, who before entering the community had worked as dressmakers, straw-bonnet-makers, weavers and domestic servants. One was the wife of a former civil servant (who had been sacked for his Socialist beliefs); another was a teacher.[5] Other communities, such as the little Ham Common Concordium, boasted a few wealthy ladies among their residents;[6] the women at the Ralahine community, on the other hand, were mostly poor peasants.[7] The London and Brighton Co-operative Societies had one or two lady aristocrats at their meetings in the late 1820s; * by the early 1830s Owen's Charlotte Street Institution in London was sponsoring large meetings of working women, who formed co-operative associations and trade unions.[8] Manchester Socialist branch reported many female domestic servants in its ranks in the early 1840s,[9] while the Leicester group noted the presence of many women schoolteachers at its public meetings over the same period.[10]

What proportion of these women were feminists it is impossible to judge. Hundreds of women attended Owenite lectures on women's rights, and scores wrote to the Owenite press on women's issues, although usually under pen-names to ensure anonymity. A broad commitment to the principle of sexual equality was expected of every dedicated Owenite, male or female; but the number willing to publicly promote that principle, particularly the number of women publicists, was always small: less than a dozen women became well-known Socialist feminist propagandists, supplemented by a slightly larger number who delivered occasional lectures on the subject. Even at the height of Owenism's strength, its self-proclaimed feminists were never more than a minority – albeit a voluble, influential minority – of its female membership.

Nor was this feminist contingent representative, in class terms, of the wider movement to which it belonged. Some Owenite feminists were from working-class backgrounds, and some few from upper bourgeois or even landowning families, but the majority seem to have come from that ambiguous region inhabited by respectable ladies of smallish means – a region on the border between the lower middle class and the upper working class where social distinctions between genteel and plebian often

---

* Byron's widow, Lady Noel Byron, was a *patronne* of the Brighton Co-operative Society in its early years. Then she went to a few meetings of Owenite workers in London and discovered that 'goodwill to men was far from being the prevailing spirit . . . not Co-operation, but spoilation of the rich was the subject of their discourses', so she withdrew her support.

blurred. This generalization, it must be stressed however, is based on evidence which is fragmentary and impressionistic. Many Owenite feminists appear only as signatures at the bottom of angry letters, or as voices in meetings, or in the occasional report from the secretary of a local Owenite society. Even some of the leading publicists remain shadowy figures, with their personal lives largely hidden from us. The series of biographical sketches which follow are, therefore, simply that: sketches whose outlines are often smudgy and obscure. Yet when these partial portraits are scrutinized together, there begins to emerge a common profile whose most marked feature, without a doubt, is its deviance from the feminine norm. Owenite feminists, whatever their social origin, tended to be, in George Gissing's phrase, 'odd women', who in their lives, as well as in their ideas, sharply transgressed social convention.[11] At a time when 'women's place' in society was becoming increasingly circumscribed, these were women who either would not or could not dwell within its narrowing boundaries: a factor which was important in determining the nature and strength of their feminist commitment.

The first women to publicly espouse Owenite feminist ideals were Anna Wheeler and Frances (Fanny) Wright. Both were women from wealthy backgrounds, with prestigious male connections – factors which served to ensure that their careers, unlike most of their Owenite sisters, were recorded in some detail.

ANNA WHEELER (1785–?)

She was born Anna Doyle, the daughter of a radical Protestant Archbishop in Limerick, and god-daughter to the leading Irish nationalist, Henry Gratton.[12] No doubt this progressive background contributed to Anna's later political development, but its influence wasn't obvious in her early years, when as the *belle* of the local squirearchy she was more interested in flirting with locals lads than in discussing social reform. At fifteen, despite parental disapproval, she married a boy from a nearby estate, Francis Massey Wheeler. He turned out to be a fool who cared only for fox-hunting and heavy drinking, and life in the Wheelers' Ballywhire home soon deteriorated into miserable scenes of wrangling resentment, with Anna constantly pregnant or nursing (she had six children, of whom two survived) and Francis perpetually drunk. Furious with her husband, and fed up with dreary domesticity, Anna gradually retreated into an intensive programme of self-education: between the births and deaths of her children she spent day after day, her daughter Rosina later recalled, 'stretched out on the sofa, deep in the perusal of some French or German philosophical work that had reached her via London'.[13] Reading away, while Francis shambled about in a stupor and the farm gradually crumbled about them, she became 'imbued with the fallacies of the French Revolution' and, eventually, with the 'corresponding poisons' (Rosina's description again) of feminism.[14] One bundle of books from London contained the *Vindication*. One imagines Anna's feelings as, pregnant for perhaps the fifth or sixth time by her loutish spouse, she opened Wollstonecraft's book . . . Easy too to imagine how she must have identified with Wollstonecraft's unhappy sexual life, for her own miserable marriage gave her later feminist propaganda a bitter edge very similar to that of the *Vindication*. One 1829 lecture began, 'Having learned only to serve and suffer, in my capacity as slave and woman . . .'[15]

But after twelve years of suffering and servicing her husband Anna had had enough, and in 1812 she gathered up her daughters and fled – first to the home of her uncle, the Governor of Guernsey, and eventually to France, where she became involved with the Saint Simonians. The next twenty years were spent moving between radical groupings in England, France and Ireland, providing an important point of contact between the emergent socialist movements in these countries. In France, she was closely associated with the Saint-Simonian feminists (whose writings she translated for the Owenite press) and also with Charles Fourier and Flora Tristan; in England, Owen and William Thompson soon became close friends and colleagues. By the late 1820s she was writing for Owenite newspapers and speaking on radical platforms, 'and always on one subject,' a friend recalled, 'the present condition of women and their rights as members of society and equals with men'.[16] In 1833 as the Owenites became drawn into a national trades union mobilization, she sat on the executive of the Grand Moral Union of the Productive Classes, Owen's first attempt to construct a 'general union of all trades'.[17]

But by then she was feeling tired and unwell, complaining of depression, neuralgia, and 'a cruel nervous malady which deprives me of the free use of both arms . . .'[18] And although she was still alive to celebrate the 1848 revolutions ('the rights of women are constantly put forth in all the clubs,' a friend wrote from the barricades, 'could you not come over?'[19]) her active political life had ended almost fifteen years earlier.

As a feminist from an upper-class background, Anna was poised between the reform-minded elite of polite society, in which she had been raised, and the far less conventional Owenite intelligentsia which developed in the 1820s and 1830s. In London, like Wollstonecraft three decades earlier, she moved in radical circles which encompassed not only leading Socialists but also the followers of Bentham (whom she 'adored as a philosopher and loved . . . as a friend'[20]), and the many progressive *literati* whom she met through her son-in-law, the novelist Bulwer Lytton. These included the young Benjamin Disraeli who described her, however, as 'not so pleasant, something between Jeremy Bentham and Meg Merrilies, very clever, but awfully revolutionary'.[21] His disapproval is revealing, for if being 'awfully revolutionary' was *de rigueur* at the dinner parties Mary Wollstonecraft had once attended, it was certainly no longer so by the 1820s, when Anna's militant feminism and her support for Owenite ideas ('system-mongering', as her son-in-law dubbed it[22]) placed her well to the left of her liberal associates. At times she felt this distance intensely. 'Before a woman inclined to do good in any way, is permitted to do so in this country, there must be a reform indeed which our Radicals do not contemplate,' she wrote bitterly in 1832, shortly after her Benthamite associates had helped push through Parliament a Reform Bill which, in her words, 'had not a word about justice to women' in it, and in fact explicitly excluded women from the expanded franchise (as well as nearly all working men).[23] The protest of the *Appeal* had been ignored. In an angry, cynical letter written to a friend at the time, she dismissed any further hopes of feminist reforms from these men who, even if they acquired greater political power, could be expected only to introduce expanded educational facilities for women 'since they acknowledge that Women would make better Servants if they were better instructed . . .'

But as to a beneficial change in the social condition of Women, that must depend on their will and energy . . . or it involves so complete a change in all human and social arrangements, as will compel men in their own interests to relinquish their shameless exploitation of half the human race . . .[24]

That tone of angry disillusionment must at least partly explain why feminists from upper- or middle-class backgrounds could be drawn towards Owenism. This is not to suggest that sexual egalitarians were to be found only in the Owenite ranks. Throughout the 1820s and 1830s the South Place Chapel in London (where Anna occasionally lectured) was the meeting place for a group of radical Unitarians including such militant women's rights advocates as Harriet Taylor, John Stuart Mill and W.J. Fox. Fox's journal, *The Monthly Repository*, carried many articles on women's position, and his own views on marriage were so advanced that they finally got him into serious difficulties with the Unitarian leadership.[25] Mary Leman Grimstone, Harriet Martineau, and Anna Jameson were all feminists of a radical-liberal hue whose writings were reprinted in the Owenite press (although occasionally with an editorial comment reminding readers that only communalized property and collectivized family life could ensure female equality).[26] But the number of non-Socialist radicals prepared to take up women's cause in the first half of the century was few; nor is it surprising to discover that the most militant among them – Fox, Mill, Taylor, Grimstone – all took a sympathetic interest in Owenism and Owenite feminism.[27]

Outside radical ranks even this limited support for feminist ideals was absent, smothered under a blanket of prejudice and anxiety which effectively suffocated any expression of women's independent aspirations. Attempting to pierce this fog of fearful conservatism, particularly among women themselves, was no doubt a daunting and exhausting task: Anna certainly seems to have found it so. On several occasions she expressed her dismay at the apparent refusal of most women around her to confront, or even to acknowledge, their oppression. 'In speaking of the degraded position of my sex, I am . . . but too well aware, that my remarks . . . will draw upon me the hate of most men, together with that of the greater portion of the very *sex*, whose *rights* . . . I attempt to advocate,' she told one audience in 1830,[28] while in a later letter she expressed pessimism as to whether 'the Emancipation of Women' would ever be achieved since 'women . . . are passive and indifferent to the suffering of their species':

> The love of rational liberty forms no part of the nature of this willingly degraded sex, and their very propensity for slavery is indeed a justification of the dogma that they originated the fall of man. Women are capable of great personal courage . . . but it is chiefly exhibited in the indurance (sic) of oppression . . . There is something very depressing in contemplating this true, but dark side of the human picture.[29]

This gloomy assessment was made at a time when Anna was ill and unhappy. But the sense of estrangement from average womanhood which it expressed reappeared elsewhere – not only in her own writings but in those of other Owenite feminists as well. Feminists clearly *were* a peculiar breed – with their unorthodox notions, their public political roles, their unconventional private lives – and this produced a sense of personal freakishness (Fanny Wright complained that respectable ladies made her feel like 'a beast from the south seas') which could be intensely isolating. In particular, such women tended to be set apart by their fierce intellectualism. At a time when the most formal schooling any woman, even a wealthy one, could generally expect to receive was a smattering of general knowledge plus training in 'accomplishments' (dancing, drawing, enough French to flirt in), genuine education was almost invariably self-acquired.[30] ' "Knowledge is power," say men,' as Anna told one audience, hence, ' "to keep women our slaves, we must keep them ignorant" . . .'[31] Her own vigorous struggle to escape this mental enslavement, buried in books and nappies in Ballywhire, exemplified a common pattern of feminist development.* For if docile ignorance was a mark of conventional femininity, so the battle for self-enlightenment was a true mark of a female

---

* 'To *speak* or *write* ideas in lucid order forms no part of a woman's mental training,' one woman wrote to *The New Moral World*, and in Anna's case the effects of this could still be seen in her later writings, in which ideas often poured out in a confused rush. Her spelling and grammar were also very bad. It is interesting to speculate whether this was one reason why Thompson took the major initiative in writing the *Appeal*, rather than Wheeler.

dissident – and Owenism contained many such fervent auto-didacts in its feminist ranks.

The lecturer who succeeded Anna as the movement's leading feminist publicist, for example, was a Bristol woman named Emma Martin who somewhere in the middle of raising a family, running a school, and working for the Baptist church (in her pre-Owenite days), had found time to teach herself several languages (including Hebrew and Italian, which she translated), basic medicine and physiology, and enough theology to put many of her later clerical opponents to shame.[32] Two other Owenite feminists, Margaret Chappellsmith and Eliza Macauley, were fascinated by economic theory. Margaret's lectures on currency reform and 'the history of British financial institutions' (copiously illustrated with charts and graphs) were among the most popular offered by the Owenites in the 1840s; Eliza had offered instruction on similar themes to London audiences a decade earlier. Other feminists wrote to the Owenite press of their explorations in mathematics, natural science, and 'the most enlightened philosophy' of the day, including the works of Godwin, Wollstonecraft, Shelley (the feminists' favourite poet) and, of course, Owen himself. 'There are, I believe, many women who, like me, deplore the irrational education they are compelled to receive,' as one of these women (who signed herself 'A Friend to Truth') wrote to an Owenite newspaper in 1839:

> and who, when they have got rid of their school-mistress, and
> can withdraw from a round of insipid and frivolous pursuits,
> strenuously cultivate their own minds, and dare to think for
> themselves . . .

She herself had had access 'to the universities modern libraries' where in struggling through 'mazes of error and prejudice' she had eventually found her way to 'the writings of the benevolent Owen'. 'Wearied with the clashing of opinions, overwhelmed with the view of the wretchedness of the worthy and unfortunate, stung with indignation at the heartless and systematic cruelty of some . . . men' she had turned 'with rapture and admiration' to the 'larger field of mental vision' provided by the New Science of Society: 'Mr Owen's hand tears down the veil, his finger points to the origin of the evil, and his comprehensive and noble mind discovers the remedy . . .'[33]

Even Frances Wright, whose own writings were nearly as popular as Owen's, was almost entirely self-taught. As a girl she buried herself in libraries, where she worked her way through everything from Byron (who inspired her to cut her hair in the mode *revolutionnaire* and write bad poetry) and Epicurus ('I think I have had done with churches,' she confided to her diary afterwards – and she had) to Mary Wollstonecraft, Bentham, Hume and countless other enlightened thinkers.[34] Fanny was a rather brash young intellectual, who by the age of twenty was already dashing off essays on Epicurean philosophy and three-act plays on political themes. But at a time when a bluestocking like Anna Barbauld could write that 'young ladies ought only to have such a general tincture of knowledge as to make them agreeable companions to a man of sense',[35] even Fanny occasionally suffered intellectual doubts and anxieties, as one eloquent autobiographical passage from her *Popular Lectures* indicates:

> Myself a scholar, not a teacher, who have purchased such knowledge as I possess, by years of self-directed study, persevering observation, and untiring reflection, I can well conceive, for I myself have experienced, the doubts, difficulties, hopes, fears, and anxieties, which beset the awakening mind in the early stage of enquiry: the indistinct and, often, evanescent perceptions which encourage, and then check, and then again encourage, again to intimidate its advance; the conflicting thoughts and feelings with which it has to struggle ere it can vanquish early impressions, and consent to receive new ones, admit ideas subversive of those which had grown with its growth, and which, associated with tender recollections, cling to the heart as well as the head . . . All this I can understand, for all this I have . . . felt . . .[36]

Such intellectual growing pains, like the estrangement from ordinary women which such growth usually entailed, were an inevitable part of the price paid by feminists for their hard-won sense of self-determination.

FANNY WRIGHT (1795–1852)

Like Anna Wheeler, Fanny Wright was the product of a well-to-do, enlightened family, and like Anna also, she was gorgeous, precocious, and totally impatient of social convention.[37] Her father, a Scottish linen manufacturer of Jacobin sympathies, died when she was only two; her mother a few months later. So Fanny's early years (along with her younger sister Camilla, who spent most of her life in Fanny's wake) were passed in the home of a conventional aunt who clearly found her brilliant, self-dramatizing niece a bit of a handful. Eventually the two girls moved in with another relative, James Milne, one of the leading members of the Scottish school of progressive philosophers. Here, among Milne and his friends, Fanny encountered an intellectual culture whose vigour and iconoclasm made a deep and lasting mark on her thought. The political and personal dare-devilry which she also began to display at this time were, however, uniquely her own. Young girls seldom write books – but by her mid-twenties Fanny had written and published several, and made her reputation as a literary lady. Young girls certainly don't set off on long treks across uncivilized lands – but in 1818 Fanny (with Camilla in tow) travelled across America (recording her impressions for posterity in a book whose strongly democratic views won her applause there and fierce criticism in Britain). And, above all, young girls must not enter into dangerously ambiguous personal attachments. But Fanny, heedless of the horror of her friends and the indignant protests of his family, formed an intense attachment to General Lafayette, the ageing hero of the French Revolution, and eventually proposed to him (he affectionately declined). Travelling with him back to America in 1824, she visited Owen at the New Harmony community which he had established in Indiana. She was immediately converted to Owenism, and within a year had sunk nearly her entire personal fortune into a co-operative community in Tennessee whose residents were mostly black slaves purchased by her to begin life anew on a communalist basis. By the end of the decade the scandals surrounding this experiment, plus a series of anti-church, pro-feminist lectures and involvement in the creation of the New York Workingmen's Party (as well as her habitual dress – a pair of bloomer-like trousers designed originally for the women of New Harmony) had all combined to make Fanny the most notorious feminist radical in America – and an object of great admiration to her fellow

Owenites back in Britain. 'May she find an echo in every instructed woman, and an active ally in every man!' as Anna Wheeler told one London audience in 1829. 'Grateful posterity will no doubt associate her name with the *illustrious men of the present age*, who, having discovered the principles of real *social science*, gave them to the world under the name of CO-OPERATION.'[38]

In her espousal of this new social science, Fanny, like Anna, never entirely lost touch with her radical-liberal origins. Her favourite doctrine of 'Free Enquiry' was really little more than a restatement of Enlightenment rationalism, while her social views clearly echoed the humanist tradition of eighteenth-century progressivism.[39] Yet in her communism, in her advocacy of class-based political organization, and – above all – in her attitude towards marriage and family life, Fanny, like all the Owenite feminists, reached past that tradition at crucial points. Sexual nonconformity in particular seems to have been a decisive dividing line, especially when it was not merely a policy position but also a mode of personal practice. 'I am a woman and without a master: two causes of disgrace in England,' Anna wrote to a friend in 1832, twenty years after deserting her husband.[40] And it was this 'masterless' sexual status, with all the disgrace it entailed, which set many Owenite women apart from even the most broad-minded liberals of the day.

When Fanny established her Tennessee community, Nashoba, she provided it with an uncompromisingly libertarian sexual code. 'The marriage law existing outside the pale of the institution (Nashoba),' she declared

> is of no force within that pale. No woman can forfeit her individual rights or independent existence, and no man assert over her any rights of power whatsoever beyond what he may exercise over her free and voluntary affection. Nor on the other hand, may any woman assert claims to the society or peculiar protection of any individual of the other sex, beyond what mutual inclination dictates and sanctions; while to every individual member of either sex is secured the protection and friendly aid of all . . . Let us enquire – not if a mother be a wife, or a father a husband, but if parents can supply, to the creatures they have brought into being, all this requisite to make existence a blessing.[41]

The result was instant notoriety among the community's conservative Tennessee neighbours and a series of turbulent liaisons among the colonists themselves (most of them involving women who, far from giving 'free and voluntary affection' appear to have been coerced and intimidated by Nashoban men) which eventually destroyed the morale of all concerned, including even Fanny who, in 1830, dissolved the settlement and shipped its black inhabitants off to a new life in Haiti.[42] Her own commitment to free unions was apparently undiminished, however, since she then promptly formed one with another Owenite, Phiquepal D'Arusmont. But finding herself pregnant, she decided to beat a strategic retreat from the high ground of sexual principle and married him – a decision which unfortunately served only to vindicate all her earlier hostility to marriage, since it eventually led to a miserable legal wrangle in which D'Arusmont managed to gain control over her entire property, including all her earnings from lectures and writings. She divorced him in an attempt to regain her financial independence, but died (of an illness following a fall) while the legal machinery was still in motion.[43]

Emma Martin, whose story is told below, left her husband, a Bristol businessman, to join the Owenites. Like Anna, Emma had become a feminist in the course of an unhappy marriage; like Fanny, she lost all her property to her husband, although in her case this was probably only a small amount.[44] As in Mary Wollstonecraft's day, this sort of unorthodox behaviour was greeted with prurient abuse by the Owenites' opponents, particularly since these women proved willing not only to leave marriages, but also to lead sexual lives outside them. Both Emma Martin· and Fanny Wright took lovers after they left their husbands (Emma had a child by hers), and it is very possible that Anna's intellectual partnership with William Thompson eventually became a sexual liaison.* Anna was a widow when their friendship was formed, and after his early death wrote

---

* Like Anna Wheeler, William Thompson was also a renegade from the Irish landowning class. 'I am not what is usually called a labourer,' ran the characteristic introduction to one of his Owenite texts, signed 'One of the Idle Classes'. 'Under equitable social arrangements possessed of health and strength, I ought to blush in making this declaration. For the last twelve years of my life I have been living on what is called rent, the produce of the labours of others.' The years which he spent living off the surplus labour of his tenants on his Cork estate

anonymously of how he had respected a woman who 'when no other obstacles existed but unequal marriage-laws, would refuse to be the legalized servant of any man', while he in his turn remained a bachelor because he was unwilling to become 'master of a slave . . . docile to his will . . .'[45] Perhaps they were able to make a more equitable arrangement for themselves. Certainly it would not have been surprising if they had, since most of the feminist publicists who did have mates seem to have chosen men in Thompson's mould; that is, Socialists with a particular interest in feminist issues. Frances Morrison, a working-class feminist, was married to a militant supporter of female unionization;[46] Catherine Barmby to a high-minded young bohemian who espoused Shelleyan views on sexual relations;[47] Margaret Chappellsmith to a man who wholeheartedly supported her activities as a feminist lecturer, and occasionally poured the tea at her public meetings.[48] Within the Socialist movement, then, these women found not only a political base but a new type of personal relationship with men, one founded not on dependence and subordination, but – as Anna Wheeler wrote of her relationship with Thompson – on 'generous feelings' and 'moral courage'.[49]

Clearly these women were not antagonistic to heterosexual relationships *per se*, nor even to marriage if by that was meant a loving union of social equals. Of all the leading Owenite feminists, only Fanny Wright ever advocated the total abolition of marriage in favour of liberated liaisons, and even she gave way at the prospect of bearing an illegitimate child. Nor were they hostile to other features of women's traditional role. Motherhood in particular most Owenite feminists valued highly in theory,

---

were also taken up, however, with building model dwellings for them, establishing local workers' educational institutes, and studying the latest developments in economics and philosophy; in return, his peasants dubbed him the 'Red Republican' and circulated stories of his cheerful contempt for the church and of the French tri-colour which adorned the top of his walking-stick. In 1822 an invitation from Bentham brought him to London, where he soon got involved in Owenism, while at the same time remaining a close, but critical, friend of the old Radical philosopher. He was Owenism's most impressive intellectual, making important contributions not only to feminist thought and the development of an anti-capitalist economic analysis, but also to a theory of trade unionism. He drew up elaborate plans for a community to be established on his own estate, but died, in 1833, before the plan could be initiated.

although in practice it often proved burdensome and traumatic. Anna Wheeler's relationship with her daughter, Rosina, was plagued by misunderstandings and by Rosina's resentment of her mother's political commitments (although later Rosina came to share Anna's feminist views).[50] Fanny Wright did eventually make a stab at conventional family life, with D'Arusmont and their daughter Sylva, but gave it up to return to radical platforms in America. Her re-entry into politics eventually cost her not only her marriage but also her daughter, who remained with D'Arusmont and became entirely estranged from her mother.[51] Emma Martin, on the other hand, managed to maintain a very good relationship with her three girls, but she had to pay friends to care for them during her lecturing tours or else risk subjecting them to the rigours of a peripatetic political life (including, on one occasion, being stoned in the streets of a hostile town).[52] Small wonder all these women looked forward to a new mode of existence – one which would allow them to combine love and maternity with wider social aspirations.

As an ideological stance, sexual nonconformity was also closely connected to the heterodox religious outlook which was so central to the ethos of early Socialism. The link between feminism and religious freethought is examined below, but its significance can begin to be measured by the fact that every Owenite feminist was, in contemporary terminology, an 'infidel' opponent of organized religion. Anna Wheeler was an avowed 'materialist' (to whom Christ was 'that eastern philosopher'), as was Emma Martin who became one of Owenism's leading secularists.[53] Fanny Wright won an awesome reputation for godless immoralism on the basis of some rather insubstantial but sharply polemical *Popular Lectures* in which she attacked the church as a citadel of conservatism, particularly sexual conservatism. And in the early 1830s one of the leading Owenite lecturers in London was a woman named Eliza Macauley, who combined vigorously feminist views with intransigent hostility to the 'superstition-mongering' clergy. Like Anna and Fanny, Eliza was an independent woman. Unlike them, however, she was also a desperately poor one who lived almost entirely by her wits and her pen: a way of life typical of many Owenite feminists, but hardly compatible with respectable Christian womanhood.

ELIZA MACAULEY (178?-1837)

According to her sketchy autobiographical memoirs, Eliza was the daughter of a poor Yorkshire farmer who died, in the mid-1780s, when she was only an infant, leaving his family destitute.[54] Casting about for a way to support herself, Eliza began an acting career: first in local barns in her neighbourhood and, eventually, in London. She arrived in London around 1805 and for the next twenty years or so went from one low-paid, badly-reviewed theatrical production to another, until finally a sustained period of unemployment (which she blamed on the philistinism of metropolitan theatre directors) led her to abandon the thespian life, or at least to turn her dramatic talents in other directions.[55] By the late 1820s she had moved from the stage to the pulpit, preaching in a little 'Jacobinical' chapel in Grub Street.[56] From there she transferred herself – how or why is not recorded – to Owenite platforms, becoming, in her own words, a 'good Co-operative woman'.[57] By the early 1830s she was deeply involved in London Owenite activities, managing the largest Labour Exchange there and delivering regular lectures on subjects as widely varied as financial reform, child development, the evils of Christian orthodoxy, and women's right to full social equality.[58] She was probably paid a small amount for these lectures, but obviously not enough, since throughout this period she also kept busy giving acting lessons (one visiting group of Saint Simonians hired her for this purpose)[59] and producing small volumes of essays on edifying topics, 'poetic effusions', and other staple ingredients of a literary lady's repertoire. But 'literary pursuits are the most arduous of any . . . and subject to the most mortifications – particularly for females', so by 1835 she was to be found publishing her memoirs (sold by subscription) from a cell in the Marshalsea debtors' prison.[60] She died on a lecture tour, two years later.

A sad, brave little tale, dominated by the types of financial dilemmas which plagued all women of her kind – women who, in her own words, 'lack goods or fortune, and, if thrown upon the world, have but the choice of industry for existence'.[61] Looking down the social ladder of Owenite feminism from Anna Wheeler and Fanny Wright to the rungs on which the majority of their sisters stood, we see many women of this sort – women who, like

71

Anna and Fanny, lived a 'masterless' existence outside conventional family life but, unlike them, lacked the income to sustain it. Some, like Emma Martin, had deliberately taken on this independent status by leaving their husbands. But many others, like Eliza, were spinsters for whom an unhusbanded life may well have been an infliction rather than a choice. Certainly getting a husband had never been harder than it was at this time. From the late eighteenth century onward the number of unmarried women in Britain had increased rapidly, while at the same time the economic prospects of such women steadily deteriorated.[62] Eliza Macauleys proliferated, eking out a precarious existence on the margins of professional or literary society. Such women were pitied for their man-less state, but as one woman sharply pointed out, the reason 'so many unmarried women are unhappy is *not* because they are old maids, but in consequence of *poverty*, and of the difficulty they encounter in maintaining a decent position in society . . .'[63]

When Emma Martin left her husband to join the Owenites, she was initially able to support herself and her daughters with the small salary paid by the Owenite Central Board for her lectures. Later, however, she was forced to take up teaching, shopkeeping and midwifery, none of which provided an income sufficient for the needs of her growing girls. Finally, like Eliza, she was reduced to a public appeal for funds.[64] Over the years Owen himself received many letters from women in a similar plight, including one who had been deserted by her husband and was currently taking in washing for a living, several who sought teaching employment, and a few who simply begged him for financial assistance (which he gave). 'I feel as if I stand alone, unaided, unblessed, without protection, support or comfort,' Jane Lewsche, a Manchester widow, wrote to him. 'All to suffer and nothing to enjoy. How long this struggle will last I cannot tell . . .'[65]

Such conditions bred feminists, and many of the most militant contributions to the Owenite feminist literature came from 'odd women' like these. From their fragmentary self-descriptions most appear to have come from petit bourgeois backgrounds . . . but the conventional class label utterly fails to convey the displaced, ambiguous quality of their lives. Outside traditional women's roles, thrust into an unwomanly independence, women like Eliza Macauley and Emma Martin soon found themselves living right at the edge of bourgeois gentility, at the point where gruelling work and poverty blurred the line between themselves and the lower orders. Lacking any route into male-controlled professions or commercial opportunities, they often entered jobs shared with women from the class below them. Emma Martin was a schoolteacher, but so also was the working-class Owenite feminist, Frances Morrison, while the many female 'teachers of infant and private schools' reported in attendance at Socialist meetings on women's rights in Leicester in the late 1830s could have been either middle or working class, and were probably some of both.[66] Needlewomen, of whom the Owenite movement contained many, were usually the wives or daughters of working men, but from the beginning of the century their ranks had been steadily swollen by impoverished 'gentlewomen', usually spinsters or widows. Certainly some jobs – governessing, writing, serving as a 'lady's companion' – were considered more genteel than others (although they were usually just as badly paid).[67] But in general it was attachment to a man of a particular class position which established a woman's social rank, not her own economic status. When a woman had to labour for a living she could all too easily find herself inhabiting a region where class differences blurred in the face of a common female oppression.

This may help to explain why women like Eliza Macauley and Emma Martin so strongly identified with the cause of working people – and also why all Owenite feminists identified women's oppression as a trans-class phenomenon. The problems which united women from different backgrounds may have seemed more important than the social and cultural differences which divided them. Yet the differences obviously remained. In general Owenite feminists tended to ignore them, but in 1833 one group of London women established a Practical Moral Union of Women of Great Britain and Ireland whose aim, in the words of its founding manifesto, was 'to combine all classes of women' in the struggle for sexual equality, so that 'the broad line of demarcation which has been drawn between different classes of women, will be effaced'.[68] This, the first separatist feminist organization established in Britain, was a short-lived venture, collapsing after only six or seven months. The reasons for its failure are unclear, but the strong opposition which it met from at least one leading male Owenite may have had something to do with it. 'Fatal to the advancement of women would be an exclusive union,' he wrote to *The Crisis* shortly after the Union was formed, 'the line of separation would be extended between the sexes . . .'

> Are the interests of man and woman separate, or is their interest one and the same? . . . If woman denounce the right usurped by man of legislating exclusively for the whole, how can she expect but every rational man will not protest against woman being the legislator, excluding man from any participation in that right? . . . woman is equal with man by the laws of our physical condition . . . Do the laws of our nature show we are destined to live together in a social state? If monasteries for men and nunneries for women be not a violation of the laws of nature, then we should return to that state; but if they are a violation of our social condition, then the projected society of women would be pernicious. Let man see his own interest in restoring woman to freedom, then will he himself be free.[69]

(In reply, the Union's organizers stated that they had never entertained 'the slightest idea th␣t the interests of the two sexes are in opposition to each other', but wished only to unite in assisting those men who 'are putting forth their moral and intellectual strength to extricate that deeply injured half of the human race from the thraldom in which they are involved' – a statement reflecting a lack of political confidence which may well have proved the Union's undoing.)

No membership lists from the Union survive, but several letters from feminists sent to the Owenite press at the time suggest that they may have been active participants. One of these was from a woman who signed herself 'a London Mechanic's Wife'.[70] She was an enthusiastic advocate of feminist organization among women 'of the labouring class', as well as a promoter of trade unions for working women. Like so many of the working-class women who became involved in Owenism, nothing is known about her personal history. But in 1834 she entered into a brief correspondence with another working-class feminist, Frances Morrison, of whom more is known since she eventually became one of the leading Owenite lecturers in northern England.

FRANCES MORRISON (1807–1898)

Frances Cooper was the illegitimate daughter of a Surrey farm-girl.[71] Her early years were spent with her grandmother, who took responsibility for her upkeep and schooling. Later she re-joined her mother in Pershore, and it was there, in 1822, that a house-painter named James Morrison, tramping for work, caught her eye. Frances, only fifteen years old and soon very much in love, agreed to return with James to his native Birmingham, where they lived together without benefit of a wedding ceremony.[72] After four or five years, however, she became pregnant and they wed: a common order of events in the early nineteenth century working class.

The first few years of Frances' married life were occupied with childbirth and childrearing (she had four daughters), running a small newspaper shop, and – with the encouragement of her husband – educating herself in radical politics, particularly Owenite theory. 'Long 'ere I began to think, my reason warred with the absurd forms of society,' she later wrote to Owen, 'but from an ill-cultivated and wrong direction given to my mind, I could never get a solid idea till on the perusal of your Essays . . .'[73] In 1833 James, who had previously been active in the parliamentary reform movement and, latterly, as an activist in the Owenite-dominated Operative Builders' Union, became editor of *The Pioneer*, a newspaper which soon became the principal organ of Owenite general unionism.[74] Frances, by then also a committed Owenite and a feminist, soon began contributing articles to the paper under the pseudonym 'A Bondswoman', while together she and James produced a series of editorials on feminist themes, ranging from the inequities of the marriage law to the demand for equal pay for equal work. 'A woman's wage is not reckoned at an average more than two-thirds of a male,' one of these editorials ran, 'and we believe in reality it seldom amounts to more than a third (and wives have no wages at all). Yet, is not the produce of female labour as useful? . . . The industrious female is well entitled to the same amount of remuneration as the industrious male.'[75]

In the late 1830s, after James' premature death, Frances became a paid lecturer for the Owenites, travelling on speaking circuits throughout northern towns where she addressed large audiences on women's rights and marriage reform.[76] Like Emma Martin, she soon discovered, however, that such employment was insufficient to support herself and her daughters, so she apprenticed the girls to the tape-weaving trade and, with Owen's help, found a teaching post in Hulme.[77] She then effectively disappeared from the Owenite scene, although according to her children she remained faithful to her Socialist feminist ideals until the end of her days.[78]

Even in a movement as densely populated with working-class intellectuals as Owenism was, Frances and James Morrison nonetheless stood out as particularly impressive theorists and publicists. Yet in all other respects they were an unexceptional couple, typical of the general working-class membership of the movement. Birmingham, where they lived and worked until James' death, was a strong Owenite centre in which most male Owenites, like James, worked in skilled trades (particularly building or metalwork), while female Owenites were employed as lacemakers, buttonmakers, glassblowers, needlewomen or, like Frances, as small shopkeepers. All were occupations characteristic of the upper stratum of the working class from which most Owenites came[79] – a stratum which they themselves almost invariably described as 'respectable'. The 'great bulk' of the Manchester Socialists, as one of their number wrote, 'belonged to the more respectable class of artisans and their families',[80] while the Huddersfield Owenites boasted of 'numerous and respectable' attendances at all their meetings.

> By respectable we do not mean lords, dukes, baronets, esquires, etc. . . . but the honest, intelligent, and industrious producers of wealth, who are the real respectables . . .[81]

Engels, surveying the movement in 1844, noted that it drew the 'most educated and solid elements' of the working class.[82] 'Their body consisted of the most skilful, industrious, steady, sober and moral portion of the working class,' another observer noted, 'those, in short, who influence the rest . . .'[83]

This proletarian respectability was a highly-specified status, bearing little resemblance to genteel notions of social refinement. It was also a status which was clearly differentiated along sexual lines. For a skilled male worker like James Morrison, the key components of a respectable lifestyle were regular employment in a recognized craft or trade which provided a steady income for his family; some small degree of education (at least to literacy level); 'steady habits', i.e. non-addiction to alcohol and a fairly sedate sexual life; and usually membership in one or more of a range of working-class institutions such as a Friendly Society, savings bank, Mechanics Institute, or a trade union. A respectable working man was a sober, industrious, regular provider of family necessities.[84] The ability of a woman to live in a respectable manner largely depended on whether or not her husband met these criteria. Access to a steady income meant regular house-keeping, clean, well-fed children, and a stable domestic life – the defining features of a decent womanly existence. Most wives of artisans also had some small amount of education, probably a few years at a Sunday school or a short period in a church-sponsored day school.* By the early nineteenth century there existed many cheap boarding schools which catered to the daughters of shopkeepers, tradesmen and the 'better class of mechanics', and Frances Morrison briefly attended one of these.[85] Many Owenite women would also have belonged to one or other female version of a local self-help institution, perhaps a female friendly society (which would provide sickness insurance and lying-in benefits) or a clothing club.[86] And some, as we shall see, were in trade unions and political organizations.

A respectable artisan home was usually financed by the joint earnings of both husband and wife. The Morrisons' arrange-ment – in which the wages James earned at housepainting and newspaper-editing were supplemented by the profits from Frances' shop – was very common. When the London Owenite, William Lovett, married a young lady's maid in the early 1820s he immediately began to look for 'some small way of business that

---

* Two-thirds to three-quarters of the British working class was literate in the early nineteenth century, with the percentage being lowest among agricultural workers and highest in the skilled sector from which the Owenites were drawn. But a marked difference between women and men was visible: far more boys than girls attended charity day-schools in Bolton in 1835, for example, and few of the early Mechanics Institutes admitted women at all. The number of those able to sign the marriage register was always higher among men than among women.

she herself could manage' which might add to the income he earned as a cabinet-maker.[87] They decided upon a pastry-shop, but after a few years Mary Lovett gave this up to become manager of the first London Co-operative shop (taking over from her husband, at one-half his salary!).[88] Owenite women married to domestic craftsmen, such as shoemakers or weavers, usually assisted their husbands at their trades, while others took in laundry, did 'slop' sewing (cheap, ready-made goods) or ran little schools for local children. In his autobiography the Owenite whitesmith, George Holyoake, recalled the wide range of jobs performed by women in his upper working-class neighbourhood in Birmingham in the early years of the century, from the housewives who ran little bakeries and grocery shops inside their own kitchens, to the small button-making workshop which his mother had at the back of their home, where little George learned to bend the button wires almost as soon as he could stand. 'She received the orders; made the purchase of materials; super-intended the making of the goods; made out the accounts; and received the money; besides taking care of her growing family. There was no "Rights of Women" thought of in her day, but she was an entirely self-governing, managing mistress . . .'[89]

A respectable working-class wife, then, was one who kept a good home, 'paid her own bread', and was 'not a burthen upon the scanty earnings of her husband'.[90] This did not mean, however, that sexual roles were any less clearly defined in the working class than in the propertied classes. A woman's primary responsibility was to her husband and children, and no other employments were allowed to take precedence over the servicing of family needs. The woman who had to neglect her home in order to earn money for its upkeep was not considered respectable.[91] Moreover, the wages women earned were usually far lower than those of men, so their financial contribution tended to be viewed as secondary.[92] And even the small sum they did receive was legally the property of their husbands who could, if they wished, spend it on themselves instead of their families. 'Many men think that the whole amount gained by their wives is so much drinking money gained for themselves,' one man, a button-maker, told a *Morning Chronicle* reporter.[93]

But if the working-class woman, like the middle-class one, was usually a social inferior within marriage, she was certainly not the decorative, dependent inferior that her wealthier sister was. She had a crucial and recognized role to play in her dual capacity as wife/mother and worker. Marriage and family responsibilities did not signal her withdrawal from the world of work and work-orientated relationships, as they did for women of the upper classes, but simply confirmed her particular place within that world. The duties of womanhood were active, demanding ones, not passive, trivial ones. The concept of femininity as graceful parasitism meant nothing to her.

Within the course of the nineteenth century, however, this situation was to undergo a radical revision, as ideals of womanly dependence and decorum forged in the middle class began to appear in the working class as well, particularly in its upper strata. One key symptom of this change was growing disapproval of any extra-familial employment for married women. From having been an essential, if secondary, contributor to family income, the ideal working-class woman became viewed simply as a 'housewife', an unwaged provider of domestic services. Men, on the other hand, were expected to earn wages sufficient to support an entire household. His the public world of work; hers the private realm of home. By the mid-nineteenth century, at the end of the Owenite period, this pattern was already clearly discernible among urban craftsmen and other 'labour aristocrats' from whose ranks many Owenites had been drawn. 'The most respectable portion of the carpenters and joiners "will not allow" their wives to do any work than attend to their domestic and family duties,' Henry Mayhew reported in London in 1849,[94] and the same was true of many other artisans: 'As a general rule, neither their wives nor children "go out to work" . . .' 'We keep our wives too respectable for that,' one coachman boasted.[95] On closer investigation, Mayhew found that the wives of many of these men did, in fact, take in washing or keep little shops,[96] so it seems likely that the dependent housewife was still more ideal than real. But it was a potent new ideal nonetheless, and one which was to have a dramatic effect on women's status in all areas of economic and social life.

The Owenites stood at the beginning of this transition, and their own views on women were not wholly unaffected by it. But in general they remained firmly within the older tradition in which women were viewed not as passive dependants but as active participants in all matters affecting themselves, their families, and their communities. Their support for women's political involvement reflected this. As a popular movement, Owenism drew on traditions of organized militancy among working-class women which, in the decades immediately preceding the rise of the movement, had reached a high point of intensity and public visibility. Throughout the war years which opened the century, and the depression which followed them, rising prices and falling wages had brought thousands of working-class women onto the streets where they led food riots, supported strikes and demonstrated in favour of popular petitions.[97] After 1815, when Jacobinism re-emerged as a mass movement for parliamentary reform, a national network of Female Reform Societies had been established in which working-class women actively campaigned for the widening of the franchise, annual parliaments, election by ballot – all the demands which were later to appear in the People's Charter.[98] This level of female activism had horrified upper-class observers, who still recalled only too vividly *les femmes de la Revolution*.[99] But reform leaders, for their part, usually welcomed the women's support. 'This array of women against the system . . . I deem the most fatal omen of its fall,' Thomas Wooler, editor of the radical newspaper, *The Black Dwarf*, chortled in 1819.[100]

Female activism of this sort, it should be emphasized, had generally been viewed not as a challenge to women's traditional family role, but as a necessary extension of it, at a time when the rights and needs of all family members were under attack. It was as 'wives, mothers, and daughters, in their social, domestic and moral capacities' that the Female Reformers of Lancashire had marched to political rallies in 1818–19, and it was as 'mothers of children' that they had called on other women for support.[101] 'Our homes which once bore ample testimony of our industry and cleanliness . . . are now alas! robbed of all their ornaments,' as Alice Kitchen of the Blackburn Female Reform Society told a rally in 1819, and 'behold our innocent children! . . . how appalling are their cries for bread!' Perhaps, she went on, women were not renowned for physical courage, yet she and her sisters were prepared to sally forth in defence of 'that food and raiment for our children, which God and nature have ordained for every living creature; but which our oppressors and tyrannical rulers have withheld from us'.[102]

This style of militant wifehood and motherhood both encouraged and limited female activism – allowing women to join social movements without being accused of unwomanliness, while at the same time usually ensuring that the role they occupied within these movements was a secondary, subordinate one. Prior to Owenism, women themselves rarely used radical platforms to raise demands related to their own status. Rather, they saw themselves as primarily engaged, in the words of the Blackburn Female Reformers, in 'assisting the male population of this country to acquire their rights and liberties'. And the types of activities which absorbed them – organizing fund-raising events, teaching in radical Sunday Schools, sewing Caps of Liberty for leading male radicals – tended to reflect this auxiliary status.[103] As in the home, so in popular protest women were seen as essential but secondary adjuncts to the men.

And yet, other ideas were also in the air. Any mobilization of women carries within it a potential challenge to sexual conventions, and from the 1790s onward there were always a number of working-class radicals prepared to openly state that challenge. The same 'Paine-ite' aspects of Wollstonecraft's *Vindication* which had led Walpole to refuse to have it in his library,[104] had placed it firmly within the intellectual culture of the radical working class, where it stimulated a small-scale but lively debate over feminist ideas. Arguments over whether women ought to be granted the franchise appeared in radical newspapers, along with discussions of Wollstonecraft's views on female education, Godwin and Spence's anti-marriage doctrines and Shelley's eloquent vision of a new age of sex equality.[105] In the 1820s and 30s the newspapers published by the leading free press campaigner, Richard Carlile, gave vigorous backing to feminist demands.[106] 'I do not like the doctrine of women keeping at home, and minding the house and family,' Carlile complained in 1832, 'It is as much the proper business of the man as the woman's, and the woman, who is so confined, is not the proper companion of the public useful man.'[107] She certainly would not have been a proper

81

companion for Carlile, who expected his female associates to sell his illegal publications, run his bookshops, stand trial for these activities, and suffer imprisonment if necessary.[108] In 1832 he established a common-law union with Eliza Sharples, who published, under his direction, a feminist freethought journal named *The Isis*, while at the same time delivering regular lectures on women's position at the Rotunda (a radical meeting-house in South London which later became an Owenite centre). 'Sooner or later it [female emancipation] must come,' *The Isis* told its readers, 'and no other reason is to be offered against the equality of the sexes, than that which tyranny has to offer on every occasion – its will and power . . .'[109]

By the 1830s most of these working-class supporters of women's rights had declared for Owenism, and merged their feminist rhetoric with that of the new movement.[110] Ideas hitherto confined to a small vanguard of radical intellectuals began to find broader channels of expression through the expanding propaganda network of Socialist organization. Not every new convert to Owenism was enthusiastic about this development. 'Why talk of making women rational until we have first made ourselves rational?' as Henry Hetherington, a leading London Owenite, demanded, 'or why talk of restoring them to their social rights until we have first obtained our own?'[111] Such hostility, as we shall see in the next chapter, was particularly pronounced among certain groups of Owenite trade unionists, for whom the feminist challenge appeared as a direct threat to their status as a labour elite. But in general the new style of sexual egalitarianism was received with sympathetic interest by the growing popular membership of Owenism. Working-class Socialists, their eyes set on the new social order to be built, took up feminism as part of the ideological equipment necessary for the task.

IV

'THE MEN ARE AS BAD AS THEIR MASTERS . . .': WORKING WOMEN AND THE OWENITE ECONOMIC OFFENSIVE, 1828–34

WOMEN WORKERS AND THE RIGHTS OF LABOUR

In the late 1820s the Owenite initiative moved almost entirely into the hands of working people, where it remained until the collapse of the movement in 1845. Although Owen always maintained that the leadership in social reform should come from benevolent-minded capitalists like himself, it soon became apparent to most of his followers that working-class self-organization, rather than upper-class philanthropy, was the ground on which a New Moral World would be built. It was those 'who give their labour for what they receive . . . who are weary of the present system, who have been groaning under the miseries inseparable from that system . . . and who are anxious to seize any probable plan that promises a speedy and effectual remedy' who were moving into the vanguard of Social Progress.[1] 'The working classes must themselves pave the way;' *The Lancashire Co-operator* told its readers in 1831, 'they must become the pioneers . . .'[2]

The direction taken by the popular movement altered course several times over the years – partly under Owen's influence, partly due to the failure of certain strategies, and their pre-emption by others, and partly because plebian Owenism was not a unitary phenomenon, but contained within it many different viewpoints and aspirations, ranging from the simple hope of material betterment to a vision of community life as a New

Jerusalem of intellectual and emotional self-fulfilment. We shall see later how some of the more far-reaching ambitions promoted by Socialist ideologues – particularly their views on conjugal relations – fared in the working-class movement. Here, however, we begin by extracting from all these dreams and aspirations the one hope which dominated Owenism's early years – the hope of a 'complete emancipation of the labouring class from the tyranny of capital and monopoly'[3] – in order to examine its meaning for working-class women and feminism. Owenism was at all times a movement based largely among working people, but it was only in the years 1828–34, and particularly in 1833–34, that it was primarily a *workers'* movement, the left-wing in a wider upsurge of labour militancy. The story of this early 'labourist' phase of Owenism has been told many times, and since it is women's involvement in it which interests us, only the highlights need be repeated here.[4]

As Gareth Stedman Jones has pointed out, 'it was not Owenism in any simple sense which forged the language of the new working class consciousness of the 1830s' but certain strands within Owenism, notably the critique of capitalism as a class-based system of labour exploitation presented in the writings of Owen and other 'neo-Ricardian' economists such as William Thompson and Thomas Hodgskin.[5] It was while Owen was still in America, according to William Lovett, that groups of workers in London and Brighton began to meet and resolved 'to take up such parts of his [Owen's] system as they conceived would be appreciated by the majority of the working classes,' and to publicize them as widely as possible.[6] By 1832 James Mill was complaining bitterly of the 'mischievous doctrines' being propagandized by Owenite workers in cheap tracts and newspapers all over the country: 'the illicit cheap publications in which the right of the producer to all that he produces, is very generally preached, are superseding all the other channels through which the people might get information', he wrote anxiously to Brougham.[7] The message delivered in these publications was simple and direct: labour, as Owen (following Locke and Ricardo) had argued, was the source of all wealth in society; therefore the poverty of working people, far from being a natural or inevitable phenomenon, was the result of a wholly unjust distribution of the workers' produce. 'The working classes have no idea of the real value of their own labour', an article in one popular working-class Owenite journal explained:

> When a man has done a week's work, and received his wages for it, he thinks he has received the whole value of his work: but this is by no means the case . . . [for] if wages were the whole value of the work, how could the master take the work to market, sell it for more money than he gave for it, and grow rich upon the profit, while the workman grows poor upon the wages? This would be impossible. Therefore it is evident that the workman does not get the whole value of his work; and it is also evident that if he did he would grow rich, just as the master does . . . We believe that this idea is quite new to the working classes . . . [8]

The obvious conclusion to be drawn from this, the writer added, was that the working classes must begin 'to work for themselves, and not for the capitalists', and this could only be done in communities where the means of production and distribution were collectively owned. But a first step in the right direction could be taken, it was suggested by some London and Brighton Owenites, through the establishment of worker-owned shops and workshops, whose profits, rather than going to retailers or employers, would be invested in land for community-building. The plan was adopted in both cities, and William Lovett became the manager of one of London's first co-operative shops: 'I was induced to believe that the general accumulation of capital by these means would enable the working classes to . . . ultimately have the trade, manufactures, and commerce of the country in their own hands . . .'[9]

Many others were induced to believe it as well. At the end of 1828 four co-operative societies were in existence, but by the end of 1830 the number had swelled to over 300, reaching perhaps as many as 500 in 1832.[10] This extraordinary growth was accompanied and encouraged by the establishment of a propaganda agency, the British Association for the Promotion of Co-operative Knowledge, and the institution of bi-annual Co-operative Congresses. 'More was done . . . to disceminate [sic] Mr Owens [sic] peculiar views, than perhaps he had done himself during his long carieer [sic]', William Lovett recalled.[11] Since this energetic campaign had begun in Owen's absence, he was considerably startled to return to England in 1829 and find himself the nominal head of a growing working-class movement. Initially his attitude towards his plebian associates and their ventures was distant and disparaging, but once he saw the level of popular excitement generated by the co-operative schemes 'he took them into more favour, and ultimately took an active part in them.'[12] In fact, by 1832 his mood had shifted from scepticism to unrestrained enthusiasm, and in that year he established the National Equitable Labour Exchange, a large bazaar-type institution where workers could exchange their products for 'labour-notes' representing the amount of labour-time invested in them, thereby receiving 'a just reward for their labour' and short-circuiting profiteering distributors. 'The Labour Exchanges will make all masters,' as one London activist wrote, 'no servants or slaves.'[13]

Several other Exchanges were established in London and Birmingham in 1832–33, and for a time they flourished. But by now Owen had devised an even greater scheme, compared to which, he assured his followers, the Exchange system was a 'mere bagatelle'.[14] In 1833 he unfolded his plan for the complete takeover of the British industrial system by combinations of workers and sympathetic employers, who would then delegate representatives to a House of Trades which would eventually supersede the capitalist state.[15] Such a grandiose strategy might never have got further than his own fertile imagination, had it not been for two factors: first, the passage of the 1832 Reform Bill, whose narrow enfranchisement provisions so infuriated plebian democrats that it drove many of them away from the reform alliance with bourgeois parliamentarians towards the idea of a Workers' Parliament[16]; and second, a concurrent upsurge of trade union militancy which, under the impact of co-operative ideas, became re-routed, at least in some trades, towards industrial syndicalism. 'The Trades Unions will not only strike for less work and more wages,' one activist in the Operative Builders Union, a strongly Owenite-influenced body, explained,

> but they will ultimately ABOLISH WAGES, become their own masters, and work for each other; labour and capital will no longer be separate but they will be indissolubly joined together in the hands of the workmen and workwomen.[17]

In Derby the silk-workers, locked out by their employers in 1833, established co-operative workshops and told their masters, 'We will be satisfied with the fruits of our own industry. We have hitherto worked for you . . . we shall henceforth work for ourselves.'[18] The two aspirations – towards worker self-management and political power – became twisted together in the struggle to establish a 'General Union of All Trades' which would serve not only as the organizational vehicle for national workers' solidarity but also as the industrial foundation of a communist government, along lines similar to those suggested by Owen.* Every trade would have 'its internal government in every town; a certain number of towns comprise a district, and delegates from the trades in each town form a quarterly district government; delegates from the district form the Annual Parliament; and the King of England becomes President of the Trades' Unions!'[19] The idea, which was promoted not only by Owen but also by leading Owenite ideologues like James Morrison, George Petrie, and John Doherty, took fire among skilled workers (many of whom had been trying to establish a General Union for some years),[20] until by 1833 *The Poor Man's Guardian* was able to report 'a spirit of combination . . . of which there has been no example in former times . . .'

> The object of it is the sublimest that can be conceived, namely – to establish for the productive classes a complete dominion over the fruits of their own industry . . . Reports show that an entire change in society – a change amounting to a complete subversion of the existing 'order of the world' – is contemplated by the working classes. They aspire to be at the top instead of the bottom of society – or rather that there should be no bottom or top at all.[21]

---

*The major difference between Owen's plan and that proposed by most of his militant working-class associates was that he wished to include sympathetic employers in the Union, an idea which seemed absurd and dangerous to most unionists. 'For the very shewing of your own Doctrines tell against the probability of the Masters and Men amalgamating from the different circumstances under which they are placed . . .' one journeyman tailor gently chided him, 'I do not entertain the opinion that you will be able to succeed, unless you wholly confine yourself to advocating the Interests of the Journeyman *alone* . . .' (Owen Corres. 604) However, the issue was not quite so clear-cut as this, since in some trades the line between a small working master and his employees was not very sharply drawn, and here Owen's proposal may have had greater support (although there is no direct evidence for this).

But alas for revolutionary ambitions: the General Union which was finally established in February 1934 – the Grand National Consolidated Trades Union – was a short-lived conglomerate of old and new unions, dominated by London craftsmen with tentacles of support spreading out into the Midlands, the Potteries, and the craft workshops of Lancashire. It was long on speeches, short on funds; different trades eyed each other with suspicion and soon accusations of misbehaviour, short-sightedness and stinginess began to fly. In the midst of this, both employers and the government – who took the new union militancy very seriously indeed – began intensive persecution of known unionists and their supporters, culminating in the trial and transportation of six Dorchester labourers (the 'Tolpuddle Martyrs') for taking a union oath. Intimidation and strikebreaking on this scale could not possibly be overcome by such a weak and divided organization, and the entire edifice crashed down only seven months after its inauguration.[22]

Short-lived as this offensive was, it attracted thousands of workers, including thousands of women workers, who produced goods for the Labour Exchanges, ran co-operative shops (one of London's first co-operative shops was a women-run operation, selling tea and coffee), and organized co-operative workshops.[23] The Society of Industrious Females was an organization of sixty women who came together in London in 1832 to win for themselves 'a fair distribution of the products of our labour' through the co-operative production of clothing which they sold at Owen's Labour Exchange in Grays Inn Road; other women workers made buttons, shoes, lace, and gloves to sell at the London and Birmingham Exchanges.[24] When the Consolidated Union was formed, women like these joined *en masse*. The official 'Articles' of the Consolidated called for the establishment of 'lodges of Industrious Females . . . in every District where it may be practicable', and within months reports were flowing in from lodges of lace-makers, strawbonnet-makers, shoebinders, laundresses, milliners, glass-cutters, stockingers, glovemakers.[25] One of the largest unions formed was that of the Leicester women stockingers, one thousand strong.[26] 'The scandalous bye word of "blue stocking" which has been thrown at every intelligent woman who happened to have more sense than her stupid

husband, has not deterred the ladies of Leicester from uniting,'
The Pioneer reported jubilantly,[27] while reports of successful
strikes of female shoemakers, weavers and washerwomen (the
washerwomen of Kensington 'all demanded an advance of one
shilling a day, with beer,' and gót it)[28] must have confirmed
employers' worst fears of a general female insurrection.
'Alarmists may view these indications of feminine independence
as more menacing to established institutions than the "education
of the lower orders",' *The Leeds Mercury* reported ironically after
a turn-out of women card-setters there.[29]

Historians who have recorded this widespread mobilization of
working-class women have described it as one of the 'more
remarkable' features of the Owenite-influenced labour upsurge.[30]
But if we recall that nearly all such women were engaged in some
form of waged employment in the 1830s (and those who were not
were still directly dependent on a wage, brought into the home by
a father or husband) the appeal of producer-based radicalism to
them is not so difficult to understand.[31] What is harder to unravel,
however, is how women's involvement in the emergent labour
movement related to their experience and consciousness of themselves as women, as members not only of an exploited class, but
also of an oppressed sex. The tale of the militant women workers
of 1834 has been told several times (albeit very sketchily), but
always as an early episode in trade union history – an approach
which has tended to obscure not only the particularity of
women's work and organizational experience, but also the
complicated connections between class consciousness and sex
consciousness which emerged in this period.[32]

General unionism, and indeed the whole of the Owenite
economic strategy, developed during a period of rapid change in
the trades and industries from which its supporters were drawn.
Up to this point we have emphasized the revolutionary, 'utopian'
aspects of Co-operation and general unionism, and these were
certainly very pronounced. As Edward Thompson has written,
the 1830s were years 'when many English people felt that the
structure of industrial capitalism had only been partly built, and
the roof not yet set upon the structure. Owenism . . . [presented]
the vision of a quite different structure which might be built in a
matter of years or months if only people were united and deter-

mined enough.'[33] This optimistic determination – this will to change – was evident within most of the Consolidated's affiliates, where it was fuelled, however, not only by visions of future alternatives but also by present economic distress. Industrial capitalism may still have been incomplete and roofless, but its construction had already had devastating effects on the lives of workers in domestic and workshop trades, who found themselves caught in a tightening noose of competition with cheap goods (machine-made, imported, or produced by sweated outworkers) and cheap labour.[34] The pattern of decline varied from one trade to another, but in general the effect on the traditional workforce was the same: lowered wage levels, increased unemployment (or, more typically for many urban artisans, periods of unemployment alternating with intense overwork), and a general deterioration of living standards.[35] 'Monopoly and competition have brought almost every trade and manufactory to a complete stand-still – I mean the working part,' as one London tailor wrote to *The Pioneer* in 1834, 'they can neither go on as things now are, nor yet stop; for at work they labour hard, and three quarters starve; and if they stop working, death . . . or the workhouse must be their fate . . .'[36]

This deterioration in working conditions and living standards had not gone unresisted. The wave of industrial militancy which swept Britain at the time of the Consolidated Union's formation represented the culmination of a long cycle of struggles in which manufacturing workers had attempted to defend themselves against the steady worsening of their position.[37] The relationship between men and women workers in these struggles had been complex. On the one hand, many of the domestic trades employed sexually-integrated workforces with traditions of industrial action involving both men and women. Leather glove-making, for example, had been a major source of employment for both sexes in the Worcester and Yeovil areas from the seventeenth century on. Male workers performed the better-paid jobs of tanning, staining and cutting the skins, while women (often their wives or daughters) did the sewing.[38] In the late eighteenth and early nineteenth century there had been strikes and riots of glovemakers in which both men and women participated, although sometimes women had taken action on their own. In

1804 Robert Southey had watched groups of women glovemakers roaming the streets of Worcester, attacking anyone wearing the new fashionable silk gloves which were eroding their trade.[39] By 1832 a combination of silk fashions and a flood of cheap French imports had brought leather-glove production in the city down by two-thirds from its 1825 level, and soldiers were brought into the area to keep order among the desperate workers.[40] By the early months of 1834 the male glovemakers had organized them-selves into a lodge of the Consolidated Union and were busy help-ing to form a union among their women co-workers: 'and such was their [the women's] intelligence and capacity to execute the business, that . . . three days after their formation, they proceeded in the most regular way', thereby putting a 'terrible fright' into the employers.[41] Soon glovemakers of both sexes, in. Worcester and Yeovil, were producing gloves in co-operative workshops and looking forward to the day when 'the dastardly tyrants, our employers, will be thus overthrown'.[42]

Buttonmaking, framework-knitting, and handloom weaving were other domestic industries, often employing entire families, in which men and women had previously organized together. The large union of women stocking-makers in Leicester who joined the Consolidated Union had been preceded by sexually mixed unions there.*[43] Similarly, the male and female handloom weavers who established large co-operative workshops in the Huddersfield area in 1832 almost certainly included weavers – of both sexes – who had participated in major disturbances during the desperate years following the Napoleonic Wars.[44] Women had not only acted in concert with men in these struggles, but had often served as violent shock-troops within them. Many of the weavers arrested in earlier battles had been women,[45] and so it was again among power-loom weavers in the early 1830s, when women led the way in riotous confrontations with the military in Oldham and other textile centres.[46] In the winter of 1833, men and women workers in the Derby silk industry were locked out by their employers (thereby initiating a struggle which generated so much anger and solidarity among other workers around the

---

*Hosiery production was a branch of framework-knitting, although women often seamed the stocking pieces, which the men had knitted.

country that it assisted in the formation of the Consolidated Union). Here women fought and stoned police and black-legs ('A poor women is now in prison, sentenced to three months confinement, for crying Ba! to a black sheep,' the Derby strike committee reported[47]). But they also established union lodges, solicited and received support from women in other industries in the area,[48] joined co-operative workshops, and marched at the head of large demonstrations. 'From the determined heroism [of these women] I could scarcely believe but that I was surrounded by the descendants of the "Maid of Orleans" ', one Nottingham unionist reported after a visit to the Derby female lodges, 'and are these, I ask . . . to be subdued by the fancied power of the monied capitalists? No, gentlemen of Derby . . . retire from the contest with these Amazonian females; defeat will be yours . . .'[49] A letter from one of these 'Amazons' appeared in *The Pioneer*:

> Be it known to the world that a female union is begun in Derby, and that the tyrants have taken fright at it, and have brought forth a document for the females to sign or *leave their employment*, not only to those who are employed in the factory, but *to the servants in their own houses also*. Here is a specimen of knavish tyranny; but, be it known that we have refused to comply with their request . . . In consequence of this, there is a great number more added to the turnout . . . Sisters! awake, arise . . . form lodges in every town and hamlet. Mothers of families, and maidens, come forward and join in this our glorious cause, and we will defy the power of our adversaries; and let the first lispings of your innocent offsprings be *union! union!*[50]

Sexual solidarity was high among these men and women as they struggled for mutual goals. Or as one observer said of the Derby workers, 'One kindred spirit seemed to "actuate the whole". . . '[51] But even where this spirit was present and the sexes collaborated in battles for common class goals, women were nonetheless viewed as a group apart. Their entry into class politics was always as women first and workers second. 'I stand here as a woman, an *operative*, and a *mother*,' ran the typical opening of one speech delivered by a 'Female Operative' in London in 1834,[52] while the 'London Mechanic's Wife', busy organizing women's unions and co-operative workshops, urged women to join her on the grounds that 'our natural and ardent attachment to our tender young should prompt us to use all our powers to obtain a far better state for the enslaved and degraded children of labour.'[53] The Grand Lodge of Miscellaneous Female Operatives based in the Charlotte Street Institution combined discussions of 'domestic matters' with their normal trade union business, and the strawbonnet-makers' union listed as its goals not only the 'protection of our labour' but also the establishment of radical schools and the provision of insurance benefits for their families, as well as assistance 'to our noble brothers in Union'.[54] Letters written by these women emphasized that it was the poverty of their families which drew them into public action. The 'London Mechanic's Wife' made this point in a particularly uncompromising letter to *The Pioneer*:

> Shall the idiot-like, the stupid and usurious captitalists tell us to look to our domestic affairs, and say 'these we understand best'? We will retort on them . . . that *thousands of us have scarce any domestic affairs to look after*, when the want of employment on the one hand, or ill-requited toil on the other, have left our habitations almost destitute . . . when we see abundance of employment, that ought to occupy our time, to make garments for our almost naked children and ourselves, and cannot get the materials to work on. Then it is of the first importance that we should know how to acquire those materials; and that is, by making ourselves acquainted with the rights of labour; and, on the other hand, with the all-absorbing and all-destroying principle of capital, as it has hitherto worked against labour . . . Ah! fellow bondswomen . . . may we live to see the whole of our sex exert themselves for their own, their children's and their country's emancipation from the cruel bondage of physical and mental taskmasters![55]

This concept of radical action as a necessary extension of women's family duties simultaneously encouraged female militancy and limited the forms which that militancy took. Sexual divisions of labour and power, rooted in the family, became superimposed on workers' organizations. Prior to 1830, it seems, no woman had led a sexually-mixed union, and within the Consolidated Union itself women were usually organized into separate lodges, even when they were employed in mixed trades.[56] The men's lodges appear to have taken all the joint leadership initiatives. None of the women involved seem to have protested at this, or suggested it should be otherwise. Like the men, they accepted that even within a common struggle the sexual division should be maintained.

Yet earlier combinations within mixed trades had often been sexually intergrated, even where women's status as secondary workers had long been firmly established.[57] In virtually all industries women had been employed on different processes from male workers and received less pay for their work, and yet they had often organized alongside the men. Now many of these mixed organizations disappeared to be replaced by segregated ones. Why? On one occasion James Morrison actually argued for the establishment of separate female unions on the grounds that these would encourage women to become self-mobilizing, instead of relying on men for organizational initiative[58] – an argument which is still heard among some women unionists today. But while a principled separatist stand might have been behind the formation of sex-segregated unions in some cases, in general they reflected a growing tension between men and women, as industrial reorganization and the debasement of craft skills made female labour a growing threat to skilled male workers. This was true across much of the manufacturing sector, including many trades which had previously been under tight male control. Indeed, it seems likely that sex-segregated unions often developed as a compromise with men who wanted women out of their industries and unions entirely. The organization of working people 'into a class . . . is continually being upset . . . by the competition between the workers themselves,' two historians of the working class have written,[59] and this was never more the case than in this period of economic upheaval, when the British working population was being torn apart in order to be put together again in the shape necessary for capitalist development. Not only women workers were deployed against male craftsmen in this process: foreign and child labour of both sexes were used extensively as well. But the woman worker posed a particularly complex and painful threat, since her deployment affected not only the balance of sexual relations in the labour market but also sexual relations in the working-class family. Competition and antagonism between men and women in the sphere of waged work often translated into disrupted patterns of patriarchal authority in the domestic sphere.

But while sex-based competition was a major issue for workers throughout the first half of the nineteenth century, it was only in one brief moment – at the height of the Consolidated Union's career – that the problem became a focus of open discussion and debate within the ranks of the organized working class. There were two reasons why this occurred. The first was the commitment of the Union's Owenite organizers to the elimination of all divisions among working people themselves, as a necessary prologue to the resolution of the capital/labour conflict. Owenite workers explicitly attacked the narrow, sectionalist outlook of existing trade societies (particularly those in the male-dominated urban crafts), and urged in its stead what they called 'universalism': the organization, on equal terms, of all workers, regardless of skill, training, or work experience.[60] The second important factor was the active presence of sexual egalitarians in the Owenite unionist ranks. From 1829 on the working-class press reported many meetings of 'female Co-operators' and women trade unionists in which women's rights was the major topic. 'We had a great number of women that evening,' ran a typical report from the Oldbury Co-operative Society regarding the visit of a feminist lecturer there who had told the women about 'the great improvement which the social system would make in *their* condition and the great injustice inflicted on them in the present day . . .'[61] A toast to women's emancipation was drunk at every Co-operative Congress. Eliza Macauley became the manageress of one of the London Labour Exchanges in 1832, and used the opportunity to promote discussions of women's position among the workers who produced goods for the Exchange.[62] 'It has hitherto . . . been the object of certain persons to keep the females in the background,' one Huddersfield activist told the Third Co-operative Congress, 'but such is not the case with the members of our body . . .'

Most of the women (and men) doing all this propagandizing were from the Owenite intelligentsia, but in 1833–34 a few of the working women they addressed joined them on feminist platforms. In 1832 Eliza Macauley addressed a meeting of the United Trades Association (a forerunner of the Consolidated) on the Rights of Women. The following year a reporter from *The*

Crisis watched while a woman at a UTA meeting rose in the back of the hall and 'in a kind of whisper' observed:

> that a great deal was said of the slavery of the working classes, and of the inadequate wages of the men, but never a word of the slavery of the poor women, who were obliged to toil from dawn to midnight for seven or eight shillings a week.[63]

'This is the still small voice of woman, which we fear must be suppressed for a season till man be served,' commented *The Crisis'* reporter condescendingly, adding 'but yet it will speak like thunder and make even the male slaves blush to think they also have been tyrants.'[64]

But as the popular base of the movement expanded, and new platforms for women developed, the suppression of that voice became impossible. In March 1834 James Morrison initiated a 'Page for the Ladies' in *The Pioneer* (which was quickly changed to 'Women' when it was pointed out that 'Ladies' was 'too aristo-cratic'[65]). In starting the 'Page', Morrison urged his women readers to use it as a medium through which to 'tell their own grievances', while Frances Morrison (writing under her pen-name, 'A Bondswoman') contributed articles which combined the usual Owenite feminist demands for marital equality and intel-lectual emancipation with protests like the following, addressed to 'The Women of the Working Classes':

> It is time the working females of England began to demand their long-suppressed rights. In manufacturing towns, look at the value that is set on woman's labour, whether it be skilful, whether it be laborious, so that woman can do it. [sic] The contemptible expression is, it is made by woman and therefore cheap? Why, I ask, should woman's labour be thus undervalued? Why should the time and the ingenuity of the sex . . . be monopolized bv cruel and greedy oppressors, being in the likeness of men, and calling themselves masters? Sisters, let us submit to it no longer . . . unite and assert your just rights![66]

It was as if a cork had been lifted, allowing a sudden, brief rush of words into the silence which surrounded the lives and consciousness of working-class women. The experience of motherhood, the desire for education, injustices in marriage and family life – all were aired in the 'Women's Page', often with timorous self-deprecation, but sometimes with the force of long-suppressed anger. The Bible commanded husbands to love and honour their wives, wrote one old woman (who asked the editor to correct her writing errors as she had 'not had a pen in my hand these seven years'), 'but how often is that pretended love converted into hatred', and affection dissolved into recrimination and abuse: 'What a bitter mixture for the poor woman to take! and if she offers the least resistance, it is thrust down her throat with his fist, possibly with the loss of a tooth or the spilling of a little of that blood which he thinks so inferior to his own. As he is lord of the castle, he is master and must be obeyed . . .'[67] Other women took up the question of women's responsibility for housework, and the miseries of co-existing with a drunken husband. There were only a handful of these letters, yet together they provide a fascinating glimpse into the attitudes and aspirations of working-class women in this period of intense hardship and conflict.*

But apart from these, the main issues in the 'Page' were those prompted by the preoccupations of the moment. In the same way that the democratic radicalism of the 1790s had opened up the question of women's rights as a citizen, so now the struggle for the 'rights of labour' opened up the issue of women's status as a worker and her place in class-based organizations. Already in 1832 there had been some controversy surrounding the under-payment of women who sold goods at the Labour Exchanges, (where the demand for equal pay had been raised)[68] and now the Morrisons and their female correspondents expanded on this and related issues, with editorials on the sexual division of labour in industry, the problem of sex-based wage differentials and the right of women to employment in hitherto male-dominated trades. 'If the women be prohibited from producing wealth . . .

---

*The ideological impact of the 'Women's Page', and its importance as a forum for working-class women, is better appreciated when we note that *The Pioneer* was the second most widely-read working-class newspaper of the period (closely following *The Poor Man's Guardian*). Estimates of its sales vary between 20,000 and 30,000; its actual readership, however, (since many copies were kept in pubs or meeting halls or coffee houses, where they would be read by dozens of people) would have been many times this figure. There can be no doubt, then, that the 'Page' was the single most important platform for working-class feminist ideas in the early 1830s. (The circulation of *The Crisis* was much lower: estimates vary between five and ten thousand.)

by making clothes, binding shoes, spinning, weaving etc., what shall they do?' Morrison demanded in one editorial. 'They must haunt the street and prowl for prey, and then be reprobated by pious magistrates . . .'[69] But the major problem preoccupying the working women who replied to his invitation to write to the 'Page' was masculine hostility to female unionism, which they were experiencing within the Consolidated itself. 'Allow me, Sir, to inform you,' an 'Initiated Weaver's Wife' wrote in the second issue of the 'Page', 'that there is a great number of men that cannot bear the idea of women's union, and yet they are unionists themselves':

> Now, Sir, I will just ask those men one simple question; do you know the fundamental principles of the noble cause you have embarked in? you will surely say 'yes'; well, then, I say, act up to your professions, and . . . do [women] justice . . . If a house is divided against itself, it cannot stand; just so, if women were all in union, I am positive that it would establish a power, that tyranny would never be able to stand against . . . therefore, they that are not for us are against us.[70]

No sooner had this letter appeared than others quickly followed, accompanied by editorials in both *The Pioneer* and *The Crisis* indicating that male prejudice against the female unionists was becoming widespread. 'What are they [the men] alarmed at?' *The Crisis* wanted to know, 'And what right have they to interfere? Are they [the women] not fellow-labourers with the men? Are they not more oppressed, and more inequitably paid, than their robust partners? . . . And how few women, now, comparatively speaking, have any support or dependence but on their own exertions!'[71] A letter from a male glovemaker protesting the unionization of women in his trade ('it seems to me not work for women, but for men')[72] evoked little comment, but one from another man, a tailor called George Edmonds, really set the fur flying. 'This is the spirit of the male', Morrison wrote in reporting Edmonds' remarks, 'We wanted to draw it out, in order that it might be exposed . . .'[73] In his letter, Edmonds claimed to support women's right to unionize while at the same time arguing that 'none but lazy, gossiping, drunken wives' would wish to leave their houses to attend union meetings. 'This will be clear to anyone, who wishes things to go on well at home,' he added.[74]

The letter immediately elicited furious responses from several women:

> I am neither a lazy, gossiping, drunken, nor tattling wife, and yet I have been to meetings alone . . . what does he think women must be? . . . either stocks or stones? But I hope he will find himself mistaken, as I . . . believe we are . . . coequal with him . . . If not then down with the Union that is now amongst men![75]

'Do not say the unions are only for men;' wrote another, 'tis a wrong impression, forced on our minds to keep us slaves! When men can do our work they shall legislate for us . . .'[76] But the most outraged response was from a tailoress, writing under the pen-name 'A Woman', who in an earlier letter to *The Crisis* had already condemned what she described as 'the tyrannical spirit of the male' revealed within some of the unions. 'In these days, when servants are rising up against their masters, and claiming equal privileges with their employers, why should the spirit of tyranny still reside in the very servants themselves . . .? But it is clear enough from this . . . that the men are as bad as their masters . . .'[77]

From these exchanges it seems obvious that the idea of women meeting and organizing outside their homes, beyond the direct control of their husbands or fathers, was a source of great anxiety to some men. Edmonds' accusations of drunkenness, idleness, 'gadding about and tattling' were standard ones which had been directed at women-in-groups for hundreds of years (in Tudor times there had even been ordinances passed preventing women from meeting together to 'babble and talk'),[78] and the female unionists of the 1830s found it necessary constantly to refute such allegations. 'We have been foolishly taught to think it preposterous for women to make herself in any way public; and . . . are told unions of women would make us idlers and . . . drunkards,' a strawbonnet-maker calling herself 'PAS' wrote indignantly, 'Let us, sisters, banish the idea . . .'[79] Another woman suggested that perhaps the tailor Edmonds didn't want his wife to go to meetings alone because she would then 'hear that he is in the wrong . . .' (presumably over the question of women's correct role), adding however that she herself was persuaded that 'a good wife . . . will not neglect business to seek that which is useless . . .'[80] In his own editorial rebuking Edmonds, Morrison claimed that one factor behind the opposition to female unionization was a desire 'to have women utterly scattered, each subject to her own husband' who having taken it upon himself to provide the major part of the family income then felt he had the right to wield complete authority.[81] Morrison then went on to give a fascinating account of how male control over the wage affected power relations within working-class households:

> If a working man should make thirty shillings a week he may drink ten pints if he pleases; go to a coffee-house every night, and read the papers, and bring in fifteen shillings a week to keep home and pay the rent withal. *He has a right to do this,* for he makes the money. But what is the woman doing? She is working from morning till night at house-keeping; she is bearing children, and suffering all the pangs of labour, and all the exhaustion of suckling; she is cooking, and washing, and cleaning; soothing one child, cleaning another, and feeding a third. And all this is nothing; for she gets no wages. Her wages come from her husband; they are optional; he can give her either twenty shillings to keep house with, or he can give her only ten. If she complains, he can damn and swear, and say, like the Duke of Newcastle, 'Have I not a right to do as I please with my own?' And it is high treason in women to resist such authority, and claim the privilege of a fair reward of their labour!

The result? 'each women [is] subject to her own husband . . . in a yoke of bondage . . .'[82]

But as a trade unionist Morrison was also conscious of other factors behind male opposition to female labour organization. It was no coincidence that the tailor George Edmonds, for example, came from a trade in which a steady influx of female labour had eroded the position of skilled workmen. For many men, it was their status in the workshop, as well as their position as authority figures in the home, which was at stake in this conflict, and it was their struggle to retain that craft status which came to the fore in 1834. In order to understand the changes underlying this struggle, we must now follow the tailor Edmonds and his tailoress opponents back into their trade.

Tailoring occupies a particularly important place in the story of working-class Owenism. More tailors' were involved in co-operative schemes than any other group of workers, and the London tailors' union was the largest union affiliated to the Consolidated. Wherever Owenite plans were afoot, tailors were to be found: depositing their garments in the Labour Exchanges (most of the goods sold in Owen's Grays Inn Exchange were produced by tailors, and they even had a few Exchanges entirely devoted to their products);[83] organizing co-operative workshops; planning community schemes; drawing up the founding Articles of the Consolidated; and marching in the Dorchester labourers' demonstrations with their shears held aloft, sharp blades exposed in a silent gesture of militant defiance.[84]

Tailors were also typical Owenite workers in another sense. The economic problems which they were confronting in the 1830s were very similar to those facing most radical artisans, employed in trades where the transformative agents were usually not steam-powered machinery and factory masters but profiteering merchant investors and sub-contracting systems which undercut the craft strength of the skilled man and introduced thousands of unskilled workers – particularly women workers – into his trade.[85] The effect of such developments, apart from growing material hardship and insecurity, was the intensification of sexual competition, which in turn encouraged a sharply defensive mentality among male workers. Labour consciousness and organization became deeply fractured along sexual lines. 'The working men complain that the masters exercise authority over them; and they maintain their right to associate, and prescribe laws for their own protection . . .' as Morrison wrote of the tailors, 'But speak of any project which will diminish the authority of the male, or give him an equal, where once he found an inferior, and then the spirit of Toryism awakes . . .'[86] And it was this sexual Toryism which flared into open antagonism during the militant union struggles of 1833–34.

TAILORS AND TAILORESSES

The tailoring workshop of the eighteenth century had been a man's world of hard work, hard drinking, and tough union politics.[87] Until the 1830s the London journeymen tailors' union had been one of the strongest in the country, with control over hours, work organization and labour recruitment. This control was exercised through the 'house of call' system: every employer who wanted workers had to apply to a union-run pub, the house of call, where he would be supplied with a 'squad' of men, each run by a 'Captain' who decided upon work allocation and wage distribution. The houses of call were segregated between highly-trained, skilled men, known as 'Flints', who worked only in the better-quality, 'honourable' sector of the trade, supplying clothing to the wealthier classes, and a minority of unapprenticed or inferior workmen called 'Dungs', who found employment in the poorer quality 'dishonourable' workshops. Until the mid-nineteenth century there were no female houses of call, and although a few women were apprenticed in parts of the trade, the overall result of the men's high level of union organization had been to confine female labour to the female wing of the garment industry (dressmaking, millinery) and to a few dishonourable workshops which sometimes employed women.[88]

Nearly all tailors, and certainly all unionized ones, worked only on workshop premises, thus allowing their wives no role in their daily labours. This did not mean, however, that tailors' wives were without employment; instead they worked as necklace-makers, embroiderers, mantua-makers, milk-sellers and small shop-keepers.[89] Only a master tailor who had done very well for himself could support a non-earning wife, and by the late eighteenth century very few journeymen could ever hope to attain such affluence. Nonetheless, a skilful union man and his wife could usually expect to earn enough between them to maintain a fairly respectable lifestyle, as measured by adequate food and clean dress, lively involvement in local cultural and political life, and the little accoutrements of a decent artisan home: brass plate, a few books, a single servant, 'small statues of Shakespeare beneath glass shades'.[90]

In the period immediately following the Napoleonic Wars, the whole economic basis of this lifestyle came under siege. In the course of the war, government contracts for cheap army and navy clothing had stimulated the development of a system of large wholesale 'warehouses' from which fabric was given out to small masters or unemployed journeymen who in turn employed other workers, often women, in their own homes or in sweat-shops. The garments produced in this way were popularly known as 'slop' clothing. Competition for the right to supply the slop warehouses was fierce, leading to the erosion of piece-rates and continual lengthening of hours. It was this process which eventually produced the metropolitan armies of indigent needle-women who so traumatized the Victorian social conscience. 'A mother has got two or three daughters, and she don't wish them to go to service, and she puts them to this poor needlework; and that, in my opinion, is the cause of the destitution and the prostitution about the streets in these parts,' one woman, herself a slopper, told Henry Mayhew in the mid-century, adding that 'the slop trade is the ruin of the young girls that take to it . . .'[91]

But once piece-work, sub-contracting and female employment had been established within the new ready-made sector, they were not to be confined to it. In the post-war period, competition with the sloppers drove many small honourable masters to the wall, while at the same time rising demand for cheaper goods and the ready availability of cheap, unorganized labour drew a new style of clothier on to the quality tailoring scene – the fabric merchant who expanded into garment production and retailing. Shops offering cheap, made-to-order clothing were opened by these men, and soon they were taking custom away from the old craft workshops. A letter to *The Pioneer* from a union tailor pointed out 'the very great increase of *show shops* . . . within the last ten or twelve years':

> These are opened by individuals (not tailors) possessing capital, who advertise such startlingly low prices . . . that they have eventually monopolized a great portion of our trade . . . These individuals generally require all their premises to make what they term a *show*, but have in very few instances room for a workshop. The consequence is, that they persuade men to take their work to their own homes, telling them that their wives, etc., might assist them . . . I know a great too many instances of seven or eight men, sweaters or dampers, as they are termed, the wife of one of them, and half a dozen children being huddled together in one small apartment . . .[92]

'I have experienced and seen good workmen work from fourteen to sixteen hours hard, for under 2s. a day . . .' another journey-man wrote; 'men working at home are scarcely ever able to earn more than 3s. 6d. or 4s. per day, with the assistance often of their wives and children,' stated another.[93] During the slack season even some Flints were forced to perform piecework and homework for these shops, and those who refused soon found themselves undercut by Dungs and other men completely outside the old union organization. In 1824 there was one Dung to four Flints; by 1849 the ratio was three Flints to every twenty Dungs. This rapid deterioration in the position of skilled union men was accompanied by the disappearance of the houses of call, until in 1830 only the best class of bespoke goods in the West End of London was subject to the same degree of control as had been exercised over the entire honourable sector in previous decades.[94]

It was at this point that many London tailors, particularly many of the unionists, became involved in Co-operation and eventually in the Consolidated. Like other urban artisans, they were already familiar with many of the practical measures on which the Co-operative strategy was based. Throughout the eighteenth century striking tailors had often established their own workshops, and journeymen sometimes sold their garments in informal bazaars, rather like the Labour Exchanges.[95] But whereas in the past such activities had been seen only as bargaining tactics or a device to supplement seasonal wages, now some tailors looked to them as a means of achieving 'complete independence' from their employers. Or as *The Times* put it, in reference to the London tailors' union in 1834: 'The blockheads, who have got some shreds and patches of second-hand Owenism for their stock of science, threaten that . . . they will operate for each other and so pocket the masters' profits!'[96] They were, Francis Place commented, 'Owenized' and 'union-mad'.[97]

The economic roots of this 'Owenization' process should now be clear. Workers like the London tailors were at a decisive turning-point. On the one hand, the expansion of show-shops, outwork and female employment had not only undermined the position of the craftsman, but had also made painfully obvious that the old dream of becoming a master – of finding an individual route out of underemployment and insecurity – was no longer viable. What point in achieving self-employed status if it only meant entering into desperate competition with show-shop owners and sweaters and thousands of other small struggling employers?[98] If self-employment was to be a genuine alternative to 'wage-slavery', it had to be *collective* self-employment across the entire trade and eventually across the whole of British manufacture, in order to eliminate competition entirely. 'Labourers must become capitalists, and must . . . regulate their labour on a large united scale, before they will be able to enjoy the whole produce of their labour,' *The Birmingham Co-operative Herald* explained.[99]

On the other hand, a craftsman on the defensive was still a craftsman, possessing the 'capital' of his own technical knowledge and experience. Although the new merchant clothiers in the bespoke sectors had soon acquired near-monopoly control over capital investment in the industry, thereby drawing direct producers under their sway, they had far less command over the actual production process itself, which in the 1830s remained largely in the hands of the skilled workforce.[100] Show-shop owners and warehousemen therefore appeared – as the Owenite economists described them – as mere 'middlemen', 'profiteering parasites' who had somehow inserted themselves between potentially self-managing craftsmen and the means of production and distribution, in order to cream off unearned profits. Who needed them? asked the tailors, shoemakers, cabinet-makers, glove-makers. 'It is only ignorance which leaves a man to do so foolish a thing as to work for another instead of himself . . .'[101] The answer then, was simply to turn one's back on the capitalist, and watch him wither away . . . 'Many parts of London have for some days been covered with placards . . . maintaining the absolute independence of the working classes from those by whom they have hitherto been employed,' it was reported in *The Times* at the height of the tailors' strike which climaxed the general union struggle: 'According to this profound doctrine, industry requires not the moving power of capital, and accumulation is altogether useless!'[102]

Far from being simply a utopian fantasy, then, the Co-operators' hope of a peaceful transition to a classless society rested on an actual balance of class forces in trades like tailoring, where workers were not yet fully subject to capitalist command, and found in their own skills and self-organization the basis for an alternative economic system. The Owenite class analysis, with its emphasis on the autonomous, value-creating power of labour, spoke directly to this sense of alternative material possibilities. At the same time, however, the Owenite emphasis on competition as a generalized social *malaise*, infecting all levels of society, pointed to a key obstacle blocking the path to this workers' commonwealth: internal hierarchy within the working class itself. 'This trade, like almost every other, is divided against itself, one part . . . rapidly undermining the other,' James Morrison wrote of the tailors in 1833,[103] while in the *Appeal* Thompson·described how these divisions developed along sexual lines. 'Men dread the competition of other men, of each other, in every line of industry,' he warned his women readers in discussing the need for women to enter the labour market:

> How much more will they dread your additional competition! How much will this dread of the competition of your industry and talents be aggravated by their previous contempt of your fabricated impotence! Hard enough, now, to acquire comforts: what will it be when an additional rivalship . . . is thrown into the scale against them? How fearfully would such an influx of labour and talents into the market of competition bring down their renumeration![104]

Women had originally entered the quality end of the tailoring trade through waistcoat-making, at the beginning of the century. 'When I first began working at this branch,' one elderly man told Mayhew, 'there were but a few females employed in it':

> a few white waistcoats were given out to them, under the idea that women could make them cleaner than men . . . But since the increase of the puffing and sweating system, masters and sweaters have sought everywhere for such hands as would do the work below the regular ones. Hence the wife has been made to compete with the husband, and the daughter with the wife . . . If the man will not reduce the price of his labour to that of the female, why he must remain unemployed . . .[105]

Initially, the tailors' union had been able to forestall this development through a series of vigorous strike actions. In 1810 and again in 1814 (when the apprenticeship laws were repealed) employers had tried to introduce women into their workshops, at half the male wage. 'This scheme was greatly applauded,' a trade union newspaper, *The Gorgon*, recalled a few years later,

> at one time the newspapers and canting Methodistical publications preaching the saving doctrine of employing women, from which the happiest results were to follow; they did not see that for every woman employed at wages on which she must be all but starved,

106

she deprived a man of his employment, and of the means of
maintaining his family; and thus by barely providing for one, they
took from at least two others the means of subsistence; that what
they gained in the morals of the woman, they destroyed in the man
and his family.[106]

On both occasions the union had been able 'to prevent the
meditated degradation' through large, well-supported turn-outs.
'It will be found universally . . . where men have opposed the
employment of women . . . their own wages are kept up to a
point equal to the maintenance of a family,' the radical tailor
Francis Place told a government committee in 1824, 'the tailors of
London have not only *kept up*, but forced up their wages in this
way . . .'[107] But as the dishonourable sector of the trade grew at
the expense of the honourable part, so the number of women
employed either in workshops or in their own homes increased.
Further strikes over the issue, in 1827 and again in 1830, were lost
– revealing a decisive weakening in the union's position.[108] 'Men
are either obliged to work for women's wages, or lose their work,'
The Pioneer commented in 1834.[109]

The respective attitudes of male and female workers throughout this long cycle of struggles are difficult to trace. Evidence
suggests that the feelings expressed by the writer in *The Gorgon*
were typical of those held by many male unionists; in particular,
the argument that men had a greater right to a living wage than
women, since they were family supporters, was one which
appeared with increasing frequency over the years, in all trades
where female competition was an issue.[110] As to the women, they
rarely had an opportunity to make their views known. But in
1834 *The Pioneer*'s 'Women's Page' provided an important
platform from which a few women workers could express their
reaction to male policies. One of these was the previous
correspondent, 'A Woman'. She was, she now revealed, a
tailoress who had worked at waistcoat-making in a West End
workshop for eighteen years. She had initially written to *The
Pioneer* because she had heard rumours that the tailors intended
to mount yet another strike against the employment of women,
and wanted to know from the union leadership whether the story
was true. 'Should this question be answered in the affirmative,
and I have good reasons for believing it will, I would ask – What

is to become of the numerous women now working at the business, many of whom are tailors' widows, who have no other means of providing for themselves and families, and between whom and the workhouse this is the only bar?' She agreed that 'some alteration' was needed,

> but surely the men might think of a better method of benefitting themselves than that of driving so many industrious women out of employment. Surely, while they loudly complain of oppression, they will not turn oppressors themselves. Surely, they will not give their enemies cause to say, when a woman and her offspring are seen begging in the streets, – This is the work of union; . . . this is the remedy proposed by the *men* of Great Britain to relieve them from their present distress![111]

Receiving no answer to this letter, she wrote again, this time outlining her grievances in greater detail. This second letter is worth examining at some length, not only because it is one of the very few documents of its kind produced by a working woman in this period, but also because of the light it casts on changing sexual relations in the working class.

The letter began by thanking *The Pioneer* for 'pressing the record of women's various wrongs upon the notice of our "lords and masters" . . .':

> An ingenious commentator has observed that woman was made of a rib taken out of the side of a man – not out of his head, to rule him, not out of his feet, to be trampled upon by him; but out of his side, to be his equal – under his arm, to be protected; near his heart, to be beloved. Alas! Alas! that poverty and oppression have so hardened the hearts of *man*kind that, instead of regarding woman in the light . . . intended by their Maker . . . they should be found amongst her worst oppressors! nay, that they should have united . . . to deprive her of the means of subsistence![112]

The only reason this exclusionist policy had not been effectively enforced thus far, 'A Woman' went on to claim, was because of the number of male unionists who relied on the income earned by their wives in the industry. In other words, female labour had created a division among the men themselves, between those who could still manage on their own earnings and those who could not. In some cases, she suggested, male dependence on a wife's earnings was a matter of choice ('instead of working themselves, they can loiter half the week in a pot-house'), but more often it was due to illness (and, although she did not mention it, seasonal unemployment):

> I myself know a woman whose husband was ill . . . for four months, and during that time . . . she supported him, herself and her three children, by the work of her own hands. That husband is now dead; and if the men succeed in their present diabolical purpose, this honest . . . woman and her children must starve, or *go to the workhouse*. This is but one . . . out of hundreds of similar cases . . . [113]

Such women, she went on to point out, had no choice but to play the breadwinning role in their families, yet at the same time they were also expected to perform all their usual household tasks. (One tailor described to Mayhew how his tailoress wife stayed up half the night to do the housework after he had gone to bed: 'she slaves night and day . . . and has less rest than myself, for she has to stop up . . . to attend to her domestic duties.'[114]) If a woman failed to maintain this double burden they lost their own sense of self-respect and often the good-will of their husbands, who 'complain that the place is dirty, their shirt is ragged, and their children neglected!'

> And how can it be otherwise? . . . Did the man so complaining do his duty as a husband and a father – make the most of his time, and procure the means wherewith to support his family, – would not his wife take a pride in rendering his home as comfortable, and his children as cleanly as possible? But while she is obliged to work, not for herself, but for him, she actually has not the time to do this; and finding, after all her exertions, instead of being thanked, she is abused, she becomes reckless; her home, instead of being resorted to as a blessing, is avoided and hated as a curse. She seeks refuge . . . in the bottle; and thus the misery and degradation of the unfortunate pair are completed![115]

She concluded by acknowledging that there were, however, 'some few good men, who, from humanity and a fellow-feeling with the female labourer, instead of wishing to banish her from the trade, would gladly join in raising the price of her labour to the male standard' – to these, she gave her 'heartfelt thanks'.[116]

This letter is obviously no more than the personal testimony of a single woman. But from other evidence it seems clear that the tensions it describes were by no means unique to the experience of this tailoress, but could be found wherever women were taking on productive roles which ran counter to the traditional sexual division of labour.[117] As male earnings and employment prospects deteriorated, increasing numbers of women were forced to perform jobs which could no longer be readily integrated with family duties, while at the same time many men found themselves pushed into an unfamiliar dependence on wife (and child) earnings. What was at stake, therefore, in the 'feminization' of the declining trades was not only the status of male craftsmen, but also the conventional balance of domestic relationships, in which men functioned primarily as bread-winners and women primarily as family servicers, integrating household tasks with casual wage-earning activities. 'Have not women been unfairly driven from their proper sphere in the social scale, unfeelingly torn from the maternal duties of a parent, and unjustly encouraged to compete with men in ruining the money value of labour?' the Secretary of the London Tailors' Union demanded in 1834.[118]

Inasmuch as this phenomenon has been examined by historians at all, it has usually been discussed in terms of the situation in the new factory districts, where the division between home and workplace created by the mechanization of former domestic trades made the problem particularly acute.[119] When Engels walked around Manchester streets in 1844 he saw many families where the husband, often an unemployed handloom weaver, had been left to tend the house and infants while his wife and older children toiled in the local mill. 'It is easy to imagine the wrath aroused among the working men by this reversal of all relations within the family,' he commented,[120] and in fact that wrath could be heard very clearly in public statements issued by male textile workers' organizations. In 1835 a meeting of Yorkshire handloom weavers passed a resolution condemning 'the adaption of machines . . . to *children*, and *youth*, and *women*, to the exclusion of those who ought to labour – THE MEN', while several years later a deputation of male spinners from the factory reform movement argued for 'the gradual withdrawal of all females from the factories' on the grounds that female factory employment represented 'an inversion of the order of nature and

110

of Providence – a return to the state of barbarism, in which the woman does the work, while the man looks idly on'. The home, not the factory, was 'woman's true sphere', they contended.[121]

These sentiments were expressed with particular force in the textile areas, where they featured within a wider struggle against the new conditions of mechanized exploitation. But neither such attitudes nor the tensions which produced them were confined to the factory proletariat; they extended throughout every sector in which older sexual hierarchies were being destabilized. One study of wife-beating in London in the 1840s has found that artisan households in which women replaced men as major breadwinners were ripe for violent confrontation, as men attempted to assert authority which had lost its material basis.[122] The opposition to married women's employment which Mayhew met among 'the most respectable' artisans in the mid-century is now easy to understand. The wage-earning wife, once seen as the norm in every working-class household, had become a symptom and symbol of masculine degradation: it 'unsexes the man and takes from the woman all womanliness', as Engels wrote of the Manchester working population in 1844, with 'womanliness' now firmly identified – as far as most working men were concerned – with home-based dependency.[123] In the late 1830s the Chartist leader, R.J. Richardson, came across a group of female calico-printers, hard at work in their trade, to whom he delivered the following little speech on Woman's Duty:

'This is the work of men', said I to the lasses, 'and you ought not to perform it: your places are in your homes: your labours are your domestic duties: your interests in the welfare of your families, and not in slaving thus for the accumulation of the wealth of others, whose slaves you seem willing to be: for shame of you! go seek husbands those of you who have them not, and make them toil for you; and those of you who have husbands and families, go home and minister to their domestic comforts.' Such were my opinions, and such are my opinions.[124]

The reaction of working-class women themselves to this development has never been systematically investigated, but scattered evidence suggests that the views expressed by our militant tailoress, 'A Woman', were shared by many other women of her background.[125] On the one hand, as we have seen, she clearly supported the idea of the man as primary bread-winner: 'did the man do his duty . . . and procure the means wherewith to support his family' his wife would be happiest 'rendering his home as comfortable, and his children as cleanly as possible'; after all, who would actually *want* to combine heavy household labour with a full-time waged job?[126] Perhaps in the New Moral World it would be possible, as the Owenites promised, to integrate collectivized domestic work with other productive and intellectual employments, but in the Old Immoral World housework and waged work had become a terrible double load which no woman would willingly take on so long as she had a husband (or some other conjugal partner) to support her. The 'ideology of domesticity' was not just a set of oppressive ideals foisted on a supine female population; it was an ideology actively adopted by many working-class women as the best in a very narrow range of unhappy options.

Yet at the same time, women like the tailoress knew only too well that many wives lacked husbands or lovers who could or would support their families. Hence her furious denunciations of the union for attempting to deny women the right to employment (her final letter to *The Pioneer* was so vitriolic that Morrison refused to publish it).[127] Once again, it was the gap between the womanly ideal and the reality of women's lives which generated female protests, rather than a direct confrontation with the ideal itself. 'I do not wish to take any power from man that he can with justice claim,' as 'PAS' wrote to *The Pioneer*, 'only let us, who bear an equal share of the evils of circumstance unite to defend our own . . .:'

> you, husbands, who have seen your wives, when you have been out of employ, toiling early and late to get a bare existence for her children and you . . . I am induced to plead to [you], from hearing . . . [you] do not like women from home. Are we not forced from home to labour, and may we not go from home to endeavour to lighten that labour without the fear of an angry husband when we return? Every feeling manly heart answers we have. Then let us sister workwomen, make a beginning in our own business; our number is great, our power equal . . .[128]

These difficult contradictions, these complex alignments and disalignments between men and women in their roles as workers and family partners, have been at the centre of working-class life and radical organization since the first half of the nineteenth century. Yet only under certain conditions have they emerged as open issues. In November 1833, a meeting of the London tailors was held where Owenite workers in the trade attempted to re-organize the union on the basis of what they called 'equalization': every tailor, regardless of his previous standing, would be allowed to join the union on the same basis 'without difference or distinction'.[129] 'Hitherto, the masters had cunningly contrived to set one man against another . . .' one man told the meeting, and 'they had created an aristocracy that had proved the workers' greatest bane and curse; for whilst they had left some destitute, these had become their worst enemies, by grasping at employment at reduced wages.'[130] Other men urged abandon-ment of the Flint/Dung distinction, the elimination of wage differentials, and the sharing-out of employment through shortening of hours. 'No sophistry . . . or tyranny shall be permitted longer to divide them,' one assured his brothers. And the tailoresses? 'Let me advise you as a brother,' George Petrie told his co-unionists, 'be not unjust to our sisters. – Remember, Equality is the order of the day . . .'[131] His position was supported by several of the most left-wing tailors, and also by James Morrison, who in a *Pioneer* editorial laid out very clearly the options currently facing male unionists, particularly those hoping to move past defensive, sectional militancy towards a new·form of egalitarian class organization. The arguments which Morrison produced are worth quoting at length, since they are unique in the history of early trade unionism.

The editorial began by pointing out that 'women have always been worse paid for their labour than the men' and thus 'by long habit and patient acquiescence, they have been taught to regard this inequality as justice.' They were therefore, 'content with merely a portion of a man's wage, even when their work is equally valuable', which meant that they could readily be used to under-cut men's wages: 'If a woman makes a waistcoat for two-thirds of the sum which is charged by a man, she will, without doubt, monopolize the waistcoat trade to herself, or compel him to lower his charges.' It was to prevent this 'diminution of wages' that the tailors had actively organized against female employment.[132]

113

The tailors claim, Morrison went on, that they 'do not want to deprive women of their means of living, provided they do not prove prejudicial to the trade at large' and this he approved so long as it meant that equal pay was the strategy, 'but where they wantonly throw out of employment a number of females, merely because they were women, we think this an encroachment on the liberties of humanity . . .' He went on to suggest that the question divided itself into two: have male workers the right to undercut each others' wages – to which the answer is always no – and 'has a woman a right to reduce the wages of man, by working for less than man?'

Certainly not, were woman considered equal to man, and did she enjoy the same rights and priveleges [sic]; but since man has doomed her to inferiority, and stamped an inferior value upon all the productions of her industry, the low wages of woman are not so much the voluntary price she sets upon her labour, as the price which is fixed by the tyrannical influence of male supremacy. To make the two sexes equal and to reward them equally, would settle the matter amicably; but any attempt to settle it otherwise will prove an act of gross tyranny.[133]

'Hear this, ye men!' wrote the West End tailoress in the following issue, 'and when next you meet to proceed against the rights and liberties of the weaker part of the creation, may the still small voice of conscience whisper in your ears the words of *The Pioneer* . . .'[134]

The tailors' union made no written response to this, but in April 1834, at the climax of the Consolidated Union's brief career, nine thousand London tailors came out on strike for higher wages, a shortening of hours, and the abolition of piecework and homework.[135] Although the strike leaders said nothing about female labour in their initial manifestoes, it was clear to observers – both pro- and anti-union – that women's outwork and show-shop employment were at stake. Morrison saw the tailors as having 'declared war against the female tailors',[136] while *The Times*, which was hysterically anti-union, stated that it was the female waistcoat-makers in particular who were under attack.[137] Since the strike was generally viewed as the beginning of an overall labour offensive (and in fact the shoemakers' and hatters' unions were both waiting in the wings, to take action if the tailors proved victorious), employers in other industries united with the government in urging the master tailors to take swift action. In particular, they urged them to bring in female scab labour: 'a few thousand women who . . . from a sort of coxcomb pedantry and jealousy are kept out of the business.'[138] Large numbers of women, probably slop-workers, were soon introduced into the striking workshops, and their products were publicly exhibited in markets around London.[139] Several Members of Parliament stated that they would wear only clothing produced by women for the duration of the strike.[140] A number of women black-legs were attacked by unionists, who seized their materials. 'The masters seem resolved to feminize the whole trade, rather than yield . . . and to stir up an uncivil war between the sexes,' *The Crisis* reported.[141]

Meanwhile, the union leadership issued contradictory statements, claiming both to support the women's right to employment while at the same time denouncing the shops which provided it.[142] The presence of female black-legs in the shops was explicitly denied: 'you must have some strange notions of our trade, to think that women can do what many men who have served seven years to it, cannot accomplish,' the opposition press was told.[143] At one point the union secretary accused *The Times* (which was acting as the employers' unofficial mouthpiece) of lying about the issue in order 'to turn our mothers and sisters against us'; they were even willing to set up a woman's union, one leading militant claimed.[144] The obvious conclusion to be drawn from this was that the men were divided on the issue, with Owenite-influenced unionists the strongest supporters of a non-exclusionist strategy. 'If women are equal in the state of human existence, what right, would I ask, has any set of mechanics to deny to them a right which they, the tailors, are at this moment claiming for themselves,' an 'old journeyman tailor' demanded in a letter to *The Pioneer*. 'Competition is the great, the only, the all-prevailing evil. Competition must be destroyed, and associated labour raised upon its ashes; all the rest must end in disappointment.'[145] Clearly he was not alone in his views, since shortly after the strike began London was plastered with placards from Owenite tailors urging their fellow-workers to establish co-operative workshops and thereby eliminate their exploiters:

115

several workshops were established and in these women workers were employed, alongside the men.[146]

By late May, however, most of the tailors had returned to work under threat of permanent dismissal if they stayed out any longer. Strike funds were exhausted (some had been embezzled by a union leader), the Executive of the Consolidated Union refused further financial support, and the strike quickly collapsed.[147] The tailors' union then pulled out of the Consolidated Union, and since it had been the largest affiliated union, this led to the speedy demise of the Consolidated as well. Sixteen years later, when Henry Mayhew was interviewing old London tailors, they remembered the strike very well, and told him that their defeat then had been decisive in finally breaking craft control of the trade: sweating, piecework, and female employment had all increased dramatically in the succeeding years. So bad had their situation become, they told him, that they would soon all 'be reduced to the position of the lowest of the needlewomen'.[148]

The defeat of the tailors, and the subsequent collapse of the Consolidated Union, marked the end of the Owenite economic offensive. The Owenites came out of the Consolidated bitterly divided. Owen, who had been terrified by the class militancy which his own rhetoric had helped to unleash, had spent the last few months of the general union agitation counselling class collaboration. His more militant followers, on the other hand, had been pushing towards a general strike (a 'Grand National Holiday') by which 'they might bring their superiors to any terms of accommodation', and were therefore opposed to 'partial actions' like those of the tailors: 'we depend for deliverance entirely upon grand and national movements,' Morrison scolded, 'and not upon the limited struggles of individual trades . . . contending for their own immediate interests.'[149] But the 'grand and national movement' had been brought to its knees; many of the new union lodges, including most of the women's lodges, had collapsed; Morrison himself was dead within a year; and only Owen emerged convinced it was all for the best. 'You seem for a time to have lost the spirit of peace and charity by which alone the regeneration of mankind can be effected,' he gently chastised his working-class followers.[150] Within less than a year he had established a new organization, the Association of All Classes of All Nations, whose goal, as he formulated it, was the establishment of a world-wide community system, to be created by a confederacy of broad-minded capitalists and enlightened workers. 'Mr Owen has this day assured me . . .' Francis Place noted in his diary at the time of the inauguration of the AACAN, 'that within six months the whole state and condition of society in Great Britain will be changed, and all his views carried into effect.'[151] It was Year One of the New Moral World.

V

EVE AND THE NEW JERUSALEM

PROLOGUE

Despite Owen's irrepressible optimism, the Socialist movement was slow to recover from the defeats of 1834. By October 1835, the Association of All Classes of All Nations had only 150 members; a year later energetic recruitment had barely doubled that number.[1] But in 1837 new groups began to appear in various parts of the country (particularly in those areas where co-operative schemes had previously flourished), and these multiplied rapidly. By 1840 Owenism had reached a new peak of organized strength.

The revived movement looked quite different, both in shape and content, from what had gone before. The loose network of co-operative societies and union branches of the previous period had been replaced by a formal organization with an elaborate branch structure, national executive (the 'Central Board'), and clearly-defined membership. This tightening of internal organization was accompanied by an important shift in strategy. Whereas in 1829–34 Owenism had been identified with co-operative shops, Labour Exchanges, and trade unionism, by the early 1840s it was an organization dedicated to community experimentation and the dissemination of heterodox propaganda. Religious freethought, women's rights, marriage reform, popular education: these were some of the cultural and social issues with which Socialism (as the movement was known by the late 1830s) was equated. This shift in political focus resulted partly from the collapse of the co-operative/trade union offensive, which had left many Owenites convinced that attempts to reclaim 'the whole produce of labour' within the existing social system were doomed to failure.[2] But it also reflected the underlying logic of the Owenite position. Even at the height of the earlier struggles, Owenite ideologues could always be heard reminding their fellows that the creation of a New Moral World depended not only on the eradication of private capital, but also on a process of moral and psychological regeneration which would transform 'the competitive system' from within. Correct Character Formation was the key to social reconstruction, it was emphasized, and only a systematic assault on all the institutions responsible for Incorrect Character Formation – authoritarian schooling, orthodox religion, patriarchal marriage and 'single-family arrangements' – would clear the psychological path to Socialist development. These doctrines, as we have seen, belonged to the committed 'core' membership of Owenism who during the militant confrontations of the early 1830s had often been unable to prevent them from being swept aside by the issues of the moment. But as hopes of building a workers' commonwealth through the union movement dimmed and died, such ideas re-asserted themselves with renewed vigour, until by 1840 Socialists everywhere were engaged in a full-scale offensive against Old World 'error' in all its forms. Universal enlightenment and cultural reconstruction had replaced economic co-operation as the major routes to the New Moral World.

Most historians of Owenism have chosen to interpret this shift in emphasis as the decline of a militant class movement into a utopian, quasi-religious sect. Before 1835, it is argued, Owenism served as the vehicle for the economic aspirations of a broad alliance of working people, but by the late 1830s it had deteriorated into a small, exclusive organization, dominated by a mystical faith in its own eccentric doctrines and indifferent to the concrete problems facing working people. In the words of *The Communist Manifesto*, it had become a 'mere reactionary sect' whose 'fanatical and superstitious' commitment to a 'new social Gospel' blinded it to the real political tasks of the moment – an assessment which has been echoed (with some variations in emphasis) ever since.[3]

One feature of this critique – the argument that in its later phase Owenite ideology became essentially religious in character – is important, and will be considered in detail below.

119

But in general, the picture thus evoked of post-1834 socialism is a remarkably distorted one. Far from being a small, exclusive organization, it was a large and fiercely evangelical one, commanding widespread popular support. By the early 1840s the Rational Society, as the Socialist body finally came to be titled,* consisted of over sixty-five branches in all parts of the country, many with their own schools, libraries and meeting halls. It produced dozens of newspapers and millions of tracts (half a million tracts were distributed in 1839 alone), employed some twenty Social Missionaries and sponsored lectures by hundreds of volunteer publicists. On any given Sunday in 1841, attendance at Socialist lectures across the country numbered about 50,000, while readership of the 'official' newspaper, *The New Moral World*, was variously estimated at between 100,000 and 400,000.[4] 'There is scarcely a town of any magnitude in which Socialism has not taken root,' *The Liverpool Standard* told its readers in 1839: an exaggerated but not wholly improbable estimate of Owenite influence at the time.[5]

This re-expansion of Owenism into a genuinely popular movement owed little, it must be said, to Owen himself – who, if he had had his way, would have turned it not merely into a sect but into an authoritarian cult. Always deeply fearful of independent working-class action, Owen had been terrified by the events of 1834, and as soon as the Rational Society was founded he tried to impose on it a quasi-dictatorial regime, 'The Paternal System', headed by himself, 'The Social Father', and a few close disciples.[6] Not only was the new organization to be class-collaborationist (Owen lectured his disciples on the inability of the working class to manage any 'large scale enterprise' and the need for middle-class leadership in the community experiments),[7] but it was also to be overtly anti-democratic. Revised plans for the New Moral World, as developed by Owen, advocated a strict hierarchy of

---

*The first organization established by Owen after the collapse of the Consolidated Union was the British and Foreign Consolidated Association of Industry, Humanity and Knowledge, which became the Association of All Classes of All Nations in May 1835. In 1837 the National Community Friendly Society was set up in order to organize the funding and development of communities; in May 1839 the NCFS merged with the AACAN to form the Universal Community Society of Rational Religionists which in 1842 became known as the Rational Society.

wealth and status in the social communities.[8] The campaign for the People's Charter was officially opposed on the grounds that working people were incapable of exercising democratic rights.[9] For Owen, none of these prejudices were new, but now they were embodied in the policies of leading members of the Central Board and in the propaganda of a number of Social Missionaries. The national leadership, in the words of one dissident Social Missionary, had 'removed itself from its earliest friends . . . and drawn around it a conventional circle, over which the poor man cannot step', and in so doing gained the reputation for conservatism and elitism for which other Socialists were to condemn it.[10]

The development of Socialism at a local level, however, usually occurred along wholly different lines. Nearly all the branches were democratically organized (despite repeated attempts on the part of the Central Board to impose the 'paternal system') and most proved highly resistant to Owen's manoeuvres.[11] As in the earlier period, their membership was predominantly working class, with a sprinkling of professionals and small business owners, and nearly all their leading activists were drawn from that same 'respectable' sector of the working population which fuelled every other radical struggle of the period. This meant that in most towns the boundaries between Socialism and other types of radical activity were very fluid: militants moved freely between Socialist branch work, union meetings, and Chartist rallies. 'Although [Owen] himself deprecated the Radical political reformers . . . most of his followers were not at all indifferent to them,' Holyoake's biographer claimed, 'They fraternised with the Chartists everywhere . . .'[12] Throughout the late 1830s and early 1840s, both *The New Moral World* and the Chartist newspaper, *The Northern Star*, carried dozens of reports from centres like Congleton where, according to the *Star*, 'many of our members are admirers of Socialism', and many of the local Socialists 'members of our branch'[13]; or Sunderland, where meetings held to debate the Charter were attended by nearly the entire membership of the local Owenite branch, most of whom voted in favour of the Charter;[14] or London, where, according to *The New Moral World*, over half the city's Owenites were active Chartists.[15] Radical movements, particularly in this period, were never isolated entities, hermetically sealed off from one another; rather they developed through a continuous interchange of ideas and personnel, particularly at a local level.*

Nonetheless, even in the most radical towns Owenism remained a highly distinctive creed, differing from other styles of radicalism not only in the goals it sought but also in the way it held and promoted them. Intense moral and intellectual purism were the hallmarks of the movement. Unlike Chartism, which developed as a loose alliance of reform-minded people with only a limited programme of democratic demands in common (and widely differing views on other ideological or social issues, such as religion or women's status), Owenism demanded of its members a commitment not only to certain practical endeavours but also to the co-operative ethos. Community schemes – and indeed the movement itself – were intended, as William Thompson put it, to 'form one grand moral as well as economical experiment'[16] for which it was necessary that every participant be morally and mentally equipped. After November 1834, anyone wishing to become a Socialist was expected to undergo a three-month probation in which they would be trained in Socialist ideas and conduct through the educational meetings and social events sponsored by all local branches.[17] As purveyors of a new way of life, the Owenites had to ensure that all who entered their ranks were genuine apostles, carrying the 'grand moral truths' of Social Science in their hearts as well as in their minds. 'It cannot be too often impressed upon persons entering into co-operative associations, that . . . their disposition to perform a fair portion of . . . labour . . . is not all which is required,' as one 'Old Co-operator' wrote, 'The mind must undergo a corresponding change; perhaps I cannot express it better than in the language of Scripture, "They must be born again . . ." '.[18]

It is in this context that the centrality of religion to post-1834 Socialism becomes intelligible. Any movement seeking to re-model and rationalize popular belief would be brought into confrontation with the dominant ideological institutions of the

---

*The main centres of Owenite activity after 1834 were London, the Midlands, the northern industrial districts, Glasgow and Edinburgh. London was the strongest urban base, with Manchester in second place (Harrison, *Owen*, pp. 224-9).

period – and when that movement also made claims on behalf of an alternative ethical code, bitter opposition from the churches was inevitable. By the late 1830s many Owenites were describing Socialism as the Rational Religion, thereby placing themselves in direct competition with orthodox Christianity. From 1838 on, the meeting halls of the working class became arenas in which the conflicting claims of Christianity and Social Science met in head-on collision. It was a battle in which a new wave of propagandists came to the fore: Owenite feminist 'infidels' for whom the struggle for sexual emancipation became inextricably tied to the struggle against patriarchal Christian orthodoxy. As in the 1820s and early 1830s, these women were mostly from the lower middle class and upper working class. Some, like Frances Morrison, were veterans of the earlier co-operative and trade union campaigns, but most had joined the movement after 1837. They were still few in number, but very voluble in presence, and it was largely through their lectures and writings that the Woman Question was taken out to audiences across England, Scotland and Wales between 1838 and 1845.

WOMAN'S MISSION

The religious revival which swept the country at the end of the eighteenth century was of a scale and intensity not experienced in Britain since the Puritan Revolution. The emergence of Wesleyanism in the 1730s had been the first stage in an awakening which gradually penetrated both Established and Dissenting congregations, generating a wave of pietistic fervour which rocked the boat of clerical passivity everywhere. The French Revolution accelerated this development and also intensified its more mystical aspects. Throughout the first half of the nineteenth century, chiliastic cults flourished in many parts of the country. Prophets rose and fell, gathering thousands of disciples one year and losing them the next to another self-proclaimed Messiah. Methodism expanded at an enormous rate, fissioning to produce a host of plebian sects. At the other end of the social scale, the wealthy Evangelical party within the Established Church busied itself with a multitude of philanthropic projects and godly propaganda schemes. Everywhere, saints and their followers were on the march, and no aspect of British social life remained unaffected by their passage.[19]

A crucial outcome of this revival, I argued earlier, was the conservatization of sexual ideology, particularly in the early Victorian middle class. This generalization now needs qualification. Sexual conservatism was not the automatic product of evangelical ideology, but rather a political triumph for certain interpreters of the Protestant moral code. Revivalist doctrines regarding women's role were, in fact, riddled with contradictions which provided a continuous undercurrent of tension and conflict.

These contradictions, like the evangelical outlook as a whole, were hardly new. Like the moralists of the seventeenth century, the re-modelled puritans of the nineteenth century revival promulgated notions of spiritual equality and companionate marriage which were highly ambiguous in their implications for women's secular status. 'Whilst the Gospel unequivocally speaks of woman as the weaker sex, subject to the authority of their husbands . . . it nevertheless represents them as helpsmeet for and like unto man: partakers by nature of the same rational and moral faculties; intitled [sic] by grace to the same spiritual privileges,' Reverend Richard Mant explained in a popular 1821 tract on 'The Female Character' – although no doubt he would have hastened to agree with *The Evangelical Magazine* when it emphasized that such 'spiritual privileges' were not intended to 'abolish the artificial distinctions of civil society . . . [or] break up the domestic circle . . .'[20] It might seem inconsistent to claim for woman a spiritual role at least equal to that of her husband and at the same time accede to her social subordination, Sarah Lewis admitted in her influential book *Woman's Mission*, but the paradox was easily resolved: 'the one quality on which woman's value and influence depends is the renunciation of self . . .'[21] This solution may have satisfied her, but some of her spiritual sisters were less easily reconciled. 'Far . . . be it from my intention to claim or uphold any privilege which would in the least degree militate against the Scriptural injunctions, "Wives, submit yourselves to your husbands, as is fit in the Lord",' one woman wrote in a militantly evangelical/feminist tract published in 1840, titled *Domestic Tyranny, or Woman in Chains*:

124

I would at the same time draw attention to the particular terms of this commandment, 'as is fit in the Lord', which certainly imply not a degraded or inferior being in the scale of His creation, or one who was unworthy or incompetent to appreciate such an injunction; but on the contrary, it is particularly addressed to them as responsible and self-governing agents, who are also required to search the Scriptures to know the will of the Lord . . .[22]

This woman's own researches into the Word had satisfied her that neither wife-beating, nor male monopoly of female property, nor an all-male franchise formed any part of the Divine Plan. 'It is indeed a feeling which seems implanted in our nature by the Almighty, to rebel against oppression . . .'

In America, which was also in the grip of a Great Awakening, these tensions within the puritan sexual strategy finally exploded into an open, organized assertion of evangelical feminism.[23] But in Britain, as we have seen, the overtly anti-Jacobin, anti-democratic content of the revival had led to a systematic suppression of any incipient emancipationist message for women within orthodox congregations. The same Reverend Mant who apostrophized women as spiritual 'helpsmeet' for men concluded his tract by contrasting the pious ladies of England to the 'inferior ranks of females in the neighbouring country mingling with unreserved devotion in all the horrors of revolutionary anarchy' including, presumably, the horrors of feminist activism.[24] The attack on Wollstonecraft consolidated in the public mind the distinction between Christian womanhood and infidel notions of sexual equality. But an undercurrent of tension remained in religious circles, eddying around attitudes towards marriage, women's education, and the respective roles of men and women within family life. One of the focal points of this tension, and the point from which various styles of Socialist feminist heterodoxy originated, was the concept of women as a moral vanguard.

The precise origins of this notion do not concern us here. Certainly the doctrine of 'female influence' had been a popular feature of bourgeois prescriptive writing well before revivalist didacts developed it into the campaigning gospel of 'woman's mission'. As Nancy Cott has pointed out, the evangelicals 'transformed the truism of etiquette books, that individual women influenced individual men's manners, into the proposition that the collective influence of woman was an agency of moral reform.'[25] More specifically, they developed a concept of femininity based on the identification of womanliness with godliness and both with the private virtues of domestic life. The 'moral power' of women, Sarah Stickney Ellis argued in her enormously influential popularizations of this thesis, derived first from God (who had endowed women with all the basic Christian attributes of love, compassion and self-abnegation and almost none of the more suspect masculine virtues such as intelligence, humour or resourcefulness) and secondly from the sexual division of labour, which provided women with the duties appropriate to a loving, self-denying nature and insulated them from the harsh realities (and unsavoury 'pecuniary objects') of male existence.[26] 'What then, is the true object of female education?' Sarah Lewis demanded rhetorically, '. . . the conscience, the heart and the affections . . .'[27] Leave to men the grimy life of intellect and action, all these women proclaimed in unison, 'the moral world is ours . . .'[28] In the performance of home duties women were not merely fulfilling their natural function but realizing a divine purpose: as chaste wives and pious mothers they became (in the words of William Wilberforce) 'the medium of our intercourse with the heavenly world, the faithful repositories of the religious principle, for the benefit both of the present and the rising generation'.[29]

A morality more convenient and yet more contradictory would be hard to imagine. Having confined all those virtues inappropriate within the stock market or the boardroom to the hearts of their womenfolk, middle-class men were then left free to indulge in all those unfortunate vices necessary for successful bourgeois enterprise. The fate of women and Christian selflessness having been thus bound together, the dependency and social powerlessness of the first become a virtual guarantee of the social irrelevance of the second: once God had settled into the parlour, Mammon had free range in public life – and the exclusion of women from virtually all areas of public existence guaranteed that this tidy division was maintained. An ideal of femininity which combined holy love with social subordination not only served to suppress women, it also tamed and contained the anti-capitalist implications of Christian love itself. Domesticated

What about Jud-----)

Christianity, like domesticated womanhood, was the most comfortable kind for a bourgeois man to live with.

The limited role offered to women within the revivalist churches only served to highlight this elision of spiritual power with social impotence. On the one hand, women were the mainstay of virtually all early nineteenth century congregations: 'We see in all places of public worship, and on all occasions in which a religious object is the motive for exertion, a greater proportion of women than of men,' Mrs Ellis noted, and a host of other observers supported her claim.[30] Yet at the same time the sphere in which they were able to exercise this enthusiasm was usually very narrow and auxiliary to that of the male leadership. William Wilberforce may have believed that women were God's own repositories, but he strongly objected to any suggestion that they should play a directing part in the philanthropic activities (such as the abolitionist movement) for which they performed all the most gruelling, least recognized labour.[31] Female preachers were unknown in the Established church and most of the old Dissenting congregations. In its early years, Methodism sponsored women preachers (Wesley himself supported them), but by the early nineteenth century they had been suppressed in the main Methodist organization, although a number of breakaway sects such as the Primitive Methodists and the Bible Christians (both with largely working-class memberships) offered platforms to preacheresses in the 1830s.[32] 'Your Society sanctions women's preaching, then?' George Eliot has a curious observer inquire of her fictional Methodist preacheress, Dinah Morris (who was modelled after Elizabeth Evans, Eliot's aunt and one of the leading Wesleyan women of the late eighteenth century). 'It doesn't forbid them, sir, when they've a clear call to the work . . .':

> I understand there's been voices raised against it in the Society of late, but I cannot think their counsel will come to nought. It isn't for men to make channels for God's Spirit, as they make channels for the watercourses, and say, 'Flow here, but not flow there.'[33]

But by the second quarter of the nineteenth century the Word had few spokeswomen within the larger churches, despite the bitter battles waged by some of these women to retain their right to speak. As the claims for women's spiritual knowledge became more extravagant, so the curbs on their right to speak this knowledge (except to their children and, if they were leisured ladies, the poor) became much tighter. Women are 'not . . . to teach virtue, but to inspire it' as Sarah Lewis wrote.[34] The presence of women on Socialist platforms was therefore viewed as another manifestation of their infidelism. On one occasion the lecture of a leading Socialist feminist, Margaret Chappellsmith, was interrupted by a young man who shouted at her across the meeting hall, 'What do you make of the following strong scriptural statements? 1 Timothy 11: Let the women learn in silence with all subjection; and verse 12: But I suffer not *a woman to teach*, nor to usurp authority over the men, *but to be in silence*.'[35] Margaret's reply was not recorded, but no doubt it strengthened her opponent's conviction that feminism was a godless creed. 'St Paul forbade women to speak in churches, and they have held their tongues in churches . . .' Eliza Sharples told her audience at the Rotunda in 1832. 'Suppressed speech gathers into a storm . . .'[36]

Under these conditions it was inevitable that the churches should begin to breed a female opposition. Having urged on women the divine mission of moral regeneration, orthodox Christians were then unable to persuade all these female regenerators that the only way to realize their mission was as dutiful wives and charity workers. 'I chose to obey God rather than man,' one preacheress wrote when she flouted the Wesleyan injunction against female ministry, and when godly duties clashed with conventional interpretations of the female role, respectable femininity was sometimes abruptly abandoned.[37] This was particularly true of that small number of women for whom the 'moral mission' of womankind acquired radical content. 'There is a principle in woman's love that renders it impossible for her to be satisfied without actually *doing* something for the object of her regard . . .' Mrs Ellis had written, and when all that loving energy was turned towards the socially oppressed, including the female oppressed, it made political activists out of a number of female moralists.[38] 'Because love must be thrust into the context of power, the moralist . . . must become revolutionary,' Edward Thompson has written of another group of 'evangelicals' in another period, and exactly the same could be said of these women, whose radicalism was simultaneously a product of their puritanism and a reaction to it.[39]

Eliza Sharples, for example, grew up in a fervently Evangelical household in Bolton, of which she herself was the most enthusiastically pious member. In her youth she was 'driven almost to the grave by prayers, hymn singing and soul searching . . .' Her mind was 'not quite of the common order,' a friend later recalled, 'and perhaps the excess of ardour with which she had thrown herself into her religious pursuits made the recoil more easy and more decided . . .'[40] Similarly, Margaret Chappellsmith had been a Baptist before joining the Socialist movement, as had another famous feminist infidel of a later generation, Harriet Law.[41] Eliza Macauley, we noted earlier, had been a Christian preacheress before becoming an Owenite freethinker.[42] Another radical, Mrs Hamilton, who lectured in Scotland in the early 1830s, delivered feminist harangues against the clergy from a pulpit, dressed in 'official white robes'. She believed she had been 'sent from Heaven' to deliver her message to womankind, she told one enquirer.[43] All these women were fierce opponents of organized religion, of whatever brand: 'Give us freedom. Give us free discussion,' Sharples exhorted her readership in *Isis*, 'LET US HAVE NO PRIESTS. Let us advance; and if Tyranny shall seek to arrest our march, let us unite to conquer it by the joint power of mind and matter moving in masses . . .'[44]

Two styles of infidelism can be traced among these women – freethought and heresy. The term 'freethought' was used very widely in the early nineteenth century, to cover almost any brand of heterodoxy from Unitarianism or Deism to outright atheism. Here, however, I am using it more narrowly, as its Owenite exponents did, to describe the anti-Christian, materialist (and, at its extreme end, atheistic) stance later known as secularism. Heresy, on the other hand, while no less anti-clerical than freethought, was based not on an outright rejection of the Gospel but on its radical reinterpretation. Heresy was schismatic; freethought was overtly anti-religious. The distinction seems clear enough, but in fact it blurred at many crucial points. The evangelical mode of thought persisted as a linking strand between all forms of feminist (anti-) theology.

The ambiguities surrounding radical infidelism were obvious at a general level within Owenism as well, where a purported commitment to Reason against Superstition was combined with a proselytizing moral stance often identical in form, if not in content, to that of the evangelical churches. By the late 1830s many branches had adopted the formal attributes of a plebian congregation. In 1837 the Owenite Congress had taken note of 'the activity of the various religious sects, in promulgating . . . their irrational dogmas, and strongly urged the necessity of counteracting them, by adapting the same means of disseminating knowledge', and within a few years this suggestion had been embodied in a panoply of devices pilfered from the clergy: Social Hymn-books, Sunday Schools, Socialist weddings, child 'namings' and funerals.[45] As the 'Rational Religion', Socialism became an alternative church for many of its adherents, albeit a radical, infidel church.

In part this development reflected the composition of the movement at its base, which included many Nonconformists with a history of politically-based schisms (a number of breakaway Methodist factions, for example, had been created by radicals, some of whom later became Socialists).[46] 'Socialism is . . . the simple transfer of the Christian religion from the Temple to the land and from the monopoly of it by the priests to the use of the people,' as one of these radical Dissenters explained.[47] But in general the creation of the Religion of Socialism needs to be understood as the outcome of a complex process of ideological development, in which a struggle to supplant dominant social attitudes found expression in the only vocabulary capable of bearing the moral and intellectual weight of that project. This can be seen very clearly in the careers of two leading Socialist feminist infidels: the freethinker, Emma Martin, and the chiliastic heretic, Catherine Barmby.

FEMINISM AND FREETHOUGHT: THE STORY OF EMMA MARTIN (1812–51)

In 1843 one of Emma Martin's many clerical opponents, a Reverend Massie of Manchester, sent her a little gift of a few tracts to assist her in finding her way back to her God. Emma's reply, issued in six thousand copies, denounced him and his spiritual brethren as conservative hypocrites, but thanked him nonetheless for his concern. It concluded in a gentle autobiographical rebuke: 'I was during the earlier part of my life, sir, a sincere and consequently *zealous* disciple of Jesus . . . It was not till I had passed twelve years of thoughtful profession of Christian principles that I became an unbeliever . . .':

> This change in my sentiments was the result of calm investigation. It was only by a long and laborous [sic] process, that my mind was emancipated from the *thraldom* of religion. I speak of its *thraldom* not because it places limits on the passions, for it possessed charms for me on that account, which it has lost only because I see a nobler way by which a purer morality can be secured; but I apply this term to religion because it fetters the reason, because it would subjugate, instead of improve the understanding.[48]

Did he really think, she wondered, that a few tracts could undo what so many years of thought and study and commitment had thus formed?

For the typical nineteenth century infidel, freethought was a stage in a cycle of belief whose beginnings usually lay in a deep religious commitment. In Emma's case that earlier commitment had been to the Baptist church. In 1829, at the age of seventeen, 'after weighing both the Socinian and Catholic controversies, as well as many others of a minor character' she attached herself to the Particular Baptists, a sternly Calvinist wing of the church now undergoing a revival.[49] 'For four years [I was] a collector of the Bible Society . . . [and] a tract distributor . . .'[50]

In her own later account of her youth Emma praised the 'facilities for the acquisition of knowledge' which had led to her conversion. 'I was brought up in such a manner as would I think present the best circumstances for the study of religion, never wearied by its compulsive exercise, yet always afforded facilities for its study and practice to which a naturally sedate . . . and a melancholy turn of mind greatly inclined me.'[51] Certainly she seems to have been allowed an unusual degree of intellectual freedom, although this was no doubt partly due to her lower middle-class upbringing. As the daughter of a family of small tradespeople in Bristol, * she would have been expected to acquire at least a rudimentary education as a training for possible future employments – in her case, teaching and writing. In the early 1830s she became the proprietor of a short-lived Ladies' Boarding School, and also the editress of an even less successful journal, *The Bristol Literary Magazine*, which no doubt proved a useful forum for her 'sedate' theological researches.[52]

But another description of Emma, written by her close friend George Holyoake shortly after her death, gives a rather different picture of the young convert. His affectionate portrait of the intelligent girl 'theoretically eulogistic of her own captivity' within her chosen faith, while at the same time 'impulsively escaping from it with unconscious gladness' sharply evokes a level of psychic conflict which, lacking any other outlet, achieved a temporary resolution through a fever of spiritual self-assertion:[53] 'The passions [of religion] . . . possessed charms for me . . .' she recalled almost nostalgically. But it was this same level of passionate engagement which also signalled what was to follow: a growing sense of the insupportable contradiction between what she demanded of her faith, both emotionally and intellectually, and the bleak offerings of orthodox religion. Her own description of the early stages in this awakening needs to be prefaced, however, with the additional information that shortly after her conversion she had married another Baptist, Isaac Luther Martin, 'a husband . . . whose company it was a humiliation to endure . . .'

> My establishment in life, which had taken place early, had multiplied my cares, and brought me to the study of realities in a different manner to that which my youth could foster. Then I devised the most magnificent remedies for those human ills with which I had a very imperfect acquaintance, but now found the magnitude of the evil and the difficulty of the remedy. I had been engaged chiefly in Education and had therefore considerable opportunity for . . . the consideration of those topics of more general interest which have of late years been so often pressed upon the

---

*Emma's father was William Bullock, a cooper, but he died while she was still an infant. Her mother, whose family owned a tea-dealing business in Bristol, soon remarried, to a man called John Gwyn, and the Gwyn household moved into the middle-class area of Clifton.

attention of the philanthropist. I had thus discovered many of the evils of our present social system . . . [for which] I could see no sufficient cure. For one of these, the degraded social condition of woman, an improved education and better employment offered hopes. After much preparation, and no encouragement . . . I announced a Lecture on this important subject.[54]

The trajectory which had brought Emma to this open avowal of feminism had taken her through many of the usual staging-posts for feminists of her class: a (limited) educational background; an unhappy marriage (which quickly produced three daughters); ill-fated career efforts; possibly the loss of an inheritance (or so she later claimed) through her husband's financial mismanagement. Had she been born forty years earlier the combination of all these factors might have made her one of Wollstonecraft's associates; forty years later and she would probably have been a suffragette. But as it was, in February 1839 she went to hear Alexander Campbell lecture on Socialism. He may have spoken on women's rights (he often did); at any rate, Emma was transfixed. Astounded to hear 'so close a transcript of many of the thoughts that had passed in my mind', she prepared to embrace the new views . . . only to discover (in Campbell's third lecture) that the Owenites denied the divine origins of the Bible.[55] Infuriated by what seemed to her a betrayal of the moral foundations of social reform, she decided that rather than retreat entirely she would fight the Owenites on the issue. She challenged Socialists to public debates on the validity of Christianity. Several accepted, including Campbell who engaged to return to Bristol for the combat. 'Since Mr Campbell has left us the sectarians are in a ferment . . .' one Bristol Owenite reported, 'They have been preaching against us in the chapels . . . Mrs Martin is going to give him a dressing, when she has the opportunity . . .'[56] Her fighting spirit aroused, Emma even began touring the countryside, calling out Socialists to take her on. 'She is a lady of considerable talent . . .' the branch secretary from Worcester told the Annual Congress nervously, adding a plea that the Central Board send 'some able advocate of the Rational System' to assist in tackling her.[57]

But even in the midst of all this public campaigning, Emma was beginning to experience her own terrible private doubts. In the months spent needling Socialist lecturers with her fine points of

Scriptural interpretation, she fell into a fever of uncertainty. Reading and re-reading her Bible, she found that once disillusionment and scepticism had caught at the corners of her faith, they ran it through and through until all those holy hopes lay in tatters around her. She teetered on the edge of her second conversion.

But it took another sort of crisis finally to bring matters to a head. Towards the end of 1839 Isaac Martin packed up his family and moved to London. Almost immediately Emma bolted . . . and with her desertion of her husband went also her church, her home, her respectability, and the God in Whom she no longer believed. She took the leap of faith and joined the Socialists as a declared freethinker and feminist. 'Long and serious was the conflict the change in her convictions caused her,' Holyoake later recalled, 'but her native love of truth prevailed, and she came over to the advocacy of that she had so resolutely and ably assailed. And no-one who ever offered us alliance rendered us greater service, or did it at greater cost.'[58]

The cost we shall see later. But initially at least the most extraordinary aspect of Emma's conversion was not how much it changed her public life, but how little. Already sharing platforms with public opponents, she simply switched sides and carried on speaking, now taking on the very clerics whom she had once led in an anti-Socialist crusade. Already a propagandist well used to the weapons of lecture and tract, she became one of Owenism's most enthusiastic orators and tractarians, covering thousands of miles and issuing tens of thousands of pamphlets in the best missionary style. Singing Social Hymns, attending meetings of the Socialist Ladies' Tract Committee, naming children at the conclusion of a Sunday School sermon . . . small wonder Emma could move so readily from Baptism to Owenism. From being an evangelical in Christ's cause, she became one of the leading evangelizers of infidel Socialism, within a milieu and style that seemed to alter very little with the transfer of allegiances.

But of course many crucial things *had* changed. Those pietistic tracts which Emma had once doled out had all been written by male divines in praise of their patriarchal God, but now she produced her own in which His existence was flatly denied.[59] The religious circles in which she had formerly moved had combined charitable professions with conservative politics, but now she worked with men and women for whom charitable fellow-feeling was part of a wider system of radical belief. Power and privilege which would have been denied her in virtually any orthodox congregation were now also hers within the Socialist organization because, as George Fleming told the 1841 Congress, the Owenites 'claimed for woman full, free and equal enjoyment of all those privileges which belonged to her as a human being . . .' He was followed in the speakers' list by Emma, who rose to say that 'she had grown up from infancy with high thoughts and strong hopes of an improvement in the condition of her sex . . .'

> For a long time she had found none to sympathise with her. But three years ago a new sun broke upon her, and that was Robert Owen. (Cheers) On looking at the position of woman, she had seen that all remunerating employment was taken from her, – that all institutions for mental improvement were confined to males, and that even the morals of the female sex were of a different stamp to those of the male. She saw no remedy for this till she saw the remedy of Socialism. When all should labour for each, and each be expected to labour for the whole, then would woman be placed in a position in which she would not sell her liberties . . .[60]

In the years which followed, Emma's struggle to win others to this creed became inseparably bound up with her personal fight for an independent life. At the same time as she was carrying the Socialist feminist message across the country she was using the small salary provided by the Central Board to raise her own little girls without her husband's assistance. Any property which had belonged to her at the time of her desertion had, of course, remained with her husband, and she was often forced to leave her daughters with friends while she moved from town to town earning the money to feed and clothe them.[61]

But she was only twenty-seven when the choice was made, and full of hope and strength. Six years of intense political activity later, both had been eroded, and she spoke with increasing bitterness of her lot as a woman while struggling to find other ways of holding her life together. And within seven years of that, she was dead.

We shall pick up the final part of Emma's story further on. But now let us follow her through those hard and exciting years as a freethinker and feminist in the Socialist movement.

THE HOLY WAR

The freethought strand within Owenism connected it to the wider working-class radical tradition. Whereas in the seventeenth and eighteenth centuries adherence to Deism or other forms of enlightened scepticism had been almost entirely confined to well-to-do intellectuals, the growth of political irreverence in the lower orders in the early nineteenth century had fuelled irreligious attitudes there as well.[62] 'Formerly infidel principles were found chiefly among the higher and educated classes; but now the humblest mechanic is heard denying . . . the inspiration of the Scriptures . . .' the Wesleyan Conference of 1840 warned, 'Many factories are . . . nurseries of sedition and heresy; and in some of our large towns nearly every street can furnish oracles of atheism and malignant impugners of revealed religion.'[63] Of the reasons for this growth of working-class apostasy the clergy had no doubt: 'Many infidels have been seduced to infidelity by the mixing up of political questions with infidelity.'[64] In the 1790s these 'political questions' had been associated wholly with Jacobinism, but by the 1840s it was the rise of Socialism which was blamed. Owen's own fiercely anti-clerical views were well known, and most of the leading Socialist publicists were no less intransigent in outlook. 'Not one of them believes *divine* the religion which our judges pronounce part and parcel of our country's laws,' Matilda Roalfe, another female infidel, wrote approvingly of the Owenites, 'they are all, aye, all, anti-Christian, and rarely open their mouths without saying something eminently calculated to bring Christianity into contempt . . .'[65] By 1839 lectures on 'theological and ethical' issues formed up to a third of the menu in the national diet of Socialist propaganda.[66] Working-class study groups which had once devoured Paine and Carlile on the evidences against Christianity now worked their way through endless Socialist tracts devoted to the same theme. 'It is very troublesome to have them attacking the Bible . . .' one Cambridgeshire clergyman sighed over the activities of local Owenites, 'for we never go among our people that we find some difficulty has been started . . .'[67]

Evangelicals busy missionizing in working-class districts in the 1840s were horrified by the level of Owenite freethought influence which they found there. In working-class London in particular, city missionaries reported, there existed a veritable 'army' of Socialists who refused to attend church, lived in common-law marriages, and preached infidelism to their neighbours.[68] 'To cure infidelity among the masses, we must cure Socialism,' one flatly declared.[69] 'The humbler ranks of society lie open and exposed to the foul effects of this most frightful malaria,' *The Christian Lady's Magazine* wailed, 'Incredible as may appear the fact, yet a fact it is, that the lectures of these wretched deceivers draw a crowded audience of *women* to listen to what ought to kindle the most burning indignation in every female bosom . . . Hundreds of rooms re-echo every night, but more particularly on the Sabbath, to such blasphemies were never before heard . . . while crowds of English females applaud them.'[70] The editor's description of these blasphemies, which was typical of the Socialists' religious opposition, reminds us that infidelism and sexual heterodoxy were never far apart in the public mind:

The main plan . . . is, first, to wholly abolish marriage . . .
secondly, to take every child from its mother at the time of its birth
. . . and to commit the infants to persons appointed for the charge,
who shall nourish them like a promiscuous litter of pigs . . .
Thirdly, to do away with that sacred and endearing thing – home
. . . There is to be no separate dwelling, no husband, no wife, no
parent, no child, no brother, no sister, no neighbour, no friend, no
pastor, NO GOD.[71]

She concluded by calling for a nationwide campaign 'to prevent this monster of wickedness [Owen] from spreading his pestilential doctrines . . .'[72]

The churches were not slow to respond to this challenge. By the late 1830s a major counter-offensive had been mounted, with clerics from all denominations busy delivering anti-Socialist sermons, writing and distributing millions of anti-Socialist tracts ('The Abominations of Socialism Exposed!', 'The Social Beasts', 'Robert Owen, Anti-Christ' and so on), attending Socialist lectures to heckle and harangue, and spreading tales of Socialist crimes and immorality. 'One woman states, that she has lived with her husband for forty years,' ran a typical report from a Leeds missionary in 1839, 'but since he has joined the Socialists, he has returned home late at night, dragged her out of bed by the hair of her head, and tells her he does not think it would be any sin to murder her, since God has given him the organs of murder. The woman has since joined the Methodists. The Lord support and guide her.'[73]

In February 1840, the Bishop of Exeter rose in the House of Lords to repeat these slanders and to demand that the Owenite organization be banned as a blasphemous and seditious sect.[74] Petitions supporting his position flowed in from respectable citizens in all parts of the country, where the oppositional campaign against the Owenites now reached fever pitch. The courage of Emma's conversion needs to be set in this context: by 1839-40 dozens of Owenite branches were virtually under siege, beleaguered by local alliances of orthodox religionists, employers and public authorities. While in some towns this offensive did not extend beyond the banning of Owenite meetings from public halls, harassment of Socialist lecturers by clergymen and their supporters, and an occasional exchange of blows along with verbal abuse in sidewalk debates, in many others the sanctions against known radicals were much harsher. Throughout the late 1830s and early 1840s innumerable reports appeared of Owenites being sacked, refused poor relief, having their homes or shops vandalized. 'The pious mill owners here make a practice of visiting the [Socialist] amusement class occasionally to see if any of their slaves are there . . .' a Hanley Owenite reported. 'Some of them have been threatened with deprivation of work if they do not cease to attend the wicked place'.[75] From Huddersfield came this account of typical opposition tactics:

'Cautions' and 'warnings' are placarded in the streets; tracts, calumny and misrepresentations are circulated; workshops and factories converted into inquisitions; workmen threatened, noticed, and discharged; spies and informers appointed . . .

But the branch worked bravely on: 'despite of all, our lectures are attended by crowded audiences, and those who dare not come only make room by their absence for those who dare . . .'[76]

The issue of women's present position and future role quickly came to occupy an important place in this struggle. Owenite marriage doctrine – with its emphasis on voluntary sexual liaisons and the equality of both partners within them – flew directly in the face of all orthodox Christian teachings, and soon accusations of adultery, prostitution, wife-swapping and other forms of libertinage were being hurled at the Socialists by their church opponents. In the next chapter this marriage controversy is examined in detail, but it is worth emphasizing here that by 1839 issues surrounding sexual relations and women's status were at the heart of the church's counter-offensive against Socialist 'immoralism'.

The effects of this campaign were mixed. Certainly many potential recruits (particularly, as we shall see when we look at the marriage issue, many women) were put off by the slanders, while others were simply intimidated by the level of repression. In a period when blasphemy was equated with sedition, the line between church and civil authority was not finely drawn, and there were probably many like the working man who some years earlier had told Owen that he had given up attending his Sunday lectures 'for fear that the Priests should pounce upon me and say that I was attending an illegal meeting, and therefore cause me to be punished.'[77] People threatened with hell-fire or, if that proved ineffective, loss of employment or poor relief if seen attending Socialist gatherings, had to keep a very firm grip on their principles if they were to resist such threats.

On the other hand, notoriety swelled the Socialists' audiences and served to spread their doctrines (or versions of them) on an unprecedented scale. In a twelve-month period between 1839 and 1841, crowds containing anywhere between one hundred and 6,000 people gathered in over 350 towns to hear 1500 Socialist lectures (over 600 on freethought issues). In the same period nearly two million Socialist tracts were read and the circulation of *The New Moral World* doubled.[78] 'Silence will not retard, and opposition will only accelerate . . . [our] progress' *The New Moral World* declared, and where publicity-minded opponents like the Bishop did not appear to assist in this, the Owenites were not even averse to stirring things up a bit themselves:

> We have found that in Sheffield, as I suppose elsewhere too, that the chief obstacle which prevents us implanting truth in the minds of our people is, that they are previously so filled with *error* . . . We intend to open a vigorous campaign against error to clear the way,

and then commence planting the seeds of truth in good earnest. We laid down a month of lectures, and placarded the town, in addition to which we had 1000 small hand-bills to give at the door, and 200 printed . . . [and] sent to ministers in the town, of all denominations, so that they might be well apprised of what was going on, and have an opportunity of opposing if they thought proper. Considerable consternation was produced, I assure you . . .[79]

Emma's early role within the movement is best understood in this context of provocation and counter-provocation. The very presence of a woman on a public platform was guaranteed to raise popular interest, and the Owenites did not hesitate to exploit this to the full. The days before her arrival in a town would see a burst of Socialist placarding ('Emma Martin Lecturing on Marriage and Divorce!!', 'Emma Martin Expounds the Principles of Robert Owen's Social System!') followed by counter-placarding from the opposition, sometimes including notices specifically warning the local female populace to keep away from the infidel lecturess. The Sunday before her lecture might well find the local clergy busy denouncing her from their pulpits. The cumulative effect of all this was to create a level of local excitement which at times reached dangerous proportions: when Emma lectured in Manchester in 1841, for example, 'the hall was opened at seven o'clock, and the people flocked in by crowds . . . [until] the outer doors were obliged to be closed . . . the public were then admitted by about twenty at a time until we were . . . crammed, almost to suffocation.'[80] Audiences of two to three thousand were not unusual, and when her subject was 'Marriage and Divorce' they were often much larger. Newcastle was one of a number of towns where such a lecture caused 'the greatest excitement . . . hundreds had to go away disappointed, not being able to hear.'[81] Jammed into these halls, the audiences were tense; violence frequently simmered near the surface and occasionally even erupted into full-scale riots. Confrontations between Emma and clerical opponents were always acerbic, with noisy audience participation. In 1843, when she debated with a Baptist minister in Hull, so many wanted to attend that the tickets were sold and re-sold at vastly inflated prices. The audience on this occasion divided itself into two camps, each indicating their response to the speakers with cheers and heckling. By popular approval, Emma won the day: 'by subtle and specious arguments . . . the infidel, as a debater, was an overmatch for the Baptist' a local paper sadly reported.[82]

Debates like these were not only doctrinal contests, but spectacles – oratorical performances in which style of delivery and audience rapport were as important as the arguments themselves. Emma was particularly favoured by the Socialist branches for what one admirer called 'her clear, pungent, often witty repartee' and her tub-thumping polemics, in which complex arguments were presented in a form which was accessible and entertaining to working-class audiences. For men and women raised on the Bible, her inverted evangelical mode was simultaneously familiar and challenging. An 1843 lecture in Bolton on the evidence for Christianity, for example, produced an 'evident impression' on a largely female audience 'who, in some instances, had their children along with them'. On another occasion her debate with a cleric was cancelled by a local official who gave as his reason the popularity of her speeches with the poor.[83] As always, however, opposition only stiffened Owenite resolve. When Emma was denied public halls she moved out into the market places and fields to speak; when denounced in a clerical tract for inciting the people to seditious blasphemy she responded by issuing thousands of copies of an inflammatory reply, sold at a halfpenny apiece. Her faith in all this propaganda never wavered. 'Where shall we find our Tract and Book Society?' one London meeting was exhorted, 'Give us the powers now wielded by our opponents – give us the thousands a year they now receive, and in two years not a poor man in the empire but would exclaim, *Socialism for me*. (Great cheering). Here is indeed a miracle, that *the poor*, the uneducated population have done *all*!! Great, indeed, then must be our progress . . .'[84]

This popular context should be kept in mind as we look at the 'subtle and specious' arguments with which Emma flummoxed her religious opponents. For while the ideas themselves were often fairly abstruse, their appearance within these mass forums of intellectual combat gave them a far more subversive edge than the words alone can suggest. This was particularly true of those doctrines which to the English upper orders still had the battle smoke from an earlier struggle lingering about them. 'Mr Owen, indeed, has done little more than adapt the leading doctrines . . . of the French school of atheism' was a typical assessment of the Socialist freethinkers, with the clear implication that those arguments put forward in the midst of one Revolution could inspire another.[85] For both sides, then, Socialist infidelism was heavily weighted with inherited political meanings as well as the new ones created by the movement's utopian strategy.

It is not necessary here to trace in any detail the myriad metaphysical doctrines and theological debating-points which went to make up the intellectual weaponry of all nineteenth century freethinkers. Most were drawn from the old and honourable armoury of Enlightenment scepticism, and partook of all the naive rationalism of that outlook as well as all of its scientistic optimism. For Emma, as for generations of enlightened apostates before her, Nature and Reason had shouldered God and Revelation out of the cosmos, and the result was an expansion of human control which made Divine intercession not only unthinkable, but unnecessary. 'Go then into the wide fields of Nature,' as the readers of one of her tracts were enjoined, 'and by the process of an inductive philosophy, collect data which will teach you how to banish crime and poverty, and cause you no longer to be the victims of Kings and Priests.'[86] Even the language of social protest employed in such tracts owed as much to the populist rhetoric of the older anti-clericalist tradition as to the anti-capitalist philosophy of the Socialists. 'Kings, Priests and Aristocrats' jostled with exploitative employers and Whig statesmen in Emma's demonology of villains, and the funeral sermon she preached for Carlile would have warmed his own heart, with its diatribes against a corrupt oligarchy and their 'spiritual jackals', the Established clergy.[87] Reason's alliance with Right may have become dangerously unfashionable in the class from which Emma had emerged, but it lived on in the writings of radical heretics like herself: voices for an enlightened morality at a time when mainstream middle-class opinion was all for the God of strict convention and swift retribution.

This older infidel tradition connected to Owenism through several popular themes. The first was working-class anti-clericalism, which was widespread among devout Dissenters and freethinkers alike and had been greatly intensified by the

development of the Evangelical movement. An 1841 meeting of
the Society for the Propagation of the Gospel in Foreign Parts
provided a typical setting for a confrontation when it was
invaded by a group of Socialists and Chartists who elected a
Socialist chairman and then proceeded to harangue the frightened
clerics: 'Hewett [a Chartist]: "We want more bread and less
bibles, and more pigs and less parsons . . . You are all robbers of
the poor" . . . The Rev. R. Crofts: "But surely you will allow us to
exercise our benevolence on . . . objects of distress . . . who is it
that build you hospitals, and visit the beds of the dying, but the
clergy (a voice . . . 'I say the people') you complain of the rich,
but you could not live without them" (cries of "Oh yes, we could;
give us the land and we will try . . .").'[88] 'The people perish for
want and you give them MORE CHURCHES,' Emma lashed out
at a group of missionaries, 'they ask for bread and you give them
stones. They pine in ignorance and you give them BIBLES . . .'[89]
That was a long way from her own days of Bible distribution.
'God *gives justly*, for the fruits of the earth *are* for *all* . . .' she
quoted back at another pious opponent after a bitter public clash
involving hundreds of her working-class supporters, 'then how is
it all do not possess them? . . . Mr Massie is not alone however in
his opinion that the fruits of the earth are for all. Some of us today
saw a procession . . . of the careworn faces . . . of honest artisans
and labourers who . . . were converts to the same opinion.'[90]

That protest was much older than Socialism. But in the context
of Owenite thinking it was reinforced by a second source of
infidel ideology: the intellectual commitment to a new Science of
Society. In the hands of Socialist theoreticians, Social Science
operated both as a critique of existing belief-systems, and as a
substitute for them. As critique, it provided a systematic
refutation of all previous 'errors', particularly superstitious
myths. As a new world-view it developed as a total alternative to
orthodox Christianity, a new 'gospel' based on a synthesis of
ethical ideals and scientific social analysis.[91] Three 'great sciences'
made up the intellectual foundations of Socialism, an editorial in
The New Moral World explained, 'the sciences of human nature
and of society, and, as a corollary, the science by which a superior
character may be imparted to every child brought into existence':

From a knowledge and practice of these sciences, will flow a
rational religion, which, discarding all sectarian creeds and superstitious mummeries, will unceasingly develop its adoration and love
of the infinite, the beautiful and the good, by the constant practice
of promoting the happiness of every man, woman and child, and
regarding with a merciful disposition everything that has life.[92]

The first task to be performed by adherents to this new faith
was to clear the ideological ground of all those 'mummeries' of
scriptural superstitions. Like most infidels, Emma later attributed
her own atheism to an awareness of internal inconsistencies in the
Bible.[93] The extreme rationalism of such an account may make it
seem rather unconvincing from a psychological standpoint; its
advantage over a more sophisticated explanation, however, was
that it offered an obvious strategy for the conversion of others. If
the 'faith of the people in the Divinity [of the Bible] was exploded,'
wrote Robert Cooper in his *Infidel's Text Book*, 'the grand corner-
stone of the priestly system is shaken . . .'[94] For Emma and her
freethinking comrades to uncover errors in the Word was to
prove (as the title of one of her tracts expressed it) *The Bible No
Revelation*, and thus to undermine the very bedrock of divine
authority; to discredit these discrepancies through ridicule was
the most potent weapon of all. 'Who was the father of Jesus?' ran
her Christmas message to the people of London in 1843:

> Luke vaguely tells us that he was supposed [to be] the son of Joseph;
> but that he 'should be called the son of God.' If HE was GOD, and
> there is but *one* GOD, two indisputable points, it means that he was
> his OWN father. Happy would it be for many a mother, could *she*
> and *others* believe that her child had been its own father![95]

'If man fell in the Garden of Eden – who placed him there?' her
friend Holyoake demanded in a favourite theme, 'It is said, God!
Who placed the temptation there? It is said God! Who gave him
an imperfect nature – a nature of which it was foreknown it
would fall? It is said, God! To what does this amount?'[96]

The general problem of the historical and cultural relativity of
scriptural language was also grist to this critical mill. How could
words whose meaning changed over time or varied between
nations be said to carry a single sacred truth? Emma demanded.
Were those who could not read the Word damned outright? Did
this mean, she hinted, that the poor were likelier to be abandoned

by God than the literate rich? And what of the rendering of the Bible into other languages?[97] Let us recall the context: in 1844 Emma stood in the marketplace in Nottingham and to a crowd of 'at least six thousand persons . . . told some amusing tales about the translation of certain passages of the divine text into other languages, which caused a good deal of mirth.'[98] Ridicule opened people's minds, it prepared them for new ideas; it exorcized demons and hell-fire by mocking their creators. 'The gospel of the New Testament contained the worst news for man . . .' the residents of the Queenwood community were told, 'It represented God . . . as a fierce and cruel God. It spoke also of a Devil; but did they believe such nonsense? Did they ever see a Devil, or smell a Devil, or chew a Devil? (Loud laughter)'[99]

Denial of the divine origins of the Bible separated hard-line freethinkers from the majority of working-class radicals for whom it was not the Word itself which was suspect, but its spokesmen. Emma's uncompromising stance on this question was typical of the smaller number of Owenites who had made irreligion their priority. 'Mistake me not, then: it is not Christian differences with which I war, but the *system* itself; – not translations or commentaries, but the BOOK. Who will confront me?'[100] Plenty would and did, only to find themselves faced with the geological evidence against Genesis, or the phrenological analysis of character formation which 'decisively refuted free will argument', or accounts of the pagan origins of Christianity. 'Mrs Martin castigated the Reverend Mr Fox in a number of observations . . . proving the identity of all religious rites and ceremonies, and tracing them to their origins . . . [in] fables, which the ancients embodied in poems . . .'[101] This final argument was drawn from numerous sources, most notably Volney's *Ruins of Empire*, but in her *Baptism, a Pagan Rite* Emma gave it a strangely Freudian twist when she argued that the baptismal ceremony had its origins in the primal birth experience. The waters in which the novitiate were immersed and then withdrawn were an unconscious reminder of the womb, she argued; and what else was Noah's Ark, riding the floods with its load of the male and female of every species? This fascinating little tract concluded on the suggestion that Jesus had been an ordinary little lad until chosen to play a part in a local fertility rite, which had given his mother all sorts of ambitions for her boy's future career . . .[102]

Feminist re-interpretation of Scripture had its part to play in these critical exigeses. Debates over the Mosaic law of marriage, the role of women in the New Testament, and the sex of the Deity proliferated; on one occasion Emma lectured on 'The Holy Ghost: HER Nature, Offices and Laws'.[103] Revisions of the story of the Fall were popular. 'The forbidden fruit story, in the second and third chapters of a book called Genesis, is a pretty picture of the allegory of liberty and necessity,' Eliza Sharples told her Rotunda audience in 1832:

> The tyrant God, Necessity, said to the subject man: 'Of the tree of the knowledge of good and evil thou shalt not eat.' Sweet and fair Liberty stepped in . . . spurned the order . . . of the tyrant, 'she took of the fruit thereof, and did eat, and gave also unto her husband with her and he did eat.' Do you not, with one voice exclaim, well done woman! LIBERTY FOR EVER! If that was a fall, sirs, it was a glorious fall, and such a fall as is now wanted . . . I will be such an Eve, so bright a picture of liberty![104]

Had the account of the Fall been 'penned by a woman', another woman wrote to *The New Moral World*, 'we should have had a very different version of it', for then the 'great folly' of Eve would not be eating the apple, but sharing it with Adam. 'Had she succeeded in concealing the extent of the power she possessed . . . she might have ruled by her reason, instead of becoming the slave of man's passions, and "multiplying her sorrows and her conception".'[105]

At stake in the myth of the Fall was not merely female culpability for the exile from Paradise but the issue of Eve's innate inferiority to Adam. In rejecting the doctrine of original sin, feminists were also rejecting the equation of femininity with innate sinfulness and depravity; in converting to the Owenite viewpoint they acquired the dogma of human perfectability which was at the centre of the new Social Science. When the Cheltenham radical, Harriet Adams, converted from Baptism to Socialism, her former minister tried to argue her out of it by claiming that the Socialists' hopes would never be realized 'as men's hearts were too depraved' for such a utopia. 'I said – I did not believe it was the depravity of man's heart, but the bad system that was adopted; and the bad education that was given to children was the occasion of people not loving one another . . .'[106] 'It was because the human heart was good at first, that it was continually going on getting better,' another Socialist assured a Northampton audience.[107] In the case of women, this meant not only (as Emma put it in one London lecture) 'that Nature had been equally bountiful to both [sexes] – that Education only had created the difference' but also that the church bore a major responsibility for this deformation of human potential. The greater religiosity of women was constantly cited as both symptom and cause of their degraded social status: 'Everywhere we find women the right arm of priestcraft' one writer in the atheistic *Oracle of Reason* complained, and while it was this writer's opinion that women's 'weaker mental capacities' were responsible, his viewpoint was not shared by most Socialists, who attributed it to women's lack of education.[108] 'Well do they [the clergy] know that if the daughters of the present and mothers of the future generation were to drink of the living waters of knowledge, their reign would be ended . . .' Fanny Wright wrote:

> So well do they know it, that far from obeying to the letter the command of their spiritual leader, 'Be ye fishers of men' we find them everywhere *fishers of women* . . . Fathers and husbands! Do ye not see this fact? Do ye not see how, in the mental bondage of your wives and fair companions, ye yourselves are bound?[109]

'The efforts woman makes to emancipate herself from domestic thraldom and the slavery of superstition, are . . . chilled and depressed by priestly power and the tyranny of custom,' Margaret Chappellsmith told one audience in 1842, adding characteristically, 'thus is her phrenological development first rendered weak . . .'[110]

Releasing women from these crippling bonds of orthodox prejudice was the first step towards feminine self-determination and, following that, the creation of a new style of sexual relation based on mutual respect and 'natural affection'. On this issue, as on most, Emma's heterodoxies were typical of the movement as a whole, although she probably addressed the marriage question more often than any other Owenite publicist. 'She saw further than any around her what the new Communism would end in,' Holyoake later wrote. 'She saw that it would establish the healthy despotism of the affections, in lieu of the factitious tyranny of custom and parliament. She embraced the Communist theory because she saw no licentiousness was included in it; and she drew an austere line between liberty and license . . . But what was thoroughly innocent she wished frankly to be avowed . . .'[111] In fact, she displayed the usual inverted puritanism of the Owenites on sexual matters, arguing fiercely for adherence to Nature's code and condemning conventional Christian marriage as a 'slave market'.[112] Far from being libertine, her tracts were crammed with injunctions against loose living and dirty thinking; she even managed to give 'Nature's chastity' a slightly mid-Victorian ring. But this moralism did not blunt the libertarian impact of her propaganda, or prevent her enemies from declaring her 'libidinous in heart and mind'.[113] 'It is under the Cross alone that woman receives the superscription that tells the world what she is, and in what sphere she is to move . . .' *Fraser's Magazine* explained in an article attacking Owenite feminism, but 'with the dethronement of woman from the pure and exalted state in which Christianity locates her, there seems to take place immediately the ruin of all those delicate and holy moralities which cluster around the fair capital of the social column.'[114] When all this delicate sentiment had been brushed aside, however, what the writer really meant could be summed up in a few words, as Emma did in 1841: 'Socialism was opposed . . . because it would give to [women] independence . . .'[115]

Unshackling women from the mythic rule of a patriarchal God meant not only freeing them from the fate (and image) of Eve, but also breaking the Pauline connection between feminine virtue and social dependency. This did not mean, however, that women's 'moral mission' was to be abandoned. Only the free woman, Emma argued, could carry the principles of a purified moral order. For her, as for so many of her sister Socialists, Socialism re-directed and concretized a 'regenerative' vision which Christian orthodoxies could never have satisfied. The answers may have been very different, but the questions remained the same. 'If we do but pierce beneath the antagonism from which all development issues,' as Holyoake wrote in reference to Emma's outlook, 'we shall see how, both with the Christian and the Freethinker, the same intention is ever at the bottom'.

We perceive a principle from different points, trace it to different roots, explain it in a different language, maintain it for different reasons, and foresee it for different conclusions: but the conflict continued . . . is for *one* morality and for *one* truth . . .[116]

Whatever religion might become within such an ideology, it could never be merely irrelevant. There *were* some individual Owenites who were genuinely indifferent to the claims of religion ('Socialism is a moral and social science . . . which neither affirms nor denies the framework of theology,' one man wrote grumpily,[117] 'and we might with equal reason oppose the science of chemistry as atheistical . . . as the science of society'), but they were few and far between. Scripture, turned first against its origins and then outward to the political needs of the moment, provided the mental framework in which new ideas could be set and ordered. A Socialist freethinker lecturing in Preston in 1844 watched a woman come to the doorway of the meeting hall and then refuse to enter because she was 'afraid of the place falling' under God's avenging Hand. But gradually she edged in and sat down. 'A friend accosted her on leaving . . . "Well, have you heard anything very bad?" No, Mr, I have never heard such a parson before: he's the best parson I ever heard . . . he's converted me.' The Socialist commented: 'There are no weapons better adapted on these occasions than their own for bringing the subject home to them.'[118]

When Emma debated with the Rev. W.J. Carpenter before his own London congregation in 1840, his flock heard both sides out and then rose to transfer their custom to the Owenites' St John Street Institution.[119] 'The people had begun to feel that the language of the Socialists was the language of truth . . . and true Christianity,' as another Social Missionary told a cheering audience at the 1841 Congress, 'but then, it was said, the infidels got hold of it first (Laughter)'.[120] The function of Social Science was not to displace those moral truths (with, for example, the Objective Laws of History) but to detach them from mystical dogmas and provide new blueprints for their realization, a route towards 'the system of co-operation and mental freedom' in which (in Emma's words) 'the religious feeling . . . would have its proper direction, and expand into universal charity and philanthropy.'[121] For how can humankind love one another 'while

149

all the institutions of society tended to make them hate one another by separating their interests?' Owen demanded of a Stockport audience in 1840.[122] 'The Religion of Socialism . . .' Emma told a London audience in the same year, 'unlike all other morality, is founded on *utility*; our sympathies are not confined to this sect or that party . . . for all are dear to *us*, all are *EQUAL*, while human hearts can feel for the benefit of all . . .' She went on to speak of the social communities, of the intellectual freedom and cultural pleasures and sexual happiness to be expected within them, and concluded:

> One great evil is, the depraved and ignorant condition of woman; this evil can only be removed by Socialism. We love Socialism, because it is more moral – we love Socialism, because it is more benevolent – we love Socialism, because it is the only universal system of deliverance that man and woman can adopt.

She sat down 'amidst the hearty congratulations of this large and crowded meeting'.[123]

Armed with this new faith, Emma spent her final years in the movement in a series of militant confrontations with the opposition. 'Mrs Martin is determined that despite of St Paul, the voice of woman *shall* be heard within the churches . . .' the freethought newspaper, *The Movement*, commented.[124] If her appearance in earlier campaigns had strikingly resembled an eighteenth-century preacheress, now it became more that of an avenging angel, sweeping down on the forces of Anti-Christ. Her vehemence even made sections of the Owenite leadership uneasy, particularly after the Central Board began to urge a more conciliatory attitude towards the clergy. In 1842, two leading Socialists agreed to take vows as Dissenting ministers in order to thwart attempts to close local meeting halls. Such compromise was heinous in the eyes of Emma and her atheistic comrades, who set up their own militant freethought league, the Anti-Persecution Union.* 'Socialists

---

*The Anti-Persecution Union was formed in the wake of several major trials for blasphemy. Its functions were therefore defensive as well as propagandistic: aid for imprisoned activists and their families was provided, while newspapers and bookshops (such as the 'Atheistical Depot' run by Emma's friend, Matilda Roalfe, in Edinburgh) were initiated. George Holyoake was the leader of the APU and editor of its newspaper, *The Movement*, which was Socialist in perspective although highly critical of the Owenite Central Board. Most of the Union's supporters outside London (of whom there were not very many) were Owenites.

think some of us go too far,' Emma told a London audience, 'that we run madly in the face of prejudices . . . but for my part, I am determined in spite of friends or foes, to pursue the path before me . . . To rouse Christians you must goad them . . .'[125]

Emma's years in the APU marked the height of her personal campaign against the church. In 1844 the London Missionary Society announced a Jubilee meeting to be held in a Manchester church. Emma immediately had placards plastered all over the walls of the city announcing her intention to attend. The clergy panicked: 'instead of calling on God, the preachers called upon the police to help them . . .' On the evening of the meeting, the church was jammed with uniformed men. Emma arrived, accompanied by dozens of supporters, and after sitting through several speeches rose in her pew and demanded the right to speak. Chaos ensued:

> . . . She was assailed with yells from all parts of the chapel, which were answered by vehement cheering from more than half the persons present . . .

'. . . cries of "Hear the Discussion!", "truth, truth" . . .' 'One female saint near Mrs Martin, threatened to poke her umbrella through Mrs M.'s bonnet.' As the police moved in to remove her 'a number of sturdy mechanics' surrounded Emma while she argued her right to speak – 'I am in a PUBLIC MEETING' – and refused to be removed. Intensified jeers and disturbance, until the police began ejecting Socialists forcibly and Emma called on them to retire. She then led her forces, now several hundred strong, out of the church.[126] Press reporting the following day was vitriolic, including one report which described the infidel lecturer as 'corpulent', to which Emma indignantly replied that she had 'never compressed her chest and waist to the destruction of the viscera within, nor sought to cut off the communication between her head and her heart, since she wants lungs for use not a waist for admiration!'[127]

This confrontation was soon followed by others. In October a Hull lecture by her on 'The Crimes and Follies of Christian Missions' was banned from one lecture room and held in another, whose owner was then promptly arrested along with the ticket-taker, a Mr Johnson. Johnson resolved to fight the case, asking that Emma be allowed to defend him in court. This was of course refused; the case was eventually lost.[128] 'The clergy are afraid of Mrs Martin – that is the truth of it,' Henry Hetherington remarked at a London meeting to support Johnson, while Holyoake wrote admiringly:

> This lady's activity is incessant. One day she sends all Hull into convulsions by an attack on the missions, next she upsets a missionary Society in Manchester, she hurls a pamphlet missive against the theists one day, . . . and ere this be well dry from the press will have a fresh paper pellet in readiness for active service.[129]

In Paisley, a few months later, what was to have been a meeting built into a mass demonstration. Having learned that a lecture on 'Home Missions' was being delivered in a church near her lecture hall, Emma informed the audience at the end of her lecture that she intended to go there. 'In another, nay, in the same minute, the audience were pouring down the stairs and long the street' until they reached the church. As Emma entered, tumult broke out, with Socialists and opponents shouting, Emma attempting to address them, and the ministers above it all trying vainly to remind her that 'women are not allowed to speak in the church . . .' Finally the police dispersed everyone.[130] And in Glasgow the next year an announcement that Emma planned to attend a sermon in the Gorbals brought over three thousand to the church and the surrounding streets, where they jeered and tussled with each other (cries of 'Burn her' from some) until the police arrived and arrested Emma and a Socialist missionary. Hundreds accompanied her to the jail and crowded the courtroom where she received a fine of three pounds.[131]

What was the significance of these struggles? In some cases they were simply forcing the issue of free speech: the Hull episode, for example, ended in a delayed victory when Emma was able to lecture openly against a cleric there some months later, while in Arbroath her arrest and brief imprisonment on arrival forced her to go underground for a few days until she emerged, triumphant, to lecture 'without the ghost of a policeman present'.[132] Most also touched the nerve of popular hostility to ruling-class philanthropy. 'The philanthropic Lady, who weeps in the most approved style . . . at the dreadful tale of Chinese ignorance of

God, wears at the moment a splendid dress over which the weaver's curse has been poured: – over which the sigh of the poor girl expiring in its making, has been expended,' Emma addressed the 'Supporters of Christian Mission': 'You grind the faces of the poor to propagate God's truth . . .'[133] But most of all, for women like Emma and her many female supporters, such moments represented the symbolic breaking of a long silence, the unleashing of that 'suppressed storm' which Eliza Sharples had prophesied over a decade before. 'I have asked the *learned* (?) clergy for rational answers to knotty questions' she wrote after one of these occasions, 'they wont [sic] answer them because they are asked by a *woman*, yet they obtained Christ from the same source. I wonder they did not object to *him* on that account.'[134] Newspaper coverage of the Manchester battle noted the remarks of the ministers as she departed: 'a humiliating spectacle of human form . . . and of woman's character', 'a weak and misguided woman . . . who degrades the very name and form of woman . . .' Emma exploded:

> and what is woman's most glorious character? Is it not to kiss the hand that strikes her, to honour and obey her lord and master, and be the tame servant of the priest? To have no will of her own. To be the football of society thankful for its kicking. You know it is! Is it not dreadful when one of the sex begins to think for herself? Why others will follow the horrible example! and where will it end? . . . Common sense will usurp the place of spiritualism, and liberty and love will supersede priestcraft. I fear I shall live to see that dreadful day![135]

Where injunctions against speech have been most harsh, they have almost deprived the silenced of a language in which to voice their opposition. For a woman, the price of breaking that silence, of 'free thinking', was to become a social pariah. Female complicity in conventional definitions of womanly virtue could be secured only by ensuring that those who voiced opposition were automatically placed outside the pale of respectable womanhood. At different times, both Emma and Margaret Chappellsmith were referred to as 'witches' and 'she-devils'; also as whores. Hysterical clergymen urged their flocks to attack them: on several occasions Emma was jeered and chased by crowds, while in Edinburgh in 1845 she and her little daughter narrowly escaped serious injury at the hands of a mob which began stoning them. 'The newspapers cry out . . . to drum the interloper out of town,' she wrote, 'so I stand a fair chance of sharing Hypatia's *fate* at least.'[136] Even to be associated with her was enough to earn charges of immoralism, as her friend Holyoake soon discovered, although he went on stalwartly defending her as a most 'womanly woman' in the face of the public slanders.[137]

But by now Emma was exhausted with it all. Ill and in financial difficulties, she returned from the Scottish tour to find the Socialist organization weakened and divided after a major struggle over the Queenwood community. Membership was rapidly falling off and the Central Board, eager to find scapegoats, accused her of alienating many former supporters through her extreme tactics. Although her own friends leapt to her defence, Emma was bitterly angry: 'some of the branches had made use of her as a tool to help fill their purses – as she had suffered much, even imprisonment . . . she thought it too bad, that delegates from these branches should turn round . . . and say she had been the means of doing them no good.'[138] No doubt this disagreement, as well as the general decline of the movement, contributed to her decision to end her peripatetic existence, although one other factor would also have been important: before her final tour she had begun living with her lover, Joshua Hopkins, whose daughter she soon bore. 'Although no marriage ceremony was performed . . . yet no affection was ever purer,' Holyoake stoutly maintained, 'and the whole range of priest-made marriages never included one to which happiness belonged more surely . . .'[139]

Joshua (who used Emma's surname as long as she lived) was a working man, an engineer, whose 'love of truth and clear sympathy with progressive action' won Emma's respect as well as her affection. 'He paid no attention to that conventional tyranny which attempts to coerce right into submission to custom,' Holyoake recorded of Joshua, which, given his lover's activities, was just as well.[140] Their little girl, born in 1847, was called Manon Roland, after the French democrat, Madame Roland. But even with four children and weakening health, Emma was not prepared to settle into a conventional existence. Having given up her salary as a lecturer, she decided to take on a new career –

midwifery. In the year when Manon was born Emma graduated as an accoucheur from the Royal Adelaide Lying-In Hospital in London, and immediately began propagandizing against the growing male domination of female health care, and for women's right to be trained as obstetricians and gynaecologists. 'I would have scientific information given to all. Especially to the future mothers of our race, would I have the "Knowledge of themselves", the laws of their own nature, the accidents and requirements of themselves and their probable offspring, imparted . . . unmixed with romantic stories . . . I would rather give my daughters a set of physiological and obstetric books for their perusal than allow them to read the Levitical Law . . .'[141]

But even in this new work, poverty and notoriety dogged her. Having exhausted her financial resources in training, she now found that she was refused work because of her infidelism: ' . . . the secretary [of the Royal Maternity Charity] wrote to say . . . that it [was] imperative on all its midwives to offer up prayer, at the bedside of the patient . . .'[142] She began practising midwifery privately from her Covent Garden home, where she and her daughters also ran a surgical bandage shop. Advertisements placed in the radical press offered lectures in gynaecology for women (six for a half-guinea and free advice to poor women every Monday),* courses in midwifery, rooms to let for invalids and trainees, medicines and bandages for sale – endless schemes to keep her head above water financially, including the preparation of a 'Young Mother's Guide' for which she required three hundred subscribers.[143] Holyoake even made an unsuccessful attempt to acquire the Rotunda for her, as a Philosophical Institute.[144] 'Now it has struck me that these endeavours . . . might be rendered successful by a few efforts on the part of those who interest themselves at all in the welfare of others . . .' she pleaded in his newspaper, *The Reasoner.*[145]

The last years of her life seem to have passed fairly quietly:

---

*It seems very probable that some of the advice and medicine which Emma supplied was contraceptive. Advertised topics for her lectures included: 'Abortion: its Causes and Prevention'; 'The Development of Foetal Life'; 'Gestation, Symptoms and Hygiene of Pregnancy'. The next generation of freethinkers was to include some of the leading pioneers in the birth control struggle.

teaching and practising midwifery; occasionally writing or lecturing (including sharing the platform with Fanny Wright at Owen's birthday celebration in 1848); producing tracts and articles on female health; caring for her family. In 1849 she nursed a number of her friends through a cholera epidemic, including Henry Hetherington, who died despite all her efforts.[146] Emma herself was very unwell at the time, and perhaps exposure to the disease weakened her further; at any rate, two years later she died of tuberculosis at her home in Finchley Common. She was reading George Eliot's translation of Strauss' *Life of Jesus* at the time. She was only thirty-nine years old. 'We have lost the most important woman in our cause,' Holyoake wrote in a tract distributed shortly after her death in order to counter false reports of her death-bed recantation, which had begun circulating as soon as she had gone.[147] He called for subscriptions to purchase a headstone for her grave, and hundreds gave, including many women (among them Harriet Martineau) who with their money offered remembrance of 'that advocacy of women's social elevation which Mrs Martin so ably rendered'.[148] She was buried in Highgate cemetery; a year later Joshua joined her. 'Ah!' Holyoake wrote after the quiet ceremony at the grave, 'what do we not owe to a woman who, like Emma Martin, takes the heroic side and teaches us . . . the truth of a gentler faith?'[149]

THE WOMAN-POWER

Woman-Saviour now we muster
To await thy advent sure,
In the cluster of thy lustre,
Come and leave the earth no
more?
Then before thy gentle look,
Swords shall quail and warriors
fail,
And the spear, a shepherd's
crook,
Shall adorn the daisied dale.
Woman-power! Incarnate Love!
Human Goddess come and be,
If the Bridegroom's tears can
move,

Bride unto Humanity.
Thou alone of all can save us
Let us be what thou would have
us![150]

(John Goodwyn Barmby,
Pontiffarch of the Communist Church)

Orthodox evangelicals had prescribed a subordinate role for godly women, but in the hands of feminist re-interpreters their Puritan code became an important source of emancipationist morality. In Emma Martin's case, this re-interpretation had led her away from God towards a Rational Religion in which social processes took the place of sacred decrees, and radical self-determination replaced pious self-abnegation. Superstitious myths were pushed aside to leave room for greater faith to flower, and Paradise moved down from the mists of Heaven to co-operative communities in Britain.

If this was not exactly a secular creed, it was certainly a godless one. But the idea of Socialism as an alternative religion provided a space in which another style of radical infidelism could develop. In the same years in which Emma and her freethinking comrades were crusading against scriptural belief, other Owenites were re-working these scriptures into a radical theology, a heretical counter-creed. These were the Christian millenarians of the movement – men and women who looked towards the communitarian future as an ascent to the New Jerusalem, and translated feminist ideas into a new, mystical gospel of female redemption. Here the idea of women as a moral vanguard – the 'Woman's Mission' doctrine of the Evangelicals – became the basis of an apocalyptic vision of sexual/spiritual revolution: the 'Doctrine of the Woman', or the 'Woman-Power'.

SOCIALIST MILLENARIANS

Millenarianism, or the belief in a Second Coming of Christ which would either inaugurate or follow the thousand-year reign of God on Earth, was an extreme version of orthodox Christian teachings, derived largely from prophecies contained in the biblical *Revelations*. As a form of religious enthusiasm, millenarianism was implicit within the evangelical revival as a whole, but in a subdued form. It was only within specific sects, often ones which had broken away from a Dissenting church, that an uncompromisingly eschatological mentality was to be found, frequently reinforced by the presence of a messianic leader. During the height of the religious revival the number of these sects operating in Britain multiplied rapidly, and the mood they invoked affected even those who did not embrace their teachings wholesale, including many radicals for whom the apocryphal rhetoric of the prophets reinforced their own sense of social crisis and their intense yearning for a new order of things.[151]

As a movement advocating the total transformation of social and cultural life, Owenism was inevitably marked by this spread of adventist sentiment, and in particular by the visionary *language* of the millenarian tradition. J.F.C. Harrison, in his detailed study of this aspect of the movement, has vividly documented the quantity and richness of millenarian references within Owenism, from the 'Advent Hymns' published in the official *Social Hymn Book* celebrating the arrival of 'Love's Millennial Year', to the inscription carved over the main entrance to the Queenwood community hall: 'C.M.', Commencement of the Millennium.[152] Owenite lecturers frequently referred to Socialism as the New Jerusalem or the Promised Land. In 1838 a Socialist missionary lecturing to the Bradford Owenite branch reported how at the conclusion of his speech his audience 'all appeared to feel that this old world must pass away, and that a new one must arise, fulfilling . . . the Scripture . . . I endeavoured to take them up to the pinnacle of the temple and show them the glories of the world to come . . .' And several years later the editor of *The New Moral World* rose at an Annual Congress of the Owenite body to deliver a toast to women's emancipation. Looking around him at the large number of women in the audience, he suggested that their presence was

> convincing proof that the time was not far distant when institutions, which would secure for woman the full and equal exercise of all her faculties, would be established all over the world. They had heard of the millennium. The millennium was come, when men assembled together in the broad light of day to proclaim their entire absolvency from all superstitious notions [regarding female inferiority] (cheers).[153]

How is the popularity of such rhetoric within Owenism best interpreted?

Historians who have considered this question have displayed a remarkable degree of unanimity as to the answer. It is claimed that after the collapse of the trade union initiatives of 1833–34, Owenism did indeed become (as Marx and Engels had argued) merely another millenarian religious sect. 'One of the legitimate ways of regarding Owenism is to class it among the Messianic religions which arose in the early nineteenth century which . . . depended for their appeal upon the promise of a heaven which . . . would shortly appear on earth,' Cole and Postgate stated in their classic *The British Common People*,[154] and J.F.C. Harrison has recently agreed: 'The Owenite working man who sang his social hymns in the Manchester Hall of Science was striving for much the same goals as his neighbour who sang Wesley's hymns in the Primitive Methodist chapel . . .'[155] In an era of extreme social and political instability, so the argument runs, balanced, realistic strategies for social reform were unable to acquire any firm hold among working people, who opted instead for enthusiastic dreams of divine intervention. 'Unable to find any rational methods of escape, it [the British working class] turned to irrational . . . prophetic religions . . . Such exactly was Owenism . . .'[156]

The argument is wrong – partly in the facts it emphasizes (the strength of secularist sentiment in Owenism is seriously underestimated) but more important in its interpretation of them. The source of the error lies in a fundamental misunderstanding of the significance of *linguistic traditions* within changing ideological contexts. Words, like ideas, are historical phenomena; they are also historical battlegrounds in which conflicting intentions and meanings struggle for space – and never more so than in this period of intense intellectual conflict. And if 'the strength of the churches resides in the language that they have been able to maintain',[157] then the strength of their radical opponents derived from their ability to appropriate that language and turn it to new psychological and political purposes.

For the majority of early Socialists, the language of prophecy and apocalypse expressed not a literal faith in millenarian change but an intensity of aspiration for which there was simply no secular vocabulary available – an imaginative straining towards future freedom which found voice in the only language of social optimism possessed by most men and women. It is important to recall that even the most uncompromising anti-Christians in the movement frequently adopted this mode of speech, not as a way of disguising their anti-theological views but as a way of communicating their own commitment to the construction of a new heaven on earth. It was also, as we saw with Emma, a way of conceptualizing and describing social reform which was deeply personal and intensely moralistic. For her, and most of her fellow Owenites, Socialism was the Rational Religion because it re-appropriated from the churches the project of human redemption and, by detaching it from any supernatural agency, placed it firmly in the hands of enlightened humanity. It was not merely another brand of religious sectarianism, but an *anti-religion*, which in claiming for itself the moral and psychic authority previously hegemonized by organized religion, posed the churches with the most serious and sustained challenge they had yet faced.

But – the story does not end here. For if Owenism as a whole was not millenarian, some Owenites certainly were. The movement contained a number of visionaries whose outlook *was* uncompromisingly chiliastic; men and women who felt themselves to be, in Owen's words, 'impelled agents' of a 'mission' to which they were directed not merely by reason or social conscience, but by the force of divine Providence.[158] Owen himself, it now seems clear, was actually a millenarian of this sort, albeit a highly complex and ambiguous one,[159] and he managed to draw around him a number of other mystics whose commitment to an eschatological interpretation of Socialism was explicit and uncompromising.[160] Some even deemed Owen himself the new Redeemer, although he did not generally aspire to that position.[161] Others proclaimed their own messianic or prophetic status, and gathered a few disciples prepared to recognize their claims, who then formed little sects which occasionally acted as rivals to the Rational Religion. By the early 1840s a small network of such sects existed across Britain and Ireland, loosely connected through overlapping membership and shared journals, as well as their common Owenite background.

They tended to be middle-class, bohemian, and highly intellectual. Nearly all were made up of dedicated communitarians who at one time or another established experimental communities, where richly unconventional lifestyles flourished. Some were activists and publicists for the wider movement, but most were committed to promulgating their own version of the radical Word and building a holier mode of existence for themselves, in preparation for the day when 'all people shall have the Church of God within them and without them and be of one heart for one work, of one possession, and of one speech, for the time of the Millennium is at hand'.[162]

Apart from their shared faith in communism as God's ultimate plan for His terrestial children, a number of these sectaries had another important feature in common. This was an emphasis, both in their propaganda and in their sexual practice, on the mystical and moral pre-eminence of women, which in some cases led to a belief in a female Messiah. The idea of women as moral missionaries, present throughout the evangelical revival as a whole, here emerged in its most extreme, mystical form, with women (or a particular woman) deemed bearers of Christ's redemptive mission. It was this vision of female messianism which, when combined with Owenite feminism, produced the heretical Doctrine of the Woman, or the Woman-Power.

JOANNA SOUTHCOTT AND THE DOCTRINE OF THE WOMAN

Faith in a female Messiah was a persistent heresy within millenarian sects in the late eighteenth and early nineteenth century. In 1770 a working-class Manchester woman, Ann Lee, proclaimed herself the female Redeemer and took over the leadership of a breakaway Quaker group called the Shakers, who shortly afterwards moved to America and established communities based on the principles of social property, female equality, and total sexual abstinence.[163] 'Mother Ann', as she was known, was succeeded in Britain by a Welshwoman named Mary Evans, who in 1780 declared herself the 'bride of Christ' and gathered a small group of followers around her; then by a Scotswoman, Luckie Buchan, who founded a sect based on the gospel of the 'Friend Mother' (herself, as Christ's younger sister); then by Sarah Flaxmer, who in the mid-1790s prophesied her victory over Satan in the Last Days; and a number of other lesser female Saviours.[164] Interest in these women was strong among some of the Owenites. Mother Ann was declared 'one of the finest types of the new system of Christianity' by one Socialist chiliast, and Owen himself was deeply impressed by both the doctrines and the success of the Shakers.[165] James Smith viewed Luckie Buchan's career as a portent of greater things to come.[166] But the woman who made the greatest impact on Socialist millenarians was Joanna Southcott, the 'Woman clothed with the Sun'.

Joanna Southcott (1750-1814) was a Devonshire upholsteress and domestic servant who in 1792 had her housework interrupted by some mysterious Voices informing her that she was the new Saviour, the 'Woman clothed with the Sun', as named in *Revelations*, sent to redeem mankind from the Fall.[167] 'These words were so terrible,' Joanna later wrote, 'they made me tremble'. She hurried off to tell her Methodist class meeting what had happened, only to be jeered down by them. But in 1802, after the publication of a little tract on the coming apocalypse, she was encouraged by a few followers (mostly clerical gentlemen with a history of allegiance to chiliastic prophets) to leave Devon for the wider spiritual pastures of London.[168] After eighteen months of intense activity, carefully stage-managed by her backers, eight thousand persons had declared themselves converts.[169] By 1808 more than 14,000 had purchased the sealed prophecy which was the token of the Joannaite, and by the time of her death in 1814 the number had swelled to about 100,000 in the London area alone, with many thousands more in the industrial areas of the north.[170]

From his analysis of a sample of these converts, J.F.C. Harrison has discovered that the majority were women (63 per cent of the sample was female), and of these many were single working women ('nurses, tailoresses, school teachers . . . servants').[171] For most of her prophetic career Joanna lived with a wealthy female believer, Jane Townley, and her companion Ann Underwood, who together tended the Bride of Christ and recorded most of her divine communications. A century after Joanna's death it was still a coterie of the female faithful who were keeping her theology alive. Such a predominance of women was in fact typical of most chiliastic sects. But an additional attraction in Joanna's case was the character of her prophecies themselves, many of which were directed at a female audience in explicit defence of women's equal spiritual status. Like Ann Lee, Joanna claimed that with her arrival womankind had been freed from the curse of the Fall and raised to a full and rightful position within the priesthood of believers.[172] To those who refused to acknowledge the justice of this claim, Christ's message (as delivered through her) was plain:

> Now I answer thee of women: they followed Me to My Cross, and stood weeping to see Me crucified; they were the first at my sepulchre to see My resurrection: now I will not refuse women . . . Let it be known unto all men, the work at first was carried on by women. The first presents that were made were from women. So they showed their love and faith before men showed any. So now suffer women to be present and forbid them not.[173]

'Is it a new thing for a woman to deliver her people?' she demanded at one point, citing Esther and Judith as earlier examples. Through her, His Bride, His Holy Spirit in female form, Christ Himself spoke in celebration of women's redemptive mission:

> Then see ye plain, ye sons of men,
> The way I've led all on.
> It was to Woman, not to Man,
> I in this power did come . . .[174]

> So Woman here in Love Appear
> You'll find my Love is strong
> To free you all from Adam's Fall.
> If Eve brought in the *first*,
> Of *Sorrow* here that did appear
> Then I'll bring in the Last;
> For joy shall come *the same* to
> Man;
> So now the *WOMAN* see!
> MY CHURCH upon HER it must
> stand,
> As WOMAN joined with ME.[175]

Unlike Ann Lee, Southcott was no revolutionary messiah; there was no hint in her writings of the communist ideals of Mother Ann. Nor did her writings to her female disciples carry an explicitly emancipationist message in the way that Shaker

prophecy did.[176] Rather, they abounded in images of male villainy
and female defiance which aroused women to an anticipation of
greater glory. As one of her female followers put it rather primly
many years later: 'The Lord has marvellously raised the position
of Woman at the end, by thus giving to the world through Her
. . . His prophecies of things to come.'[177] But the Lord also assisted
Joanna in the rather less cosmic but equally satisfying task of
defying the male sex. In her writings, Satan was castigated as 'the
liar', the 'betrayer of women' who, when he was not
masquerading as a serpent, was busy philandering with innocent
girls. Joanna had had bitter experience of Satan's little ways: one
lover, a man called Rigsby, had been revealed as the seducer of
another woman to whom he had given an abortifacient – savine
– which had killed both herself and her unborn child;[178] another,
a married man called Wills, professed love for Joanna only to
abandon her for his adulterous wife. And it was after Wills'
betrayal that Joanna felt the Eternal Spirit rising within her:

> The Type of Wills goes deep
> For just like he ten thousands be,
> And so their end will break.[179]

So goes one of her many prophetic poems; and in an account of
her dispute with Satan – held in a barn over a seven day period
– the devil revealed a number of recognizably masculine prejudices when, exasperated with Joanna's verbal abilities, he
harangued her for being a 'poor, low-bred bitch of a woman' who
should learn to hold her waspish tongue. 'It is better to dispute
with one thousand men than one woman,' he was said to
complain, finally exploding, 'O, thou bitch of hell! Call me no
more the woman's friend. I hate the sex.' Joanna's fierce reply is
worth quoting at length:

> If man can't tame a woman's tongue, how shall the devil? If God
> hath done something to choose a woman to dispute with Satan at
> last, Satan did something to dispute with the woman at first; if
> Satan down-argued the woman at first, she ought to down-argue
> him at last. If Satan scarce gave the woman room to speak or think
> at first, the Woman ought not to give him room to speak or think at
> last . . . If Satan paid no regard to the weakness and ignorance of
> the Woman at first, the weakness and ignorance of the Woman will
> pay no regard to him at last. If he took advantage of her weakness,

she will take the advantage of *her strength*. If the Woman's fall has tired Men, I hope it will tire the Devil also. If a Devil could not shame her at first, how shall he shame her at last? . . . For he glorieth in what the woman doeth that is wrong; so IF THE WOMAN IS NOT ASHAMED OF HERSELF, THE DEVIL CANNOT SHAME HER![180]

Satan thus vanquished, his opponent was able to proceed on her mission, unhindered by any further displays of masculine contempt. In 1813, after numerous tours around the country and the publication of over sixty volumes of prophetic writings, Joanna was told by her Voices that the Bride was soon to give birth to Shiloh, the new Messiah. Her poem on this occasion celebrated the unique mission of womankind:

> Woman brought to Man the GOOD Fruit at the
> first,
> And from the Woman shall the good Fruit burst
> . . .
> Because no Fruit did ever come from Man,
> Though it is often grafted by his Hand.[181]

The Voices commanded her to wed. And although she wrote, 'I looked upon matrimony as worse than death',[182] she did write to a certain Mr Pomeroy to whom she had made such a proposition before. Spurned by him once again, she married a disciple. In 1814 she had an hysterical pregnancy and died, leaving her followers to dispute the implications of the tragedy and to await Shiloh's later arrival.

It is an extraordinary story, and one which exemplifies many features of the millenarian tradition: the richly symbolic language of personal self-assertion; the spiritual democracy of God's Call to Grace; the enormously enhanced status of those who were believed to have received that Call. For a woman like Joanna, whose only education had been from the Bible and whose only forum was the church, such advantages were obvious motives for messiahship, particularly since she received her Mission only shortly after the Wesleyans barred women from public preaching. For what a mere woman was denied, a Redeemer might easily claim; thus becoming a living symbol of what a touch of God's Hand can do for even a humble working woman.

But more than this, Joanna's career also serves to illuminate a connection between religious enthusiasm and sexual heterodoxy which was evident in the writings and works of nearly all female chiliasts and their followers in this period. Her poems, as Harrison has noted, were 'full of the imagery (mostly biblical) of brides, bridesmaids, bridegrooms, marriages, wedding feasts, wedding guests, as well as adultery, fornications, and sodomy'.[183] The dreams which she recorded in elaborate detail read remarkably like Freudian case-histories, dominated by fantastic symbols of unconscious desire.[184] In Joanna's case, this subliminal preoccupation reached its climax with the conception of Shiloh, in which she felt she had realized her own mission both as woman and redeemer, and she had little to offer in the way of sexual prescriptions to her followers. This was not true, however, of Ann Lee and Luckie Buchan, both of whom translated a similar obsession with sexuality into a definite code of holy conjugal conduct: in Luckie Buchan's case, free unions untrammelled by priestly or legal ties;[185] in Ann Lee's case, celibacy. 'No soul could follow Christ . . . while living in . . . the gratifications of lust,' Mother Ann wrote.[186] For all these women, the realization of their divine mission was directly tied to a transformative sexual practice, and also to a widening of women's moral jurisdiction. These were connections which had been forged early on in the puritan tradition, but here they appeared in their most explicit and mystical form – the form in which they then entered into Owenite chiliasm.

Southcottianism, as it developed after Joanna's death, was not a radical creed. Its leadership was mostly in the hands of conservative male clerics, while the mainstream of its membership (which remained in the thousands until the 1840s, when it rapidly dwindled) preoccupied itself with keeping up the faith in anticipation of Shiloh's imminent arrival, and did not get involved with social or political questions.[187] But there were a number of radicals on the edge of the church, sometimes forming rival sects, who linked Southcottian prophecy to the language of social protest. One of these was a man called Zion Ward, who claimed to be Joanna's Shiloh and argued in favour of social communities and a libertarian sexual morality: 'if you love one another, go together at any time without law or ceremony'.[188] He preached in the Rotunda in 1831–32, and managed to attract a few Owenite supporters before being imprisoned for blasphemy. But it was the man who then replaced him, James Elishama Smith, who forged the first real link between Southcottianism and Socialism. We briefly encountered Smith in an earlier chapter as the editor of *The Crisis* and a leading Owenite ideologue, but here we meet him as he was when he first appeared on the London Socialist scene – a young prophet of the Coming Age, armed with the most avant-garde chiliastic beliefs and that aura of spiritual entrepreneurship which was so typical of all these radical heretics.

James Smith (1801–57) was born in Edinburgh, and trained there for the Presbyterian ministry.[189] Like Emma Martin and a number of other Socialist infidels, his background was sternly Calvinist – an upbringing which seems to have induced in all of them the combination of obsessive religiosity and imaginative restlessness which was soon evident in Smith's life. By his late twenties he had thrown in Presbyterianism to become a disciple of the fashionable millennialist, Edward Irving, only to abandon Irvingism for the more exotic heresies of the Southcottians. He travelled to join a Southcottian faction, the Christian Israelites, in Ashton-under-Lyne. A couple of years spent in that town, which was also a hotbed of radical politics, probably taught him more than just the intricacies of Joannaite doctrine. At any rate, by the time he left he had acquired a liberality of outlook which pre-disposed him to social as well as theological heterodoxies. 'I am not a bigot or fanatic, I assure you, for I believe in all religions,' he wrote his family on his departure for London in 1832.[190] On arriving there, he soon made contact with a number of Owenites, including Anna Wheeler who became his friend and political mentor. In 1833, on Owen's invitation, he transferred his lectures from the Rotunda to the Charlotte Street Institution, and later that year became editor of *The Crisis*. By now, his politics were firmly Owenite, but his chiliastic fervour remained undiminished, and he used the columns of *The Crisis* to promote a combination of Christian eschatology and anti-capitalist militancy which reached its apex in prophecies that 1834 would see both the Second Advent and the revolutionary victory of the working class.[191] When neither materialized, Smith's enthusiasm for the Owenites diminished, and after a series of quarrels with Owen he departed from *The Crisis* to begin his own newspaper, *The*

Shepherd. Thereafter he became a successful newspaper publisher with a continuing sideline interest in esoteric religions, but his active career as a Socialist effectively ended in the mid-1830s.[192]

It was during this brief period as an Owenite ideologue, and then as the editor of *The Shepherd*, that Smith translated his Southcottianism into the 'Doctrine of the Woman'. This doctrine was based, as he pointed out in one article, on an amalgamation of two prophecies, one mystical and one secular: 'the one setting forth woman as the mother of Messiah, and the other laying claim to the equality of woman and her emancipation . . .'[193] The many female prophets of recent years, he claimed, were 'not imposters, but forerunners of a great change of system' in which both these prophecies would be realized; they were harbingers of the final great female messiah, the Free Woman, whose Coming would not only fulfil the promises of Scripture but 'put an end to marriage, and introduce an entirely new era in the social and domestic system . . .':[194]

> At present woman is a dependent; then she would become equal to man in political and personal privileges. Now, the marriage tie binds together for life two parties, who are frequently destructive of each other's happiness; then, each would be free to make such change of circumstance as was necessary for their own comfort; love would become a perpetual courtship, and not a domestic prison . . . This is the marriage of nature. *She* is the only priest, or rather, priestess. Hitherto the world has been ruled by priests; let a priestess be substituted in their stead. Hitherto God has been worshipped as a man; let us now worship the female God; the goddess Nature – the bride – the Lamb's wife; thus fulfilling the words of scripture, 'Behold I create a new thing in the earth, a woman shall compass a man.'[195]

Three influences can be traced behind this prophecy. The first was Southcottianism. The second was Owenite feminism, as Smith had learned it from his new acquaintances and particularly from Anna Wheeler (despite his numerous quarrels with her over her atheistic 'materialist' philosophy).[196] The third, a slightly later and even more complex addition to Smith's doctrinal repertoire, were the teachings of the Saint Simonians, who by 1833 had also embraced the heresy of female messianism. In that year the sect's

leader, 'Père' Enfantin, announced that he had received a message
from God informing him that the establishment of the *système
sociale* would be inaugurated by the advent of a woman saviour,
La Femme Libre, La Mère, with whom he would spiritually unite,
thereby creating a divine androgyne, the new messiah. An 1834
manifesto issued by his followers in London proclaimed 'the
advent of the Mother . . . the advent of a new Church, wherein
the spirit of emancipated woman will unfold its germs of moral
feelings and be instrumental in building up the new heaven and
the new earth.'[197] Thanks to a message received by two female
members of the sect when in a hypnotic trance, a number of the
faithful hurried off to seek this New Woman in Constantinople,
and reports of their progress were eagerly awaited by members of the sect and their sympathizers in London as well as in
Paris.*[198]

Smith soon became one of the key English promoters of the
Saint Simonian gospel: writing the introduction to an English
version of Saint Simon's *New Christianity*; publishing Wheeler's
translations from their feminist newspapers in *The Crisis*;
expounding their views in public lectures and editorials.[199] It is
clear that one of the features of the French sect which fascinated
him was their faith in a female redeemer, and more specifically the
elaborate sexual cosmology which they had produced to substan-
tiate such a faith. According to the Saint Simonians, Smith
explained in one article for *The Crisis*, human nature was divided
into three departments: the physical, the intellectual, and the
moral. The moral side of humanity was based on the 'feminine
principle' since it was there that 'the tender, affective sympathies
of human nature are developed'; the others were 'decidedly male':

---

*In November 1833 a meeting was held in London to report on the progress of the
Saint Simonian emissaries. It was attended by many Owenite women, some of
whom cheered loudly at the mention of *La Mère* (*The Destructive*, 2 November
1833). The only dissenting voice to be heard was that of an elderly woman who
rose to argue that English radicals ought to follow their own female messiah,
Joanna Southcott. After she spoke a young Owenite responded, saying that

> he thought it a matter of gratification to see a woman rise to declare her
> sentiments in a public meeting. He knew many Southcotians [sic] and as their
> social views were in unison with their [the Owenites'] own, he did not see
> that it mattered whether the cause was the spirit or man's reason, provided
> the glorious result was obtained. (Hear, hear).

but neither of the three is exclusively male or female; inasmuch as each individual is supposed to be placed in a condition suited to his or her particular organization.

This threefold division, however . . . may be reduced to a twofold division, which the Saint Simonians call 'material and spiritual'. The material is the physical department of industry; the spiritual is the scientific and moral in one. This double department is what may be called the priesthood; comprehending the man and the woman . . .[200]

The triumph of the Spirit, then, would occur in the union of masculine intellectualism and feminine moralism, from which a new race of men and women would be formed, carrying within themselves the best elements of both genders. As in Joanna's theology, it was through the 'marriage' of the Bridegroom (the male Christ) and the Bride (his female equivalent) that the reign of the saints would be inaugurated. In a later series of articles in *The Shepherd*, Smith developed this argument into an evolutionist cosmology based on a sexualized vision of the universe – a theory he called 'Universalism'.

Universalism was essentially an idiosyncratic version of eighteenth-century progressivist doctrine. It was founded on a Manichean vision of reality as a unity of polar opposites, in which the masculine half included God, the Spiritual and the Physical, and the feminine half comprised Nature, the Material and the Moral. The historical development of humanity could be traced, Smith argued, as a dialectical progression through stages in which these masculine and feminine principles diverged, warred, and finally united. 'The two extremes . . . are equal, and both are positive and negative to each other,' one article in *The Shepherd* explained:

The positive and negative forces seek each other . . . Hence it follows that man, who represents the spiritual, holds the material sword; but woman, representing the material, has the moral power, which will ultimately overcome the former. Woman is a refinement of man . . . she is the end of the old world and the new can only begin with her complete emancipation from the curse of the first.[201]

In Smith's Doctrine of the Woman, then, gender was interpreted not merely as a biological distinction based on anatomical difference, but as a division around which all other spiritual, psychic and social distinctions grouped themselves: an organizing principle for difference itself. The cosmos is sexualized; its *primum mobile* is sexual attraction; and, as a result, sexual relations between men and women become a matter of cosmic significance, the key to a new historical and moral order. 'The universal Harmony of Nature and Spirit is found only in truly chaste marriages, in marriages of the affections . . .' The puritan-romantic mentality displays itself once again, draped in the language of apocalypse.

This preoccupation with sexual difference was an important feature of the evangelical revival as a whole. In following Smith's ideological career, we can see how under certain conditions this preoccupation translated into a subversion of rigid gender definitions, while at other times reinforcing them. Thus during his Owenite phase he insisted on the equality of the masculine and feminine principles, and on this basis gave vigorous support to feminist demands (including women's right to work and unionize, and equal political rights).[202] But when he left the movement to edit *The Shepherd*, his emphasis shifted towards an insistence that women's superior moral capacities actually disqualified them for certain tasks, including direct participation in the 'male' political arena: 'the moral government [of women] is . . . an invisible government . . .'[203] Underlying this was an even more significant shift, away from the Saint Simonians' ideal of the androgynous personality towards a strict re-drawing of the boundary between male and female characteristics:

> Woman can never be elevated by becoming more masculine, nor men by becoming more feminine. The tendency of civilization is rather to increase than diminish the difference of sex.[204]

By the time he was editing *The Family Herald* his views on women's character and social role seem to have become as conventional as any other middle-class Victorian paternalist.[205]

For Smith, then, radical notions about sexuality and women's position were part of a wider radical-chiliastic vision, and when the link was broken between his millenarian outlook and his Owenite commitment, his mystical vision of a revolution in gender relations went with it. But the Doctrine of the Woman did not disappear from the Socialist ranks. The cluster of ideas which it represented – Southcottian eschatology, feminism, and a theory of sexual evolutionism which challenged conventional definitions of womanhood and manhood – reappeared in the writings of the most interesting chiliastic sect associated with Owenism: the Communist Church.

THE COMMUNIST CHURCH

The Communist Church was the creation of Goodwyn (1820–81) and Catherine (? –1854) Barmby, two young, middle-class intellectuals, and a handful of dedicated followers.[206] Like James Smith, Goodwyn was from a respectable, religious background. As the son of a Suffolk solicitor he had been intended for a solid Church of England career. But his father died before this ambition could be realized, and thereafter young Goodwyn was left to find his own way into the world. At the age of sixteen he could be seen haranguing groups of local agricultural labourers on the iniquities of the New Poor Law; at nineteen he was an active Chartist, busy organizing the East Suffolk Chartist Council which he then represented at both the 1839 and 1842 National Conventions. In 1841, at the age of twenty-one, he was chosen as the Chartist Parliamentary candidate for Ipswich (but apparently withdrew before the election). Over these years, he also became involved in Socialist movements both in England and abroad, contributing articles to *The New Moral World* on Fourierism, Saint Simonianism, medical theory (a pet concern), and various millenarian themes, as well as publishing a good deal of bad poetry which he heralded as the new Language of Truth. 'The reign of the critic is over, the rule of the poet commences,' an early Communist publication announced, 'All Messias [sic] will be acknowledged.'[207]

Much less is known about Catherine, but from her writings it is easy to guess that her background was very similar to that of Emma Martin and many other Socialist feminist propagandists. From 1835 on she produced a series of articles for *The New Moral World*, under the pen-name 'Kate', which contained that typical blend of lower middle-class women's concerns and Owenite politics which we have met throughout our story. One titled 'The Condition of Woman', for example, attacked the hypocrisy of those who preached 'family interests and family affection' while at the same time supporting laws of inheritance and marital property rights which 'oppose husband to wife, and the father against the mother of their children'.[208] Immediate reforms in this area were essential, she argued, although ultimately only Socialism could create a happier mode of family existence: 'individual accumulation, and the consequent desire for private property . . . are the root of the evil; and unless we place the axe to the root what do we effect?' Other articles examined the restricted job opportunities for women in shop and office employment, the educational needs of girls, and the particular hardships faced by working-class women (which were addressed with great sensitivity, despite the distance which separated her own life from theirs).[209] General topics of 'societarian' interest were also explored, including (several years before she met Goodwyn) the 'Religion of the Millennium', a religion 'free from the spots and stains of imaginative ignorance . . . and sectarian bigotry', founded on 'moral purity and moral liberty':

> How quick would be the transition from sadness to delight, were society made to understand how its welfare depends upon . . . an unremitting love and practice of the truth . . . the Religion of the Millennium![210]

Possibly this romantic-religious outlook predisposed Catherine to look favourably on Goodwyn when they met – or maybe his 'gentlemanly manners . . . soft, persuasive voice' and 'light brown hair parted in the middle . . . à la Byron' had something to do with her rapid conversion . . . At any rate, in 1840 they became acquainted and by 1841 they were working together in the 'Central Communist Propaganda Society', soon to be the Communist Church. They were wed in the same year. 'I announce love to be the sacred bond of marriage,' Goodwyn wrote at the time, 'I declare that two only at the same time can feel that particular love that is completed in marriage. I affirm that divorce begins when love ends.'[211]

The Communist Church survived until 1849. The size achieved by the sect over this lifetime is difficult to assess, but it seems likely that it remained very small: from five branches in late 1842 it could claim only an additional seven or eight by 1845, and even this may well have been an exaggeration.[212] As always, however, propaganda reached out much further than card-carrying members. The Church's newspapers had respectable circulation figures, while the Communist Temple established at the Circus, Great Marylebone, drew large audiences for regular lectures on 'Communitive' principles. Lecturers also toured the countryside, and no doubt here and there new Communists were made, but the sect's strongholds were Cheltenham (where a former Swedenborgian edited various journals for them) and Goodwyn's political constituency in Ipswich, where nearly the entire local leadership of both Socialism and Chartism moved into the Communist Church branch.[213] The sexual composition of these branches is not known, but several women were involved in the Church's central council at different times, including Catherine and her sister Maria. Communists also toured with other Owenites and often joined them on platforms. Emma Martin presided over one Communist meeting on the marriage issue, while her good friend George Bird, medical officer for the Queenwood community, was on the Church's Central Council.[214] This overlap of personnel would seem to indicate that the Communists remained pretty much under the Owenite umbrella although Barmby himself made a point of emphasizing the Church's doctrinal superiority: 'God has made us, Communists, . . . more than Socialists,' he explained in 1843.

> Owenism has material benevolence which is more than the Christianity of Sectarianism has; but it wants religious faith, it is too commercial, too full of the spirit of this world, and therefore it is rightly damned; and God through us is raising up the white, the pure, the true, the only Catholic Communist Church.[215]

Despite these exclusivist claims, in the early 1840s the Communist Church was in fact linked to several other sects of a similar sort, including the White Quakers of Dublin and the Ham Common Concordium, which resided in a communal house in Richmond. The White Quakers, who were led by Joshua Jacob and Abigail Beale (a couple united in a free union) were dedicated to restoring Fox's original teachings, which they interpreted in communist and eschatological terms. They preached and practised free love; wore only white linen and sandles; and left their hair and beards uncut.[216] The Ham Common Concordists, who included several Southcottians and some female followers of James Smith, were inspired by the 'Sacred Socialist', James Pierrepont Greaves, who advocated vegetarianism, celibacy, and cold baths . . .[217] The Concordium produced a journal called *The New Age*, to which Goodwyn contributed. Several of its residents published chiliastic tracts of their own, including one (by Henry Wright) advocating the 'Harmonic Elevation' of the sexes as the prelude to the New Age:

> Man and woman, as the outer forms of Divine Wisdom and Divine Love, must be consorted: but none short of the Divine Power may be the uniter. So united, Man cannot oppress Woman, nor Woman torment Man.[218]

In common with these sister sects, the Communists were a highly cerebral and intensely romantic lot, vigorously experimental in their approach to everyday life (with enthusiasms ranging from vegetarianism and hydrotherapy to meditation and something called 'philanthropic philology'), and passionately evangelical in their theological/political causes. Goodwyn himself became an increasingly Shelleyan figure over the years, with blonde hair flowing down to his shoulders (to the joyful amazement of the crowds he addressed, who occasionally demanded locks as souvenirs), and volumes of sentimental verse to his credit, while Catherine in turn published poems in praise of her husband, 'my dear Master-Messiah', and acted as his faithful co-worker ('under the guidance of the Holy Spirit') in all their projects.[219] Together the young couple travelled the streets of London in the early 1840s with a hooded cart from which they dispensed tracts calling on their compatriots to refuse to pay taxes to the 'impious imposts of an unjust government' and demanding that the Archbishop of Canterbury dissolve the Established Church and reinstate the communist practices of the early Christians.[220] Occasionally they invaded churches to publicly criticize the sermons and harangue the congregation:* why was

---

*These sort of activities generated a hostile article in the Quaker journal, *The Friend* (vol. 7, no. 73, January 1849), which contrasted Communism to Christian charity:

the 'demoralizing practice' of private trade and competition banned only on Sundays? Goodwyn demanded of one Southall congregation; 'Every day should become the Lord's Day . . .'[221] Throughout the early 1840s they produced a series of apocalyptic tracts on the final state of 'Communization' which mankind was about to enter, which was depicted as an age of enlightened elegance, set in a pastoral landscape with numerous fountains, large libraries, air-ships (for easier transport to neighbouring communities) and an eastern style of architecture 'which would even far excel the temple and the palace united together, and surpass the most gorgeous conceptions and glorious imaginings, which even the most advanced among us can at present conceive or imagine . . .' The 'most probable site' of this utopia would be Syria, 'that most delicious country, that earthly paradise . . .'[222] But alas for Syrian dream kingdoms: when the Barmbys finally did establish their first community, it was in a small house at Hanwell, Middlesex, 'a place well known for its Lunatic Asylum'. The compromise was accepted with the cheerful resignation of true philosophers.

> It thus seems that God has decreed the first Asylum for the sane to be situated near the Asylum for the insane . . . in accordance with that Divine Law by which extremes meet . . .[223]

The Moreville Communitorium (as the household was called in honour of that first great modern Utopian) opened in 1843 with Goodwyn and Catherine as its sole occupants and folded slightly less than a year later. During that period various others came and went ('His eye could not see the light of the religious spirit of

It is one thing when christians hear the precept of the Saviour, 'Give to him that asketh of thee' – nay, when they even anticipate the request; making inquiry into the wants of the poor and supplying them; *another*, when persons, pretending to the name [of Christian] are found affirming that the very possession of aught to give is immoral, tyrannical, unlawful from the creation! when the command to the wealthy, *to give*, is to become a *demand*, on the part of the needy or covetous, to have; when associations are formed under the specious name of a 'church' and the public mind to be agitated to promote the impossible scheme of a possession in common of the goods of this world!

Nor was the feminism of the Communists spared: 'we have, some of us, seen quite enough . . . of such attempts to break up families . . .'

communism'; 'She . . . proved irreclaimably wedded to the habits of individualized selfish life . . .'; and so on), while Catherine and Goodwyn slaved away over domestic routine (there were no servants), wrote advertisements offering 'juvenile education for both sexes', and reproduced.* The birth of little Moreville Watkins Barmby in early 1844 seems to have brought things to a head, however, for very soon after Goodwyn realized that God was recalling him to London 'to combat Babylon in its stronghold', and the experiment was abruptly dissolved.[224] Thereafter the Church concentrated on profession rather than practice, arguing that until mankind had been educated to Communist principles there was no hope of establishing the New Jerusalem.

Throughout these years the politics of the Communist Church, and in particular its feminist commitment, developed as a typical blend of popular radicalism and mystical enthusiasm. The Communists were not Southcottians in any 'orthodox' sense (although Goodwyn did reprint some of Joanna's poetry and initiated a campaign to have her famous Box of prophecies opened).[225] But, like Smith, they saw Joanna's career as a symbol of the emancipationist mission of womankind: 'The communication of the Free Woman in history is providentially beautiful,' Goodwyn wrote to a feminist acquaintance, Anne Knight, 'even Joanna Southcott, in whose strange but wrongfully despised scriptures most of the woman's mission is to be found in mystery . . . But the Free Woman who shall give the womanly tone to the entire globe is not yet manifested.'[226] What was meant by this 'womanly tone' was elaborated in an 1841 article he wrote for *The New Moral World* called 'The Man-Power, the Woman-Power, and the Man-Woman-Power', a fascinating statement of the Church's chiliastic feminist vision.[227]

The article began with a quotation from Shelley's *Revolt of Islam* (Shelley's own version of the myth of a feminist messiah),

---

*The Communists strongly disapproved of the Ham Common Concordists' celibacy rule. 'It is the duty of the new world . . . of the communitive life, purely and chastely to give birth to their children, so as ultimately to overcome by their good generations the evil generations of the wicked,' Catherine wrote to her friend Abigail Beale, who was toying with the idea of following the Concordists' example. But they absolutely agreed with the Concordists that the issue was of transcendental as well as social significance.

and then went on to outline an evolutionist theory in which the influence of James Smith ('a friend of mine, a truly religious spirit' as Goodwyn referred to him) was plainly visible:

> In the times of barbarization and feudalism was the man-power strong and dominant. Physical force reigned triumphant. Gentleness ruled only secretly in the bosom of woman. Hence we have learned to term gentleness and its sentiment equations as the woman-power. Long was it in abeyance to the man-power, or physical empire; but now, at last, it is beginning to prevail. Love is its God . . . and it beams like the sun itself, from the heart of every true Socialist, irradiating the heart of every real communist.

Various tables and diagrams were then supplied to illustrate this historical oscillation through the stages of mankind's social development. 'Except during the fabled golden age, the man-power has been *generally* in the ascendant . . . Now the vacillation increases to a grand extent, and as civilization expires, the woman-power will be immeasurably in the ascendant, preparing the way for the equilibrium harmony of community.' This was, Goodwyn argued, the hidden meaning of Joanna's mission:

> When an enthusiastic woman proclaimed the reign of women upon earth, and asserted their future empire over men, she knew not what she said, but yet she was a prophetess.

Her mistake, however, had been in equating the ascendancy of the feminine principle with the actual rule of women. 'She saw the might of gentleness in women, but knew not that their natures were really common with those of man, although the better natures of man were actually dormant.' The important issue now facing humanity is 'not of woman nor of man, but of . . . gentleness and of force . . .'

> which we wish to behold united in every human individual, without relation to sex. In fine, to be a true communist, or Socialist, the man must possess the woman-power as well as the man-power, and the woman must possess the man-power as well as the woman-power. Both must be equilibriated beings.*

*The union of the woman-power and the man-power, Barmby added here, would also represent the re-union of Adam and Eve: 'In the primitive paradisaical state of the world . . . Adam and Eve were not divided, being hermaphroditically one. But when Adam formed, as they tell us, a separate body for Eve from his rib, we can only interpret it as the disunion of the man-power and the woman-power, imaged

The new social order must have at its foundation a harmony of the sexes based not only on the eradication of women's subordinate status, but on the gradual elimination of psycho/sexual differences. Androgyny is divine; its realization in the individual psyche is the fulfilment of the 'Love-spirit', the 'Messiah-spirit' . . . 'the Woman-Man-Power':

> Grace be to those in whom woman-nature . . . and man-nature are at present equilibriated and active. We hail them as true priests of humanity, as the veritable social apostles . . .

The two examples which Goodwyn then offered of these equilibriated revolutionaries were Mary Wollstonecraft and Shelley, and he obviously had himself and Catherine in mind as their successors* (with a little note that 'the existence of the woman-power does not necessarily imply that the man or woman possessing it is endued with what we call effeminateness . . .'). The article concluded on a strongly chiliastic note – 'Let the Messiah be within us, it will socialize our planet and establish true communism amid our globe' – which was more than echoed in an article written by Catherine on the same theme:

> The mission of woman is discovered by Communism: will she hesitate to perform it? The grass is growing, sorrow is accumulating – waves are rushing, the world is warring – life and death, soul and body, are in the conflict, the saviour is in the hearts of the redeemed, the prophet is the inspired one, WOMAN LEARN THY MISSION? DO IT? AND FEAR NOT? – the world is saved.[228]

These texts, along with several others produced by the Barmbys on similar themes, represented the apogee of the Communist Church's chiliastic-feminist vision, and also the most explicit critique of the concept of an essential masculinity and

---

by the separation of the man and the woman bodies.' This heresy seems to have been a fairly common one; an interesting article in the atheistic newspaper *The Investigator* (vol. 1, no. 1, 1843) traced it through a variety of eighteenth century theologians (including a French woman who claimed that the Fall was the disunion of the original hermaphrodite which then created 'monsters in nature, divided into two imperfect sexes, unable to produce their like alone . . .'). Blake's visionary writings were also based on a version of this myth.

*At several points he suggested that Catherine was a 'manifestation' of the Free Woman, although not her 'final realization'.

femininity to be found within Owenism. When the Communists' Love-Spirit set out to emancipate, She would not only revolutionize sexual relations, but also transform the meaning of womanhood and manhood. The pantheistic notion of the personal 'Messiah-spirit' became a manifesto for a new type of androgynous personality: 'tender as a saint, brave as a martyr'. Seen in this light, Goodwyn's shoulder-length hair and soft voice appear Christ-like in more than just the obvious sense, just as the masculinizing bloomers of the Saint Simonian women, which Catherine lauded and possibly emulated, signalled an 'inner emancipation' from rigid sexual definitions. Elsewhere the Barmbys retreated somewhat from this position: 'although we would equalize, we would not identify the sexes. Such identification would be unnatural, unbeautiful . . .' Catherine assured her readership at one point.[229] But its continuing influence was reflected in their militant opposition to all restrictions on women's social role. The summary of Saint Simonian doctrine provided by Robert Southey was wholly applicable to the Communists as well:

> They teach that the wife ought to be equal with the husband, and that . . . she ought to be associated with him in the exercise of the triple functions of the church, the state, and the family: so that the *social individual*, which has hitherto been the *man* alone, henceforth shall be the *man and wife*, presenting politically thus the perfect Androgyne of philosophical fable.[230]

It was on this basis that the Communists not only supported the usual Owenite demands for egalitarian 'marriages of the affections', improved education for women, communalized housework and so on, but also mounted the first campaign for female enfranchisement. The Barmbys were Chartists as well as heterodox Socialists, and in 1841 they issued a 'Declaration of Electoral Reform' in which they demanded that the People's Charter be amended to include women's suffrage. 'We assert that man and woman are equal to each. We are opposed to sex legislation as we are opposed to class legislation. We therefore ask by the names of Mary Wolstonecraft [sic] and Charlotte Corday, for universal suffrage to woman and man, for unsexual Chartism!'[231] Editorials in the *New Moral World* supported the Communist position, but did not urge action on it, and it was left to the Barmbys and their comrades to produce a stream of statements on the issue, for 'how can we allow the political subalternity of woman when we advocate her social equality? If woman is not free, man must ever be a slave.'[232]

The most important tract published by the Communists on the suffrage question was one written by Catherine in 1843 in which she raised three demands: for the political, the domestic and the ecclesiastical emancipation of women.[233] The first, for equal political rights, was supported with arguments which soon became a stock part of the enfranchisement case: that women were subject to laws over which they had no control; that they were taxed by a state which they had no part in administering; that they were at least the equals of men in political ability; and so on. By women's 'domestic emancipation' was meant 'her freedom at the hearth and board' which could only be secured by 'her independence in the pursuit of those labors [sic] for which she is particularly adapted, and which alone can be her security from the tyranny of her husband, and her preservation from the oppressions of society':

> In fine, we demand her emancipation . . . from mere household drudgery . . . the means for which are to be found only in that communitive state of society of which these tracts are the advocate.[234]

Catherine then went on to argue, here and in another article on 'Women's Industrial Independence', that only when domestic labour was wholly collectivized would sexual equality become a practical possibility, since women would then become independent of men and able to engage in the 'common labours' of society alongside them. Until then, the 'isolation of domestic life' and intense sexual competition within the labour market would inevitably drive women back into a ghetto of dependent subordination: 'no enfranchisement through work – no independence by industry . . ' Only 'a community of goods and labors [sic] properly organised' could remedy this.[235]

Women's natural allies in the struggle to create this new social system, Catherine argued, were the men of the working class, 'and should they not at once perceive the justice of her demands, it will prove indeed that evil example worketh much mischief' since they would then be treating women 'as the Tories have evilly acted towards them . . .'[236] Catherine had no patience with those who counselled forbearance or conciliation. The issue facing women and working people of both sexes was essentially one of power, 'the mighty agent for all societies and all worlds . . .' Christian love was all very well as a final goal, but a little fear in the hearts of the ruling classes would probably be more effective in the short run: 'And fear may by some of the varied changes that are ever on the wing . . . produce love . . . between all classes . . .'[237]

Finally, from the struggles of the present would emerge a new Holy Order, a social priesthood united by Wisdom and Love, 'the masculine and feminine principles which blent in the man, the woman, and the child, should rule over society . . .'[238] Woman's redemptive mission lay in the creation of this Divine vanguard. 'We have the priest, we therefore demand the priestess, the Woman teacher of the word, the woman apostle of God's law!'[239] But now the Priestess is no longer seen to be an individual Messiah-figure, the Bride of Joannite theology, but womankind in general, womankind in struggle:

> The means for effecting the ecclesiastical emancipation of woman appear to us to consist in the formation of a 'woman's society' in every city, town and village possible. In this society women might converse, discuss, and speak upon their rights, their wrongs, and their destiny; they might consult upon their own welfare and that of the great human family, and thus prepare each other for the mission of the apostle in society at large . . .[240]

Thus in Catherine's writings the doctrine of female messianism was eventually translated into the vision of autonomous feminist organization which would reshape not only the future of women, but the destiny of humanity as a whole. The evangelical emphasis on women as carriers of a new moral order became in her writings, as in Emma Martin's, the basis for a style of feminism which demanded freedom for women not merely on their own behalf, but as the precondition for general social liberation. Despite the profound divergence in their religious outlook, ultimately both women were involved in a similar project, the transformation of the Christian concept of Womanly Duty into a rallying-call for Socialist feminist militancy. Eve must organize to make the New Jerusalem.

VI

LOVE AND THE NEW LIFE: THE DEBATE OVER MARRIAGE REFORM

THE POPULAR DEBATE

The attack on the marriage system was one of the most controversial issues handled by the Socialists after 1835. As usual, their fiercest opponents were the clergy, who viewed Socialist sexual doctrine as the apogee of infidel degeneracy. But on this matter the churchmen also managed to draw in behind them conservatives of almost every religious and political stripe, until by the late 1830s the whole topic had become a major battleground for competing ideologies. No other issue touched so many nerves of popular anxiety, or generated so much excitement and acrimony. 'Upon no subject has antipathy to change, been more violently manifested, than that of Marriage and Divorce . . .' a *New Moral World* editorial commented at the height of the debate, 'It is scarcely possible to travel anywhere . . . or enter into any mixed company, without hearing this subject broached, and the most licentious, vicious and brutalising opinions ascribed to the Socialists . . .'[1]

The initial target of all this opprobrium, and the text which first brought the marriage issue into the public eye, was Owen's *Lectures on the Marriages of the Priesthood in the Old Immoral World*, which was published as a tract in 1835 and re-issued in four further editions in the following five years. By 1840 the *Lectures* had been torn apart in dozens of anti-Socialist publications; quoted aloud in endless public debates; denounced in pulpits from Canterbury Cathedral to the Primitive Methodist chapels of Belper; banned from many public bookstalls; and on one occasion publicly burnt by an opponent with a flair for the

183

dramatic. 'Let no man, let no woman especially, dare to become a Socialist without first reading these ten lectures . . .' *The Evangelical Magazine* warned.[2]

Apart from its strident anti-clericalism, the aspect of the *Lectures* which most infuriated these critics was its blueprint for a remodelled sexual life in the new communities. At one level, as we saw in Chapter Two, Owen's speeches had been a plea for certain legal reforms, notably civil marriage and divorce, which were widely supported by other liberal thinkers – and had he confined himself to these demands the controversy would never have reached such a pitch of intensity. But it was where his argument moved from marital reform in the Old Immoral World to promises of 'marriages of Nature' in the New Moral World that it provoked a reaction not far short of hysterical. The combined assault on Christian morality and patriarchal power contained in his more revolutionary proposals seemed to shake the very foundations of civilized life. 'The Socialists require us to break up house, to tear asunder our household ties, and put to death the strongest and dearest affections of our hearts,' ran a typical piece of anti-Socialist propaganda, 'they call on us to throw our wives and children into one common stock . . . No man is to be confined to one woman, nor is any woman to be confined to one man; but all are to yield themselves up to be governed by the unrestrained instincts of nature, in imitation of dogs and goats.'[3]

Thousands of tracts and sermons pumped out a similar message, accusing Owen of everything from open advocacy of adultery to the introduction of contraception and sex education at New Lanark to proposals to limit the community population through the murder of surplus infants. One particularly virulent tract even managed to speculate on the incestuous possibilities inherent in Socialist childrearing arrangements ('since none shall know their natural parents'), and went on from there to offer a quick history of the London Co-operative Society, which the author claimed had been forced to dissolve because the promiscuous mating of its members had produced so many offspring that the society was no longer viable.[4] 'Every community is to be one vast brothel . . .'[5] By the late 1830s, according to Thomas Frost, this propaganda had been so effective that just the mention of the word Socialism was sufficient to evoke in the minds of most people 'a system behind which all took refuge who wished to cast off the restraints of society and make free with his neighbour's wife and chattels'.[6] If Chartists 'were suspected of designs tending to the wholesale infraction of the Eighth Commandment,' he added, 'a Socialist was held in horror as certainly capable of violating the entire decalogue.'[7]

The Socialists' own campaign on the marriage issue developed under the pressure of this assault. The *Lectures* were acquiring notoriety during the years when the movement's priorities were shifting away from economic struggles to a wider concern with cultural and social questions, including sexual reform; and this, combined with the outcry from their opponents, led to the initiation of a major propaganda offensive. Throughout the late 1830s and early 1840s a continual stream of publications poured from the pens of Socialist ideologues, defending, re-interpreting and occasionally even wholly revising Owen's proposals. Lecturers began to give the issue pride of place within their repertoire of Social topics, particularly when they discovered that topics like 'Marriage and Divorce' or 'Robert Owen's Marriage System Defended' were great crowd-catchers, attracting audiences of up to five or six thousand people. In addition, Owenite publicists began to challenge opponents to public debates, and these confrontations became major events with enormous audiences and much excitement.

When Owen debated his arch-antagonist, John Brindley, in Bristol in 1840, for example, at least five thousand tickets were sold and many more people were turned away. The whole city was in an uproar for days, and the debate itself proved a very noisy affair, with opposing camps cheering their champion and jeering his adversary.[8] The same level of excitement was evident on many other occasions, including one confrontation between the Socialist James Clarke and Reverend Bromley in Macclesfield, where the meeting room 'which is calculated to hold about 600 persons, was crowded to excess, and hundreds who could not gain admittance, had to retire disappointed; others crowded at the windows outside, and broke them to gain a hearing, so great was the anxiety.' This time even the speakers found the turmoil so upsetting that they began to misplace their notes and forget their arguments; at one point Bromley quoted several passages from a free love text which he claimed was written by Owen but turned out to be from Shelley's *Queen Mab* . . . ('great noise and confusion'). Despite the hullabaloo, however, Clarke finally emerged triumphant, which (in the words of the local Socialist branch secretary) 'clearly demonstrated that the people are ready for a change'.[9]

Although there were many women at all these events, nearly all the Socialists' platform opponents were men, who seemed to view Socialism either as a future sexual anarchy in which men would wage bitter warfare for women's favours ('The value of women differs as much as any of the goods of life . . .' as one opponent explained, 'and were they not appropriated by marriage, the contests that would ensue for the possession of the most estimable would be furious and unceasing') or as a terrifying prospect of female sexual independence.[10] 'In a community, the woman you have won today may be tired of you tomorrow, and choose another,' Joseph Barker gasped in his *The Overthrow of Infidel Socialism*, 'and what sort of remedy will there be for such a calamity as that?'[11] Slanders directed against the Socialist women ('lascivious whores', 'prostitutes . . . in whom infidelity and debauchery have eaten up natural affection') displayed an intense apprehension lest other women take up their 'hideous example' and remove themselves from patriarchal control.* Female chastity, it was constantly hinted, was a very precarious virtue, maintained only under the strictest surveillance. In the words of one man, 'it is marriage alone which makes a woman honoured and honourable'.[12] The reply which a Socialist made to another cleric who had expressed similar misgivings went to the heart of male anxiety:

> You have . . . *taken it for granted* that nothing but fear hinders our wives and daughters from defiling their minds and polluting their

---

*One short-lived newspaper titled *Antidote, or the Anti-Socialist Gazette* ('The Uncompromising Enemy of Socialism, Chartism, and Mormonism') took Margaret Chappellsmith as its particular target, accusing her of deserting her husband and acquiring a string of Socialist lovers. The editor, John Brindley, even made a lengthy detective trip around various towns to try and find the cuckolded husband, presumably to offer him sympathy. When Mr Chappellsmith was located, however, Brindley was forced to report that he appeared to be as degenerate as the 'filthy female lecturer' with whom he happily lived, and whose views he wholly endorsed.

bodies by wholesale prostitution . . . really, the sex you affect to honour have little cause to relish your opinion *that nothing but fear of the law restrains them from the practice of lewdness and immorality.*[13]

But if this was the implicit message of most of the anti-Socialist propaganda, its explicit appeal was usually to women themselves, who were encouraged to believe that Socialism was only an ideological cover for male libertinism. Well-known Socialist men were repeatedly accused of crimes ranging from wife-desertion and adultery to child-abuse and incest, while tales of innocent matrons lured into Owenite meetings only to find themselves embroiled in behind-the-scenes debauches were very common. Newspapers began to report wife-murders and desertions with side-heads such as 'Effects of Owenism' or 'Domestic Socialism', and dubbed free unions 'Socialist marriages'.[14] Tracts carrying apocryphal tales of 'lovely maidens' who had been seduced and abandoned by Socialists were distributed all over the country.* 'For the honour of the sex – for the rights of women

*In 1840 the streets of Manchester were showered with copies of a newspaper published by a local religious society (*The Watchman*, 12 February 1840) which carried a little cautionary tale titled 'Moral Harmony'. It began by depicting the humble home of a rural cottager, whose virginal daughter 'sits knitting near the door, with its perfumed porch of honey-suckles'. Into this idyllic scene wanders a young man:

> He wears the garb of a mechanic. He converses about science and the march of intellect. He declaims, fluently, concerning political rights and moral organization, and talks of signing the People's Charter.

Fascinated by his deadly charms, the 'simple village maiden' soon falls in love, only to find that her paramour does not believe in God or marriage ('he would burn the Cross of Christ for firewood'). But inclination prevails over conscience, and the innocent girl agrees to a ceremony at the local Hall of Science. Several months pass, and she becomes pregnant.

> 'How tiresome!' said her reputed husband, as he took the last shilling from her pocket during her calm sleep, and escaped from their little home, two hours before daylight.

Thus abandoned, our miserable heroine betakes herself into a workhouse (where she has been sent by a 'weeping magistrate') and bears her child, only to travel from there to a madhouse where

> she moans and walks alone. The keeper will tell you
> that she is near the grave. WHO IS SHE? WHO
> IS SHE? And a madman answers, dolefully, she is a
> SOCIALIST'S BRIDE! . . . a bonny SOCIALIST'S BRIDE!

187

– in the name of all that is dear and lovely – never give your hand or your heart to a Socialist!' a London City Missionary implored his female readers.[15]

All this produced the anticipated results. When the Bishop of Exeter denounced Socialism in the House of Lords, he received dozens of petitions from women supporting his stand. A typical one, signed 'The Ladies of Hertford', begged the Queen to intervene and prevent the establishment of the Queenwood community, where casual coupling would be the norm, babes would all be 'torn from their mothers' arms', and various other mysterious innovations introduced 'too revolting to pain your Majesty's chaste ear by an allusion to them'.[16] Meetings called by anti-Socialist clergymen drew large numbers of women (which prompted the editor of *The New Moral World* to make some uncharitable remarks about feminine susceptibility to priestly dogmatists).[17] When Lord Melbourne presented Owen to the Queen in 1840 he was immediately inundated with protests from defenders of female virtue, male and female. 'Never will the females of England forget the insult offered to them, as virgins and matrons, by Lord Melbourne's introduction of Owen to the Queen,' boomed *Fraser's Magazine*, while *The Christian Lady's Magazine* urged its readers to mobilize against this new threat to English domestic life.[18]

Many of these women were conventional middle-class churchgoers who were antagonistic to Socialism on class grounds as well as religious and moral ones. For them, the movement reawakened all those old fears of plebian degeneracy which had been whipped up during the Jacobin period, transforming even modest proposals for marriage reform into symptoms of revolutionary upheaval. But if these were Socialism's most respectable female opponents, they were by no means its most virulent ones. In town after town throughout the 1840s crowds of working-class women (usually described by the Owenite press as 'rough and disreputable') gathered outside Socialist meetings to boo and jeer and sometimes to make rough music with pans and sticks. In

---

Her career terminates in a pauper's funeral, attended by many angry women, while her former lover dances the night away at a Social Festival. 'ENGLISHWOMEN', the tale concluded, 'THIS IS SOCIALISM'.

Dudley in 1839, for example, a meeting was disrupted 'by the shouts and yells of a party of boys and women perched on a brick wall' who 'beat old pans', while in Whitehaven in 1842 a crowd of women, egged on by a Methodist preacher, assembled outside the Socialist meeting hall where Robert Buchanan was scheduled to speak 'and commenced a clamour which very soon drew to the spot a crowd . . . of several hundreds'.[19] In this case, however, the women were not content with noisy disruption. The hall was broken into and torn apart; the Socialists inside were attacked and Buchanan was badly beaten (although none of the Socialist women were injured). Buchanan's son later wrote, in an account of his father's career, that it was the belief that the Socialists were advocating male promiscuity and wife-desertion which 'drove the wives and mothers of the toiling classes to absolute frenzy, and made them the chief leaders and abettors of many acts of violence' – and so it clearly was in this case.[20] Two nights after the Hall of Science riot the mob re-formed and

> a considerable crowd, consisting principally of females, assembled in front of the shop of Mr Wm. Wilson, printer, King Street, who was known to be one of the leaders of the Socialists . . . On the present occasion popular indignation was excited against him, – and especially on the part of the women – by a report that he had induced several of his wife's apprentices, young girls learning the business of straw bonnet making, to embrace the doctrines.

All Wilson's windows were smashed by the angry women before they were dispersed by the police. The local newspaper expressed its gratification 'at the decided tone in which public opinion has expressed itself'.[21]

On other occasions it was Socialist women who became the target of female anger. This was particularly true in Scotland, where Emma Martin and her daughter were chased by violent crowds, and where Margaret Chappellsmith (whose arrival had been announced by a Paisley newspaper which described her as a 'she-devil') was met by a group of women who threw stones and called her names. Margaret also had trouble in South Shields, where 'as usual, a great mob of insolent women and children' surrounded her in the streets, threatening and shouting 'Which is she with the seven husbands?' 'Are you her with the seven husbands?' In sending in her report on this incident Margaret commented:

'Poor creatures, they might well be angry with me, since they have been taught to believe me such a monopolizer.'[22]

On the other hand, the Socialists also commanded a good deal of female support, particularly on all issues relating to women's status within marriage and their right to divorce. Hundreds and sometimes thousands of women would turn out to hear them speak on such topics, and a Methodist preacher who attended one such meeting in 1839 was 'very much surprised' to find that 'the ladies present . . . could see no morality in forcing people to live together when their affection for each other had ceased'. On this occasion, when the issue was put to the vote the women in the audience supported the Socialists' demands.[23] When George Fleming lectured on marriage and divorce in Great Yarmouth in 1840 his lecture was attended by a large number of women 'many of whom had never been at a social lecture before' who at the conclusion 'pressed forward . . . to shake hands with the lecturer, and to wish him health and strength to spread his glorious tidings of emancipation, equality and justice to poor, ill-used women'.[24]

Margaret Chappellsmith and Emma Martin both spoke regularly on divorce to large female audiences, who often interrupted their speeches with cheers. At one meeting this level of female support so annoyed an opposing Methodist minister that he snarled 'in the most insulting and indelicate manner' that 'if the ladies were *satisfied* there was no more to be said about it'; the report added, 'all this time the excitement was extreme'.[25] And in 1839 when a man rose in a London meeting to criticize a Socialist lecturer for his immoral views he was suddenly interrupted by his deserted wife who had spotted him across the hall and used the occasion to publicly denounce him.[26] 'A woman in becoming the wife of a man, becomes also his property and servant,' ran a letter from one of these women to *The New Moral World*, 'and he may sell, half starve, beat, confine and deprive her of many of the necessaries of life, and yet not be punishable by any law . . . Indeed woman, in the words of the divine Shelley, – "As the bond slaves dwells/Of man a slave; and life is poisoned in its wells". And as long as man continues to be a slave, so long will woman be his bond-slave; the oppressed ever seeking to become oppressors in their turn.'[27]

Most of the women at these meetings were working-class, with the usual substantial minority of lower middle-class ladies. Some were Socialists, or the wives and daughters of Socialists. Yet even within the Owenite movement itself female support for marriage reform was by no means unanimous, and some of the same divisions and tensions appeared there as within the wider audiences. 'It unfortunately appears, that, in our various branches, there is a great dearth of the [female] sex, owing, to a great measure, to their having been prejudiced against the system, from . . . statements having been promulgated relative to our principles of marriage,' it was reported in 1838, while a few years earlier a number of women had expressed their unease over the issue, including the feminist 'Concordia' who warned Owen that meddling with marriage relations was a very dangerous business: '. . . let not the change be attempted at the expense of women's tears, of women's sorrow . . .'[28]

There was male opposition to the issue within the movement as well, but this was usually from sexual conservatives who disapproved of the whole project of marriage reform.* In the women's case the reasons for opposition were more complex. The Owenites themselves usually ascribed all female hostility to the slanders of their religious opponents, and clearly this was often true. But it did not explain either why those slanders were so

---

*William Lovett was one of a number of Owenite men who took strong exception to Owen's marriage views. According to his autobiography (Lovett, *Life*, p. 41), he first became aware of them at a dinner party held by Owen to discuss William Thompson's community proposals, in about 1830:

> When we got back from dinner our friend Owen told us very solemnly, in the course of a long speech, that if we were resolved to go into community upon Mr Thompson's plan, we must make up our minds *to dissolve our present marriage connections and go into it as single men and women*. This was like the bursting of a bomb-shell in the midst of us. One after another, who had been ardently anxious for this proposal of a community, began to express doubts, or to flatly declare that they could never consent to it; while others declared that the living in a community need not interfere in any way with the marriage question.

Whether Owen ever made such a proposal seems doubtful, since there is no mention of it elsewhere. But Lovett's apocryphal recollection of the incident probably accurately reflects his own anxiety at plans for radical revisions in marital conventions. In later years he went on to write a book in which he condemned all those who 'rail' at marriage, and elaborated his own version of companionate marriage philosophy.

readily believed or why women who were closely connected to the movement were so divided in their reactions to its ideas. Part of the answer to this, as I suggested earlier, was the difficult and sometimes sharply contradictory relationship between feminism and sexual radicalism. But behind that ideological problem lay certain changes within marriage and sexual culture, changes which were having a direct impact on the Socialist propagandists and the audiences they addressed.

SEX AND MARRIAGE IN THE EARLY NINETEENTH CENTURY

Owenism arose during a period of critical transition in popular sexual conventions. We have already seen that the 1830s and 1840s were a highly unstable, treacherous time in male/female relations – and nowhere was this instability felt more strongly than in the sexual arena. Inherited patterns of sexual behaviour were shifting and crumbling under the weight of new economic and social pressures, giving way to attitudes and practices which were often as unwelcome as they were unfamiliar. Since the history of sex and marriage (particularly working-class marriage) in this period has yet to be studied in any detail, the outline given here is necessarily fragmentary and impressionistic; yet from it we can locate certain developments which would have had important consequences for women in and around the Socialist movement.[29]

Inasmuch as these changes have been considered at all, it has usually been in terms of middle-class domestic life, which had hardened into the familiar 'Victorian' pattern even before Victoria ascended the throne. For women, this meant a narrowing of their occupational possibilities to marriage and motherhood, and a corresponding idealization of the dependent domestic role as woman's life-mission. Yet in the same years when femininity was becoming thus family-defined, it was becoming much more difficult for middle-class women to establish their own families. By the 1830s a combination of male preference for late marriage and a high ratio of women to men in the population had created large numbers of middle-class spinsters – 'surplus women', in the language of the day. Since single women of this background faced an almost total lack of employment opportunities, most were either forced into unhappy dependence on some male relative, or left to face destitution and social marginality. 'If a portionless woman, trained – accomplished only for marriage, – miss her fortune and remain single, unless she is . . . required or tolerated as a nurse or unpaid upper servant, what to the cruel world is any longer the use of her?' one woman demanded in the *Monthly Repository* in 1844, adding bluntly, 'the matrimonial market is overstocked . . .'[30]

It was from the ranks of such women, as we have seen, that many Socialist feminists emerged, just as they were later to supply the womanpower for many post-1850 feminist campaigns. The contradiction in which they were caught – increased dependence on marriage at a time when marital partners were hard to come by – highlighted the subordination inherent in conventional views of women's role. But there is also evidence to suggest that many working-class women were finding themselves trapped within a similar double-bind, both in terms of their reliance on a male provider and their difficulty in maintaining the type of stable sexual relationship which ensured such support. Among these women, however, the issue was further complicated by the changing status of legal marriage itself.

In the early nineteenth century most working-class women and men shared a household with a sexual partner at some stage in their lives, and the majority of these shared households were based on a legal marriage. But this was by no means universally true, nor were marital relations as clearly defined, in both legal and social terms, as they were in the second half of the century. Consensual unions were common in many parts of the country; separations were frequent and often succeeded by other temporary relationships. Sexual attitudes seem generally to have been far more pragmatic and flexible than in the middle class during the same period, or in the working class half a century later. These changes need now to be considered in greater detail.

Resistance to legal marriage had several sources. One was simply the expense. A marriage licence could cost anywhere between five and twelve shillings: up to a week's wage for a poorer artisan. Many of the couples cohabiting in London in the 1840s told social investigators that it was this which had deterred them. 'He's willing to marry me the first day that he can afford,' a needlewoman who lived with a dock labourer assured Henry Mayhew, 'but he hasn't the money to pay the fees.'[31] Moreover, even those who had the price of a licence were sometimes reluctant to pay it into the coffers of the Established Church. In the 1840s and 1850s dismayed churchmen reported meeting couples who refused to wed not out of lack of personal commitment 'but because they had got it into their heads that marriage was only instituted by the clergy, for the purpose of drawing money out of the public . . .'[32] The Owenites constantly drummed on this anticlerical theme, and it is clear that far from being merely an ideological idiosyncrasy of their own, their attitude reflected the widespread hostility to the Established Church which existed in most working-class areas.

Apart from these financial and principled motives for refusing wedlock, many districts simply had traditions of doing without. Among the weavers of Norwich, for example, 'in general the woman is treated as if she were a lawful wife and when a man dies she assumes the character and the assumption is recognised as his widow'.[33] Clergymen in this area often commented on the small number of weddings they were required to perform, while similar reports came from parts of the North and Wales. The needlewomen of London, the female straw-plaiters and lace-makers of Bedfordshire and Nottinghamshire, the women glove-makers of Dorset – all were said to have 'a very bad reputation' for cohabitation and illegitimacy, while the factory women of Lancashire were constantly accused of a casual approach to marital matters.[34] One visitor to a Lancashire mill 'was told that many of the most respectable looking women refused to take upon themselves the responsibility of husbands; not at all, however, from Malthusian principles, as I have understood they had not in all cases the same objection to a family. I was told, also, that matrimony was not considered a very permanent institution, and that many young couples, from jealousy and other causes of quarrel, frequently separated and took up with the original causes of jealousy or others, as it suited either inclination or convenience.'[35] Agricultural labourers, other observers claimed, were also extremely lax in these matters, although city dwellers were deemed to be the worst offenders. Manchester, Liverpool and

194

London were all said to be cesspools of sin. 'It is somewhat surprising how large a number of persons the missionaries have found living together unmarried,' one London City Mission report ran.[36] 'It is found in every street . . . ' declared another stationed in Marylebone,[37] while from Westminster came a horrified report of an area in which only 200 of the 700 couples resident were wed.[38] Some of these cohabiting couples had been together for over thirty years.[39] 'Reproof might be administered again and again to the parties themselves and the only reply would be . . . "We don't see any need of such a thing; we have agreed between ourselves and that is enough . . ." '[40]

Commentators in the early nineteenth century were particularly surprised to find these customs were 'not only a characteristic of low rural life', but even of the educated and 'respectable' portions of the working population. In Cornwall, for example, it was found that among the orderly and temperate fisherfolk cohabitation was the rule, while the miners

> are much more under the influence of constant religious teachings than is the rural labourer; and yet they are no better than he is, so far as the practice alluded to is concerned.[41]

Even among the skilled artisans of the towns, the backbone of Owenism, sexual arrangements had long remained flexible. Tailors and weavers in London often moved from one relationship to another, while among the shoemakers the cohabiting mistress was often called a 'tack'.[42] In his autobiography, Francis Place recalled with a mixture of nostalgia and distaste the casual sexual mores of respectable working people in his youth, although he hastened to add that all was much improved by the 1830s.[43]

Although such evidence is very impressionistic and frequently distorted by the combination of prurience and outrage with which middle-class observers recorded it, from it a picture of acceptable sexual behaviour begins to emerge. Sensitive witnesses of customs like 'tallying' and 'bundling',* for example, noted that when pregnancy occurred it nearly always led to the establish-

---

*'Tallying' usually referred to sexual intercourse prior to marriage, although sometimes it was used to describe cohabitation. 'Bundling' was sexual play between unmarried couples in which intercourse was not supposed to occur.

ment of the common household, and indeed in many areas marriage or cohabitation was not initiated until pregnancy had occurred.[44] In rural parishes, according to one study, between one-third and one-sixth of all brides were pregnant at the time of marriage.[45] In a case where the man involved could not or would not live with the woman, a sum of money was paid. When the weaver-radical Samuel Bamford found himself in this position he could not 'make up my mind to become the husband of the one I had thus injured. I was somewhat relieved, however, by learning that . . . the obtainment of a handsome weekly allowance was with her as much a subject of consideration as any other.' When he did wed some years later, he and his wife were already proud parents.[46] Sex was part of courting, and courting led to family responsibilities. If a man tried to enjoy the first without doing his duty by the second, community pressures and sanctions would often be brought into play, including public humiliations and loss of employment: '. . . so binding was this engagement,' one observer noted, 'that the examples of desertion were exceedingly rare'.[47] For in an old working-class community the pressure towards sexual conformity was usually very strong.

This was hardly the unregulated, unstructured 'promiscuity' which many middle-class critics believed it to be, but a code whose norms were no less compelling for their lack of legal status. This is not to suggest that such a code was any less patriarchal than the highly formalized marital arrangements found in the middle class in the same period; in itself, informality was no guarantee of greater flexibility in social roles, or greater power for women within a sexual union. For as long as women's lives were held within the constraints of child-bearing and child-rearing their material dependency on men was virtually inescapable, and their subordinate status ensured. 'The children all cling to the mother,' as James Smith noted in *The Crisis* 'whilst the means of supporting them belong to the father. She therefore is *bound* to the man by a tie, which is stronger than legal marriage itself . . .'[48] Maternal responsibilities and the sexual division of labour, rather than the marriage institution, were the primary determinants of domestic power relations.

Nonetheless, the pragmatic and relatively tolerant atmosphere found in many working-class districts in the late eighteenth and early nineteenth century probably allowed for a wider range of options in women's sexual conduct than at a later period, while the correspondingly weaker emphasis placed on female chastity meant that penalties for overreaching those options were less severe than in other classes at other times. This point is only speculative, but evidence for it is scattered throughout contemporary sources, not least those relating to the personal behaviour of working-class radicals themselves. Frances Morrison's premarital pregnancy comes to mind, as do the free unions established by the 'avowed Infidels' whom City Missionaries discovered in London in the 1840s.[49] Richard Carlile's 'moral marriage' with Eliza Sharples was part of the same pattern; and when they went to visit his native village they were given a flitch of bacon by the admiring inhabitants – a traditional gift given in social recognition of a stable consensual union.[50] Sharples herself, however, was originally from the middle class, and it is interesting to speculate whether she saw her relationship with Carlile as a way of culturally identifying with the working-class movement in which she actively participated. Certainly her willingness to enter such a relationship must have depended upon its general acceptability within plebian radical circles, or else she would have faced the same social ostracism there as she experienced in her own family. This was also true for Emma Martin, whose decision to live with her lover Joshua had no affect on her popularity with working-class audiences. An advertisement for a wife placed in *The Crisis* noted that applicants must be radically-minded but not necessarily virginal – 'no Socialist could insist upon it'.[51]

How widespread such attitudes were among the Owenites is impossible to judge, but there are hints that they were fairly common. In his memoirs of the movement, Thomas Frost recalled those 'ardent disciples of Owen who would fain have anticipated the legislature by constructing a new code of divorce and marriage for themselves', and on several occasions Owen found it necessary to warn his followers against such 'premature actions'.[52] At least one community established by a group of Owenites, Manea Fen in Cambridgeshire, was notorious as a centre of sexual heterodoxy. Its leader, William Hodson, lived in unwedded bliss with his dead wife's sister, while his followers established relationships among themselves.[53] No doubt such behaviour was often prompted by the spirit of social experimentation, but for some it simply represented conformity to existing norms. The radicals discovered living in sin in London in the 1840s, for example, resided in areas where such conduct was commonplace.[54]

More speculatively, it is possible that the widespread support for legal divorce expressed in the movement was based partly on changing attitudes towards older, informal divorce procedures which were still fairly common in parts of the working class at the time. Mutual agreement to separate, witnessed by friends or neighbours, was one method; the 'wife-sale' was another. Neither was merely a ritualized way of abandoning a partner, but rather a socially-recognized device for dissolving unions which many working people, even in the 1840s, regarded as legal divorce.[55] The Owenites highly disapproved of these procedures, particularly the wife-sale which they regarded as very degrading to the woman involved, who was harnessed and 'auctioned' in a public place.[56] But in 1842 three Cheltenham Socialists drew up a contract which 'divorced' two of them – Amelia and James Vaughan – and 'married' Amelia to the third, William Stanbury. The contract read as follows:

> This is to certify that I, James Vaughan, and I, Amelia Vaughan, do mutually and peacably propose, consent, and agree to separate and live apart; and especially I, James Vaughan, hereby do agree that Amelia Vaughan, my wife, *may live where she likes and with whom she pleases*, so long as she does not contract any debt, or cause any debt to be contracted, or trouble James Vaughan, her husband, or refuse to give up her son George when required after two years of age; and I, James Vaughan, do agree and consent that the said Amelia Vaughan should be *as free*, as regards the disposal of her person and property (should she hereafter possess any) as though she had never been married . . .

Stanbury's statement ran:

> I, William Stanbury, do hereby promise and agree to become liable for all debts the said Amelia Vaughan may hereinafter contract, and pay the same, if any be so contracted, so long as this contract is abided by . . .

The document was signed by all three and witnessed by two local members of the Communist Church – Henry Fry and Caroline

Brown – of which the other three may also have been members. When the agreement was discovered some years later the local newspaper reporting it noted that in the interval the happy couple had had several bastard children and that – most shocking of all – all three remained very good friends.[57]

Far from being the *product* of Owenite 'immoralism', then, much of the sexual behaviour found within the Socialist membership reflected older conjugal customs. This does not mean, however, that the movement did not attract a few sexual adventurers. In 1839 a young barmaid, Mary Ann Bennet, applied to the London magistrates for assistance to support her baby after being abandoned by its father, an engineer called John Joyes, who had wed her in a ceremony performed by Owen at the Manchester Carpenter's Hall (in which she claimed they had agreed that 'if either of them found anybody else who would do them greater good, and with whom they could be more happy to separate and have them'). After he left her she discovered that she was the second woman to have joined Joyes in such a Rational partnership; the first woman he had also deserted, along with her infant.[58] Naturally the Owenites denied the entire story, and since a hostile press was only too likely to print any such slanders, true or false, it is hard to assess other similar charges. George Fleming, for example, was persistently accused of deserting *his* wife until finally Mrs Fleming herself appeared at a public meeting expressly to exonerate him, where she was received 'with cheers'.[59] But if Fleming proved faithful, other Socialist leaders did not. Robert Buchanan, who was attacked and beaten by women in the Whitehaven incident, was in fact having a series of illicit relationships at the time, which made Mrs Buchanan (who was also an active Socialist) very miserable. Eventually they separated, he to a career in journalism and she to the Ham Common Concordium.[60] And Charles Southwell's story of his early sexual career reads like a poor man's version of *Tom Jones*. After a youthful marriage with a young woman who left him for another man (apparently a bi-sexual), Charles fell in love with his wife's aunt, herself a jilted unmarried mother. She became his mistress, only to be challenged by his repentant and jealous wife to whom he finally returned. 'My experience . . . has shown that keeping a *good* mistress was more productive of happiness than keeping a *bad* wife,' Southwell later reminisced, adding with a Shelleyan flourish, 'And who, after all, are the prostitutes? Not those, assuredly, who are held together by the strong tie of affection but those who own no other than a legal bond . . . The woman with whom I lived was faithful; the woman I married was false . . .'[61]

But such attitudes and behaviour were probably no more common among the Owenites than in any other male-dominated political setting. It was the misfortune of these particular philanderers to be part of a movement which had fallen under the spotlight of public censure, thereby making their everyday infidelities a source of political as well as personal difficulties.

The years in which such latitudinarian traditions of plebian sexual behaviour were making their appearance within the Owenite ranks were also, however, years in which these traditions were coming under systematic assault from several directions. The major attack came, of course, from the church, and in particular from the new puritans of the evangelical sects, who had made the task of 'taming the passions of the poor' one of their key goals. By the 1840s there were armies of volunteers engaged in this endeavour, from the City Missionaries who hunted out unwed couples and harried them to the altar; to the tens of thousands of lady 'visitors' who descended on working-class households to examine their moral condition; through to the Sunday Schools and Mechanics Institutes which constantly preached the virtues of stable family existence.[62] Within working-class communities themselves, the growth of the Methodist presence proved an indigenous source of conservative sexual ideology,* although not without a struggle in which more permis-

---

*Middle-class anxiety about working-class sexual morality was also fuelled by Malthusian fears of plebian overpopulation. In 1834 these fears found concrete expression in the New Poor Law, which established sex-segregated workhouses for the indigent and removed the right of unmarried mothers to claim financial support from the fathers of their children (which had previously been done simply by swearing an affiliation order against the man, who then had the choice of either marrying the woman or giving her an allowance towards child upkeep). Seldom was the underlying unity of evangelical and Malthusian mentalities so obvious as

sive attitudes continued to find a voice for some time. By the 1830s, the effects of all of this could be seen in a gradual hardening of the line which divided sexual respectability from 'irregular' behaviour, and the appearance of anti-erotic attitudes similar to those which prevailed in the middle class.

---

in this second measure – the Bastardy Clauses – which was defended with a judicious combination of pious moralism and economic logic. By throwing the full weight of child support on the woman, government spokesmen argued, she would be punished for the 'terrible sin' of fornication (thus satisfying God's commands) and also dissuaded from further 'imprudent' pregnancies (thus lowering the rate of population growth). In the words of Lord Althorp, women would learn 'always to bear in mind their individual responsibility and be either the wives of their lovers, or nothing at all'.

Radical response to the Clauses was very hostile, but for reasons which are revealing of a general approach towards sexual politics among many male radicals. According to nearly every radical newspaper of the period, the reason the Clauses had been introduced was 'to screen a vile aristocracy, who seduce and ruin more young girls than all the other male population put together . . .' (Davenport, *Life of Spence*, p. 22). Torrid tales of innocent daughters of the people seduced and ruined by dastardly blue-bloods or lascivious employers filled the radical press. No doubt many young women *did* meet with sexual mistreatment at the hands of their social superiors, but in general this scenario functioned less as a genuine social protest than as a powerful metaphor for class exploitation – the rape of class by class. It was, however, a wholly androcentric image whose force largely derived from the concept of women as male property. Virtually every man who wrote on the topic described how the maiden had been 'stolen' from the home of her father/brother to be 'ruined' by the upper classes. The implication was that trans-class sex only occurred when a girl had been removed from the patriarchal control of her own class, thereby becoming prey to another. 'How many of your once affectionate daughters have become careless and undutiful; and how many, being thus removed from your care, have fallen victims to the lust of selfish and unpitying monsters, whose wealth has enabled them to prey upon your unwary . . . offspring . . .?' as one Owenite man wrote to *The New Moral World* (7 October 1837), 'As fathers, as husbands, as brothers, and as lovers of your race, will you, can you, go timely on and not seek for emancipation?'

Apart from anything else, this equation of sex exploitation with class exploitation was a clear evasion of the reality of sexual power within the working class itself. It was not a lusty nobility which 'ruined' most working-class girls, but the men of their own class. 'Ah Sir,' a Welsh woman told the government commissioner investigating the effects of the Bastardy Clauses in her area, 'it is a fine time for the boys now . . . it is a bad time for the girls, Sir, the boys have their own way.' (Quoted in U.R.Q. Henriques, 'Bastardy and the New Poor Law', *Past and Present*, no. 37, 1967, p. 119)

The Clauses were amended in 1844, in the 'Little Poor Law', but the provisions which resulted still made it far more difficult for women to claim maintenance funds than in the past.

As far as the churches were concerned, then, the battle against Socialist immorality was part of a wider campaign to uplift the lower orders, while the Socialists' own sexual philosophy was formed in conscious resistance to this new prudery. The imposition of 'Victorianism' did not go uncontested. 'There is nothing unchaste . . . in the natural desire which one organized being has of being united to another,' *The Working Bee*, newspaper of the Manea Fenites, declared defiantly. 'On the contrary, it is the basis of the highest virtues and highest happiness, which can be built up by humanity. "To the pure all things are pure." This is chastity – to behold no evil in gratifying all our natural desires *in the most perfect manner of which our natures are capable . . .*'[63] It is important to realize that this libertarian strand within Owenite thinking was not merely a romantic mental posture, but also the ideological expression of a sexual tradition far more pragmatic and openly hedonistic than the one currently developing around them. When Owen polemicized against 'the priests and the rich and the powerful . . . who have united to contrive an artificial conduct for the industrious and the poor, and to call that conduct by high-sounding names, and especially to *call it virtuous*', he touched a nerve of popular resistance to puritanism which reverberated throughout large parts of the working class in the early nineteenth century.[64] 'We would not have the strongest passion of our nature shamed out of existence by the fanatical absurdities of Monks and Methodists,' as one *New Moral World* editorial declared.[65]

The appeal to a natural sexuality, unfettered by religious scruples, was a crucial part of this oppositional outlook. 'There was nothing which the priests hated more than the law of nature,' as Lloyd Jones told one Liverpool audience, 'because the law of the priests and that of nature were opposed'.[66] But sexual relations, we must recall, are never in fact 'natural' events in the way that this anti-puritan propaganda suggested. They are complex social interactions which constantly evolve and change. The Owenites, like their audiences, were living through a series of economic and social developments which ultimately undermined their older sexual culture much more effectively than the intervention of repressive religious moralists.

Generalizing about these changes across the whole of the working class is clearly impossible, but if we look again at the lives of male and female workers in the old skilled trades we can see a developing pattern of family instability and sexual insecurity. In 1833 the journal of the Journeymen Printers' Union, *The Advocate*, carried the story of 'Tom', a young printer just completing his apprenticeship, who decided to wed his childhood sweetheart. Up to this point, Tom's prospects had seemed excellent, but 'here was almost the end of Tom's felicity and the beginning of his misfortunes: not that matrimony in itself is a misfortune; for we agree . . . that early marriages should be encouraged. But . . . not for England in its present state.'[67] The rest of Tom's story – unemployment following the introduction of new print machinery into his workshop; children weeping with hunger; days looking fruitlessly for work and nights of drunken despair in the pub; followed at last by eviction and homelessness on the London streets – may seem something of a Malthusian morality tale, but the circumstances described were only a melodramatized version of difficulties facing many working people. The same changes which were undermining the economic strength of craftsmen were pulling apart family economies based primarily on male earnings. Young men who had once prided themselves on their potential as home providers were now often forced to delay marriage until they could find stable employment (which frequently led to pregnant fiancées and illegitimate children), or else chose to wed only to find themselves in 'Tom's' position.[68] 'No man who defends the present matrimonial system can defend the cause either of justice or chastity . . .' James Smith wrote:

> Let not the women deceive themselves; their situation is becoming every day more deplorable; marriage is becoming more and more formidable to the other sex; the difficulties of life are becoming every day more perplexing; and men dread the prospect of precarious warfare, with a wife and children in dependence upon them.[69]

Since these same men were usually unwilling to live a celibate existence, however, the position of women became increasingly insecure, particularly after the introduction of the Bastardy Clauses. This was a major problem in cities like London to which large numbers of girls were drawn, away from their families and communities, in search of employment. Here the transferral of traditional modes of sexual behaviour, particularly sex during courting, into an environment in which community and state sanctions no longer existed to enforce fatherly responsibilities, led to a high rate of desertion and illegitimacy. Consensual unions were common, but they were also unstable and often very short-lived. 'I'm often out of work, and the last fortnight . . . I've nothing to do,' as one needlewoman working in the London slop-trade told Henry Mayhew, 'I've got no husband, but am compelled to live with a man to support me, for the sake of my child . . .'[70] Many other needlewomen told of being in a similar position, often with tailors as their cohabitees. Relationships frequently ended when the man had to move to another part of the city to find work, or when cycles of economic depression made the prospect of growing family responsibilities too frightening. Ann Westmoreland and William Richey lived together in the Barbican district while he worked as a journeyman tailor in 1809. He was called away to the militia, and returned to find Ann expecting a child. He had other financial responsibilities, and trade had just suffered a collapse, so all he felt he could do was write to apologize and leave her to her own resources: 'For I am very Short at Present and any Business is Extremly [sic] Dead'.[71]

Sometimes the women themselves terminated the relationship, usually for fear of additional pregnancies. One needlewoman who had 'found it impossible to get on' by herself accepted the proposition of a man lodging in the same house:

> . . . the result was that I was in the family way . . . The man did his part as well he could, but the work he got was so little . . . that I told the man that he and I must part; for I had seen nothing but starvation with him.[72]

In their interviews with social investigators these women often emphasized that their lovers would have married them had not their joint economic prospects been so appalling.[73] Such statements cannot be taken entirely at face-value, since they were no doubt made partly in deference to the moral sensibilities of the middle-class inquirers, but it seems likely that they also reflected a real shift in the women's own attitudes. As practices which had been perfectly acceptable in some contexts (such as premarital pregnancy or free unions) became symptoms of domestic insecurity and personal degradation in another, so the comparative stability of legal marriage became more desirable. Women who were forced to continue living in a casual, permissive mode – like the needlewoman – often spoke of their situation with real shame. Their poverty and vulnerability made them too close to prostitutes, and as the canons of sexual respectability pulled away from such 'irregular unions' they were left stranded on the margins of decency – sexual victims, almost fallen women. 'I was virtuous when I first went to work . . .' a young slopworker told Mayhew, 'but I found that I couldn't get food and clothing . . . so I took to live with a young man . . . a tinman. He did promise to marry me, but . . . I have not seen him now for about six months, and I can't say whether he will keep his promise or not . . . I know how horrible all this is . . . But no one knows the temptations of us poor girls in want.'[74]

FEMINISM AND MARRIAGE REFORM

The combined effect of pressure from above and a changed social environment below was to narrow women's options and increase their sexual vulnerability. Under these circumstances, women were usually more interested in enforcing the obligations of marriage than in abolishing them. Safer relationships, rather than freer ones, were a common goal. It was at least partly for this reason that many women turned to the church, in the hope of imposing its conjugal code on men whose inclinations and circumstances frequently carried them beyond the reach of dependent women. When City Missionaries arrived on the doorsteps of cohabiting couples in the 1840s they were often welcomed by the women, who were only too willing to deplore the sinfulness of their condition and join with the churchmen in urging their obstinate mates towards the altar.[75] Evangelical tracts constantly harped on the edifying effects of Christian fellowship on wayward spouses. 'Religion which extends the sanctity of the marriage vow to the husband, as well as to the wife, has rescued her from a condition in which her best and most tender affections were the source of her deepest misery,' one puritan woman wrote.[76]

The success of anti-Socialist propaganda among these women, despite its explicitly male supremacist overtones, was also a sign of just how deep their fears went; fears not only of abandonment and material deprivation, but also of loss of womanly respectability. That this respectability could now be had only within patriarchal marriage was clearly stated in all the anti-Socialist literature. Woman's sexual virtue mattered because it was, in the words of one man, 'her most valuable portion', her market-value to men who didn't want shop-soiled or independent-minded property.[77] It was this quintessentially bourgeois notion which underlay the constant accusation that the Owenites intended to create a 'community of women'. 'A woman in common would be like a field in common,' as one man explained, 'there would be no concentration of care upon any particular female; all those ties and obligations which unite parties in marriage . . . would be dissolved. The effect of this would be a depreciation of women in society . . . [since] not being appropriated, they would have no exchangeable price.'[78] The same point was made in many other speeches and articles, including one which argued that this devaluation of the female sex could be mathematically calculated, since as a woman passed from one lascivious Socialist to another there would occur 'a progressive depreciation . . . at a fixed ratio of say, every 2 or 4 or 6 years. At each exchange it is abundantly obvious the unhappy female would sink in value . . .'[79]

The argument, as the Owenites never failed to point out, could only have been made by men 'so depraved by the present system of legalised prostitution, and so long accustomed to look upon women as property . . . [that] they can form no conception of a society in which both sexes would be equally in possession of social, moral and political rights . . .'[80] This was perfectly true, but unfortunately it ignored the fact that until such a feminist society was established, women's status was indeed determined by her relative value to men. In the New Moral World, women might well be free to choose their sexual partners according to love and inclination, and belong to no-one. In the Old Immoral World, however, it had not only become harder to acquire a man, but it had also become much more difficult to survive as a decent woman without one. 'Hence the fairest daughters of our isle are doomed, by a harsh necessity, to outrage their own instinctive

206

sense of propriety, of morality, and of decency, in order to procure the means to drag on a miserable existence,' Frances Morrison wrote, '[and] any individual thus violating the moral and social laws . . . [is] held to blame, in order to deter others from similarly committing themselves.'[81]

The major weakness of the Socialist marriage position, as it was initially formulated, was that it tended to overlook these present realities in favour of future hopes, substituting lyrical descriptions of love in the New Life for a political programme based on the actual conditions of female subordination. This was, understandably enough, a brand of utopianism which many women were unwilling to accept. 'The women who profess to think with you [are not] prepared for accepting . . . the change you propose', 'Concordia' warned Owen, 'to them, indeed, it would be no boon; and woe to them should it be . . . acted upon as such . . .'[82] Increased sexual freedom for men would only be compatible with increased social power for women, she pointed out, when all other sources of sexual inequality had been eliminated. Until then, greater liberty could only become greater libertinism. This contradiction, which had been implicit within all the early theoretical writings of the movement, became explicit within the popular controversy, showing itself to be not merely an intellectual disagreement but a division rooted in the changing *realpolitik* of contemporary sexual life. 'The women will not allow men to become the fathers of their children without having a pledge of their attachment,' an Exeter Socialist warned after discussions about community plans there, while reports from other branches revealed a similar disquiet in the female membership.[83] Catherine Barmby's brother wrote that he had 'personal knowledge' of some women, 'the partners of some of our best socialists' who were 'opposed to our proceedings' for this reason. He urged that free lectures be delivered to women in which they would be told 'that in our first community the present marriage ties will be held valid, and that not till we have educated man to be a rational being . . . do we intend placing him in that relation to the other sex, that the laws of nature require . . .'[84]

A few years earlier, James Smith had received a letter from a couple who had decided to 'anticipate the natural freedom of the sexes' by establishing a moral marriage. His response to this was sharply disapproving. 'Such unions as these are much more unequal than legal marriages,' he warned, for they provided no protection for women whose menfolk 'are always tempted to desert, by the consciousness of freedom, the pleasures of release, and the pecuniary saving it would effect'.

> Nothing indeed can be more binding than love while it continues . . . but where [love] fails . . . the case of a simple and confiding female . . . is at present very hopeless. There is some respect acknowledged to be due to a woman who is deserted of her husband; but society has no pity for one who is foresaken of her gallant. He is acquitted; she is loaded with reproach . . . and left with the burden of a family, whom she is unable to support by her own earnings, and with whom she may be left to struggle in pauperism, while the father is raising up another brood elsewhere . . .

'A moral marriage,' he concluded, 'is not so much an emancipation of woman as an emancipation of man.'[85]

Under the pressure of this dissent, the Owenite 'line' on marriage, which had originally been represented only by Owen's *Lectures*, began to dissolve into a range of positions, veering between various re-workings of his libertarian philosophy and a belated recognition of the vulnerability of women, particularly unmarried women. On one side, a steady flow of propaganda began to emerge aimed at reassuring women that neither Owen nor his male followers intended to abolish marriage entirely. The *Lectures* continued to be published, but with a lengthening string of appendices supporting the new Marriage Act, laying down regulations for marriage and divorce in the new communities, and guaranteeing the permanence of marriage and 'the happiness of the . . . Female Sex' under Socialism. When they were re-issued for the third time in 1838 it was with an accompanying editorial in the *New Moral World*: '. . . no change in the present marriage system can take place, unless it be preceded by an entire change in our religious, educational and economical institutions; for so long as woman is trained to be the helpless dependent of man for mere subsistence, and only tolerated by courtesy in the enjoyment of any social or moral rights, it would be a mockery and delusion to talk of change in any other respect.'[86] This point was made with increasing force over succeeding years. 'WE DO NOT

PROPOSE ANY ALTERATIONS IN THE LAW OF MARRIAGE UNDER THE EXISTING INSTITUTIONS OF PROPERTY . . .' Charles Southwell's 1840 tract (addressed to 'the women of England') stated, '[nor] before . . . woman . . . takes her place in the social scale, not as the cringing slave, but as the FRIEND AND COMPANION OF MAN.'[87] In the same year the annual Congress of branch delegates voted in favour of a resolution declaring their adherence to the existing marriage laws, and calling only for a new law of divorce. It was accompanied by a statement from Owen in which he distinguished 'promiscuous intercourse' ('of savages, without affection') from 'natural intercourse' ('the intercourse of refinement, sentiment, and affection') and warned against confusing the former with the latter – a warning which was quoted and reprinted endlessly. Natural sexual affection, he now argued, was not merely transitory sensual excitement, but 'lasting emotions of love', which under Socialism would 'almost always' lead to lifelong unions. 'Permanent marriage is natural,' one Social Missionary wrote in 1841, 'or, in other words, the inclination of the human mind is to permanency of the marriage contract . . . which is best calculated to promote health, happiness, and harmony . . . Thus far we go with the majority of legislators, priests and philosophers in the world . . .'[88] And when Socialists in the local branches gathered together to sing from their Social Hymnbook, the hymn they sang titled 'Marriage' ran:

> United by love then alone
> In goodness, in truth and in heart
> They both are so perfectly one
> Their bonds they never can part.
> Their union has love for its
> ground,
> The love of the man and his bride;
> And hence in affection they're
> bound
> So close they can never divide.[89]

In 1840 the Owenites began providing weddings for their own members (since under the terms of the new Marriage Act any building could be certified for this purpose), and these were usually dignified public demonstrations of Socialist propriety.[90] When two members of the London A1 branch wed in 1845 'a large

Eve and the New Jerusalem

number of persons . . . assembled in the Hall, curious to witness an act of which a great portion of the public believe we take no cognizance'. They were treated not only to the ceremony itself, but also to a good deal of organ music and a few Social hymns ('we never saw our choir more spirited in their performance'), followed by an address from another branch member in which he congratulated the happy couple 'on the example they had shown of our appreciation of the marriage law, apart from the trammels the priesthood of this and other countries have continually encircled this natural law of nature [sic]'. The ceremonials concluded, everyone retired to a wedding breakfast and a discussion of the problems of the Queenwood community.[91] When Alexander Campbell wed another couple in the same year he reminded them of the seriousness of the step they were about to take, warning them that 'selfish considerations of any kind' were wholly out of place in love-marriages. He could not resist concluding, however, with a reminder that the affections were not governable by the will: 'I do not ask you to promise to love each other to death, for to do that is beyond your control; and I might as well tell you to be beautiful or to fly.'[92]

Public debates between Christian men and Socialist men became lively competitions over whose moral system produced happier wives and more dutiful husbands. The following exchange between Reverend John Bowes and the Owenite Lloyd Jones occurred during a Liverpool debate in 1840:

Bowes: 'With respect to what Mr Jones had said about a man changing his affections, was it because a wife did not always retain her virgin beauty that she was to be deserted? His . . . wife was not now what she was fourteen years ago, but was she to be less beloved by him on that account – was he to cast away from his breast the rose which had regaled his smell because it had lost a little of its verdure . . .? Woman was the friend and companion of man, not his slave . . . and should not be thrown aside to please a capricious love of change.'

Jones: 'Mr Bowes has said his wife was not what she was fourteen years ago. He was ashamed that Mr Bowes should have made such an assertion . . . He . . . was a married man, and his wife was older now than on the day he married her; but to him she was as young and lovely as ever . . . It was not the formation of a face, the shape of a nose . . . which caused an attachment; but the affectionate and kind soul . . .'

210

Jones then went on to refute Bowes' claim that Christianity elevated the status of women ('woman in the present state of society was the slave of man – he was the lord of the creation'), and argued that only under Socialism would 'woman . . . stand recognized by man as his equal, in all the dignity of her own nature'. When Bowes attempted to come back on this by claiming that in a Socialist community all women would be held in common and degraded accordingly, Jones leaped in: 'Mr Bowes has taken it for granted that if a man's wife was not his own property, she was the property of everyone else; and if she was not his property, she was nothing . . .' Both men called for a vote from the audience (which included a 'great number of respectably-attired females'), resulting in a resounding victory for Jones.[93]

Earlier in this dispute Jones had tried to repudiate Owen's *Lectures* as an unrepresentative statement of the Socialist position. At a later point, however, he declared himself willing to defend even its most libertarian passages, and topped this off by quoting Shelley on the 'crime' of loveless marriages. Arguments seesawed back and forth, one often contradicting the other, leaving opponents plenty of room to expose all the inconsistencies. When Owen confronted his arch-opponent John Brindley in Bristol he was so confounded by the hostility of the audience that he tried to deny authorship of certain embarrassing passages from the *Lectures* and insisted that his position was identical to that of the Quakers (who married by simple declaration before their congregations). Eventually, however, he was forced to admit that the words 'all couples married without affection are living in prostitution' were his, which nearly caused a riot. When he tried to clarify this by saying that it was 'marriage for money' he abhorred, he left the course wide open for Brindley, who immediately turned to the audience of five thousand working people and demanded 'Who among you has married for money?' One hand was raised and the man to whom it belonged – who had misunderstood the question – severely heckled. 'Women of Bristol . . .' Brindley exhorted his audience, now in a state of great excitement and anger, 'hurl back upon these Sensualist Socialists the foul slander that your affections are to be purchased with "money"! Let every husband bring his wife, every brother

211

his sister or aged mother, and let the expression of female indignation prove once and for ever that English women will never forget what is due to female virtue!' Great cheering; and then hisses for Owen, who finally, after being hounded mercilessly by his opponent and the crowd, shouted out that he had never intended to destroy female virtue or family life, that 'he did not mean that individuals should not have their own wives and their own children, and everything else within their own house, but that they should have all these and tenfold more'. This was followed by loud cheers, presumably from the men.[94]

The most important shift in the Socialist campaign occurred, however, when the female lecturers took up the issue. 'It is by the teachings of such instructors alone,' as one branch secretary wrote of Margaret Chappellsmith's marriage lectures, 'that we can hope to see woman emancipated. The lessons which might be looked upon suspiciously when proceeding from men, will be listened to with attention and without prejudice when uttered by one of themselves . . .'[95] It was not only the sex of these propagandists, however, but what they said, that won female approval. Frances Morrison's 1838 tract was the only major piece of writing by an Owenite woman on the marriage issue.[96] It began by insisting that strict enforcement of marriage laws would be necessary until the 'licentious libertinism' of the present age was replaced by the egalitarian unions of Socialism. 'Under existing circumstances . . . it is necessary that the majesty of the law should interpose in order to insure that fidelity which the vehemence of temporary passion could never guarantee.' And even when Socialist communities had been widely established, it was not 'indiscriminate wantonness' which would be encouraged but what Engels was later to call 'individual sex-love' – permanent partnerships based on monogamous affection. 'But you ask,' Frances went on 'what external security is there for mutual fidelity?'

> I will tell you. In the first place, they will not be strangers to each other, which causes so much suspicion as well as danger in parties going together. In the second place, being equally intelligent, there could be neither chance nor inducement for knowledge to triumph over ignorance, which is invariably the case under the old system. And thirdly, in a rational state of society, when the sum of human

happiness would be equally felt by all, and where the general
interests would be indissolubly united, it is difficult to imagine how
any human being, so connected, could cause pain to another, and
thereby disturb the general harmony that prevailed.[97]

The echoes from a past community life, where no-one had been
a stranger and everyone had been tied into common rules of social
intercourse, are not difficult to hear. Similarly, a letter from
Margaret Chappellsmith to *The New Moral World* emphasized
how the experience of 'continuous association' in the sexually-
integrated pursuits of a community would create feelings of love
between women and men 'more binding, more enduring, than
any legislative enactment'. But where love alone did not suffice it
would be necessary to use 'public opinion' to ensure that no
'desecration of character' occurred. Hence the public declarations
which would be made before the assembled community as a
whole before either marriage or divorce was allowed. 'Under such
circumstance, infidelity or jealousy are not likely to arise . . .'[98]

All the feminists used their lectures to dwell on the miseries of
sexual exploitation in the Old Immoral World (often in terms not
so different from those employed by their pietistic opponents),
and to promise women a new life of sober husbands, well-fed
children and personal dignity. A reporter at a meeting in Bury
where Margaret spoke to 'a large number of ladies' recorded how
'cheering' it had been 'to see their countenances brighten up, as the
fair lecturer opened to them . . . the happy and lasting unions
which would be formed under new and rational arrangements;
every sentence was loudly responded to by the audience . . .'

> She described with glowing eloquence the homes of both rich and
> poor; the licentious profligacy, and promiscuous intercourse of the
> present absurd system . . . the manner in which children are now
> trained, and the superior advantages which must result from the
> adoption of the rational system.[99]

This talk ended with two men getting up on the stage to oppose
Margaret, only to be 'literally hissed off the platform' by the
largely female audience.

These women almost never described sexual relations in the
celebratory language employed by male libertarians. For them,
sexual passion was usually 'the animal propensities' (Frances

213

Morrison) or 'the fleeting vapour of an excited fancy' ('Concordia') which, if experienced by women at all (which some doubted) was usually discounted in favour of emotions of a more solid and civilized sort, such as sympathy and mutual respect. None would have used the language of Owen's *Lectures* or written a passage like the one in Charles Southwell's tract where he characterized sexual desire as 'an instinct of reproduction' which 'impels men to women by a law as certain as that which points . . . the needle to the pole . . .'[100] (Laws could never confine it, he added, for 'like steam' it would always 'force its way . . .') The equation of sex with compulsive processes was a male mode of thought; women, on the other hand, firmly asserted the ruling place of reason in all properly-ordered human relations. This had been a characteristic of nearly all feminist thought from Wollstonecraft onwards, but was particularly pronounced in the writings of poorer women (whether indigent middle-class or working-class) whose material insecurity would have made the price of 'natural' behaviour that much higher.

A hostile little exchange in the correspondence columns of *The New Moral World* illustrated very well this difference in attitude. It began with a letter from a needlewoman (probably the mistress of a small establishment) calling herself 'Syrtis' (who at one point described herself as an Old Maid) arguing that men and women experienced the sexual relation in fundamentally different ways. 'I am no man-hater – no enemy to matrimony . . . and far from me is removed any desire to deprecate a tie which if contracted wisely and virtuously must have a beneficial influence: but I have the fullest conviction that love with men rarely exists as a senti-ment, and with women, as seldom sinks to a passion.' The 'only foundation' on which a happy marriage can be based, she went on, is 'esteem and respect' and not that temporary 'state of excitement quite unfavourable to moral observation and reflection . . .'[101]

If Syrtis did not regard her views as 'those of a *man-hater*', they were 'certainly not those of a *man-lover*', came the indignant response of a man calling himself 'Homo' a few issues later. He went on to deliver a spirited defence of the sexual drive – 'the deeply-rooted, all-pervading, and indestructible attraction between the sexes', the 'dammed and pent-up stream that bursts

214

its banks', the 'eagle . . . of the air, soaring twixt heaven and earth', and so on and so forth – concluding in an apocalyptic assessment of the historical importance of sexual energy: 'what noble undertakings and heroic deeds – what desire to please – what cultivation, moral and intellectual – what masterpiece of literature and art; in a word, how much of excellence in all that MAN [sic] undertakes and achieves, is inseparably connected with, and in reality proceeds ultimately from, that "mere propulsion of nature which guides all animal creation"!'[102] Syrtis did not directly respond to this, but a letter from her a few months later returned to her earlier themes, warning that the sentiments which drew women into relationships often blinded them to the 'mire and wretchedness, the poverty and anguish of spirit, which awaits the wife of a poor man' until at last they found themselves in the 'iron grip' of marriage to men 'who require of their wives the labours of Hercules, with the servility of the spaniel'.[103] What of the 'romantic passions' then?

> Yet am I willing to admit that the ills of love may be the effects of an ill-organized state of society, on one of the greatest blessings of which our nature is capable, but stimulated to the detriment of much that requires attention and encouragement, and that this powerful passion should rather be watched with jealous eyes lest it extinguish virtues of more modest . . . origin.[104]

None of these women ever openly raised the issue of contraception, although lack of control over reproduction was obviously a crucial factor shaping their views on sexuality. Of all the Socialists, only William Thompson and Robert Dale Owen had argued for birth control as a way of separating sexual pleasure from reproduction, thereby allowing women the same measure of sexual freedom as men. (Although there were hints of similar ideas in the Manea Fen community.)[105] Instead, the collectivization of child-rearing was always posed as the solution to this fundamental inequality, since it would allow women to 'divorce' men without fearing for their children. 'Here, my friends, is the grand *advantage* which a state of rational community provides,' Frances Morrison told her female readers, 'namely, that your children are secure from want, or the fear of want. This we cannot too much dwell upon . . .'[106] But that sex should be enjoyed for its own sake, by being entirely separated from the prospect of motherhood, never entered their writings. This was no doubt due to the strong anti-Malthusian feeling in radical circles at the time ('What? should the working classes now be told *when they may breed . . .!*' as one woman wrote), but it also reflected more complex factors, such as the identification of unreproductive sexuality with prostitution, and a deep, half-conscious fear of making themselves wholly accessible to masculine desires – of becoming, in Syrtis' words, 'mere toys of man'.

Yet these women were no prudes. Socialism gave them an alternative to sexual conservatism. By imagining a society based on women's social and economic independence, they were also able to envision a time when men and women would offer a sweeter life to each other, emotionally and physically. Frances' tract quoted Robbie Burns on the joyful passions of sensual love and sighed for a time when such pleasures would be shared by social equals. Even Syrtis believed that someday all those 'ills of love' which women experienced would be transformed into 'the greatest blessings of which our nature is capable . . .' In the meantime, they supported marriage as a civil contract only, and argued for the right to divorce on both feminist and class grounds. They rejected the new puritan dogmatism as vigorously as they eschewed the free-love ideology of some of their male comrades, hoping to find a route between these two unacceptable options which would be palatable and credible to the women in their audiences. Often they succeeded. But more often their voices were drowned in the mutual slandering of male ideologues, Christian and Owenite alike, arguing over the limits of sexual liberty in terms which remained largely male-defined. Had the Owenite position been a less ambiguous, more female-oriented one from the beginning, its popularity among women would no doubt have been much more widespread. But as it was, the contradictions within the Socialists' own propaganda left it wide open for an oppositional campaign which undermined Socialist feminist support, and ultimately destroyed the movement's credibility among large numbers of women.

VII

WOMEN AND SOCIALIST CULTURE

Socialism was not only a political commitment – it was a way of life. Joining a Socialist branch meant automatic *entrée* to a wide range of cultural and social events intended not only to educate and entertain their participants, but also 'to bind them together with ties of communal fellowship', thereby providing an emotional preparation for the New Life to come. Or as the Brighton Owenite leader, William King, wrote in the early years of the movement, 'friendly feeling, among the members generally, must not be left to chance and accident. It must be . . . enforced as an imperative and paramount duty and obligation. When a man enters a Co-operative society, he enters upon a new relation with his fellow men' . . . and also with his female associates, for whom the duties of collective sociability had particular meaning.[1]

Central to this radical culture was the joint participation of the sexes. In general, the 1830s and 1840s were a period of sharpening cultural segregation between men and women, in both the middle and working classes. The Owenites' insistence on sexually-integrated dining tables, for example, was in direct contrast to the usual public arrangements (whether in a genteel gathering or a plebian Friendly Society dinner) where women were either excluded from male company entirely or else placed in overhead galleries where they could, in the words of one Owenite, 'see the lords of creation enjoy themselves'.[2] In 1840 Catherine Barmby attended a Socialist dinner at the John St Institution in London and was so pleased by the mixed seating policy there that she immediately wrote an enthusiastic letter to *The New Moral World* congratulating her comrades on their principled behaviour. 'There is no custom so unimportant as not to deserve attention . . . for we know that habit and example are the great

217

teachers of the world . . . therefore it is especially agreeable to see that our social brethren have sufficient moral courage to come forward, and furnish society with a better example. May it be imitated, for good effects must follow it.'[3] She went on to suggest that the usual male rationale for women's exclusion from such gatherings – that they were potentially offensive to feminine sensibilities – was really only a chivalrous mask disguising the conviction that any female presence in a public setting *must* be a sexual presence – an argument amply borne out by the reaction which the Socialists' dinner-table reforms provoked in their opposition. The shiver of titillation with which the arch anti-Socialist, Edward Hancock, viewed the social life of the London Owenites in the late 1830s was typical:

> On certain nights they held a Social Supper . . . and when they met, it was customary for a member to take the first seat that was unoccupied, and so on in rotation, the women sitting on one side of the table and the men on the other, no distinction made between married and single . . . the consequence was that a common intimacy arose between all parties, and . . . a number of illegitimate children were begotten . . .

Such, he concluded, were the inevitable results of the 'promiscuous mingling of the sexes' practised in the Socialist branches.[4]

In addition to welcoming women into all their assemblies, many Socialist branches made active efforts to ensure that female voices would be heard on these occasions. When the Huddersfield branch established weekly discussion classes for its members, for example, they adopted the Methodist class system, in which ten-member groups each elected their own 'conductors' for three month terms, on a rotational basis. During the class meeting itself every member was required to speak in turn on a subject chosen at a previous meeting, in order that each 'might have the opportunity of expressing their views and feelings, their doubts and confidence, concerning the Social System'. This highly democratic system was the most effective, the branch emphasized, in encouraging active female participation.[5]

Theoretically, women were also expected to play an equal role in the government of the movement, both at a local and national level. Branches which proved backward on this issue were occasionally made the target of official reproof. When the Social Missionary Alexander Campbell visited the Cambuslong Co-operative Society and discovered that they allowed their women members no vote in their meetings he insisted that this policy should be amended:

> The ignorance of man and delicate feelings of woman, have hitherto done much to deteriorate the female character. Instead of being brought forward into the midst of public assemblies, to hear and take part in the discussions on local or national subjects . . . they are generally left at home . . . If you want to secure your success, you must take your wives and little ones along with you in the march of improvement, and give a vote to your female members when of age.[6]

But if the women did vote in most branches, it was apparently not for each other, since the number of female officials was always very low. After 1835, only a few branches had female Presidents or Secretaries, and only one – the Finsbury branch in London – had a continuous history of female leadership through-out the late 1830s and early 1840s. Even branches with a high level of women's involvement (like the Bolton branch, where in 1836 'the sisters' were said to 'outstrip' the Owenite brethren in 'the march of progression')[7] were dominated by men at the executive level. In 1839 a woman member of the Edgbaston branch complained to *The New Moral World* that 'having, for some time, attended the lectures and discussions of the socialists, and heard much talk about emancipation, education, etc. of females, and their right to equality with the other sex, – I wonder our social friends should . . . preach one thing and practise another.' Why, she demanded, were women not automatically assigned an equal number of seats with men on all the Owenite councils? 'This being done, I think many women would soon acquire sufficient strength of mind to speak their sentiments in public . . .'[8]

Similar complaints were also voiced over the lack of female Social Missionaries (only Emma Martin, Margaret Chappell-smith and Frances Morrison were employed as lecturers, although many other local women spoke on a voluntary basis), and over the level of women's representation at the annual Congresses. Mary Wiley, the Secretary of the Finsbury branch for several years, seems to have been the only female delegate to attend a Congress (in 1843), although a large number of women attended in an unofficial capacity.[9] The issue was raised year after year, but with no visible result. *'No female delegate* has been elected for Congress,' a London Socialist newspaper noted indignantly in 1840:

> Why is this my friends? Why? ask yourselves! . . . We know many females who stand high in the estimation of their fellow Members, who have, notwithstanding, been passed over – not one, I believe, has been, at least to our knowledge, ever nominated. Is it that the iron hand of Conventionalism, pressing hard on the destinies of one-half the human race, has not found, even amongst the most advanced ranks of Social Reformers, one who has shaken off the shackles of civilized bondage and who dare, in the face of the day, proclaim the 'Equal Rights of All', woman not excepted?[10]

What provision did the Central Board intend to make for the representation of female interests within the organization? another woman ('Astrae') demanded the following year: 'At the last two Congress meetings the necessity for the appointment of women delegates . . . was most apparent . . . how can . . . so large a proportion [of the membership] as the women constitute, be left without opportunity or means to explain the judgements or opinions they have formed?'[11]

Exactly why the feminist principles of the movement had so little effect on its own power structure is not entirely clear, although no doubt the 'iron hand' of male prejudice was partly responsible. Female diffidence was also a problem. 'It being so novel a thing for females to speak in public assemblies, and the idea of all eyes being, at once, directed towards them, is it at all marvellous that . . . a sufficiency of courage is wanting to speak their sentiments?' as one woman demanded.[12] But in addition, it is necessary to see this marginalization of women as part of a broader development within working-class politics as a whole – a shift away from locally-based, direct-action mobilizations towards the more formalized structures of national political organization. Dorothy Thompson has argued that it was this process of formalization within the Chartist movement which led to a decline in active female participation there.[13] And a similar transition can be traced within post-1834 Owenism, as the trade unions and early co-operatives were replaced by the regularized, representational structures of the Rational Society, with the result that women who had been very active in organizing and leading local unions moved to the sidelines of Socialist policy-making forums. Executive councils, delegate meetings, minuted conferences with agendae and elaborate rules of order: all this paraphernalia of formal democracy was time-absorbing and intimidating to women who had far less free time than their husbands, and much less public confidence. Direct action on grievances, particularly when entire communities were involved, was very different from incessant meeting-going and complex organizational issues, and women who had been militant and vociferous in the earlier context often fell silent in the later one – a problem which remains very much in evidence in radical organizations today.[14]

In addition, prejudice against a public role for women was growing within the working class, and although the Socialist leadership officially set its face against such views, attitudes within the wider movement varied. Narrowing definitions of feminine respectability made it difficult for women to take on active political roles without risking the sort of public slandering endured by Emma Martin and Margaret Chappellsmith. Politicking was increasingly seen to be not only a disreputable activity for women, but de-sexing: '. . . females are too often found to forget the modesty and diffidence which alone makes them estimated by the other sex,' one Manchester woman wrote to *The New Moral World*, 'they seem to forget, while railing against what they consider the restriction imposed upon them by the tyranny of custom, that, even if these laws were altered, it is a very doubtful question whether mankind . . . will ever recognize a woman who has not made her conduct strictly agree with the sentiments of virtue which mankind at present tolerate . . .' She went on to add: 'These, from experience, I well know to be the sentiments of many of the Socialists . . .'[15]

Egalitarian principles tugged in one direction while the tightening claims of respectable femininity pulled in another. This tension had been present within feminism from the 1790s on. But within Owenism it was heightened by an internal emphasis on the moral and cultural 'improvement' of working people which often involved a deliberate re-orientation of plebian social life around a feminized ideal. Women's family-centred, nurturing culture came to be seen as a desirable alternative to masculine, work-centred, competitive culture: a development which had important implications for the status of Socialist women.

FEMINIZED CULTURE

The drive for collective self-improvement was a keynote of Socialist life. A puritan zeal for personal reform, combined with a burning thirst for 'useful knowledge' and social respectability, were typical of the upper working class in general and of radical workers in particular, whose radicalism almost invariably implied an overt rejection of the more debasing features of popular culture.[16] In the Owenites' case, all these impulses were further stiffened by their faith in the revolutionary power of Correct Character Formation. To make Socialism, it was emphasized, it was first necessary to make Socialists, and nearly every item on the movement's internal agenda was geared to this task of cultural 'elevation': a collective bootstrap-pulling operation on a grand scale.

This project, it should be noted, was in sharp contrast to the integrationist and disciplinarian goals of other would-be 'improvers' of the working class in the same period, although the means employed were often strikingly similar. Teetotalism, educational reform and 'rational recreation' were campaigns which engaged both Socialist and bourgeois-philanthropic energies in the 1830s and 1840s. But whereas most Owenites saw these reformist endeavours as 'stepping stones to a New Social System', their competitors fervently hoped they would lead working people into sober, industrious behaviour within the existing system – a difference in political emphasis which led to numerous clashes between, for example, Socialist temperance advocates (who urged that the money saved through abstinence from alcohol should be invested in communities) and Evangelical temperance advocates (who banned Socialists from their meetings and tore up their temperance tracts).[17] In town after town, Owenites invaded local agencies of moral improvement in an attempt to convert them into vehicles for Social Regeneration, and in town after town this led to acrimonious meetings, the expulsion of Socialist agitators, and often the establishment of Owenite counter-institutions, such as the Halls of Science which were founded as radical alternatives to the bourgeois-sponsored Mechanics Institutes.[18] The improving spirit, in other words, could take many directions, and in the Owenites' case the route chosen was usually fiercely independent, democratic and class-conscious: a style of working-class respectability which soon became as detestable to its upper-class opponents as the cries of an angry rabble. A letter from Sir Charles Shaw to Lord Ashley, written in 1843 in response to his lordship's request for information on the state of the lower orders, informed him that the 'best legally conducted people' to be found in the working population were 'the Socialists, who are all teetotalists and readers' yet no less abhorrent for that: 'all know their morals to be bad for society . . .'[19]

One of the two major prongs of this Owenite improving campaign was a drive to create a new style of working-class recreation; the second was the development of an alternative educational programme. Let us begin with the recreation issue.

With the collapse of the Consolidated Union in 1834 'the area to which first principles could be applied in [Socialist] branch life' was narrowed 'from everyday working life' to 'leisure-time . . . alone' where Socialist activities competed with a host of other, less edifying recreations available to working people.[20] 'When we see how the leisure hours are employed . . . by the masses of people . . . it is lamentable enough,' one Cambridgeshire Owenite sighed in a letter to a community newspaper there. He went on to list 'alehouses, race courses and skittle alleys' as a few of the 'low and debasing' amusements which absorbed the time and money of workers – or rather of working men, since none of these were female pleasures.[21] The alternative to these masculine entertainments which he and others urged was a sober, gentle, family-oriented social life which allowed for the maximum participation of women and children. This was the philosophy behind the multi-functional Social Institutions established in most branches whose aim, in the words of the prospectus for the Worcester Social Institution, was to provide 'large public rooms wherein the working class might assemble with their wives and children to acquire and communicate useful knowledge, and wherein they might have innocent recreation and rational amusement at so trifling an expense as to be within the means of the poorest'.[22] In 1840 one of the leading activists in the Manchester branch told the story of his early years as a radical organizer in that city, when the only meeting venues were pubs whose inebriated clientele indiscriminately cheered progressive orators and reactionary opponents alike. Fired by this experience, he and his fellows had 'determined upon attempting to elevate the character of the working classes . . .':

> At first everyone said it was a mad trick – it was the greatest
> absurdity to talk about the working classes having halls of their
> own – schools of their own – music halls of their own – libraries of
> their own; why it was said the plan was preposterous . . . it was the
> rich, and the rich alone (it was said) for whom these things were
> intended; but he and his friends were determined that the poor
> should have them too. They therefore called the working classes
> together, and explained . . . how easy it would be for them to get
> instruction for themselves and their children, and how much more
> enjoyment there would be in the family circle if they joined in music
> and song at home, instead of the son being at the public-house, the
> daughter roaming the streets, and the poor mother breaking her
> heart at home. Proud was he to say that they had succeeded to a
> considerable extent; the working classes were now determined to be
> elevated; they were determined no more to be slaves . . .[23]

By 1840 the Manchester Owenites had built their own Hall of Science (an enormous Gothic edifice with 'Doric columns' and seats for three thousand) with funds raised by selling one pound shares to local working men who (in the words of one) 'having tasted the sweets of education, sobriety, and strictly moral habits, are desirous of facilitating the means of imparting the like character . . . to their brother workmen'.[24] Within a few months, the Hall was able to offer its members a rich agenda of activities, from evening classes and Sunday Schools ('for interested persons of both sexes'), to dances, picnics, day-outings and an occasional Grand Social Festival with dinner and dancing. A band was formed which practised during the week for its regular Sunday morning performances. Tea parties (to which 'female members are particularly invited') were frequent and popular, and often provided the occasion for a short lecture on women's rights by a local speaker. 'Community dress' was sometimes worn at these functions, as a way of symbolizing the connection between present comradeship and future communalism.[25]

Similar halls were established in more than two dozen Owenite centres by 1842, although in some cases (as in the Worcester branch) they were really only small workshops which had their fittings altered, benches added and a plaque hung proudly over the door, 'Hall of Science' – 'not that we had much science,' the local Social Missionary in Worcester, George Holyoake, recalled, 'only a preference for it . . .'[26] In every case the building became the focus of a cultural life whose closest equivalent, in Old World terms, was undoubtedly the plebian chapel. In the Salford Social Institution, for example, 'a good book of music was formed, singers were drilled, a hymn book published, a form of service arranged . . . [for] the Sunday meetings' when a sermon would be delivered on some Social topic. In 1836 the branch purchased a 'delightfully toned seraphania' to accompany its congregational hymn-singing.[27] Other branches rehearsed choirs and held regular Sunday services, while some even provided their own funerals and child-namings, in addition to the weddings which we have already described.* Christian holy days, no matter how solemn,

---

*This pilfering of the sacramental rites did not increase the Socialists' popularity with the clergy, particularly when these ceremonies were then invested with 'blasphemous' content. Naming rituals, for example, were often the occasion for a little diatribe against the doctrine of original sin, while funerals were not only displays of mournful appreciation of a lost brother or sister, but also infidel demonstrations on a large scale. The Socialist who had died an unrepentant freethinker ('No fearful terrors – no false hopes, depressed . . . or . . . excited him . . .') would often be followed to the grave by hundreds or even thousands of comrades. Hymns were sung and sermons delivered (the chosen text on one occasion being 'Whatever thy hand findeth to do, do it with thy might, for there is no work, nor device, nor knowledge in the grave whither thou goest'). If there had been opposition from local clergy, huge mobs of curious or hostile townspeople would also arrive, sometimes to jeer, occasionally to stone or attack the procession, but often to stand awed by the solemn scale of the event. 'We are glad to hear of . . . these solemn and catching ceremonials,' James Morrison wrote after one such funeral in 1834 (*The Pioneer*, 22 February 1834), 'they make a powerful impression on the public mind, and produce more permanent and decided results than the most eloquent speeches . . .':

> make a new ceremonial for yourselves – a rival ceremonial – which shall win the people on your own side, by the very same arts by which kings and generals, bishops and monks, have in all ages secured popularity to themselves. Theirs was the tyrant's ceremony – let yours be the people's ceremony . . .

were celebrated with a blasphemous gusto which would have made even hymn-singing suspect to most Methodists. Christmas Day 1839, for example, was observed by the London Owenites with a party whose 'entertainments' included 'music, dancing, singing' and various 'scientific' experiments with laughing-gas, electricity, 'electro-magnetism, chemistry, geology, phrenology, optics'.[28] On the same day the Liverpool branch also held a Social Festival which was duly reported in *The New Moral World*:

> A good band was in attendance. We had country dances, quadrilles, hornpipes, marches, recitations, glees, songs, etc.; and . . . an address suitable for the occasion, recommending strict adherence to the great principles of our profession . . . It made my heart glad to see so many of the wives and children of our married members there, all enjoying themselves, more than they had done since the pleasing days of courtship; and I believe it was the wish of us all that the time may speedily come, when we shall be enabled to meet in community, where we shall enjoy these and much greater pleasures, without measure and without end.[29]

Such events usually attracted (in the words of one Manchester man) 'many who have hitherto held aloof from us', particularly many women. When the Bradford branch introduced an orchestra into its menu of entertainments as a way of luring women, they met with great success: soon female attendance was 'uncommonly numerous'.[30] Dance classes, balls and concerts were all very well attended; so well attended, in fact, that they encouraged further sneers from the opposition, who accused the Owenites of turning their Halls of Science into dance-halls with political speechifying as a mere 'tax on admission'.[31] In at least one case the accusation came uncomfortably close to the mark. In 1844 the secretary of a London branch wrote to *The New Moral World* bewailing the collapse of all activities in his branch except dance sessions, which were held three or four times a week. 'Our friends have paid by far greater attention to their lower than their upper understandings,' he concluded dolefully.[32]

But if the social medium occasionally drowned out the Social message, in general the opposite was true: not only did these playful events attract women and men for whom lectures would have been too dry an initiation, but they also provided an important training-ground in Socialist principles. Before the dancing began at one Social Festival in Liverpool, for example, John Finch rose to remind those assembled of the natural equality of all mankind. 'You will not, therefore, be found quizzing each other's dresses, language and manners,' he urged them, but 'will treat each other with the greatest kindness, like children of one family'.[33] Fellow-feeling and mutual respect were the emotional foundations on which Socialism would be built – including mutual respect between the sexes which was encouraged in a host of little ways, from censure of obscene language (Robert Dale Owen was 'girlishly sensitive to the coarse and ribald jests in which young men think it witty to indulge at the expense of a sex they cannot appreciate')[34] through to constant reminders to male Socialists to smarten up before attending Social functions, and always to remove their hats. 'To sit covered in the presence of *one* female is a breach of decorum.'[35] (Apparently these admonitions were necessary, since complaints of dirty clothes and rowdy behaviour at Owenite events were fairly common. One report from Manchester complained of members talking during lectures and lounging about in the aisles 'as in a promenade'.[36]) If a certain confusion between comradely courtesy and conventional etiquette was evident in all this,* at least the motivating impulse was always the same, for 'each individual [to] do all in his and her power to . . . increase the general happiness . . .'.[37]

For female Socialists, this style of social life had a three-fold significance. First, it drew on strands within working-class culture which were traditionally associated much more closely with women than with men. This was most evident in activities

---

*The line which divided mutual respect between the sexes from high-minded prudery was a very fine one indeed, and Socialist feminists occasionally crossed it. In 1841 Margaret Chappellsmith wrote a letter to *The New Moral World* (18 September 1841) in which she criticized certain branches for allowing waltzing at their Social Festivals, thereby encouraging an extension of 'that revolting familiarity which has arisen' from large numbers of boys and girls being congregated in the same workshop, without anyone to check impropriety or sustain modesty'. This familiarity arose, she went on to add, because of the 'pernicious error that industry is a badge of disgrace, which subjects every milliner, dress-maker, and servant, or factory girl, to the rude touch and offensive speech of any vagabond . . . We should strive to create virtuous dignity in females, and respectfulness towards them in males, and this, it appears to me, we do not if we allow the familiarity of the waltz.'

modelled on the plebian church, which had long been a centre of feminine sociability, but it could also be seen in all the other gentle and genteel 'entertainments' on offer, which appealed to well-established female tastes. Secondly, this was a much more accessible form of political culture than the one it was trying to replace, based almost entirely on the male domains of workshop and pub. The pub in particular had acted as a focus of radical organization throughout the early nineteenth century, and the Owenites' decision to abandon it in favour of their own institutions was a deliberate step towards a feminized form of political development. 'It would be injudicious to bring families to a public house, but this is only another reason why a society should have a house of its own . . .' an early article in *The Co-operator* explained, 'why should females be so studiously excluded from cheerful and friendly meetings?'[38]

Finally, the Owenites' campaign for moral and cultural improvement led to an immediate enhancement of women's social status, if only by providing them with respectable and respectful male companions. Here again the question of drink is an obvious case in point. Throughout the early nineteenth century, male alcoholism wreaked havoc on poor homes and the lives of women within them, soaking up wages which were desperately needed for family necessities and often leading to the wife-beating for which Englishmen were notorious.[39] Socialist temperance propaganda always played on this theme of male selfishness and female misery, and since most Owenites were temperance supporters there was rarely any drink served at Social functions. 'Excess, intoxication and noisy revelry, have too often attended the banquetings of the "old world", as the secretary of the Socialist London District Board noted in 1841, 'but these we have put from us', thereby also allowing them to terminate 'the old practice of excluding the ladies' from such gatherings.[40] A Huddersfield Socialist on his way home from a Social Festival there could not help but contrast

> the sobriety and civil manners of those who had participated in our 'feast of reason' with the brutal language and bullying conduct of the unfortunates who were reeling from the public houses; and when I consider that those who were *now* so sober and courteous might, but for the circumstances of our festival, have been similarly

situated to the individuals around me, the good moral results of these kind of institutions, and the general want of them appeared to me clear and self-evident as light amid darkness.

'The attendance of females is larger than formerly . . .' his letter concluded.[41]

In creating an atmosphere of cheerful respectability within their branch meetings, then, the Owenites not only provided women with 'a foretaste of the pleasures to come' in community life, but also allowed them the more immediate satisfactions of sober husbands and courteous treatment. The enforcement of moral discipline was in itself a modest version of feminism, as the high level of female involvement in the temperance movement and later 'social purity' campaigns demonstrated.[42] But cultural puritanism and moral discipline, although they served to protect women from some of the harsher features of male dominance, also had the effect of policing women themselves. The Socialists' attempts to order their branch activities in ways which met women's particular needs became inextricably connected with a wider cultural re-definition of female needs themselves. The issue of drink serves again as an example of this process.

In insisting that meetings be held outside pubs so that women could attend, the Owenites were actually helping to enforce new standards of *female* temperance. Before the early nineteenth century, working-class women's presence in pubs, either alongside men or in all-women groups (like the Female Friendly Societies), had usually been taken for granted. It was only with the rise of the moral reform movements – conservative and radical alike – that alcohol and respectable womanhood came to be seen as wholly incompatible.[43] Even the working women of the 1834 unions had often met in pubs, but by the 1840s few Socialist women would have done likewise. Nor, of course, would most of their husbands, and no doubt many women found the benefits of a teetotalling husband outweighed the loss of their own drinking rights; but it is important to see how the self-improvement mentality of the movement could actually serve to promote narrowed definitions of feminine respectability.

In all cases, opposition to women drinking was bound up with a higher valuation of their significance as wives and mothers, and this was as true of the Socialists as it was of other moral improvement campaigners. The whole drive towards sober, family-oriented leisure activities within the Owenite movement was fuelled by an underlying belief that the type of emotions and experiences associated with domestic life were the ones which should be nurtured in the collectivist environment of the branches. And although in principle these values and emotions were supposed to be generalized across the membership as a whole, in practice they frequently devolved on to the women alone. No one ever suggested, for example, that the way to prepare men for the New Moral World was to have them teach children or perform child-care at branch meetings. Fatherhood was never the ground on which men entered political life. Instead, the 'moral preparation' of children was seen as women's prerogative and one of their central contributions to the building of a Socialist society. In 1839 the women of the Manea Fen community were addressed by a leading male resident there:

> Sisters of the community! you who have all to gain and nothing to lose, – you who have been counted politically dead in law, – you whose rights have never been recognized except by the social system, remember, I say, you must get knowledge; on you mainly depends the character of our youths; on you depend mainly the peace and happiness of the community circle. Without you the superstructure would be unfinished; you, the chief cornerstone that the builders rejected, have become the bulwark of our peace and unity.[44]

The 'self-improvement' of women would lead to the moral regeneration of society as a whole. The practical implications of this idea were most obvious in the Socialists' policies with regard to women's education.

FEMALE EDUCATION

The most important self-help aspect of Owenism was its internal educational programme. 'Educate! Educate!! Educate!!!' the branches were exhorted in 1840, 'Let every institution forthwith have its Sunday and Day school, distribute tracts and works explanatory of the Social System with unsparing liberality, let the lecture rooms be made as attractive as possible, and be as seldom empty and unused. Commence, where possible, private classes, lyceums, reading rooms and other means of instruction and innocent recreation. Let us not be outstripped in the endeavour.'[45] Two years later delegates to the Seventh Annual Congress were able to report that twenty-nine branches had 'Social Institutions' of which eight seated over 1,000. In addition, twenty-two branches held regular classes, nine had day-schools and twelve operated regular Sunday Schools where both adults and children received elementary and 'social' instruction. Twenty branches had libraries of their own.[46]

Women were usually encouraged to participate on an equal basis in all these educational activities, from the sexually-integrated class in chemistry held in a hired room over a pub at Dalkeith branch,[47] to the separate 'female classes' offered in many branches from 1830 on. Special emphasis was placed on women's attendance at all membership discussions, partly to coach them in Social Science (like the men, all women members of the Rational Society were supposed to pass a test in the Social principles before admission), but also to give them a forum in which to discuss their own condition. An agenda of discussions in the Ipswich branch, for example, included: 'The Emancipation of the Female Sex', 'May the Fogs of Religious Animosity be speedily dispelled by the Genial Sunshine of Universal Charity', 'The Formation of Character', 'The Connection between Woman and Civilization', and a discussion of the question of Miracles.[48] In the Manchester Hall of Science, it was reported, 'the evils of marriage are among the favourite topics; the women are told that they live in slavish dependence upon the men; the men are in their turn, flattered that they are the producers of all wealth; they are the bees, the rich the drones . . .'[49] Classes like the one held in the Huddersfield branch, modelled on the Methodist class system, were adopted elsewhere, as a method of ensuring women's active participation.

The popularity of these classes and lectures among women was at least partly due to the very low level of educational opportunities available to them elsewhere. Throughout the first half of the nineteenth century most working-class girls acquired what little schooling they could in dames' schools (schools run in the homes of local women who were often minimally educated themselves) or Sunday Schools, which generally provided children with only enough education to allow them to carry out their religious duties.[50] Charity day-schools, most of them church-sponsored, provided a rudimentary literacy training, heavily supplemented by courses in needlework, cooking, and so on. But even this was beyond the reach of girls whose home duties or paid employment left them no time for daily attendance. 'The education of the females of the lower classes, in many cases does not extend even so far as a knowledge of their letters,' one woman complained bitterly to *The Pioneer* in 1833, 'in the agregate [sic] to sew and read (and that but very indifferently) is the sum of their acquirements. Yet these females are to be the bosom friends of the most useful portion of our population . . .'[51]

Adult women were no better served; partly, it was claimed, because of the hostility of their husbands who, in Frances Morrison's words, 'tremble at the idea of a reading wife . . .'[52] The autodidacticism so central to the lives of radical working men usually played little part in the busy daily lives of their women-folk. 'Most working men now feel to read a newspaper is a want as urgent almost as the desire for food . . .' as one journalist in a radical newspaper noted, 'yet few of them take any trouble to create in their wives this taste for reading', fearing that it would lead to all sorts of problems with dirty homes and untended kitchens.[53] The Mechanics Institutes established by middle-class educationalists for working men in the early decades of the century did not admit women either, probably for similar reasons. This policy soon elicited protests from Owenite feminists.

The Owenites' role in relation to the Mechanics Institutes is a good example of how the question of women's education arose in the context of a wider struggle over the control of working-class education.[54] The Institutes were established by philanthropic industrialists who aimed to provide male workers with the skills and, more important, the disciplined work attitudes required in the expanding manufacturing sectors. The intrusion of radical elements into these Institutes was therefore viewed as a highly dangerous development. Socialist speakers were banned; Socialist texts were weeded out of Institute libraries and some-times even destroyed.[55] Political and religious disputation was prohibited, and radicals who persisted in trying to initiate such debates were often expelled. A number of the Owenite Halls of

Science were founded by men who had either been expelled or
seceded from a local Institute, including the Halls in Manchester,
Coventry and Sheffield. (The Sheffield Hall was established after
a local Socialist leader had been sacked from his post as the
Mechanics Institute's secretary for placing Socialist books in the
Institute library. The new Hall announced its independence with
a defiant inscription over the door: 'Under the Patronage of
Nobody'.[56]) A fierce competition then developed between these
radical Halls and the Institutes, in which the question of women's
education became one lively point of dispute, along with issues of
democratic control, class aims and political affiliation. 'Would
you improve intellectually and socially the *men* of the industrious
classes, improve the *women* also,' William Thompson urged in an
early article supporting working-class control of the Institutes,
'Let your libraries, your models, and your lectures . . . be equally
open to both sexes. Have not women an equal right to that happiness which arises from an equal cultivation of all their faculties
that men have? . . . Long have the rich excluded the poorer
classes from knowledge: will the poorer classes now exercise the
same odious power to gratify the same anti-social propensity
– the love of domination over the physically weaker half of their
race? By such conduct the best fruits of their own knowledge
would be lost . . .'[57]

In 1830 a fierce struggle developed over democratization of the
Manchester Mechanics Institute, in which female admission was
one of the reforms demanded. A breakaway Institute was eventually established which immediately initiated classes for women
and urged radicals in other towns to do likewise.[58] By 1840 the
Owenite reputation for supporting reforms in this area was so
well known that when a group of women petitioned the
Birmingham Mechanics Institute for classes and were refused
('such a thing would ruin the Atheneum in a month' the directors
told them) they immediately turned to the Owenites. Delighted,
the local branch provided them with classrooms and instructors
and then used the incident as a handy stick with which to beat
their middle-class competitors.[59]

When one considers the reasons proffered by some Owenite
leaders for this female instruction, however, it is difficult to see
how even the staunchest sexual conservative could have objected.

The men who seceded from the Manchester Mechanics Institute in 1830, for example, urged women's classes on the grounds that 'young women should be taught the duties of housewifery', and a decade later the founders of the Manchester Hall of Science were defending their own decision to provide instruction for women on the basis that 'numerous scenes of domestic thriftlessness, discomfort and contention' would be thereby eliminated. 'Elevate women everywhere, and the effects will speedily show themselves throughout society . . . *That* is the keystone of the arch . . .'[60] When the Mechanics Institutes finally did begin to admit women in the mid-century, it was for exactly these reasons, since 'the absence of a systematic provision for female instruction' had proved to be 'a fertile source of improvidence and domestic unhappiness' in the homes of working men.[61] 'Even the zealous friends of female education are afraid to press its claims on other than utilitarian and comparatively low grounds,' one feminist complained in the mid-century; 'Women are to be educated . . . in order to qualify them for the duties of wives . . . and servants . . . How rarely is it argued that women should be educated in order that whatever capacities they possess may be permitted to grow to their full height . . .!'[62]

Yet within Owenism there were others willing to defend women's intellectual development on those higher grounds as well, including a number of feminists who demanded education precisely in order to free women from the narrow boundaries of domestic concerns ('the stupid, mind-destroying, mill-horse routine of domestic slavery' as one woman called it).[63] Arguments veered back and forth. Articles defending women's innate mental equality ('are the sensations of woman weak . . .? All persons affirm just the contrary. Then I argue that they ought all to admit . . . that the associative power infused into her ideas is also equal . . .') appeared in the Socialist press alongside letters explaining that women ought only to be trained in non-analytical subjects, since their concerns were with 'matters of the affections' rather. than 'the cold calculations of masculine intellect'.[64] A good deal of this propaganda, whatever its particular line, was produced by the lower middle-class wing of the movement, but it was generalized to apply to working-class women as well, who were alternately exhorted either to educate themselves for home duties or to prepare for 'a wider sphere of action'. 'To be a good wife, nowadays, means nothing more than to be a *good drudge,*' George Fleming told the 1840 Rational Society Congress, but under Socialism all this would change:

> The Socialists want women to be educated equal to themselves; they want to place women in such a position, as that the lecture-room, the ball-room, the study of the stars and earth, might be to her, as to others, a source of amusement and pleasure. (cheers) They wished women to be free – to assert their own dignity . . . as the wives and daughters of free men, enjoying equal benefits with them. They wished her no longer to be the inhabitant of the cellar and the kitchen. (cheers)[65]

It was this blend of ideals – the emancipationist and the 'utilitarian' – which lay behind the classes which Owenite women themselves organized, of which the best-documented example was the Ladies Class established by the women of the London A1 branch in 1844. The class began with a few women in March and quickly grew to over sixty members. Its goals were laid out in a statement of 'Objects and Laws':

> To promote the individual and collective happiness of every man, woman and child, without regard to country, colour, or class.
>
> 1st.   By the circulation of useful, practical information.
>
> 2nd.   By the cultivation of social and industrial pursuits, and the taste for literary and scientific pursuits, – including the song and the practice of the pianoforte.
>
> 3rd.   By acquiring a practical knowledge of the science of human nature, the science of the formation of character and the science of society, as developed in the outline of the Rational system of society; and by giving all possible assistance to the establishment of Communities of mutual interest.
>
> 4th.   By taking an active part in the business of the Branch, and assisting each other in times of affliction.[66]

The cost of membership was 2d. a week, and another 1d. for those wishing to contribute to a 'health insurance fund' for themselves and their families – an echo of the old Female Friendly Societies. Like most Female Friendly Societies also, the class was self-governing, with its own elected executive whose President (first a Mrs Skelton and then a Mrs Hornblower) also sat on the local branch executive.[67] Classes in reading, writing, arithmetic, grammar and history were reported to go so well that 'an advance from this elementary instruction to the more arduous studies of moral and physical science' was urged, 'for the time when woman shall, by equality of education, assume her rightful place in society . . .'.[68] Discussions were wide-ranging, moving between 'abstract rights, and the principles of political and social economy' to topics which conventional society would have deemed most improper for feminine ears. On one occasion, for example, a Mr Ellis was brought in to deliver a lecture on 'The Duty of Man as a Father' in which he

> dwelt at some length on the transmission of moral and physical
> diseases – the evils of near alliance – the want of a proper
> knowledge of anatomy, physiology, etc., and trusted much to the
> effects of the Ladies' Class to remove the existing false delicacy
> which prevented its acquirement.[69]

This class was obviously considered a model of its kind. Its members, according to some male supporters, were 'consistent demonstrators of our principles, living exponents of the superiority of morality and intellect over the stupid negative requirements of theology'[70] – a reminder that one of the other functions of education for women was to wean them away from pious 'superstition'. The intellectual preparation for Socialism, in other words, involved not only mental enlightenment but a change in those characteristics thought feminine: instead of 'false delicacy' there would be frank discussion; instead of religiosity, rationality; instead of 'foolish giddiness', intellectual courage and moral strength. But always there remained the suggestion that these were merely 'relative virtues', developed not to meet women's own expanding needs, but those of their husbands and children. 'The wife to an almost unbounded extent determines the happiness of her husband and children,' the men of the A1 branch reminded their sisters in a solemn public address, 'If she is ignorantly selfish . . . she is a drawback upon his improvement, a poison to his existence. On the other hand, if she is enlightened . . . she pacifies and improves him, and sweetens the paths of domestic life . . .' It was to this end, they assured the women, that they offered the class their heartfelt support.[71]

Attempts to prefigure the egalitarian social relations of the New World within the boundaries of Old World existence were obviously going to run into practical limitations set by women's existing needs and responsibilities. In many ways Owenite branch life represented a genuine attempt to come to terms with those conditions and offer women an improved status within them. Certainly there were few other contemporary milieux which offered as much to women, intellectually and socially, as the Socialist movement. Nevertheless, the lack of female leadership in the branches was symptomatic of underlying ambiguities in Owenite thinking which were never resolved. Even the communities themselves reflected similarly divided and ambivalent attitudes towards women's role – but here such problems were further complicated by a series of practical and political crises which not only made feminist reform difficult, but eventually undermined the Socialist movement as a whole.

VIII

PARADISE LOST: WOMEN AND THE COMMUNITIES

Between 1821 and 1845 seven Owenite communities were established in Britain, along with a host of smaller experiments in which individual Owenites participated. Nearly all had short, crisis-ridden lives. The longest-lived community was also the only one initiated and supported by the national Owenite organization: Queenwood, in Hampshire, which survived from 1839 to 1845. All the others were founded either by individuals or small groups who received sympathetic encouragement from their fellow Socialists, but no centralized financial backing.

All the larger communities, with one exception, were built in the countryside, often on the personal estates of their founders. They supported themselves through a mixture of agriculture and domestic manufacture, although in many cases the preponderance of skilled townsmen in the membership made the agricultural side of production problematic, to say the least. Most suffered from overproduction of goods for which they lacked local markets, plus problems of general economic mismanagement and considerable personal tension within the membership. Under the weight of such difficulties they usually lurched from crisis to crisis before finally collapsing into financial disorder, lively recriminations, and bitter disillusionment.[1]

Given this pattern of rise and decline, it is perhaps not surprising that most of the communities failed to meet the expectations of Owenite feminists, as far as improvements in the position of the female residents were concerned. Survival was top priority, and there was often little space in which genuine social experimentation could occur. Nonetheless, even within these limits some attempts were made to restructure sexual relations, and the question of women's status remained a lively issue among the community builders.

The women who joined the Socialist communities appear to have been typical of the Owenite female membership in general, being mostly working class, married, and – as all the communitarians themselves emphasized – eminently respectable. The women who lived in the Queenwood community (the only one whose membership was really documented in any detail) certainly fit this description, although since Queenwood drew its residents from Socialist branches all across the country its population was more heterogeneous than communities which were locally based.

Membership lists for Queenwood published in 1843, 1844 and 1845 show that of the twelve women living in the colony in May 1843 (out of a total population of forty-three) all but one were married (and the single girl was only sixteen years old); by 1844 four more spinsters had joined (and one married woman had left); by 1845 there were fourteen married women in residence, and four single.[2] Almost all the women living in the community in 1843 were still there two years later (an extraordinary testimony to women's power of endurance, as we shall see). The 1844 census also listed the former and present occupations of some of these women. Harriet Hornsey was a dressmaker, married to a whitesmith. Amelia Cotterrill was a former Worcester straw-bonnet-maker whose husband, Charles, had worked in the building trades. Elizabeth Robinson was an unmarried twenty-year old from London who was listed as a former 'domestic', but whose payment of fifty-five pounds into the Community Fund suggests a more affluent background (although this sum may well have been subsidized by her local Owenite branch). Lucy Rowlett and Catherine Ingham had been servants in Northampton and Manchester respectively; they were aged thirty-seven and twenty-three and were both unwed – an interesting reminder of how difficult it was for women in service to find husbands. The remaining two single women – Emma Marsden of Edinburgh and Mary Ann Deane of Halifax – had been a dressmaker and a 'weaver of lastings' in the Old Immoral World.[3] The occupations of all the other women were unlisted, which probably meant that their income-earning activities had been restricted to such part-time, home-based employments as they could fit in along-side their domestic duties. (The founder of another community – Manea Fen in Cambridgeshire [1838–41] – claimed that the women there had all been unemployed in the Old World, 'and boldly stated . . . that they would do no more here than there'.[4] But since the husbands of these women, like those at Queenwood, were all working men [tailors, shoemakers, wheelwrights, engineers and so on], it seems likely that they too had formerly been employed in that sort of hard 'women's work' which is usually invisible to those who simply take it for granted.)

Although there were only a few single women in the communities, others expressed interest in trying out the communal life. Unmarried women of poor backgrounds were frequently cited in the Socialist literature as one group most in need of a supportive, communal environment. In his will, William Thompson had left a sum to be used specifically in assisting spinsters to enter the Cork community which he hoped would be built after his death.[5] (In fact the entire estate was lost after a lengthy legal battle in which Thompson's views on marriage were cited as evidence that his money would be used for immoral purposes if handed over to the Owenites.) Several branches appear to have had a large number of single women either as members, or hovering about on the edge of their organization, and in 1842 Owen received a touching letter from one of these women which no doubt spoke for many more:

Sir, – Having seen at the house of a friend *Cleave's Gazette* of February last, in which there is some account of the 'Social Community' at Tytherley, in Hampshire, I take the liberty of addressing you respecting it . . . I am a solitary female, the survivor of all my family, without any ties or connections on earth; and the sense of loneliness, of living, acting, thinking, always for self – self alone – without one heart to reciprocate one feeling, or share a joy or sorrow with me, is at times painful in the extreme. I at present obtain a livelihood by keeping a day school. I am a good needle-woman, and can turn my hand to any feminine employ, not absolutely laborious, for hard work I have never been accustomed to. I am middle-aged, – single – and sighing to be part and parcel of and with some of my fellow-creatures. It struck me, when I perused the account above-named, that I should like to join the Social band, if there were no impediments in the way. I did years ago, when the

idea of such communities was first thought of, consider how delightful they would be could they be brought into operation; but they
appeared completely Utopian, nor did I understand that the plan
had met with success till this paper of Cleave's fell into my hands.
You will, I trust, be so good . . . as to give me any other information which would be requisite for a stranger to learn . . .[6]

Not every Owenite, it is important to emphasize, was as
entranced by the possibilities of community life as this woman.
Some were not community advocates at all. It was the commitment to constructing a New World inside the shell of the Old
which characterized early Socialism, not the community strategy
per se. In the 1830s, it was the quasi-syndicalist scheme for a
workers' government which captured the imagination of general
unionists, some of whom openly repudiated the idea of colonies
on the land. Communism had to begin 'in cities; in trades and
manufactures; by combinations of intelligent workmen, continuing to prosecute their own employments . . .' James Smith
wrote in *The Crisis* in 1833, 'to leave the city, to commence
digging and scraping with a spade and a hoe, is a retreat to
savagism nearly'.[7] Many early co-operative societies made no
mention of communities in their plans, while others viewed them
only as distant goals rather than the immediate object of co-
operative endeavours.[8] Even in later years, when nearly every
branch of the Rational Society subscribed to the National
Community Friendly Society (the 'official' body responsible for
the establishment of Queenwood), many branches invested far
more energy and funds in local propaganda work than in
communitarian projects (although this might well have been due
to the stranglehold Owen was acquiring over the centralized
community plan.)[9]

Nonetheless, Communities of Mutual Association remained
the primary route to the new life for most Socialists throughout
the 1830s and 1840s, and their dominant image of the utopian
future. There were several reasons for this, of which one in particular needs to be strongly emphasized. At a time when class relations across Europe were at a high pitch of tension, and the spectre
of bloody insurrection overhung all political developments, the
Owenites were deeply committed to a peaceful path to social
reform. Having set their faces firmly against demands for violent

revolution, they built a strategy which relied not on coercive power but on the potency of human hope and the force of human example. 'If we have neither the wealth, nor the power, the persuasion, to induce all around us to give their exertions a new direction,' William Thompson wrote, '[we] must be satisfied with attempting to carry into effect, on a small scale, for and with a few able and willing, in their several stations, and as an example to all, that system of united exertion which will accomplish for the few who voluntarily engage in it, the greater part of those advantages which the same system, if universally and voluntarily adopted, would produce for all.'[10] Particularly after the bitter struggles of 1833–34, it was clear that employers were not going to stand by and watch a workers' commonwealth built within their own industrial establishments, so to move off and do it elsewhere seemed the only pacific solution – as well as the only one which, in the words of *The Pioneer*, would succeed not merely in 'lopping off the branches of oppression' but 'eradicate it in its deepest roots'.

Moreover, by initiating these exemplary colonies outside the range of competitive social relations, the Owenites provided themselves with a space in which to work towards the fulfilment of their socialist ideal in its broadest sense – a society based not only on new modes of production and distribution, but also on new patterns of personal relationships. 'A co-operative community is not a simple Joint Stock Company, composed of unselected persons, residing . . . in dispersed and isolated dwellings, employing other people to do their work . . . and meeting only occasionally to divide the profits,' as one Birmingham Socialist wrote sternly in *The New Moral World*:

> The essential externals of community are closely connected residences and constant, intimate, and familiar association . . . [in which] the work of moral and intellectual training must be systematic and unremitting, and of a higher character than that which can at present be anywhere pointed out . . .[11]

It is necessary to stress these aspects of the communitarian strategy, since so many studies of Owenism have tended to ascribe the community-building zeal of the movement to a series of external social influences rather than the internal logic of the

Owenite position itself. The communities were the necessary out-come of a specific style of Socialist thought, which relied on example and personal transformation. Nonetheless, certain social factors were also important in determining the specific directions which community thinking took.

Most accounts of early nineteenth century communitarianism have described it as a reaction to the alienating effects of indus-trialization and urbanization, combined with a romantic faith in the land as a source of material independence.[12] Land-hunger was certainly very evident in the movement, even among workers who had been city-dwellers for generations. 'The great remedy for poverty amongst the operative classes is the possession of land . . .' a 'Female Operative' told a London Owenite audience in 1834, 'the rich mine from which all wealth proceeds . . . the source and foundation of all life; the garden of all production . . .'[13] When this agrarian communism was combined with the type of romantic pastoralism found in virtually all utopian writings, it struck a responsive chord in workers living in crowded, unhealthy conditions, with growing unemployment and persistent fears of total destitution. One man wrote to *The Crisis* that he found it 'very pleasant' to turn his thoughts away from the 'crowded and still increasing town' in which he lived towards an image of sunny meadows, filled with quiet cattle and laughing children, where 'as soon as the demon competition shall have been expelled from human transactions, we shall hasten to resort in . . . societies of hundreds and thousands . . .'[14] 'Ah! for that happy day . . .' Moreover, with the enactment of the New Poor Law in 1834 the contrast between Owenite community hopes and that other alternative now facing indigent workers – the workhouse – must have persuaded many that it was better to build a new society for themselves than be thrust into the one provided by a Chadwickian administration.[15] 'Working men and mechanics . . . put your shoulders to the wheel, and those same houses you have built for pampered wealth build for yourselves, your wives and children; those walls you have plastered, those iron balconies and railings, those splendid doorways and porticoes; the cabinet furniture, sofas, pianos and organs; build them for yourselves, on your own land, under your own regulations; and be assured that without you do so . . . ruin must overtake you, and sore distress follow . . .'[16]

Such a vision obviously had important implications for family life. Earlier I argued that the Owenite model of communist social organization was essentially that of an 'enlarged' family, an extended kinship network bound together by affective ties of love and mutual obligation. The construction of this quasi-familial ideal, I suggested, was at least in part a reaction against the growing impersonalism of everyday life in a commercialist society. But did it also, as some commentators have suggested,[17] reflect specific changes in the familial experience of the Owenites themselves?

To identify any common pattern of family change within the Owenite ranks is difficult, since the pressures exerted on family structure by the economic and social developments of the period varied from one group of workers to another. This was true even within the relatively narrow sector of the working population to be found in Socialist branches and communities. The Salford textile workers who joined the Queenwood community had a very different domestic experience, for example, from that of their fellow colonists who had formerly been employed as shoe-makers and tailors in London and Liverpool. For whereas in the first case the coming of the factory system had meant the decline of home-based industry and the subsequent separation of family and home from work and factory, in the second the rise of the outwork system had led to an expansion of home-based industries employing entire families (although at such an appallingly high rate of exploitation that little time was left for anything resembling home life).[18] Despite the dissimilarities, however, both cases also shared certain features common across a wide sector of the manufacturing population in these years, notably a rising level of male unemployment accompanied by a disruption of internal family economics – changes which, as we saw in the case of the tailoring workers, often generated serious tensions between husbands and wives. Men dependent on the earnings of their wives and children; women unable to integrate waged work with domestic tasks, either because waged work had moved outside the home (as in the factory districts) or simply because there was too much of both to do (as in the sweated trades); the subsequent disintegration of older patterns of authority and shared expectations – these were experiences shared by families from Spitalfields to Salford, in both the declining trades and the new industrial regions. Moreover, these developments were accompanied by others – increased labour mobility, urbanization, the decline of older community and kinship networks – which together served to isolate the individual family unit and place it under enormous stress.[19] The Owenite protest against 'single-family arrangements' needs to be seen in this context of increased isolation and insecurity in working-class domestic life, just as their communalist strategy needs to be understood partly as an attempt to recoup a wider context for domestic existence.[20]

Interesting evidence for this can be found in the familial language employed by Socialist community propagandists, and also in the eager attempts made by small groups of Owenites, or even Owenite couples, to set up communal living arrangements: 'bigger homes for ourselves and our families' as one man called them. Socialist newspapers carried many advertisements and notices from would-be experimenters like these, including one placed in *The New Moral World* by 'two married individuals' asking for a third 'intelligent Socialist' to join them in a cottage outside London;[21] another from a Liverpool man, suggesting that twenty families there should set up a collective household (by which he estimated they would save £253 annually in domestic costs);[22] and one from four fustian cutters who had set up house together with all their families in Failsworth.[23] The intended atmosphere of all these enterprises, as one ardent communalist wrote, was 'that of diffuse and extended affections'.[24]

As well as intending to restore and extend the affective features of family existence, Owenite community schemes also aimed to re-create the unity between home and work which had characterized many artisan trades prior to the Industrial Revolution.[25] Here, as in so many things, Owenite proposals involved a complex blend of the conservative and the innovative. The communalized work and living arrangements of the communities, it was claimed, would restore what many workers perceived as a golden age of home-based industry – but now on a collectivist basis. Production and consumption would be re-united, not in the isolated family unit as before but in communities where labour could be deliberately allocated between domestic and productive tasks on the basis of the general needs of the 'Social Family' as a whole.[26] It was only in this way, William Thompson claimed, that industry could be simultaneously modernized and 'domesticated'. 'The isolated domestic manufacturing system, unaided by machinery, is gone, never to return . . . [and] only by co-operative industry, can domestic manufactures be rendered compatible with machinery . . . with increased and increasing knowledge, thus only will they be rendered compatible with universal intercourse, and include a thousand times more than all the advantages . . . of that supposed happy and simple state of human society when domestic manufactures, carried on by hand labour, prevailed.' To think otherwise, to look back longingly to a golden age of 'cottage economy', was a 'sickly' nostalgia, he added.[27]

Once this new, technologized version of 'domestic' industry had been established, it would permit a reduced division of labour and flexibility of work roles. Men would no longer have to think of 'trudging down town to work in cold mornings with your tin kettle in hand, and at twelve o'clock eating a cold dinner in your fist out of it away from home', as one man wrote, but instead would be able to labour in their own fields and workshops 'beside your wife and children and friends'. Women would no longer be left 'drudging at the wash tub, up some . . . garrett', but would join in all the work of the community, alongside their menfolk.[28] A romanticized vision of both sexes reaping hay in the golden fields provided the paradigm for this ideal. A play published in *The New Moral World* titled 'Community, a Drama' was typical of Socialist propaganda in its depiction of male and female communitarians sowing wheat, gathering in the harvest and – in the evening – teaching classes in natural philosophy to their children, who had spent a happy day in the collective nursery.[29] Other publicists portrayed women nursing, working in 'bright, airy workrooms' on various manufacturing jobs, and – of course – performing domestic chores 'under the most scientific arrangements possible'. 'Great as are the advantages of co-operation to men, they will be found . . . to be much greater to women', the leading female character in the 'Community' play enthused.[30]

But what did these ideals mean in practice? Evidence on the role of women in the Owenite communities is fragmentary, and in the

Owenites' reports themselves it is often difficult to detect where fantasy ends and reality begins. Male supporters of the feminist cause frequently made extravagant claims about the reforms achieved in community life. At Ralahine in Ireland (1831–33), for example, 'in all respects women were upon terms of equality with males':

> they received the same education, they engaged in the same kinds of labour (but the easier parts were allotted to them), every means were adopted to remove or lessen domestic drudgery, and the performance of such services belonged to youths under seventeen. The wages of the wife made her independent of her husband for support . . . she, therefore, was a help-mate, companion, friend, and equal, and not a servant, cypher, or slave . . .[31]

Similar statements were made about nearly every other community at one time or another, usually by men and usually to audiences outside the community itself.

The reality, at least in terms of the working lives of the female communitarians, seems to have been based on a rather uneasy blend of principled experimentation and economic expediency, and in most cases the results conformed fairly closely to existing patterns of female labour outside the communities. Communal housework was the major innovation. At Spa Fields community in Islington (1821–23), for example, domestic work was performed by the women 'under a system of combination' which freed them for other types of labour, including teaching in the community school and taking paid employment 'for a moderate portion of the day'.[32] Their wages were pooled to pay for the children's education. Since Spa Fields was inhabited by twenty-one families of London craftsmen, most of these women probably continued either to assist their husbands in their trades or to work in one of the traditional female industries. Sewing, drawing and dress-making were among the services listed in the circular with which the Spa Fields colonists solicited custom from the 'Nobility and Gentry' in 1821.[33] No doubt shared housework lightened their overall workload, but it hardly revolutionized their existence.

Similarly, the two dozen women at Ralahine community* were

The Ralahine Agricultural and Manufacturing Co-operative Association was established by a philanthropic landlord in County Clare, John Scott Vandaleur, on his own estate in 1831. The residents were mostly his own tenants. The all agricultural workers who had worked on the land all their lives, and continued to do so on the communal land.[34] An infant school was established which provided full-time childcare (from six in the morning until six at night) while the women were in the fields, and a collective housekeeping system was initiated, but whether these reforms had the emancipating effect that Socialist commentators later suggested seems unlikely (particularly when we read that the wages of the women were – as they had always been in the agricultural areas – about half that of the men . . .)[35] Another early community, Orbiston in Scotland, employed women on the land, in traditional female manufacturing trades, and as teachers, but attempts to introduce a co-operative cooking and housework system were so ill-organized that 'the wives, disillusioned at the disorder, wanted to march out'.[36] Far from providing women with the flexibility and independence which propagandists had promised, the integrated domestic economy of the communities seems mostly to have generated an enormous amount of hard work, frequently under chaotic conditions which made those tasks much more difficult than they had been in the Old Immoral World.

This was certainly true at Queenwood (or Harmony, as it was also known). Since this community was the 'official' project of the Owenite body as a whole, slightly more information was provided on the daily lives and collective progress of its inhabitants, usually through the medium of regular reports to the Central Board and the annual Congress. Its members, as we have said, came from Socialist branches all over the country (most had

---

community was eventually to be taken over and governed by the tenants themselves, and it was doing quite well until Vandaleur gambled away his fortune in late 1833.

*Orbiston was the largest Owenite community: at one time the 291 acre estate in Lanarkshire had over 300 residents. Founded in 1825 by Abram Combe, it survived on a mixture of agriculture, iron-founding and domestic crafts for two years. Disagreements within the membership over the principles on which economic rewards should be dispensed, and the death of Combe, brought about its collapse in the autumn of 1827. One interesting feature of the community was its 'personal monitor' system: every member was assigned a monitor, who observed and criticized his/her behaviour in an early version of 'criticism/self-criticism' sessions.

in fact been heavily subsidized by their local branches, since few could afford the fifty pounds-per-family entrance fee); therefore interest in events there was very widespread.[37]

When the community first began on a 533-acre Hampshire estate leased from a merchant banker, its fifty-odd residents were housed in rough, uncomfortable accommodation, which made even routine cooking and cleaning very laborious.[38] Two years later the situation had not greatly improved. 'With regard to the cooking apparatus,' one typical report ran,

> it is in operation, but . . . there is no oven attached thereto, and we find that the hot plate is incapable of baking any thing; and only one pan can stand on the fire at once, which is an inconvenience to the cook, and we can never have anything baked except by heating the large oven which makes the kitchen all over litter . . .[39]

Gradually, an efficient rota was devised in which every woman was required to perform one domestic task for one month, leaving the heaviest work to be done by hired labour.[40] This freed the rest for work in the fields, which took up the bulk of the community's time. Everyone rose at six, and those women who were not on cooking duty went out to the fields with the men, returning at eight for breakfast and then back to work until the supper hour.[41] Evenings were taken up with singing, dance sessions and regular classes; a 'female class' was held every Thursday.[42] In 1841 Owen embarked on a controversial building programme which included the construction of a kitchen. It was, according to visitors, probably the most elaborate and expensive kitchen to be found anywhere in the country, equipped not only with the 'most advanced' cooking technology available, but also with various ingenious gadgets such as a little train 'which, through a tunnel, conveyed the dishes and the dinner . . . to the door of the dining-hall' and from there back to the kitchen once the meal was over.[43] No doubt all this represented a genuine attempt to lighten the women's workload, as did the decision to have no hot meal on Sunday, so as to allow the women more time off.[44] But the possibility that exclusive female responsibility for certain tasks might in itself lead to an inequitable division of labour never seems to have occurred to the residents, nor did any of the Owenite leaders raise this issue. It took a woman delegate to the 1843 Congress (the only one) to elicit the following admissions from the (male) Queenwood delegate:

'I ask you whether the females of this Establishment are worked more hours per day, or per week, than the males are?'
  'Yes, by a great deal.'
'Have they the same means of instruction and recreation . . .?'
  'I suppose they have.'[45]

To another question about whether the women, like the men, had their Sundays free: 'They cannot altogether so; they are as much as possible.' And to the general question: 'Are your labours harder here to obtain the same comforts which you would have in the old world?' the answer was unequivocal: 'Undoubtedly they are.'[46]

It is perhaps not surprising to discover, then, that the threatened walk-out by women at Orbiston was succeeded by similar expressions of female discontent in other communities, including Queenwood (where the women were at one point described as being 'very inattentive to orders')[47] and Manea Fen, where according to its founder, women who came 'buoyed with large expectation and ardent enthusiasm' often 'cooled into disappointment and settled into discontent . . . and left'.[48] Women's unwillingness 'to enter into the . . . communional views' was cited as one of the main reasons for the collapse of Orbiston, and anxieties that women's disillusionment would lead to similar results elsewhere were frequently expressed.[49]

'Women . . . are attached to their own notions about comfort and privacy – and cannot easily admit that a residence in community, without individual property, individual staircases, and individual wash-tubs, side covers, and kitchen fires, can be consistent with domestic happiness,' one man argued in a letter to *The New Moral World* in 1836, and certainly it seems true that women were wary of collective living arrangements.[50] But this had less to do with any innate partiality for individual wash-tubs than a fear, often justified, of becoming embroiled in a hard life over which they would have too little control, and in which they would bear the brunt of utopian impracticality. In 1833 a woman calling herself 'MCO' wrote to *The Crisis* asking whether the wives of prospective community residents would be given any independent choice as to whether they followed their husbands into a community, 'for the women now depending upon their husbands for existence, are obliged to obey *his* feelings, in place of following sometimes her own . . .' She also wanted to know what sort of living arrangements would be made and whether they would be permanent, or merely a temporary sanctuary for those who had failed to support themselves in conventional society. 'These questions may not appear very important to the men, but they are very important to the co-operative women . . .'[51]

The man who replied to her letter claimed that no woman would be forced to enter a community when her husband did, although he did not explain what would happen to the man's family if he left them for the communal life.[52] (A few years later the rules of the Community Friendly Society required that no married man or woman could enter a community 'without the consent of the partner, unless they are separated for over a year'.[53]) The living arrangements, he went on to tell her, 'would be the most scientific known at the time . . . uniting all that is good in the chace [sic], pastoral, agricultural and manufacturing departments, in such proportion as shall be found beneficial to the general happiness.'[54] Whether 'MCO' was reassured by this we do not know, but clearly other women did not find such sweeping promises a sufficient substitute for a larger voice in the planning of the communities, and what William Thompson described as 'the natural discontent of women at being treated like sheep instead of rational beings' occasionally boiled over (as Thompson had warned it would) in 'counteractions'.[55] In his own community schemes he insisted that women should be given an equal role in all aspects of communal life, including its planning and government – and had this always been done the communities would no doubt have developed somewhat differently.[56] Most *did* allow women full voting rights in their councils: Queenwood held 'family meetings' where all its general decision-making was done, while both Orbiston and Ralahine held separate women's meetings as well as mixed assemblies.[57] But all three remained very male-dominated nonetheless, and it was no doubt this balance of internal power, as well as the inequitable division of labour, which engendered resentment among the resident women.

This resentment should not be exaggerated, however; many

women were deeply committed to the communities, and the fact that the Queenwood female population remained stable over its last terrible years indicates just how much some women were willing to endure in the hope of a brighter future. No doubt it was those who had been unwillingly dragged into community life by their husbands who were most bitter about the failure of the experiments, like the common-law wife of Manea Fen's President who was, as he admitted, 'no Socialist' and who urged him to withdraw his support from the community as soon as it began to run into difficulties.[58]

Even in the face of feminine dissidence, most of the community-builders persisted in claiming that genuine improvements had been made in women's status within their colonies. The most important reform which all claimed to have made, and the one most difficult to assess, was a re-vamped marriage relation, based on mutual economic independence and social equality. 'Look at the women in our community,' the Governor of Queenwood exhorted an audience of four hundred local farm labourers meeting in the community barnyard in 1840:

> they are as women ought to be; Educated in such a manner as to make them equal with men. We have none here but married women, but they are not tyrannized over by their husbands: no, they are equal with them. They are not depending on them for support; they derive their subsistence from a community which they admire and to which they contribute . . . See, my friends, how happy we live; and look at your own miserable condition . . . [59]

Regulations for marriage and divorce at Queenwood followed the rules Owen had laid down some years earlier, with a declaration of intent to wed followed by a ceremony, and divorce only allowed after a year had elapsed.[60] But since most of the residents arrived wed and stayed that way, the rules had little practical significance. The few young single women living there, however, each had two rooms of their own and a seat 'at our Council Table with the Men with whom they become acquainted before marriage, living with each other, and knowing each other before that time . . .', and it is perfectly possible that this was intended as tacit approval for pre-marital sexual intercourse (as one shocked observer, who reported this speech to the Home Office, obviously thought it was). But if so, it was all done so discreetly that no scandal resulted.[61]

At Ralahine, according to one report, couples married according to the law, but if they found themselves to be incompatible, 'they had a very easy mode of separation':

> John had only to say to Mary, or Mary to John, 'I cannot put up with your ill tempers, scolding tongue, dirty habits, etc.; if you do not behave yourself better, I will leave the cottage, eat my meals in the public dining-room and sleep in the dormitory of the single members . . .'[62]

Since the children were all collectively cared for 'this could be done without any inconvenience' and the public humiliation of having one's partner move out of one's bed 'and . . . the taunts and ridicule that would attend such a circumstance', would induce couples to treat each 'like sweethearts' – an interesting reminder of how Socialist communality restored a type of public sanction which had controlled marital relations within earlier village communities.[63] Again, there is no evidence as to whether individuals actually took advantage of this situation to 'divorce' their partners, but, if they did, it went unnoticed by the Owenites' opponents, who were usually quick to pounce on any signs of sexual indiscretion.

The Manea Fen community, however, gave scandal-mongers plenty to talk about.

Manea Fen was a renegade community in a number of ways. It was established in 1838 by a young adventurer called William Hodson whose career, by the time he arrived in the Owenite ranks, already included stints as a Methodist lay preacher, a sailor, and a local radical in Cambridgeshire politics.[64] Somewhere along the way he had also managed to accumulate enough money to buy a small estate at Upwell, and it was here that he decided to build the first instalment of the New World after his conversion to Owenism in the mid-1830s. Reaction from the Central Board of the Owenite movement to this interloper was fiercely hostile, partly out of jealousy, partly because Hodson emphasized that his community – unlike the one projected by the Central Board – was to be democratically organized.[65] 'None will spoil their hats in bowing to others . . .'[66] Many of the Owenite branches, however, welcomed Hodson's initiative, and criticized their own Board for its pettiness. One woman, 'Sophia' (who claimed to have been an active Socialist 'since the commencement of the labour exchanges') even wrote a letter to the newspaper published by the new community, *The Working Bee*, in which she urged her Socialist sisters to threaten the Central Board that unless it too began 'practical operations' immediately, the women would all move to Manea Fen. 'Some of the chicken-hearted would be forced to exert themselves to rescue us and our children from the pandemonium which environs us – or lose us.'[67]

Queenwood began a year later, and a fierce competition ensued between the two colonies, in which Manea Fen gradually became a rallying-point for many who opposed the autocratic policies of Owen. *The Working Bee* carried letters and articles censored from *The New Moral World*, including several in which Owen was denounced for his class-conciliationist views and the Central Board was attacked for supporting his 'paternal government' schemes.[68] Since both communities attempted to combine agriculture and manufacture (in Manea Fen's case, the production of bricks, floor tiles, and stockings), rivalry over whose land was richest and whose industries most efficient was very lively, and when one of the leaders of Queenwood visited Manea Fen and departed with its master builder, 'Social ties' were strained almost to breaking point.[69]

Nevertheless, by 1840 discussions about a possible amalgamation of the two communities had begun, and had Manea Fen survived a bit longer they might have borne some results. But by the winter of 1840 a series of crises – the collapse of a bank in which Hodson had funds invested, the overproduction of goods for which the colonists could find no market, growing tensions between Hodson and his fellow residents, plus the opposition of his common-law wife, made Hodson decide to give up the experiment.[70] When this decision was opposed by some of the other members, factions were formed and a violent conflict ensued in which buildings were vandalized and one man shot at. Finally, Hodson disappeared and the community collapsed in disarray.[71]

Not surprisingly, Manea Fen attracted a great deal of interest from local people, who were fascinated by the way of life and appearance of these radical eccentrics, who dressed 'like Robin

Hood and his foresters', the men in green habits and the women 'with trousers, and the hair worn in ringlets'. 'They are quite the lions of the villages round about', it was reported.[72] Not all reaction to the community was favourable, however, partly due to its communist principles but more specifically because of its reputation for marital misdoings, particularly in the first six months of the community's existence.

Two separate versions of what happened in the early months of Manea Fen can be traced. In Hodson's own account, presented to a later group of residents in the pages of *The Working Bee*, he claimed that the first colonists recruited for the community had been 'penniless in pocket and bankrupt of moral qualification'; the men interested only in 'beer shops and the company of the lowest prostitutes', while their wives were no better suited:

> One person brought his wife, who was a Methodist, she of course was unfitted for such an undertaking. Another woman, the wife of a very good member, who was from the sister land, would call out for whiskey repeatedly. The wife of another declared that she would never stop in the community, for she believed in heaven and hell.[73]

By the New Year, according to one of Hodson's lieutenants, the situation had deteriorated into constant drunkenness, fights, and uproar in the local brothels. Finally most of the residents were told to pack up and leave; a new batch was recruited; and business began over again.[74]

Or so the story went . . . In fact, as a number of letters written during this period reveal, the issues underlying the conflict between Hodson and his recruits were not quite as he later represented them. 'We have had a little confusion in our society owing to . . . parties not knowing that there is something more in your system than an improved mode of producing and distributing wealth,' the community's secretary wrote to Owen at the time.[75] And what that 'something more' had been was revealed by a former colonist, Mr Woofenden, when he told the London and Manchester Owenites that Hodson and his supporters had intended 'to dispense with the present matrimonial arrangements'.[76] They 'were impressing on the minds of the young single men that the union of affection is an evil and that indiscriminate connection of the sexes is the true principle.' All the married couples were leaving, he added, and Hodson had begun advertising in the local newspapers for young, single women to enter the community.[77] These revelations threw the Owenite branches into an uproar, and Hodson was promptly called upon to explain himself.

It was quite true, Hodson acknowledged, that he was an opponent of conventional marriage, and lived with his dead wife's sister in a free union.* But the rules regarding marriage and divorce at Manea Fen, he claimed, were only those advocated by Owen himself, and adopted in other communities; there was nothing for anyone to get excited about.[78] (It was also true that he had welcomed single women from Manchester into the community, he later stated, but only in order to rescue them from Old World perils.[79]) Be this as it may, a letter which he wrote at about the same time to a Manchester female friend (and which she decided to publish) clearly indicated that Hodson did not merely want to see marriage reformed in the community, but abolished:

> We have had a revolution in our community already. This arose from my calling a meeting of the members; stating the objects I had on view, viz., the abolition of private property, more particularly the traffic in human flesh, the buying and selling of each other. I told them that those who wished to be tied together could be. But were they prepared to see each other act rationally – that is, were they prepared to cherish a mother and child provided there was no legal husband? The answer was – No. Upon my declaring that I could not convey the property on any *other* condition than that all should enjoy personal freedom. [sic] This has caused a secession from our body . . .[80]

Even the departure of this first batch of colonists did not alter Hodson's convictions, however, and it seems likely that the second wave of recruits were told of his intentions in advance and accepted them, since the tone of the propagandà coming out of the community after the change of membership was, if anything, even more uncompromising than before. 'As to being very lax on the subject of marriage, we have the pleasure to . . . plead guilty,' the editor of *The Working Bee* boasted in response to a protest

---

*Under the existing laws at the time, marriages between a man and his dead wife's sister were illegal, so Hodson could not have married her even if he had been willing to do so.

from a scandalized local farmer.[81] And when this bluntness brought cries of outrage from some of the national Socialist leaders they were in turn taken sharply to task for having much the same views on marriage, according to the irascible editor, as 'holy Apostle Peter'.[82] 'We are happy to say we know many of the social members whose lofty minds will never stoop to ask leave of their fellow men (whether superstitious or 'Rational Religionists') to have sexual connexion,' *The Working Bee* snorted, 'Bah! The man of intelligence would as soon ask liberty to sneeze, as ask his fellow mortal permission to love a female.'[83]

What effect these views had on life in the community itself was not revealed, although a letter to the newspaper from 'Alice, a Resident in the Hive' pleading with her fellow Socialists to 'be kind to those who have moral courage to carry [principles] into practice' suggests that she, at least, may have been living with the consequences of a liberated lifestyle. 'Why should the sexual connexion be more fettered than hunger or thirst?' she demanded, 'Mr Owen has often said we cannot pledge to love for twenty-four hours. If we cannot love as we like, why attempt to bind parties who do not mutually love? . . . A time is fast approaching when this important subject must be fairly met . . . [and] woman, abused, ill-treated woman . . . placed upon an equality with man, and love of the most disinterested nature be experienced by both sexes.'[84] It is perhaps also significant that one of the only references to birth control to appear in any Socialist newspaper occurred in *The Working Bee,* in a letter advising women to read William Thompson's prescriptions for keeping down the population rate.[85]

This was as close to genuine 'free love' as Owenism ever came, and it is interesting to find that it appeared in a community which, rhetorically at least, was strongly committed to democracy and equality, including female equality. Some of the most militantly feminist statements ever to be voiced within the Owenite ranks came out of Manea Fen, but accompanied by others whose male-centred view of sexual freedom must have led to tensions even among the second group of residents.[86] Thus in the ignominious collapse of the community we see not only the inevitable fate of a crisis-ridden social experiment, but also the failure of a certain brand of sexual libertarianism which was so heavily riddled with

257

contradictions that it fell into disarray almost at the moment of its articulation.

But if Manea Fen's demise was tragi-comic, the collapse of its major competitor – Queenwood – was tragedy pure and simple, for it meant the collapse of the Owenite movement as a whole.

Even in the early years of Queenwood's operations the tensions which were finally to tear the community – and the movement – apart were in evidence. Initially Owen refused to have anything to do with it on the grounds that it was a plebian community run by working men 'who thought they knew sufficient to carry forward those measures which required the most experienced individual to guide'.[87] Then, in 1842, he re-entered by the back door, bringing with him a group of middle-class investors (the 'Home Colonization Society') who were prepared to support the community only if they could have governing control over it.[88] Since the little colony was already in desperate financial straits (due mostly to lack of support from the branches, in turn probably due to a combination of depressed economic circumstances and suspicion about Owen's intentions),[89] they had no choice but to accept HCS rule, which ultimately meant accepting Owen's dictatorship.[90] Having thus regained control, Owen used it to spend thousands of pounds building sunken walk-ways, promenades, and the famous kitchen, thereby exhausting all the movement's central funds.[91] Social Missionaries were fired; grants for the building of local Halls of Science ended; the whole Socialist propaganda machine slowly began to grind to a halt. Soon the fate of Socialism as a national organization was tied to the fate of the community. 'Failure at Harmony would not only entail severe loss and suffering on the best supporters of the cause,' ran one prescient warning issued at the time, 'but . . . would inevitably scatter beyond the possibility of recall the members and friends of the Society . . .'[92]

By the end of the summer of 1842 it was clear that Owen's expenditures had virtually bankrupted the movement, since few of the funds promised by his capitalist friends had actually materialized.[93] 'Strenuously have Mr O. and his coadjutors inculcated the sad doctrine of the absolute dependence of the working classes on capitalists,' Holyoake wrote with furious sarcasm at the time. 'Behold, Socialists! in your hour of need, what assistance you get from them!'[94] Somehow the community continued to lurch on, but by the following summer the residents' diet had been reduced to bread and water, and all their hired labour dismissed, so the work load was very much heavier.[95] Owen continued to issue chirpy reports on their progress from the large comfortable house which he and various 'paying guests' inhabited on the same estate (and where he took his own large, regular meals while the colonists munched their bread nearby*).[96] In 1843 he established a school there whose fees were so high that few working-class Owenites could afford to send their children to it.[97] By late 1843 the level of anger and disillusionment created by all this within the community was reflected in the demoralization of Socialist groups outside it as well: only half the branches existing in 1840–41 were still in operation, and even these reported declining membership.[98]

In May 1844 the inevitable revolt finally occurred. The majority of delegates at the annual Congress threw Owen out of the Queenwood governorship and replaced him with a Manchester calico-printer who was committed to transforming it into a democratic, working-class-controlled community.[99] 'Now what idea can a working man have of government?' one of Owen's supporters spluttered in a last-ditch attempt to retain control, 'he is a creature of circumstances and how can he acquire ideas of governing as a working man? If they did, they could cease to be working men . . .'[100] For one last valiant year the new regime sought to undo the damage created by their social superiors, exercising even greater economic stringencies than before, but with a spirit of comradeship which had been noticeably lacking under past administrations. Hope reawakened in the remaining branches, who sent in gifts of money and messages of support: one woman tried to organize a subscription among all the female members of the Rational Society, reminding them that it was their own emancipation which was at stake. 'My sisters, remember the bundle of sticks. Unity *is* strength. The trees at Harmony must not blossom in vain . . .'[101] But even with these efforts, the financial burden proved impossible to lift, and in mid-1845 the

---

*Owen always disliked eating with his working-class colleagues, and finally refused to do so; a decision which was defended by one supporter on the grounds that socialism did not mean 'dragging all down to one level'.

experiment officially ended. The annual Congresses stopped, and the few branches still in existence closed down completely, or else turned themselves into 'Literary and Scientific Institutions', Friendly Societies, secularist associations.[102] 'I can scarcely persuade myself that this is a reality,' the last secretary of the Owenite Congress wrote from Queenwood Hall in August, 1845:

> I look back on what we have been and what we are; we were a Society united for the holiest of purposes; we had a leader in whom we reposed the most unbounded confidence – nay, by many of us he was almost worshipped, and all were ready to follow to the death for the accomplishment of our object . . . and now we are dis- jointed, cast down and powerless. A spirit of discord has been among us, and blown our strength and purpose to the winds . . .[103]

The first phase of British Socialism had come to an end.

IX

SEX AND CLASS IN
THE POST-OWENITE ERA

With the collapse of Queenwood, Owenism died as a unified radical force. The Rational Society staggered on until 1848, but with a tiny fraction of its peak membership and little popular support. The disillusionment engendered by the demise of the Hampshire community had been too intense – the conflicts over its fate too bitter and divisive – to permit any unitary organization to survive. Whereas earlier community failures had shaken but never destroyed Socialist confidence, this failure – with its complex interplay of class and personal conflicts, and its enormous investment of movement energies and hopes – had pushed a dagger straight into the strategical underbelly of Owenism. Disunity and competition, it now seemed painfully evident, were not just 'ignorant and irrational habits' which would automatically be eliminated through mental enlightenment and the communalization of social conditions; their resilience, even among men and women of Social good-will, had become all too obvious in this last tragic phase of Owenite endeavour. Thus an idea which had seemed both plausible and necessary – the peaceable supplantation of the Old Immoral World by classless, democratic communities – gradually lost the widespread support which it had commanded among working people from the late 1820s onward, and slid into the realm of dreams that had failed.[1]

This decline of Owenism as a popular force cannot be entirely explained, however, in terms of the internal divisions and strategical weaknesses in the movement itself, so sharply exposed in the Queenwood debacle. It must also be considered in relation to wider economic and cultural changes. The faith in the perfectibility of the human condition which lay at the heart of the Owenite philosophy in turn relied on a belief (very widespread at the time) that the capitalist system was a transitory, fragile form of socio-economic organization which would inevitably be swept away in the tide of co-operative progress. Or as Holyoake put it, in his usual terse fashion, 'the social seers expected that the "old immoral world" was played out . . .'[2] But by the end of the 1840s it was becoming obvious to everyone, Owenites included, that the competitive system was by no means as impermanent as they had thought. In the years after 1848, the crisis-ridden pattern of boom-and-slump which had characterized British industrial development during the first half of the century (and which must occasionally have left even the captains of industry wondering about the viability of the capitalist mode of production) stabilized into a period of sustained growth. Capitalist command over the economy was steadily extended and consolidated, while the capitalist state enacted certain reforms (the Ten Hours Bill of 1847, various Public Health Acts, the 1867 Reform Bill) which reduced class tension while at the same time maintaining and reinforcing ruling-class power. By the 1860s, capitalism had shown itself to be not only more resilient than any of its early critics could have anticipated, but also capable of internal reconstruction and restabilization – processes which the Owenites themselves could not have foreseen and for which their own theories provided no explanation. The hope of simply moving beyond the boundaries of the competitive system into a new mode of co-operative, communal existence faded as it gradually became evident that there was no longer any 'outside' left to go to. Capitalism itself had become the terrain on which the struggle for its own supersession would have to be fought.[3]

Nor was it only in economic life that the horizons of alternative possibilities seemed to narrow. In the years just prior to the mid-century, as Dorothy Thompson has noted, 'the Victorian sentimentalization of the home and the family, in which all important decisions were taken by its head, the father, and accepted with docility and obedience by the inferior members, became all-pervasive, and affected all classes', including the working class, where women who had previously been considered economic help-mates to their husbands gradually acquired a sense of 'homecentredness and inferiority' very similar to that found among women of the wealthier classes.[4] The idea of a domestic, dependent, private 'women's sphere', rigidly segregated from the male sphere of work, politics and public life, became for the working class, as for the middle class, central to their concept of social respectability.

Thus for both women and working people, 'a period of openness and experiment, in which people seemed prepared to accept a wide range of ideas, was followed by . . . a narrowing down of expectations and demands'. The last Owenite feminist text to be published was an essay by Catherine Barmby, written in 1848.[5] Thereafter Catherine, along with her husband, abandoned the Communist Church and millenarian feminism for more prosaic forms of political activity.[6] Emma Martin continued to lecture against religion and for women's emancipation, until her premature death in 1851. Margaret Chappellsmith seems to have ended her career as an Owenite propagandist in 1843; she emigrated to New Harmony a few years later.[7] The debate over marriage reform, which had served as the central focus of feminist discussion at a popular level, had already spluttered to a halt in 1843–44, as the Owenite propaganda machinery wound down. This does not mean that Socialist feminism left all its adherents and propagandists behind in the 1840s. Movements never die all at once, nor do the individuals who comprise those movements disappear once organizations decline. Owenites who had been young in the 1830s and 40s were energetic and active – and sometimes still propagandizing Owenite feminist ideals – in the 1850s and 60s, while many of the organizational forms created by early Socialism survived into the later period as well. But whereas in 1820–45 all these ideas, organizations and hopes had been held together in one great, united surge towards the New Moral World, now they moved apart into separate channels: trade unionism, practical co-operation, social science, spiritualism, freethought (which after 1850 was known as Secularism) and the new women's movement itself, which had a small left-wing. Moreover, this dispersal of Owenite energies also signalled the disintegration of what had been a crucial element in the Owenite vision: the link between women's freedom and class emancipation. The utopian dream which foresaw women's liberation as part of a general process of 'social regeneration' had dimmed and died – and with it went the ideological tie between feminism and working-class radicalism. After 1845, sex oppression and class exploitation increasingly became viewed not as twin targets of a single strategy, but as separate objects of separate struggles, organized from different – and sometimes opposing – perspectives.

In considering this divergence between feminism and the organized working class, it is important to recall that the ideology of 'women's sphere' did not appear suddenly within the working class, at the point of Owenite decline, but had its roots within the Owenite period itself. The hardening line of sexual apartheid which emerged within the most 'respectable' strata of the working class in the 1830s and 40s developed not in emulation of middle-class attitudes and lifestyle, as has often been suggested, but in response to certain fundamental changes which had occurred in the wake of the Industrial Revolution. In the home, as we have seen, family economies previously based on a primary bread-winning role for men and a combined wage-earning and domestic role for women were disintegrating under the impact of new employment structures. In the workplace, changed labour requirements in both old and new industries brought increasing numbers of men and women workers into direct competition, as employers drew on an expanding pool of cheap female labour in order to undercut male wage levels, skills, and union organiza-tion. These were complex changes, varying from one region and industry to another, but their cumulative effect was the creation of a sense of sexual crisis noted by many observers of the early nineteenth century working class, and heard very clearly in all the popular movements of the period, including Owenism and Chartism. In Owenism, it turned the movement into an arena where competing views on women and sexual relations fought for ideological foothold, but always with the strongest voice coming from those who advocated the equalization of sexual roles and status within a communal society. Within Chartism, however, public support for such a radical solution was very slight, and instead its membership sought to restabilize older patterns of sexual power, rather than replacing them entirely. Looking briefly at the role of women within the Chartist movement highlights those dominant tendencies within working-class sexual relations which had a formative effect on the relationship between sex and class politics in the post-Owenite era.

CHARTISM AND FEMINISM

The Chartist movement, as we have seen, was directly contemporaneous with Owenism and to a certain extent overlapped with it, at least at a local level. But the two movements were, nonetheless, philosophically and organizationally distinct, not least because of the ideological purism of Socialism. Although any Socialist could become a Chartist – simply by committing him or herself to the agitation for the Charter's Six Points* – a Chartist could only become a Socialist by accepting the entire doctrinal package advocated by the Owenites, from the Doctrine of Character Formation through to the demand for female equality. Chartism therefore remained a much more loosely-knit movement than Socialism, incorporating a far wider range of social views. It was also, of course, a much larger movement, with a popular membership several times that of Owenism. Its female membership also appears to have been very large, and, as in earlier radical-democratic agitations, very militant: throughout the peak years of Chartism tens of thousands of women campaigned for the Six Points, leading mass demonstrations, organizing 'exclusive dealing' campaigns, teaching in Chartist Sunday schools, praying in Chartist churches, and sometimes acting as violent shock-troops in struggles with the military and the police.[8] In 1839 a leading male Chartist from Hyde noted that his Chartist society contained three hundred men and two hundred women, 'and all he could say was that the women were the better men . . .'[9] But with all this female militancy there does not seem to have been much in the way of feminist consciousness or organization. Few of the leading propagandists of Chartism were self-proclaimed feminists, and the movement never produced women publicists of the stature or influence of Emma Martin, Margaret Chappellsmith, or Frances

*These were: universal male suffrage; annual parliaments; vote by ballot; equal representation; payment of members of Parliament; no property qualification.

Morrison. Thus throughout the 1830s and 1840s concern with the question of women's own status was much more closely identified with Socialism than with Chartism.[10]

A comparison of the public rhetoric of the two movements over this period, however, shows that although Chartist ideologues seldom spoke from a self-consciously feminist perspective, they were almost as voluble as the Owenites on the subject of women's correct social and political role. Throughout the late 1830s and early 1840s male Chartist ideologues used the movement as a platform from which to make some very firm pronouncements about the duties of womanhood, while female Chartist societies (of which several dozen existed at the height of the movement) issued a steady stream of memorials, public addresses, and open letters to government and Chartist leaders, most of them highly stylized in form and very similar in content. Typical of such statements was one written by the Female Political Union of Newcastle upon Tyne in 1839, which began with an exhortation to women to rally to the support of their menfolk in the battle for democratic freedoms:

> FELLOW-COUNTRYWOMEN, – We call upon you to join us and help our fathers, husbands, and brothers, to free themselves and us from political, physical, and mental bondage . . . Is it not true that the interests of our fathers, husbands, and brothers ought to be ours? If they are oppressed and impoverished, do we not share those evils with them? If so, ought we not to resent the infliction of those wrongs upon them? We have read the records of the past, and our hearts have responded to the historian's praise of those women, who struggled against tyranny and urged their countrymen to be free or die.[11]

'We have been told,' the women wrote, 'that the province of woman is her home, and that the field of politics should be left to men', but 'this we deny' since 'the nature of things renders it impossible': 'We have seen that because the husband's earnings could not support his family, the wife has been compelled to leave her home neglected and, with her infant children, work at a soul and body degrading toil . . . our husbands [are] over wrought, our houses half furnished, our families ill-fed, and our children uneducated . . .' They had 'searched and found that the cause of these evils is the Government of the country being in the hands of a few of the upper and middle classes' who not only 'robbed the poor of their inheritance' but then proceeded to pass laws which drove the pauperized into workhouses where the policy was 'to separate those whom God has joined together, and tear the children from their parents' care':

> . . . the solace of our homes, the endearments of our children, and the sympathies of our kindred are denied us – and even in the grave our ashes are laid with disrespect.[12]

The only solution to these injustices, the Newcastle women concluded, was to place the government in the hands of 'the working men who form . . . the strength and wealth of this country' who would then 'drive poverty and ignorance from our land, and establish happy homes, true religion, righteous government, and good laws'. This message – that it was through the representation of the male working class in Parliament that the 'white slaves of England', women as well as men, would be freed – was echoed in statements from many other women's Charter associations around the country, who despite their very active role in the movement clearly saw themselves as auxiliaries ('glorious auxiliaries' as the Female Radicals of Ashton-under-Lyne dubbed themselves)[13] to a male cause. 'While we are compelled to share the misery of our fathers, our husbands, our brothers, and our lovers, we are determined to have a share in their struggles to be free, and to cheer them in their onward march for liberty,' the Female Chartists of Aberdeen told Feargus O'Connor,[14] while the Female Radical Association of Carlisle promised him that 'if need be' they would 'follow our husbands, our fathers, and our sons and our brothers, to the battlefield, to cheer and comfort them in the hour of danger, bind up their wounds, and instigate them to fresh deeds of valour . . .'[15]

This was not a new emphasis within female radicalism. From the beginning of the century, as we saw in an earlier chapter, women's democratic activism had generally been viewed as a militant extension of their family role, thus reproducing divisions of labour and power found within the plebian household. It was as 'wives, daughters, mothers and lovers' that women had rallied to the side of their male kindred in 1815–19 and again in 1829–32, and so it was within Chartism where, in the words of the London

Female Democrats, 'even woman, domesticated woman, leaving her homestead, will battle for the rights of those that are dear to her . . .'[16] But what was new within Chartist rhetoric was an explicit preoccupation with sexual/familial relations themselves, and in particular with their dislocation through the substitution of women for men as primary breadwinners and the introduction of the New Poor Law, both of which were constantly described as violations of a 'natural order'. 'The order of nature [is] inverted,' when 'the female is driven to the factory to labour for her offspring, and her husband unwillingly idle at home, dependent . . . on female labour,' the National Female Charter Association of Upper Honley and Smallthorn wrote to *The Northern Star*.[17] This theme was also taken up vigorously by male radicals, especially in the northern textile districts where both the Anti-Poor Law campaign and the factory reform struggle flowed into Chartism. Joseph Rayner Stephens, the Anti-Poor Law leader, was cheered by audiences in the north when he defended the sanctity of proletarian family life against Malthusian social legislation and argued against women's employment outside the home.[18] Chartists active in the factory reform movement frequently linked the campaign for the Six Points to the demand for the gradual withdrawal of all married women from industrial employment. 'If the Charter became a legislative enactment tomorrow, I would not thank for it unless men were returned to Parliament who would make laws to restrict all females from working in factories . . .' one Manchester Chartist told an audience of factory women in 1842, 'Her place is in the home . . .'[19] Similar statements, stressing the need for a male wage high enough to support a dependent wife and children, and the confinement of women to domestic responsibilities, were repeated again and again in Chartist propaganda.[20]

Such rhetoric should not be interpreted merely as a reactionary protest against the disintegration of the old patriarchal family economy of the pre-industrial period. Rather, it should be seen as an attempt to recoup the traditional balance of sexual power which had existed within such family economies by radically transforming the meaning of family life itself (and in particular women's role within the family) in a way which brought it much closer to the bourgeois ideal. Evidence for such an interpretation is abundant within Chartist writings, in which female domesticity and the joys of privatized home life were often eulogized in terms so effusively sentimental that they could easily have been confused with Evangelical tracts. One particularly sugary specimen was a book by William Lovett, who even in his Owenite salad days had been horrified by the unconventional sexual notions of Owen and some of his followers. Now, some years after leaving the movement and becoming a Chartist, Lovett expounded his own views in a text (*Social and Political Morality*) in which he described the home as a private retreat from the harsh world of masculine endeavour, extolled the female homemaker whose 'chief duty' was 'to gratify the mind and console the heart of man' by rendering his little household sanctum cheerful and attractive, and argued that waged employment for women undermined family happiness and the manliness of husbands. 'A man must indeed have lost all self-respect to allow himself and his offspring to be dependent on a wife's labour.'[21] His description of his own wife (on whose earnings he had nevertheless relied at various points) as a 'guardian angel o'er my life presiding'[22] underlines Dorothy Thompson's point that the Victorian image of the wife as 'the Angel in the house' was far from being confined to the leisured upper classes.

Within Chartism, it is true, such notions still vied with the older ideal – and reality – of women as active economic partners in the household and in the labouring community as a whole. The Lancashire General Strike of 1842 involved thousands of working women, who led marches from town to town and openly confronted employers and the military with demands for bread for their starving families.[23] Sentimental concepts of 'women's sphere' meant little to such women. In addition, these concepts also vied with the Jacobin inheritance of *egalité*, which still survived within sections of the Chartist membership. Cheap re-editions of Wollstonecraft's *Vindication* were advertised in Chartist newspapers, and her name was occasionally evoked, along with that of Shelley, in discussions of women's position.[24] This brand of equal rights philosophy could be rendered compatible with the cult of feminine dependency, but only through the sort of convoluted argument produced by Lovett, who drew a sharp distinction between woman's *rights* – which, he asserted, should be equal to those of men – and woman's *duties*, which were wholly dissimilar to those of her male partner. 'His being to provide . . . for the wants and necessaries of the family; *hers* to perform the duties of the household . . .' The confinement of women to a domestic, dependent sphere did not in itself produce inequality between the sexes, he (and other Chartist men) claimed, in direct contrast to Owenite feminists who insisted that it did.[25]

The contradictions and strains within such a position, and indeed within the Chartist approach towards women's issues in general, became most obvious in relation to the one feminist issue on which the movement leadership could not avoid taking a position – the question of women's suffrage. Here the bruised tradition of 'women's rights' came into direct collision with old prejudices and new anxieties generated by the sexual instability of the times.

When the People's Charter was first drafted by William Lovett he inserted in it a clause advocating the extension of the franchise to women, but this was speedily removed on the urging of 'several members' who 'thought its adoption in the Bill might retard the suffrage of men . . .'[26] Several attempts were made to reintroduce the clause (often by Owenite-Chartists), but these met with little encouragement.[27] The campaign for 'a-sexual Chartism' launched by the Barmbys in 1841 seems to have died still-born, and other sexual democrats who raised the matter at later Chartist meetings did not meet with any greater success. In 1843, a leading Birmingham Chartist (not an Owenite) tried to push the women's suffrage issue forward at a delegate Convention there (Birmingham had the biggest female Charter association in the country, over 2,000 strong). He was dissuaded from doing so by other male delegates (there were no female ones present) who argued that the demand would distract men from the struggle for their own enfranchisement.[28] The previous year, a Shoreditch Socialist Chartist who had argued for women's right to the vote at a local meeting of Chartists had been laughed down by the rest of the assembly (although there were scattered cries of 'Hear, hear' from some in the audience).[29] 'What is this but . . . moral cowardice . . .?' *The New Moral World* demanded furiously in an editorial devoted to the issue, 'What is this but saying, we are Radical Reformers, but we will not hold fast to that which is good?'[30]

Political expedience was clearly one reason for this 'moral cowardice', but there were others as well. In 1841 the Rochdale Social Missionary, William Spier, debated the Manchester Chartist, James Leach, in Rochdale. In the course of his speech Spier reminded the audience that although the Charter claimed to stand for 'the principle of universal suffrage . . . women were excluded from its benefits, – this was one half of the population: how could it be called universal suffrage?'

> This should not be the case; women are as fit to enjoy the suffrage as men; they lie under the same liabilities, and ought to possess the same privileges. The system he advanced was superior to the Charter; it ranked woman as the equal of man . . .[31]

In reply, Leach stated that 'he did not think that such a wide difference existed between man and woman as to make it necessary for woman to enjoy the suffrage: he thought that men, as fathers, husbands, and brothers, would secure the best interests of women.'[32] Many of his fellow radicals agreed, with the additional proviso that even if women *thought* their political interests were different from those of their menfolk, this was just a further reason for denying them the vote since then they might 'arrive at political conclusions adverse to those of their husbands . . . and then there is one more . . . subject of domestic discord . . .!'[33] Or in the words of Feargus O'Connor, an adamant anti-feminist, 'IT WOULD LEAD TO FAMILY DISSENSIONS . . .'[34] Even men who supported voting rights for widows and spinsters, baulked at the idea of giving the franchise to married women.[35] Fear of female self-assertion, when combined with a narrowing view of women's role, fuelled an anti-egalitarianism which boded ill for the fate of future feminist demands in working-class organizations. 'No;' as one man summed up, 'let [woman] endeavour to make *her home happy* to all about her. Let her encourage her husband, brothers, and sons, to perform their political duties, and then she will have performed her own . . .'[36]

These complex and rather contradictory views were those of the policy-makers, who in turn were nearly all male (no woman was ever a delegate at a national Chartist Convention, and only a few women sat on the executives of local Chartist associations, except for all-women associations).[37] Uncovering women's own attitude towards the issue is obviously much more difficult. Certainly few of the statements issued by female Chartist societies actually raised the demand for political equality, although there are hints that such demands were discussed by them. In 1843 the Nottingham Female Political Union was addressed by a woman on 'The Political Rights of Woman',[38] while a few years earlier the Female Radicals of Gosforth presented Julian Harney with a silk handkerchief in appreciation of his 'able advocacy of the "Rights of Women" '.[39] A letter written by the Female Radicals of Ashton-under-Lyne to *The Northern Star* indicated that although at present they were willing to support manhood suffrage they also looked forward to the day when 'we shall enjoy the elective franchise as well as our kinsmen . . .'[40] Probably a detailed examination of the female membership would reveal many more women with similar views, who were either unwilling or unable to impress their own aspirations on the movement leadership.

There is no evidence, however, to suggest that such women ever linked the demand for equal political rights to plans for reconstructed family life or marriage relations, in the way Owenite feminists had. In a period when women's prospects outside marriage were worsening and the burden of family support falling on many women inside marriage was intolerably heavy, it is not surprising that women themselves tended to look towards a home-centred existence, supported by a reliable male breadwinner, as a desirable goal. Or perhaps more accurately, they found it almost impossible to imagine any real alternative, except the current reality of economic insecurity and overwork. Owenite feminists might well argue that the solution to such insecurity lay not in dependence on a single man, but in the com-munalization of the family system. But their views had been too heavily tarred with the brush of sexual immorality to attract much support beyond the Socialists' own ranks (and even there, as we have seen, they sometimes met with a sceptical or hostile response from women, fearful of the intentions of male sexual libertarians). And the failure of the community experiments can only have confirmed most women's views that it was respectable, well-paid husbands which they needed, rather than visionary schemes for collectivized conjugal arrangements. The New Moral World must have appeared to them, as it ultimately did to the Owenite women, as a very distant horizon indeed.[41]

Within Chartism, then, it is possible to see certain ideals being advanced and consolidated which were to have a crucial influence on later working-class organizations. Chartism itself lost its mass base in the 1850s, and for a time independent working-class political organization declined. But economic organization strengthened, particularly among skilled male workers in expanding industries whose employment prospects were becoming stable enough to allow them to aspire to

> such components of middle-class family life as the comfortable
> home, the regular income, the dependent (and less exhausted) wife
> and children looking securely for support to the man. The successful
> trade unions of the 1850s and 1860s were formed by skilled workers
> with this in mind – wages, conditions and benefits sufficient to
> ensure financial security for a family, including a woman at home to
> provide all domestic comforts.[42]

The way these goals were achieved, however, was by building unions on what the Owenites had earlier dubbed the 'exclusivist' model, i.e. organizations which excluded unskilled male workers and women workers from their ranks, which allowed them to make considerable economic gains for their own members while ignoring the needs of the broad mass of working people, particularly women. 'The exclusion of women and the demand for a breadwinner's wage for men', as one historian notes, 'was an industrial bargaining strategy, enabling [some] men to make sectional gains while women provided employers with a pool of casual labour at below-subsistence wages.'[43] It was also a strategy which served to intensify divisions within the male workforce itself, between a small elite of organized craftsmen who could afford to support an unemployed wife and children, and the vast majority of working men who could not. Throughout the whole of the nineteenth century most male workers continued to require the supplementary income earned by their wives (often in casual, home-based employments) in order to sustain their families, while other female-headed households were wholly reliant on women's earnings.[44] But the fact that such female wage-earning was now, despite its continuing prevalence, considered exceptional and undesirable, served as an ideological justification for the confinement of women to the low-paid, 'unskilled' sector of the waged workforce. 'Ideological and economic considerations thus combined to set a tone in attitudes towards women . . . which is reflected in trade-union records and history' throughout the mid-Victorian decades,[45] and which continued to exercise a conservative influence on sexual politics within the labour movement even after the revival of working-class political organization in the last years of the century.

Thus, whereas in 1834 Owenite unionists were still able to win support for female unionization by reminding their male comrades that women were also working people with economic rights to defend, by 1877 the Secretary of the Trades Union Congress was being cheered when he defined the aim of the labour movement 'as to bring about a condition of things, where wives could be in their proper sphere at home, instead of being dragged into competition for livelihood against the great and strong men of the world'.[46] The early years of the Labour Party were marked by vigorous disputes over the status of women, in which strong opposition was expressed to married women's employment. 'Women were accused of taking jobs away from men, undercutting their wages, neglecting their children and their husbands, and encouraging their husbands to be idle.'[47] Working-class women who became involved in the suffrage battle at the turn of the century, like the Manchester suffragist and Socialist, Hannah Mitchell, soon discovered that many men in the labour movement were 'quite content to accept Manhood Suffrage, in spite of all their talk about equality',[48] and that such men almost invariably expected their wives, even if they held full-time jobs, to act as willing servants in the home. Working-class women thus entered the struggle for their own liberation, Hannah concluded bitterly, 'with one hand tied behind us . . .'[49] Even some of the leading lights of the various socialist organizations, as they re-emerged in the final decades of the century, were fiercely anti-feminist: 'some of the bitterest opponents' of women's enfranchisement, Hannah recalled, were 'found . . . among the Socialists'.[50]

There were important counter-tendencies to this development. But in general the attitude of Victorian working-class leaders towards women seems to have been one of combined prejudice and paternalism, while their views on the Woman Question (as the question of women's status became known in labour circles) tended to be suspicious and hostile. Within trade unions, and particularly skilled craft unions, this was part of a wider process of social conservatization, as they and their leaders often became absorbed into the mechanics of capitalist life.[51] But even within the new socialist organizations which appeared towards the end of the century, where the challenge to capitalist institutions was once again heard, the voice of feminism was often very muted – or even deliberately suppressed. Much of the responsibility for this lay within the socialist movement itself, which had undergone many changes since the Owenites' day; but the internal transformation of feminism itself was also a factor. The women's movement, as it emerged in the mid-century, was very different in ideological tone from the feminist radicalism which had preceded it, particularly in terms of its class perspective and long-term social aims.

THE VICTORIAN WOMEN'S MOVEMENT

Throughout the first half of the nineteenth century, as we have seen, feminism was identified with a revolutionary humanism which challenged hierarchies at all levels of social existence. As Jacobinical ideals of *liberté* and *egalité* were succeeded by Socialist schemes for communist-feminist communities, feminism became continuously linked in the public mind with images of a 'world turned upside down', a wholesale transformation of private and public life. Conventional reaction to this prospect, particularly with the example of the French Revolution before them and the pressure of the evangelized churches behind them, was one of outraged horror. This had a dual effect. On the one hand, it led to the radicalization of a number of upper- and middle-class feminists, whose uncompromising commitment to sexual equality pushed them well past the boundaries of mainstream liberal opinion. On the other hand, it meant that anyone attempting to articulate a 'less radical style of feminist thought – and there were a number who made such an attempt – had great difficulty in distinguishing their own position from that of the 'ultra-radicals', whether of a Jacobinical or Owenite stamp. In 1843, when a woman named Marion Reid took up her pen to advocate the extension of the franchise to those 'superior classes of British women' who were 'more capable of exercising those rights than the lower classes of the present electors', she still found it necessary to emphasize that in supporting this limited equalization of political rights she was by no means advocating any major transformation in women's social role nor 'any irrational system of levelling, such as that the poor have a right to share equally with the property of the rich . . .'[52] Whether or not such qualifications were heeded by her readers, it remained true that throughout the early decades of the century feminism was far too closely associated with 'levelling systems' of one sort or another to attract more than a handful of middle-class liberals, and even these (like William J. Fox and his South Place associates) tended to be on the left of the bourgeois-Radical spectrum.

But in the years following the demise of the Owenite movement, the political location of feminism began to shift. In 1851, Harriet Taylor was still complaining about how few respectable ladies of the 'literary class' were prepared to advocate feminist demands,[53] but by the end of the decade this was no longer the case. 'Women's rights' had by then acquired many more respectable middle-class adherents, and in doing so became a much more respectable cause. Only detailed research will eventually reveal all the factors which lay behind this change, but several were clearly of major importance.

The most obvious was the demise of the Owenite movement itself, which made it possible for middle-class women to begin to organize various feminist reform campaigns without being constantly accused of socialistic aims or immoral sexual intentions. With the decline of Chartism as well, the connection between feminism and working-class radicalism became even dimmer in the bourgeois mind, opening a space in which respectable women could begin to voice demands which no longer automatically placed them on the side of plebian militants or implied wholesale social subversion. The concept of feminist reformism had room to develop.

Many of the women who pioneered this new brand of feminist

agitation had been active within two important bourgeois reform campaigns: the slavery abolition struggle, and the battle for the repeal of the Corn Laws.[54] The victories won in these struggles had revealed to their female participants the possibility of effecting major reforms through sustained pressure group tactics, tactics which some then brought into the emergent women's movement. The anti-slavery crusade was a particularly important training-ground for many feminists, since the analogy between the position of the black slave and the female sex was readily drawn, and the weapons used to win one freedom fight could readily be transferred into another. This connection had been very important in America, where female abolitionists had been in the vanguard of feminist politics from 1840 on. Their success in building national support for the freeing of 'the female slaves' was an additional impetus to the emergence of the British movement, many of whose leaders were in direct contact with their American sisters, learning from their example. 'Yes dear Angelina dear Sarah [sic],' the British feminist abolitionist, Anne Knight, wrote to the American Grimke sisters after the notorious 1840 Anti-Slavery Conference in London where all the female activists had been refused delegates' rights (thus sparking off the first feminist organization in America), 'your noble spirits lighted a flame which has warmed . . . [British women who had] thought not of *our* bondage . . .'[55]

Another important factor was the involvement of many middle-class women in philanthropic schemes directed at women (such as 'rescuing' prostitutes, or providing for unwed mothers), which in the hands of feminist militants could easily take a feminist direction. The idea of 'women's mission' promoted by the evangelicals was never intended to spur women towards radical action, but – as we saw in the case of women like Emma Martin and Catherine Barmby – it frequently did. After 1850 there were a number of evangelical women who if they did not interpret that mission in a Socialistic light, certainly viewed it in a feminist one, as a call to assist all their sisters towards their own emancipation. Josephine Butler, with her mission against the brutal Contagious Diseases legislation, was the most eminent among a host of these salvationist feminists.[56]

Finally, by the late 1840s it was possible to discern certain definite improvements in the position of upper middle-class women, particularly in the area of education – improvements which encouraged some ladies to contemplate the possibility of achieving genuine equality with men of their own class.[57] The spirit of this new optimism was expressed very clearly in the writings of two influential mid-century feminists: Harriet Taylor, author of *The Enfranchisement of Women* (1851) and her husband, John Stuart Mill, author of *The Subjection of Women* (1867).

In the 1830s Harriet Taylor had been a member of the Unitarian circle at South Place Chapel, where Owenite ideas were sympathetically ajred, and her 1851 essay is an interesting blend of standard liberal philosophy and quasi-Owenite sentiments, but with the Owenite side now definitely on the descendant. For in the section of the essay which discussed, *inter alia*, the question of women's economic dependence, Harriet remarked that although she still 'did not believe that . . . the division of mankind into capitalists and hired labourers, and the regulation of the reward of labours mainly by demand and supply, will be for ever, or even much longer, the rule of the world', so long as competition remained 'the general law of human life' it was 'tyranny to shut out one-half of the competitors . . .'[58] Women should, in Mill's later words, be allowed to enter 'the free play of competition' in order to realize their natural abilities. 'Nobody asks for protective duties and bounties in favour of women: it is only asked that the present bounties and protective duties in favour of men should be recalled.'[59] Once women were placed in a position of civil equality with men, and allowed unrestricted access to the same educational and commercial opportunities, ability and enterprise alone would govern individual destinies: 'Whatever women's services are most wanted for, the free play of competition will hold out the strongest inducements for them to undertake . . .'[60] In sexual relations, as in business life, enlightened *laissez-faire*, not 'levelling', would now prove the liberating principle.

This ideal found practical expression in the new feminist organizations of the 1850s and 1860s, which sought to remove from the paths of women some of the major disabilities blocking their route to the 'free exercise of individual ability . . .' So little research has been done on these organizations that it is difficult to offer more than speculative generalizations about them, but from evidence thus far presented a picture emerges of a mode of feminist thought and organization which was both narrower and wider than the Socialist feminism of the preceding decades. It was narrower in its ultimate social goals and also in its base of active support, which throughout the mid-Victorian period seems to have been almost entirely confined to women of the middle, and particularly the upper middle, class.[61] But it was wider in the sense that it eventually involved a far larger number of feminists than Owenism had ever attracted, organizing in independent, women-led associations. By the late 1860s feminism had become (as a number of Owenites had argued it should) an autonomous movement led almost entirely by women themselves. Moreover, if the vision of post-1850 feminism was narrower than that of earlier Socialist feminism, it was also much more sharply focused on what was possible and attainable. In place of the Owenite dream of a communal egalitarian utopia there arose a sustained, pragmatic strategy for the piecemeal reform of women's social and economic condition: what Millicent Garrett Fawcett later described as the struggle for 'the successful removal of intolerable grievances'[62] which had to be uprooted before the foundations for sexual democracy could be laid.

In 1855, Barbara Leigh Smith, a young woman of liberal but far from levelling convictions, called together a group of women to campaign for the introduction of a Parliamentary Bill allowing married women to retain ownership of their own property. In 1857 she and a handful of other feminists established the Association for the Promotion of the Employment of Women whose aim was to relieve 'the unhappy condition of women who had to earn their bread' by establishing training programmes and encouraging employers to consider hiring women for expanding job areas, particularly clerical work.[63] 1858 saw the inauguration of *The English Women's Journal*, the first feminist newspaper to be written and published entirely by women. Over the years the *Journal* and its editorial group, located in Langham Place in London, became the focus of an expanding network of feminist agitators, including pioneers in the campaign for women's higher education, for entry into the professions, for married women's property rights and – eventually – for the vote. Most of the women who led these campaigns were from well-to-do professional or business-owning families; many were the wives or daughters of leading Radicals (later Liberals) or progressive Tories.[64] The movement which they built was bold in its political demands; militant in its opposition to masculine privilege; charitably philanthropic in its attitude towards working-class women (who were generally viewed as objects of sisterly compassion and concern rather than as active agents in their own liberation); highly respectable and decorous in its day-to-day proceedings ('tea-cups and *conversaziones* were the tactics', as one woman wrote, rather than mass meetings or marches);[65] and very cautious in its approach to all sexual matters, eschewing almost entirely the type of libertarian sexual philosophy which had been voiced, and practised, by some Socialists in preceding decades. Its ideology was still far from acceptable to most members of the British upper classes, but it was also a very long way from the radicalism of the Owenite period, which was allowed to slide into the movement's pre-history, as a phase best abandoned and forgotten.

Yet although few of the new movement's leaders would have wished to acknowledge their ultra-radical foremothers (or when they did they generally presented a softened version of them, as in Millicent Fawcett's description of Mary Wollstonecraft as a paragon of domestic virtue[66]), the radical past had left its mark. 'We must not be surprised to find that a diversity of practical aims has existed among the supporters of . . . the women's movement,' noted one of its pioneers,[67] and this diversity often reflected profound differences in social background and outlook, as women who had been raised in the turbulent, polarized atmosphere of the 1830s and 1840s found themselves in a movement dominated by the staider, liberal-reformist mentality of the mid-century. Even a staunch liberal like Barbara Bodichon had had a fairly frisky intellectual past (including an early education from an Owenite teacher),[68] while other women brought both the cultural style and intellectual emphases of those earlier years directly into the new movement.

Emilie Venturi, for example, was the daughter of William Ashurst, Owen's lawyer and personal friend.[69] As a girl, Emilie grew up in the midst of Ashurst's Socialist associates, from whom

280

she imbibed a strong distaste for religion ('she talks of the "Carpenter's Son", meaning Christ, with some respect, but she
considers our faith in him an old and injurious superstition,' the
Evangelical feminist, Josephine Butler, lamented[70]); unconventional social habits (including cigar-smoking); republican
political sentiments (she was Mazzini's literary executor); and a
militantly feminist outlook (which she shared with her sister, who
ran away to France in order to emulate the career of George
Sand). In the 1860s and 70s, Emilie became involved in a host of
feminist campaigns, including the suffrage movement and the
struggle to repeal the Contagious Diseases Acts, where, however,
her divorced status and pronounced radical views made her
something of a black sheep in the feminist flock. Yet she was by no
means unique. A number of other women sympathized with her
ideas, including her friend and fellow-feminist, Elizabeth
Wolstenholme Elmy, who 'modelled her life on . . . [that] of
Mary Wollstonecraft' and cohabited with her lover until she
became pregnant and was persuaded to wed by some of her
suffragist friends. 'The fact that such women existed at all,' Judith
Walkowitz has noted, 'contradicts the common assumption of a
universal prudery and sexual repression among mid-Victorian
feminists'.[71] It also reminds us that many members of the
post-1850 women's movement had served their political
apprenticeships in a period when progressive movements were far
less decorous than they had become by the 1860s and 70s.

No doubt further research will reveal many more women like
these, on the fringe or perhaps even at the centre of some early
feminist organizations – women like Mary Smith (1822–89), a
poor Carlisle spinster who, having supported moral force
Chartism in the early 1840s, became an active participant in the
campaign to repeal the Contagious Diseases Act and the women's
suffrage movement;[72] or Anne Knight (1786–1862), the Quaker
anti-slavery campaigner and Chartist sympathizer who was
friendly with the Barmbys and various other Owenites in the
1840s and helped found the first women's suffrage society;[73] or
other Owenites and Owenite fellow-travellers like Catherine
Barmby, Lady Noel Byron, Mary Leman Grimstone, all of
whom, in the 1850s and 60s, found themselves drawn into 'the
Cause', the multi-pronged movement for women's emancipation.

Even a cursory examination of the movement at a national and local level reveals too a number of Owenite men busy lending a hand. It was Isaac Ironside, the leading Sheffield Socialist, who contacted Anne Knight with the names of seven Chartist women (quite possibly members of the former Owenite branch there as well) who were eager to take action on the women's suffrage issue.[74] Anne immediately wrote to them, and a month later the first recorded Women's Suffrage Society began meeting in Sheffield.[75] Lydia Becker, one of the leaders of the suffrage struggle, was introduced to some of her fellow coadjutors by Goodwyn Barmby, who was a member of the National Society for Women's Suffrage in the 1860s, along with his second wife, Ada.[76] From 1843 on the Barmbys, particularly Catherine, had made various attempts to found a feminist journal, and one of their supporters in these efforts was George Holyoake, who in 1847 wrote a series of articles urging the establishment of such a magazine.[77] In the same year Holyoake had also approached Barbara Leigh Smith, Bessie Rayner Parkes, Emilie Venturi, Harriet Martineau and various other 'ladies interested in the public action of women' with the suggestion that they begin a journal, 'but none thought that my suggestions practicable . . .'[78] A decade later two of these women founded *The English Woman's Journal*. 'Women have organized associations of their own now,' Holyoake wrote several decades later. 'They hold meetings of their own sex, preside over them themselves, speak from the platform, make themselves an independent power in the State, and have come to excel in University contests.'[79]

But despite these tantalizing hints of Owenite involvement in the new feminist organizations at their inception, there is little indication of any real Socialist influence within the Victorian women's movement proper, at least until the left-wing revival of the 1880s and 90s. The legacy of Owenite feminism, in fact, was felt most strongly outside the boundaries of the women's organizations, within another popular agitation of the post-1850 period. This was religious freethought, which under the new name of Secularism not only survived the decline of Owenism, but rapidly became a national movement in its own right, with a number of feminist leaders who saw themselves as direct ideological descendants of Emma Martin.[80] The movement as a whole was a child of Owenite freethought (its leader until the 1860s was Holyoake, and much of its local leadership was in the hands of Owenites). Throughout its history it took women's emancipation as one of its goals, along with (as one branch manifesto stated) 'universal suffrage; the rights of labour; secular education by the state; nationalization of land; Home Colonization . . . and freedom of opinion.'[81] Secularist branches attracted a large female membership, and several of the movement's leading publicists were women, including one woman whose story, it is hoped, will eventually be told in much greater detail – the freethinking socialist feminist, Harriet Law.

Like Emma Martin (who was her heroine) Harriet Law was a lower middle-class woman who, in her early years, had had to support both herself and her family (her father was a failed farmer) by running a school.[82] Like Emma also (in fact the resemblance between the lives of the two women is rather eerie) she was a fervent Baptist (in her case a Strict Baptist) and a dedicated propagandist of Jesus. But in the early 1850s she encountered a number of Owenite infidels lecturing in East London (among them Holyoake and Southwell) and challenged them to public debates, and in the course of these discussions she lost her own religious convictions. Characteristically, as one biographer has noted, her first real doubts arose over St Paul's injunction to women not to speak in the church . . .[83] By the mid-1850s she had openly embraced atheism, feminism, and 'Owenite co-operation' (and also another freethinker, Edward Law, whom she married in 1855). In 1859 she began lecturing on these subjects and soon became Secularism's leading female publicist, using her own journal, *The Secular Chronicle*, to promote 'free enquiry into social, political, and theological questions', including a 'Ladies' Page' which was devoted to 'the advocacy of those political, social and domestic matters that especially affect women'.[84] She was the only woman to sit on the General Council of the First International.[85] One of her greatest admirers was Eleanor Marx, who described Harriet as one of the first women 'to recognise the importance of a woman's organization from the proletarian point of view'. 'When the history of the labour movement in England is written,' Eleanor prophesied, 'the name of Harriet Law will be entered into the golden book of the proletariat . . .'[86] In fact her name has been virtually forgotten, like most of the other Socialist feminists who preceded her.

In the 1870s, Harriet was joined on Secularist platforms by Annie Besant, whose later involvement with women's trade unionism (notably the matchgirls' strike of 1889), the early birth control campaign and Marxist socialism made her a much better-known figure than Harriet.[87] Annie also wrote and spoke very critically on marriage. Her *Marriage as it was, as it is and as it should be*, published in 1882, was an influential text within freethought and socialist circles for several decades; in 1906 a young Marxist cited it, along with Robert Dale Owen's writings, as examples of a continuous tradition of sexual radicalism from which twentieth century socialists had much to learn.[88]

The audiences which Harriet, Annie and other women free-thinkers addressed were largely working class. Secularism was, as Logie Barrow has written, 'the sole nationally organized plebian current of [radical] opinion to last through the mid-Victorian decades'.[89] In London in particular, as Stan Shipley has shown, there existed a network of freethinking working-class clubs where both radical-democratic and socialist ideas continued to flourish in years when, according to most historians, the working-class intelligentsia had all turned from socialism to embrace Liberalism.[90] In the 1860s, one leading freethinker wrote a letter commenting on the interest shown in feminist issues within this radical-secularist network,[91] while in the 1870s Karl Marx complained bitterly to a correspondent about the 'follies and crotchets' of these London clubs, including one 'crotchet' which he described as the 'false emancipation of women'.[92] Over these same years, other former members of the Rational Society kept themselves busy establishing spiritualist associations (which despite their mysticism operated on an ideological terrain bordering on Secularism) as well as small-scale, short-lived community experiments, educational reform schemes, co-operative shops and workshops – and in nearly all these activities they continued to promote feminist ideals. Spiritualism in particular attracted a substantial number of Owenites (including Robert and Robert Dale Owen), and its propaganda, which had a very wide circulation in some working-class districts, frequently dwelled on feminist themes, filtered through the spiritualist perspective.[93]

284

Such evidence, fragmentary as it is, points to the persistence of an Owenite-inspired feminist tradition within plebian circles which ran counter to the increasing sexual conservatism of mainstream labour organizations, and also to the pronounced anti-feminist bias of some later Marxist socialist associations. As Shipley has argued, we need to know far more about the 'crotchets' of these mid-Victorian radicals, particularly their feminist ones, 'which Marx treated as an eccentricity, which diverted the energies of revolutionary-minded men, but which may be better understood in the light of movements of our own day'.[94]

⟡

The 'stupendously grand'[95] vision of a communist-feminist society promoted by the Owenites was ultimately foredoomed both by the inadequacies of their social theory and by the insurmountable practical difficulties which they faced. When socialism revived in Britain towards the end of the nineteenth century, it was with a new set of conceptual tools (those of Marxism, which began to be used systematically at the close of the century) and a new strategic awareness of the obstacles facing a revolutionary movement: developments which gave the struggle for communism a clearer direction and focus. But if certain things were gained in this transition, others were lost. 'At any point after 1850,' Edward Thompson has written, 'Scientific Socialism had no more need for Utopias (and doctrinal authority for suspecting them). Speculation as to the society of the future was repressed, and displaced by attention to strategy.'[96] One result of this was the collapse of the 'moral self-consciousness' necessary to sustain a genuinely libertarian movement; another, I argued earlier, was the decline of the feminist impulse within socialism, as certain issues which had been fundamental to Owenism (such as sexual liberation and the democratization of personal relations) were pushed to the far side of a revolutionary agenda now increasingly dominated by the class-based economic struggles of the industrial proletariat. As the boundaries of the Socialist project thus narrowed, so women's independent aspirations became stranded outside them – to be either ignored, attacked as bourgeois deviationism, or relegated to the category of secondary issues which would be tackled once the primary battle against capitalist exploitation had been won. This development was visible not only within Marxist organizations like the Social Democratic Federation but also within larger, non-Marxist bodies like the Independent Labour Party, signalling a general process of sexual retrenchment which, although by no means universal (all the new Socialist organizations continued to harbour some feminists, and support them) nonetheless marked a significant shift away from the radical feminist commitment of the 1830s and 40s.[97]

In the introduction to this book, I suggested that scrutinizing the socialist tradition in the light of its contribution towards the emancipation of women would produce a rather different image than the one currently dominating most socialists' view of their past. The assumption of a steady progress within socialist thought, from the primitive utopianism of its early years to mature, scientific socialism, has rarely been questioned. Yet when the various phases of socialist development are re-examined in terms of women's liberationist aspirations, it is clear that this description must be challenged. The fact that the Owenites' vision – the vision of a society freed from the deformations of both class exploitation and sexual oppression – proved unrealizable at the time and in the way that they attempted it, in no sense invalidates that hope itself, or makes its suppression within later socialist organizations any less tragic. It was not the ambition for a New Moral World of loving equality between women and men which was 'utopian' (in the pejorative sense) but how the early socialists sought to achieve it. And those who later abandoned that ambition in the name of science and proletarian revolution did not thereby raise the socialist project onto a higher terrain, but contracted it around a narrow programme which left little space for women's needs or women's demands. 'I repudiate that there is any sex antagonism,' as one labour leader told working-class suffragists in denying them his support in the franchise struggle; the women's suffragists, he went on, had 'placed sex first, but . . . we have to put Labour first in every case . . .'[98]

Yet the older dream *did* survive, if only as an imaginative undercurrent flowing against the dominant stream of socialist thought. One need only read Eleanor Marx and Edward Aveling's 1886 essay on the abolition of 'sex-slavery' under socialism;[99] or

Edward Carpenter's 1890s manifestoes for a New Life socialism which would free women and men not only from the crippling effects of sex-based hierarchy but also from the rigid enforcement of heterosexual self-identification;[100] or Hannah Mitchell's account of feminist propaganda in the Labour Churches at the turn of the century;[101] or Stella Browne's writings on women and sexual freedom, produced in the teeth of the Communist Party opposition in the 1920s,[102] to realize how many of the ideas, and sometimes even the vocabulary, of Owenism persisted into later socialist feminism. And in the 1960s and 70s, as a new generation of socialist feminists began to organize, we too looked back to the pre-Marxian socialists: not out of nostalgia for an ideological moment long since past, or in rejection of the lessons learned since, but as a way of tracing the beginnings of a communist-feminist project with which we still identify.[103] It is a project for which we also have been dubbed divisive and utopian, but as one leading Socialist suffragist said in 1913, when describing her dream of a 'beautiful Socialist order' constructed on the twin foundations of sex and class equality: 'Utopian it may be called. We care not. It is a dream worth living for . . . working for . . .'[104] From the Owenites onward, then, it would seem that what has counted as utopian answers has depended on who has been raising the questions.

NOTES

The place of publication, unless otherwise indicated, is London. Where anything other than a first edition has been used, the date of the first edition and the edition used have both been given.

Abbreviations:

Public Record Office, Home Office Papers ...   .   HO
(followed by relevant file number)

The New Moral World ...   .   *NMW*

Correspondence (as in Owen Correspondence) ... ... Corres.

Introduction (*pp. ix–xiii*)

1 Charles Fourier, *Théorie des Quatre Mouvements, Oeuvres Complètes* (Paris, 1841-5), p. 43.
2 For Owen's career see, among many others, A.L. Morton, *The Life and Ideas of Robert Owen*, first ed. 1962 (1969); G.D.H. Cole, *The Life of Robert Owen*, first ed. 1925 (1965); S. Pollard and J. Salt, eds., *Robert Owen, Prophet of the Poor* (1971); J.F.C. Harrison, *Robert Owen and the Owenites: the Quest for the New Moral World* (1969).
3 Harriet Martineau, *Biographical Sketches*, first ed. 1869 (1876), quoted in Harrison, *Owen*, p. 157.
4 Robert Owen, *Life of Robert Owen, by Himself*, first ed. 1857 (1971), p. 184, 176.
5 *ibid.*, p. 241.
6 *The Liverpool Standard*, 7 September 1839.
7 Frederick Engels, *The Condition of the Working Class in England*, first ed., 1845 (Moscow, 1973), p. 274.
8 J.S. Mill, *The Principles of Political Economy, Collected Works*, vol. 2 (Toronto, 1963), p. 209; J.S. Mill, *Autobiography* (1873), pp. 167-8. Mill personally favoured the Saint Simonian version of socialism (by which he

was deeply influenced in his youth), but admired all of the 'Utopian' pioneers – the Saint Simonians, Fourier and Owen – for their views on women.

9 The few studies which do consider it include Harrison, *Owen*; J. Saville, 'Robert Owen on the Family', in M. Cornforth, ed., *Rebels and Their Causes* (1978); G.K. Malmgreen, *Neither Bread Nor Roses: Utopian Feminists and the English Working Class, 1800–1850* (Brighton, 1978). See also Sheila Rowbotham, *Women, Resistance and Revolution* (1973), pp. 47–58 and her *Hidden From History: Three Hundred Years of Women's Oppression and the Fight Against It* (1973), pp. 38–46. There is a useful discussion of Owenite feminism in John Killham, *Tennyson and the Princess: Reflections of an Age* (1958), ch. 3.

10 Frederick Engels, *Socialism: Utopian and Scientific*, first English ed., 1892, in K. Marx and F. Engels, *Selected Works* (New York, 1968), p. 401.

11 *NMW*, 20 July 1839.

12 Karl Marx and Frederick Engels, *The Manifesto of the Communist Party*, first ed. 1848, in *Selected Works*, p. 60.

13 *ibid.*, p. 61. Marx and Engels are here discussing the doctrines of all three major 'Utopian' socialists – Fourier, Saint Simon and Owen – but the point applies equally to all three.

14 Certain aspects of Owenism, it should be noted, are seen as assimilable to this class-based view of 'real' socialism, notably the co-operatives and trade unions of the early 1830s which are generally regarded as early chapters in the evolution of the modern labour movement. The post-1835 phase of Owenism, when cultural, educational and sexual issues were paramount, cannot be assimilated to the 'labourist' model in this way, however, and is therefore described either as mere utopian crankery or as an ideological throwback to certain brands of religious sectarianism. A discussion of this phasing of Owenism, and the character of the post-1835 movement, is to be found in Chapter Five.

15 Quoted in E.P. Thompson, 'Romanticism, Moralism and Utopianism: the Case of William Morris', *New Left Review*, no. 99 (September–October 1976), p. 107.

16 *ibid.*, p. 98.

17 See, for example, the critiques of 'women's rightsers' offered by Bebel, Eleanor Marx, Rosa Luxembourg, and Louise Kautsky, collected in Hal Draper and Anne Lipow, 'Marxist Women Vs. Bourgeois Feminism', *The Socialist Register*, vol. 13 (1976), pp. 179–226. Obviously there were individuals and organizations which swam against the tide, and persisted in presenting a version of socialism which addressed personal/sexual relations as well as class ones. But they were definitely (particularly in this century) in a small, and often beleaguered, minority (for a further discussion of this see the Conclusion).

18 *ibid.*, and see also 'Some Responses to Feminism in the Socialist Movement before 1914' in Rowbotham, *Hidden*, ch. 16.

19 The literature on all but the suffrage phase of feminist struggle in nineteenth century Britain is still very small, but nonetheless remarkably homogeneous in its presentation of the ideology, membership and aims of feminism. See, for example, W.L. O'Neill, *The Woman Movement* (1969); Duncan Crow, *The Victorian Woman* (1971), ch. 10; Richard Evans, *The Feminists* (1979),

especially chs. 1,3; Marion Ramelson, *The Petticoat Rebellion: a Century of Struggle for Women's Rights* (1972); J.A. and O. Banks, *Feminism and Family Planning in Victorian England* (Liverpool, 1964). For a challenging essay on feminism as a bourgeois egalitarian ideology, see J. Mitchell, 'Women and Equality', in J. Mitchell and A. Oakley, eds., *The Rights and Wrongs of Women* (Harmondsworth, 1976). A number of these accounts do mention individual Owenites (particularly Anna Wheeler and William Thompson) and their views on women, but make no attempt to place them in the context of Owenite feminism as a whole.

20 For some recent books which are reshaping our view of post-1850 British feminism, see Jill Liddington and Jill Norris, *One Hand Tied Behind Us: the Rise of the Women's Suffrage Movement* (1978); Judith Walkowitz, *Prostitution and Victorian Society: Women, Class and the State* (1980); and Sheila Rowbotham's pathbreaking studies, cited above. All these books, it is worth noting, are by women active in the contemporary women's movement.

21 See Chapter Eight.

22 For socialist-feminist critiques of present-day socialist movements, see S. Rowbotham, H. Wainwright and L. Segal, *Beyond the Fragments: Feminism and the Making of Socialism* (1980); Anne Phillips, 'Marxism and Feminism' and Rosalind Coward, 'Socialism, Feminism and Socialist Feminism', both in Feminist Anthology Collective, *No Turning Back* (1981). And for an essay which, from a rather different direction, provides the basis for a modern utopian challenge to 'actually existing socialism', see Raymond Williams, 'Beyond Actually Existing Socialism', *New Left Review* no. 120 (March-April 1980), pp. 3–19.

I   The Rights Of Woman: A Radical Inheritance

1 Quoted in Claire Tomalin, *The Life and Death of Mary Wollstonecraft* (Harmondsworth, 1977), p. 144. Tomalin's book contains a good account of radical circles in the 1790s. Other studies of Wollstonecraft and her times include: Ralph Wardle, *Mary Wollstonecraft* (Kansas, 1951); Margaret George, *One Woman's Situation* (Illinois, 1970); Eleanor Flexner, *Mary Wollstonecraft* (New York, 1972); H. N. Brailsford, *Shelley, Godwin and their Circle* (1913); Ruby Saywell, 'The Feminist Idea in England, 1789–1833' (MA Thesis, University of London, 1936); M. S. Storr, *Mary Wollstonecraft et le Mouvement Feministe dans la Litterature Anglaise* (Paris, 1932).

2 Thomas Paine, *Rights of Man*, first ed. 1791–92 (Harmondsworth, 1977), p. 181.

3 Mary Wollstonecraft, *An Historical and Moral View of the Origin and Progress of the French Revolution* (1795), p. 20.

4 Mary Wollstonecraft, *A Vindication of the Rights of Men, in a Letter to the Right Honourable Edmund Burke* (1970), p. 149.

5 Mary Wollstonecraft, *A Vindication of the Rights of Woman*, first ed. 1792 (1970), p. 9.

6 For an interesting discussion of anti-patriarchalist ideas in the work of Locke

and Hobbes, see Elizabeth Fox-Genovese, 'Property and Patriarchy in Classical Bourgeois Political Theory', *Radical History Review*, vol. 4, no. 2–3 (1977).

7   Wollstonecraft, *Rights of Woman*, p. 11.
8   *ibid.*, p. 12.
9   *ibid.*, p. 51.
10 For a discussion of these changes in the position of middle-class women, see Ivy Pinchbeck, *Women Workers and the Industrial Revolution, 1750–1850*, first ed. 1930 (1969), pp. 282–3; Alice Clark, *The Working Life of Women in the Seventeenth Century*, first ed. 1919 (1968), pp. 291–308; Fabian Society, *The Economic Foundations of the Women's Movement* (1914), pp. 5–7; J.D. Milne, *Industrial and Social Employment of Women in the Middle and Lower Ranks*, first ed. 1857 (1870), pp. 326–9.
11 Wollstonecraft, *Rights of Woman*, p. 38.
12 *ibid.*, p. 62.
13 *ibid.*, pp. 63–4.
14 Wollstonecraft, *French Revolution*, p. 19.
15 *ibid.*, pp. 518–9.
16 Mary Wollstonecraft, *Letters Written During a Short Residence in Sweden, Norway and Denmark* (1796), p. 170.
17 Mary Wollstonecraft, *Maria or the Wrongs of Woman*, first ed. 1798 (New York, 1975), p. 8.
18 Wollstonecraft, *Rights of Woman*, p. 161.
19 Wollstonecraft, *Rights of Men*, p. 148.
20 Franco Venturi, *Utopia and Reform in the Enlightenment* (Cambridge, 1971), pp. 97–100.
21 William Godwin, *Enquiry into Political Justice* (1793). For a detailed discussion of Godwin's proposals, see Brailsford, *Shelley*, pp. 94–141.
22 Thomas Spence, *The Meridian Sun of Liberty: or the Whole Rights of Man Displayed and Most Accurately Defined* (1796), p. 8, 12. For Spence's life and writings, see O.D. Rudkin, *Thomas Spence and His Connections* (1927) and the biography produced by one of his followers who later joined the Owenite ranks, Allen Davenport: *The Life, Writings and Principles of Thomas Spence* (1836). For an interesting examination of the role of communalist ideas within late eighteenth century English radicalism, see Stephen F. Wolfe, 'The Rhetoric of English Radicalism, 1780–1830' (Ph D Thesis, York University, [1976], chapter two).
23 See chapters five and eight for further discussions of this tradition.
24 Thomas Spence, *The Right of Infants; or, the Imprescriptable RIGHT of MOTHERS to such share of the Elements as is sufficient to enable them to suckle and bring up their Young* (1797). This tract is in the form of a dialogue between a woman and an aristocrat, in which the woman declares that having found the menfolk unwilling to defend their own rights, 'we women mean to take up the business ourselves' and act on behalf of their starving children. For Spence's views on marriage see also 'The Marriage Act Censured', in *Pig's Meat*, vol. 1 (1793).
25 Godwin, 'Of Co-operation, Cohabitation and Marriage' (*Political Justice*, Book 8, Appendix).
26 The extent of Godwin's influence on Owen is difficult to judge since Owen rarely acknowledged intellectual debts to anyone, preferring to present his

ideas as wholly original. But the resemblance between his ideas on marriage and those put forward by Godwin is too close to be coincidental, particularly as we know the two men were well acquainted: Godwin's diary for the years 1813–18 records frequent visits from Owen, sometimes as many as four a week. It was on one of these visits, Godwin claimed, that he converted Owen 'from the system of self-love to benevolence' (i.e. from capitalism to communism) in a single conversation (Frederick Rosen, 'Progress and Democracy: William Godwin's Contribution to Political Philosophy', Ph D Thesis, University of London [1965], pp. 287–90, 214–5). Thanks to Greg Claeys for this reference.

27 Coleridge, quoted in Tomalin, *Wollstonecraft*, p. 133n. For the story of the Pantisocratic plan, see Brailsford, *Shelley*, pp. 51–5; W.H.G.Armytage, *Heavens Below: Utopian Experiments in England, 1560–1960* (1961), pp. 62–8. William Blake's visionary utopianism was obviously another current flowing into this stream of thought, but his was far too complex and ambiguous a contribution to be dealt with here.

28 B: Cone, *The English Jacobins* (New York, 1968), p. 114.

29 M.J. Quinlan, *Victorian Prelude* (New York, 1941), p. 72.

30 Brian Simon, *The Two Nations and the Educational Structure, 1780–1870*, first ed. 1960 (1974), p. 79.

31 Jeremy Bentham, *The Theory of Morals and Legislation* (1802); quoted in T. Nairn, 'The English Working Class', in R. Blackburn, ed., *Ideology in Social Science* (1972), p. 192.

32 E. Burke, *A Letter from the Right Honourable Edmund Burke to a Noble Lord* (1796), p. 21.

33 Richard Polwhele, *The Unsex'd Females*, first ed. 1793 (New York, 1800), p. 12.

34 *The Monthly Visitor* (1798); quoted in Tomalin, *Wollstonecraft*, p. 290. The publication of Godwin's *Memoirs of the Author of a Vindication of the Rights of Woman* (1798), with its revelations about Mary's sexual history, was a decisive factor in turning public opinion against her (R.M. Janes, 'On the Reception of Mary Wollstonecraft's *A Vindication of the Rights of Woman*', *Journal of the History of Ideas*, vol. 39, no. 2 [1978], pp. 293–302).

35 Saywell, *Feminist Ideas*, pp. 46–7.

36 'The Old Woman – No. III', *The Ladies Monthly Museum*, vol. 1 (September 1798), p. 186.

37 John Gale Jones, *Sketches of a Political Tour* (1796), p. 91.

38 E.P. Thompson, *The Making of the English Working Class*, first ed. 1963 (Harmondsworth, 1972), p. 60.

39 Arthur Young, *An Enquiry into the State of the Public Mind* (1798), p. 25.

40 William Wilberforce, *A Practical View of the Prevailing Religious System of Professed Christians in the Higher and Middle Classes in This Country, Contrasted with Real Christianity* (1797), p. 40. The religious revival actually began, in the form of Methodism, in the 1730s, but it was in the 1790s that it acquired the momentum, particularly in the middle and upper classes, which carried it into Victorian England. For an excellent discussion of the relationship between the revival and counter-revolutionary ideology, see V. Kiernan, 'Evangelicalism and the French Revolution', *Past and Present*, no. 1 (1952). For an interesting account of the impact of

Evangelicalism on 'manners and morals' see Quinlan, *Prelude*, chapters four to ten.

41 'Will Chip' (Hannah More), *Village Politics* (1792), p. 19.

42 Hannah More, *Life and Correspondence*, 4 vols. (1834) vol. 3, p. 453; quoted in Catherine Hall, 'The Early Formation of Victorian Domestic Ideology', in S. Burman, ed., *Fit Work for Women* (1979), p. 25. I am grateful to Catherine Hall for letting me see this essay prior to publication. For a longer discussion of the impact of the religious revival on sexual attitudes, see below, pp. 123–128.

43 Thomas Gisborne, M.A., *An Enquiry into the Duties of the Female Sex* (1813), p. 124.

44 D.M. Stenton, *The English Woman in History* (1957), p. 313.

45 Polwhele, *Females*, p. 37.

46 See below, pp. 128–182.

47 G.K. Malmgreen, *Women's Suffrage in England: Origins and Alternatives, 1792–1851* (MA Thesis, Hull University, 1975), pp. 27–30. For Wollstonecraft's views, see *Rights of Woman*, p. 161.

48 The *Essay on Government* in which Mill argued this was first printed in the Supplement to the fifth edition of the *Encyclopedia Britannica* (1821) and then re-printed many times. It was, according to Ernest Barker, 'the classical statement of the political theory of the Benthamites' (introduction to *Essay on Government* [Cambridge, 1937], p. xiv). The actual statement on women (p. 45) ran:

> One thing is pretty clear, that all those individuals whose interest are indisputably included in those of other individuals, may be struck off without inconvenience. In this light may be viewed all children, up to a certain age, whose interests are involved in those of their parents. In this light, also, women may be regarded, the interest of almost all of whom is involved either in that of their fathers or in that of their husbands.

For his remarks relating to working-class suffrage, see pp. 47–51, 71–3. Mill's position on female enfranchisement was immediately criticized by some of the young Turks of Utilitarianism, including his son John Stuart Mill (always a man uneasy with the limits of the liberal perspective) who claimed that Bentham also opposed his father's view (J.S. Mill, *Autobiography* [1867], p. 68). There is, however, very little evidence that Bentham was particularly favourable to feminist ideals, despite his close friendship with feminists like Anna Wheeler and Fanny Wright. (Miriam Willisford has claimed to the contrary in her 'Bentham on the rights of Women', *Journal of the History of Ideas*, vol. 26, no. 1 [1975], pp. 167–76, but her evidence for Bentham's feminism is not very convincing. See Malmgreen, *Women's Suffrage*, pp. 95–7, for a more critical assessment of Bentham's contribution to feminist thought.)

49 P.B. Shelley, 'Queen Mab', *Poems of Shelley* (1970), p. 93, 92.

50 Robert Owen, *Report to the County of Lanark*, first ed. 1821 (edited and with an introduction by V.A.C. Gattrell, Harmondsworth, 1969), pp. 232–3, 257. See also G.D.H. Cole, *A History of Socialist Thought: Volume 1: The Forerunners, 1789–1850* (1953), p. 88.

51 The full title of the book was *Appeal of One-Half the Human Race, Women, against the Pretensions of the other Half, Men, to retain them in political,*

and thence in civil and domestic Slavery: in Reply to a Paragraph of Mr Mill's celebrated 'Article on Government' (1825). It was published under Thompson's name (for a discussion of its authorship, see pp. 22–23). For the background to the book and its authors, see R.K.P. Pankhurst, *William Thompson, 1775–1833, Britain's Pioneer Socialist, Feminist and Co-operator* (1954).

52 *ibid.,* p. xi.
53 *ibid.,* pp. ix–xiv.
54 Shelley, 'Queen Mab', p. 120.

II Women And The New Science Of Society

1 Marx and Engels, *Communist Manifesto,* p. 89.
2 *The Crisis,* 31 August 1833. She signed this letter with a pseudonym, 'Vlasta'.
3 John Gray, *A Lecture on Human Happiness* (Edinburgh, 1825), pp. 31–2.
4 *The Economist,* 3 February 1821.
5 Robert Owen, *A New View of Society,* first ed. 1814 (edited and with an introduction by V.A.C. Gattrell, Harmondsworth, 1969), p. 140.
6 Norman Hampson, *The Enlightenment* (Harmondsworth, 1968), chapter three. See also Harrison, *Owen,* pp. 83–7 for a discussion of the Enlightenment intellectual background to Owen's ideas.
7 Owen, *New View,* p. 101.
8 *The Crisis,* 22 March 1834.
9 Owen, *Report,* p. 232.
10 Owen added marriage to religion and private property in his 'trinity of the most monstrous evils that could be combined to inflict mental and physical evil upon the whole race' in July, 1826. See *The New Harmony Gazette,* 12 July 1826.
11 Charles Bray, *The Philosophy of Necessity,* 2 vols. (1841), vol. 1, p. 434; quoted in Eileen Yeo, 'Social Science and Social Change: a Social History of Some Aspects of Social Science and Social Investigation in Britain. 1830–1890' (Ph D Thesis, University of Sussex, 1972), p. 61.
12 For a discussion of Owenite economic doctrine, see Chapter Four.
13 For a very interesting discussion of the contrast between early Socialism (including Owenism) and Marxism, see Gareth Stedman Jones, 'Utopian Socialism Reconsidered – Science and Religion in the early Socialist Movement', forthcoming *History Workshop Journal.* I am grateful to the author for allowing me to see this essay prior to publication.
14 *The Crisis,* 31 August 1833.
15 James Smith writing in *The Crisis,* 22 March 1834.
16 Marx and Engels, *Communist Manifesto,* pp. 90–1.
17 Thompson, *Appeal,* p. 209, 213.
18 Thompson, *Appeal,* p. 107.
19 *ibid.,* pp. 12–14.
20 William Thompson, *An Inquiry into the Principles of the Distribution of Wealth most conducive to Human Happiness; applied to the newly*

proposed system of Voluntary Equality of Wealth (1824), p. 373; Thompson, *Appeal*, p. 199, 211, 213.

21 *The Co-operative Magazine*, August 1826; Thompson, *Appeal*, p. 93.
22 *The Crisis*, 31 August 1833.
23 *ibid.*
24 Wollstonecraft, *French Revolution*, p. 17.
25 Charlotte Elizabeth Tonna, *The Wrongs of Woman* (1843), p. 4.
26 Gisborne, *Female Sex*, pp. 10–11.
27 Wollstonecraft, *Rights of Woman*, p. 104.
28 *NMW*, 19 July 1845.
29 *The Crisis*, 17 August 1833.
30 *ibid.*
31 *NMW*, 27 July 1839.
32 *The Co-operative Magazine*, August 1826.
33 *The British Co-operator*, April 1830.
34 *The Crisis*, 22 March, 5 April 1834.
35 *ibid.*, 3 May 1834.
36 *NMW*, 27 July 1839.
37 *The British Co-operator*, April 1830.
38 See, for example, John Millar, *The Origin of the Distinction of Ranks* (1777); Baron d'Holbach, *Système Sociale* (Paris, 1774).
39 See, for example, Lady Morgan, *Woman and Her Master* (1844); Mrs Hugo Reid, *Women's Rights and Duties* (1840); Anna Jameson, *Winter Studies and Summer Rambles*, 3 vols. (1838). See also Gisborne, *Female Sex*, p. 8, for another, anti-feminist use of the evolutionist argument – also very popular in the early nineteenth century – in which Christian marriage doctrine was claimed to represent the triumph of Civilization over Barbaric sexual practices (such as polygamy).
40 Charles Fourier, *Théorie des Quatre Mouvements* reprinted in J. Beecher and R. Bienvenu, *The Utopian Vision of Charles Fourier* (Boston, 1971), pp. 194–6. For Fourierite influence and community-building in America, see J.H. Noyes, *Strange Cults and Utopias of Nineteenth Century America* (original title: *History of American Socialisms* [Philadelphia, 1870]), edited and introduced by Mark Holloway (New York, 1966).
41 Frances Wright, *Course of Popular Lectures* (New York, 1829), p. 24.
42 Thompson, *Appeal*, p. 113.
43 Thompson, *Appeal*, p. 110.
44 *The British Co-operator*, April 1830.
45 For the classic anti-feminist version of the argument see Sarah Lewis, *Woman's Mission* (1839). The concept of women as a moral vanguard is discussed in greater detail below (pp. 124–128).
46 'Syrtis', 'The Social and Domestic Condition of Woman', *NMW*, 9 August 1845.
47 W.R. Waterman, *Frances Wright* (New York, 1924), p. 74.
48 Thompson, *Appeal*, pp. ix–x.
49 *The British Co-operator*, April 1830.
50 Mary Astell, *Reflections upon Marriage* (1700), no pagination.
51 Wollstonecraft, *Rights of Woman*, p. 46.
52 *Ladies Monthly Museum*, Vol. 1 (September 1798), p. 145.
53 Thompson, *Making*, p. 178.

54 *NMW*, 1 March 1843.

55 Wetenhall Wilkes, *A Letter of Genteel and Moral Advice to a Young Lady* (1740); quoted in Lawrence Stone, *The Family, Sex, and Marriage in England, 1500–1800* (1977), p. 327.

56 Daniel Defoe, *Complete English Tradesman* (1726); quoted in Stone, *Family*, p. 326. The emergence of the romantic marital ideal in the English middle class has been the subject of many studies, of which I have found the following most useful: Ian Watt, *The Rise of the Novel* (Harmondsworth, 1977), esp. chapter five; Christopher Hill, 'Clarissa Harlowe and Her Times', in *Puritanism and Revolution* (1958); Keith Thomas, 'The Double Standard', *Journal of the History of Ideas*, vol. xx, no. 2 (1959); J.T. Johnson, 'The Covenant Idea and the Puritan View of Marriage', *Journal of the History of Ideas*, vol. xxxii, no. 2 (1971); R.P. Utter and G.B. Needham, *Pamela's Daughters* (1937) and Stone's uneven, exasperating and fascinating study, *Family* (especially chapters six, seven, and eight).

57 Hill, 'Clarissa Harlowe', p. 384.

58 Thompson, *Appeal*, p. 79.

59 *ibid.*, pp 55–7.

60 Wollstonecraft, *Maria*, p. 27.

61 Thompson, *Appeal*, p. 67, 63.

62 *The Pioneer*, 15 March 1834.

63 Thompson, *Appeal*, p. 86. For the legal status of married women in this period, see Caroline H. Dall, *Woman's Rights under the Law* (1861); Erna Reiss, *The Rights and Duties of Englishwomen* (Manchester, 1934); O.R. McGregor, *Divorce in England* (1957).

64 Mrs Johnstone, 'Plea for Women' (review of Mrs Hugo Reid's *A Plea for Women* [1843]), *Tait's Magazine* (July 1844); reprinted in *NMW*, 17 August 1844.

65 Wollstonecraft, *Rights of Woman*, p. 164.

66 Thompson, *Inquiry*, p. 373.

67 Frances Morrison, *The Influence of the Present Marriage System Upon the Character and Interests of Females, etc . . .* (Manchester, 1838), p. 10.

68 Thompson, *Appeal*, p. 201.

69 *ibid.*, p. 180, 179, 192; *Inquiry*, pp. 372–3.

70 *The Co-operative Magazine*, August 1826.

71 Thompson, *Appeal*, p. 71.

72 See, for example, W.J. Fox, 'The Dissenting Marriage Question', *The Monthly Repository*, vol. 7 (1833), pp. 136–42; *The Westminster Review* vol. 1 (April 1824), p. 537; *The Moral Reformer*, 1 December 1831.

73 See McGregor, *Divorce*, for the story of nineteenth and twentieth century divorce law reform, and its supporters.

74 Robert Owen, *Lectures on the Marriages of the Priesthood in the Old Immoral World . . . with an Appendix containing the Marriage System of the New Moral World*, first ed. 1835 (Leeds, 1840), p. 30, pp 36–7.

75 For descriptions of the American communitarian sects who influenced Owen, see R.L. Muncy, *Sex and Marriage in Utopian Communities: Nineteenth Century America* (Bloomington, 1973), pp. 9–63; Noyes, *Cults*, pp. 10–58. His most important contacts were with the Rappites and the Shakers, both of whom not only lived collectively but also practised complete sexual abstinence. Owen strongly disapproved of this celibacy rule.

76 Noyes, *Cults*, p. 143.
77 Quoted in Muncy, *Sex*, p. 62. For the story of the New Harmony community, see G. Lockwood, The *New Harmony Movement*, first ed. 1905 (New York, 1971). Whether Owen's hostility to conventional marriage stemmed from his own marital experience is unclear. Certainly he seems to have spent a good deal of time away from his wife (Caroline Dale, the daughter of his former employer at New Lanark) and Harrison has suggested that she was a 'rather sad and lonely figure' (Harrison, 'A New View', p. 5). He left her in Britain when he went to America in 1824–29 and she died in 1831, so a good deal of his political career occurred in her absence.

  By contrast, Robert Dale Owen married a feminist, Mary Robinson, who lectured on women's rights in New York in the 1850s, and actively supported her husband in his career in the Indiana legislature, where he fought for major reforms in women's legal position (Lockwood, *New Harmony*, pp. 201–8).
78 Fanny Imlay (Wollstonecraft's illegitimate daughter) recorded Owen telling her how much he admired her mother (Tomalin, *Wollstonecraft*, p. 174n.). On several occasions Owen argued that women, like the working class, were unequipped to organize for their own emancipation, but had to await the assistance of those whose 'moral qualities' and 'intellectual capacities' were more fully developed – presumably middle-class men (see, for example, *The Crisis*, 24 August 1833; *NMW*, 16 September 1843).
79 Owen, *Marriages*, pp. 20–5. For a recent discussion of Owen's views on the family and marriage see Saville, 'Owen on the Family', pp. 107–21.
80 Owen, *ibid.*, p. 16.
81 *Old England*, 26 October 1839.
82 See, for example, Charles Southwell, *An Essay on Marriage, Addressed to the Lord Bishop of Exeter* (1840), p. 6; *NMW*, 17 May 1845; *The Man*, 29 September 1833.
83 *The Man*, 29 September 1833.
84 Owen, *Marriages*, p. 75.
85 *ibid.*, p. 12.
86 *ibid.*, p. 71,63.
87 *ibid.*, pp. 44–5.
88 P. B. Shelley, *Queen Mab, a Philosophical Poem, with Notes* (1813), p. 145. Quotations from Shelley (especially *Queen Mab* and *The Revolt of Islam*) appear throughout the Owenite feminist literature: see for example, *NMW*, 3 April 1841; Catherine Barmby, 'The Demand for the Emancipation of Woman, Politically and Socially', *New Tracts for the Times*, vol. 1, no. 3 (1843), p. 39; letter from Anna Wheeler to Owen, Owen Corres. 426. Owen's views on marriage were constantly equated with Shelley's (by both supporters and opponents) in the late 1830s and 1840s. It is interesting to note, however, that although Owenite women frequently quoted Shelley on women's right to social equality, they rarely quoted his comments on marriage.
89 Godwin, *Political Justice*, pp. 243–4.
90 Shelley, *Queen Mab*, Canto IX.
91 *NMW*, 17 May 1845.
92 Hill discusses this suppressed erotic component of the ideology of romantic marriage in 'Clarissa Harlowe', p. 391. Compare, for example, Shelley's or

Owen's views on the 'transitory nature of the affections' to this seventeenth century Puritan moralist:

> As *Faith, so Love cannot be constrained*. As there is no affection more forcible, so there is none freer from force and compulsion. The very offer of enforcement turneth it oft into hatred.
>
> (Thomas Gataker, *The Good Wife* [16?]; quoted in W. and M. Hadler, 'The Puritan Art of Love', *Huntington Library Quarterly*, vol. 5 [1942], p. 263).

93   W.E. Houghton, *The Victorian Frame of Mind, 1830-70* (Princeton, 1957), p. 379. 'The study of Victorian love,' Houghton comments, 'is a study of how this tradition [of Romanticism] embodied mainly in the works of Rousseau, Shelley, and George Sand, was domesticated under the powerful influence of Evangelical family sentiment' (p. 375).

94   *NMW*, 19 December 1835 (written under pseud. 'Kate').

95   For the story of the Saint-Simonian mission in England, see R.K.P. Pankhurst, *The Saint Simonians, Mill and Carlyle* (1957). Their activities can also be traced through the major radical working-class periodicals between 1832 and 1834, particularly *The Crisis, The Poor Man's Guardian, The Destructive and Poor Man's Conservative, The People's Conservative*. Pankhurst discussed their feminist views; for a more detailed account see M. Thibert, *Le Feminisme dans le Socialisme Francaise* (Paris, 1926).

96   For Anna Wheeler's relationship with the Saint Simonians, see R.K.P. Pankhurst, 'Anna Wheeler: a Pioneer Socialist and Feminist', *Political Quarterly*, vol. 25, no 2. (1954), pp. 134-5, 140, 142; and also J. Gans, 'Les Relations entre Socialistes de France et d'Angleterre au debut du XIX[e] Siecle', *Le Mouvement Social*, no. 46 (1964), pp. 161-74. For her translations of Saint-Simonian feminist texts, see, for example, *The Crisis*, 15 June 1833.

97   *The Destructive*, 4 January 1834. Both Anna Wheeler and Eliza Macauley lectured for the Saint Simonians (*The Poor Man's Guardian*, 11 January 1834).

98   Quoted in *The People's Conservative*, 22 February 1834.

99   See below, pp. 168-169.

100   *The Crisis*, 31 August 1833.

101   *ibid.*

102.   Wollstonecraft, *Rights of Woman*, p. 92. 'In order to fulfill the duties of life, and to be able to pursue with vigour the various employments which form the moral character, a master and mistress of a family ought not to continue to love each other with passion' (*Rights of Woman*, p. 33).

103   *ibid.*, p. 36.

104   Robert Owen, *Book of the New Moral World*, Parts IV-VII (1844), Part VI, p. 48.

105   Joshua Hobson, *Socialism as It Is!* (Leeds, 1838), p. 134.

106   *NMW*, 25 July 1835.

107   *ibid.*, 3 December 1836.

108   See, for example, the exchange between a woman Owenite and the editor of *The Crisis*, in *The Crisis*, 28 December 1833, 4 January 1834.

109   Thompson, *Inquiry*, pp. 372-3, and William Thompson, *Practical*

Directions for the speedy and economical Establishment of Communities on the Principles of Mutual Co-operation, united Possessions and Equality of Exertions and of the Means of Enjoyments (1830), p. 61.

110   Thompson, *Practical Directions*, p. 3.

111   *NMW*, 2 May 1840.

112   *The Economist*, 21 April 1821.

113   *NMW*, 24 June 1837. See below, pp. 247-252, for a discussion of how plans for collectivized housework worked out in practice.

114   *ibid.*, 4 June 1836.

115   *ibid.*

116   Thompson, *Appeal*, p. 179.

117   *The Man*, 29 September 1833.

118   Thompson, *Practical Directions*, p. 3. The argument that the introduction of machinery would allow women a greater role in production was popular among the Owenites: see also, Henry McCormac, *On Improving the Moral and Physical Condition of the Working Classes* (Belfast, 1830), p. 13.

119   Robert Cooper, *A Contrast Between the New Moral World and the Old Immoral World* (Hulme, 1838), p. 8. Like all the community proposals, Cooper's contained plans for a collective nursery: 'their parents, however, might see them (the children) at any moment they pleased' (p. 10). For Owen's plan, see *Book of the New Moral World*, Part VI, pp 59-77.

120   Owen, *Marriages*, Appendix, pp. 88-9.

121   Thompson, *Practical Directions*, pp. 246-7.

122   *ibid.*, 'Apprehended Evils from Increase of Numbers', pp. 233-41.

123   *ibid.*, p. 229.

124   'In those alarmed days, when politicians and capitalists were as terrified as shopkeepers of Co-operation, Mr Owen countenanced the discussion of a new question which has strangely passed out of the sight of history . . . This question concerned none save the poor, and he boldly counselled them against supplying offspring to be ground up alive in the mill of capital; or be cast aside when the labour market was glutted to fall into the hands of the constable or the parish overseer' (G.J. Holyoake, *The History of Co-operation*, first ed. 1875-79 [1906], p. 47). Others have challenged Holyoake's account, however: see Norman E. Himes, 'The Place of J. S. Mill and Robert Owen in the History of English Neo-Malthusianism', *Quarterly Journal of Economics* (August 1928). See also Angus McLaren, 'Contraception and the Working Classes: The Social Ideology of the English Birth Control Movement in its Early Years', *Comparative Studies in Society and History*, vol. 18, no. 2 (April 1976).

125   Robert Dale Owen, *Moral Physiology; or a Brief and Plain Treatise on the Population Question*, first ed. New York, 1830 (1870), p. 15.

126   Richard Carlile, *Everywoman's Book, or What is Love?* (1828), p. 23.

127   Owen, *Moral Physiology*, p. 151.

128   Thompson, *Appeal*, p. 151.

129   Catherine Barmby, 'Reply to Anne Knight', in *Some Account of the Progress of the Truth as It Is in Jesus*, no. 31 (1844), p. 39.

130   *NMW*, 3 April 1841.

III   Feminist Socialists: Some Portraits

1   *The Whitehaven Herald,* 15 January 1842. Estimates as to the numerical strength of Owenism vary enormously, ranging anywhere between 3,000 supporters and half a million, indicating how difficult it is to assess the size of the movement. During the years 1829–34 there was no Owenite 'membership' as such, but rather a large number of working people involved in Owenite-influenced schemes, such as the co-operative societies (of which there were about 500 by 1832), the labour exchanges, and the general union mobilization. It is impossible to judge how many of these people considered themselves 'Owenites', although it was certainly far less than the total number involved in these projects. After 1835, however, the movement was much more formally structured, with branches and official membership lists. Even then, however, actual figures for Owenite adherents still remain elusive: Harrison (*Owen*, p. 229) has accepted a membership figure of between 70,000 to 100,000 for the Association of All Classes of All Nations, but Mary Hennell's estimate of 3,000 enrolled members in 1841 (*An Outline of the Various Social Systems and Communities Funded on the Principle of Co-Operation* [1841], p. 170) seems more realistic (and since she was at least tangentially involved in the movement in Birmingham, her guess was probably a well-informed one). To this 'official' membership would have to be added, however, thousands of sympathizers who regularly attended meetings, participated in Owenite social events, and generally identified themselves with the movement's aims (the Hall of Science built in Manchester in 1840 held 3,000 people, while the total capacity of all the Socialist halls opened in the late 1830s and early 1840s was well over 20,000). The few membership figures from individual Socialist branches which are available indicate that these usually contained about the same number of women as men, although in some cases recruitment of women was slower (see, for example, the reports from Manchester in *NMW*, 2 April, 21 May 1842).

   In 1840 Flora Tristan claimed that there were at least a half million Socialists in Britain (*Promenades dans Londres,* Paris [1840], p. 383), and although the figure was obviously exaggerated, it is an interesting indication of how impressive Owenite influence seemed to many observers.

2   Gustave d'Eichthal, reporting to 'Pere' Enfantin; quoted in Pankhurst, *Saint Simonians,* p. 71.

3   *The Christian Lady's Magazine* (1840), p. 378.

4   There has been little systematic research on the social background of the Owenite membership. Harrison's book (*Owen*) is rich with detail on individual Owenites, and gives a good general sense of the upper working-class/lower middle-class milieu from which most Socialists were drawn; Thompson's account of the artisan base of the movement in its co-operative phase is very good (*Making*, pp. 868–7). But the bulk of the 'Owen' literature disregards the question of who these ideas and schemes attracted (and there has been no study of the female membership).

5   Queenwood membership lists were published in *NMW*, 3 June 1843; 8 June 1844; 24 May 1845. For a more detailed discussion of the female residents, see below, pp. 239–240.

6   The Ham Common Concordium was a small Richmond commune whose

president for a time was Sophia Chichester, while one of its residents was her friend Mrs Welsh. Both were wealthy feminist mystics who also helped finance the career of the Owenite millennialist James Smith (W. Anderson Smith, 'Shepherd' Smith the Universalist: the Story of a Mind [1892], pp. 191–8, 205).

7   For the women of Ralahine, see below pp. 247–248.

8   For meetings of working women at the Charlotte Street Institution, see The Official Gazette of the Trades Unions, 12, 21 June 1834. See Chapter Four for a discussion of women's co-operative associations and trade unions in the early 1830s.

9   The Working Bee, 12 December 1841.

10 NMW, 11 August 1838.

11 George Gissing, The Odd Women, first ed. 1893 (1980). Gissing's book is a fictional account of Victorian feminists, but his portrait of the self-educated women who made up the backbone of the movement in the later period applies almost as well to the Owenite feminists of a quarter century earlier.

12 The most useful source for Anna's life is the brief but detailed study by Pankhurst, 'Anna Wheeler'. Other sources are: M. Sadlier, Bulwer Lytton and His Wife (1933); Louisa Devey, Life of Rosina, Lady Lytton (1887); Smith, 'Shepherd' Smith; Gans, 'Socialistes'.

13 Pankhurst, 'Wheeler', p. 133.

14 ibid.

15 The British Co-operator, April 1830.

16 Smith, 'Shepherd' Smith, p. 148.

17 The Crisis, 19 October 1833.

18 Anna Wheeler, 'Letter to M. Jullian' (15 November 1832); reprinted with an introduction by Stephen Burke, Studies in Labour History, vol. 1, no. 1 (1976), p. 22. See also Smith, 'Shepherd' Smith, p. 205, for letters from her to Smith complaining of illness.

19 Pankhurst, 'Wheeler', p. 142.

20 Wheeler, 'Letter to Jullian', p. 22.

21 Sadlier, Lytton, p. 38.

22 Pankhurst, 'Wheeler', p. 135.

23 Wheeler, 'Letter to Jullian', p. 20.

24 ibid.

25 For the feminism of Fox and his circle, see F.E. Mineka, The Dissidence of Dissent (Chapel Hill, 1944), pp. 284–96. The other major liberal journal which published feminist contributions was The Westminster Review; see for example, the article on women's education which appeared in The Westminster Review, vol. XV (July–October 1831).

26 See, for example, NMW, 15 July 1837; 2 February 1839; 17 August 1844.

27 For Mill's favourable comments on Owenism and Owenite marriage doctrine, see F.A. Hayek, John Stuart Mill and Harriet Taylor (1951), p. 74, 300; and also his Autobiography. Both Mill and Harriet Taylor later described themselves as Socialists. Fox praised Owen in an 1823 article in The Monthly Repository and later claimed that his exclusion from the Unitarian hierarchy was due to his promotion of Owenite-type sexual doctrines (Mineka, Dissidence, p. 188). Even Harriet Martineau contributed towards the cost of Emma Martin's gravestone, in recognition of Emma's contribution to the feminist cause.

28 *The British Co-operator*, April 1830.
29 Wheeler, 'Letter to Jullian', p. 21.
30 I.B. O'Malley, *Women in Subjection* (1933), pp. 54–92. See also M. Phillips and W.S. Tomkinson, *English Women in Life and Letters* (1926), pp. 164–223.
31 *The British Co-operator*, April 1830.
32 For Eliza Macauley, see below, pp. 71–72.
33 *NMW*, 4 May 1839.
34 Waterman, *Frances Wright*, p. 26; Lane, *Frances Wright*, p. 5.
35 Mrs Barbauld, *Works*, 2 vols. (1825), vol. 1, p. 57.
36 Frances Wright, *Course of Popular Lectures* (New York, 1829), p. 86.
37 For the life of Fanny Wright see her *Biography, Notes and Political Letters* (Boston, 1849), and also: W.R. Waterman, *Frances Wright* (New York, 1924); A.J.G. Perkins and T. Wolfson, *Frances Wright, Free Enquirer* (New York, 1939); M. Lane, *Frances Wright and the 'Great Experiment'* (Manchester, 1972).
38 *The British Co-operator*, April 1830.
39 Harrison, *Owen*, p. 86.
40 Wheeler, 'Letter to Jullian', p. 22.
41 Quoted in Lane, *Frances Wright*, p. 29.
42 Perkins and Wolfson, *Frances Wright*, pp. 166–71.
43 *ibid.*, pp. 370–81.
44 For Emma's marriage see below, pp. 132–133.
45 'Vlasta' (Anna Wheeler), 'Letter to John Minter Morgan', in John Minter Morgan, *Hampden in the Nineteenth Century*, 2 vols. (1834), p. 323, 320.
46 For Frances Morrison's marriage see below, pp. 75–77.
47 Catherine and Goodwyn Barmby were the leaders of a tiny but fascinating sect called the Communist Church (see below, pp. 172–182.)
48 *NMW*, 25 April 1840.
49 'Vlasta' (Anna Wheeler), 'Letter to Morgan', p. 324.
50 Lady Lytton and her husband eventually became embroiled in a public scandal, involving mutual accusations of sexual misconduct. Her Ladyship emerged from the marriage a militant feminist (see her exchange of letters with James Smith in Smith, *'Shepherd' Smith*, pp. 325–401). Lady Lytton's grand-daughter was Constance Lytton, a famous suffragette.
51 Lane, *Frances Wright*, pp. 40–5.
52 See below, pp. 130–156.
53 For Anna Wheeler's religious views, see Smith, *'Shepherd' Smith*, p. 335, and her letter to Owen, Owen Corres. 426.
54 Elizabeth Wright Macauley, *Autobiographical Memoirs* (1834 and 1835).
55 She departed the stage in a flurry of tracts denouncing their owners and the rest of the acting profession. See, for example, *Facts Against Falsehood, Being a Brief Statement of Miss Macauley's Engagements at the Winter Theatres; the Subterfuges by which she has been driven from the regular exercise of her profession and withheld from at least two-thirds of the Public of this Metropolis. etc. . . . .* (1824). She also shared the platform with Eliza Sharples at the Rotunda in 1832 (*The Isis*, 3 November 1832).
56 Iorwerth Prothero, *Artisans and Politics in Early Nineteenth Century London: John Gast and His Times* (Folkestone, 1979), p. 260.

57 *The Lancashire and Yorkshire Co-operator*, May 1832.
58 *The Crisis*, 7 July, 25 August 1832; *The Isis*, 3 November 1832; *The Poor Man's Guardian*, 11 January 1834.
59 Pankhurst, *Saint-Simonians*, p. 130.
60 Macauley, *Memoirs*, see the newspaper clipping glued in the back of the 1834 edition for her obituary.
61 Elizabeth Wright Macauley, *Poetical Effusions* (1812), p. ix.
62 For a more developed discussion of this, see below, pp. 192–193.
63 (Anon.), *Can Women Regenerate Society?* (1844), p. 117.
64 See below, pp. 155.
65 Owen Corres. 470.
66 *NMW*, 11 August 1838. One local study of female school-teachers has shown that most were widows or spinsters for whom 'opening a school was a simple . . . response to poverty . . . not unlike taking in laundry or becoming a needlewoman' (John Field, 'Private Schools in Portsmouth and Southampton, 1850–1870', *Journal of Educational Administration and History*, vol. x, no. 2 (July 1978), pp. 9–10). At the lower end were the dame schools run mostly by working-class women; at the upper end were boarding schools, which were more genteel and usually run by women from slightly better-off backgrounds (like Emma Martin).
67 The poverty of women employed in ladylike occupations was notorious. In 1804 the Ladies' Society for the Education and Employment of the Female Poor issued a statement in which they condemned the lack of employment opportunities for the 'unprovided daughters of clergymen, officers and others', most of whom became teachers and governesses, and appealed for funds for their support. For accounts of charitable provision for journalists, governesses and schoolteachers in the mid-nineteenth century, see C. Kent, 'The Whittington Club; a Bohemian Experiment in Middle-Class Social Reform', *Victorian Studies*, vol. XVIII, no. 1 (September 1974), p. 37; M. Jeanne Peterson, 'The Victorian Governess', in M. Vicinus, ed., *Suffer and Be Still: Women in the Victorian Age* (Bloomington, 1973); Lee Holcombe, *Victorian Ladies at Work* (Newton Abbot, 1973), p. 54.
68 *The Crisis*, 24 August 1833.
69 *ibid.* The Union was still meeting in March 1834, under the leadership of a woman named Mrs Brooks. It disappeared from the Owenite records after this, but Mrs Brooks went on to organize a women's trade union which may well have been a successor to the original Union.
70 *The Pioneer*, 18 January, 8 February, 22 February 1834.
71 John Sever, 'James Morrison of *The Pioneer*' (typed ms. in British Museum), pp. 7–10.
72 Sever suggests that she was living with Morrison's relatives all this time, but this seems unlikely (particularly given her pregnancy, which preceded their marriage).
73 Owen Corres. 476.
74 James Morrison was an active radical before his conversion to Owenism. Birmingham in the 1820s was a lively political milieu, and not long after his marriage James became caught up in local political and trade union agitations, combining involvement in the city's Mechanics Institute with the editorship of a short-lived radical paper, *The Artisan*, and authorship of reams of sentimental poetry. His speeches from the period reveal him to

have been, as he later described himself in a letter to Owen, 'a stickler for vulgar liberty': a passionate and intensely optimistic reformer whose support for the unstamped press and trade union organization both had their sources in a craving 'for a *practical knowledge* of the means whereby to effect a change in the conditions of my fellow workmen and to devote my whole energies to their complete emancipation' (Owen Corres. 649). In 1831 the workers in the building trades in Birmingham came together to form a single union – the Operative Builders' Union – whose programme for inter-trade solidarity and worker self-management was heavily Owenite-influenced. By 1833 Morrison was deeply involved in the OBU and also with the Labour Exchanges in Birmingham; in that year he offered to launch *The Pioneer* as the official organ of the OBU. The paper began that autumn, and very soon became one of the most important forums for Owenite trade unionist ideas; in 1834 it became the newspaper of the Grand National Consolidated Trades Union. (This account of Morrison's career is largely drawn from J. Saville's study of Morrison's collaboration with James Smith in 'J.E. Smith and the Owenite Movement' in Pollard and Salt, *Robert Owen*, pp. 126–38).

75 *The Pioneer*, 12 April 1834.

76 James died after an accidental fall. Immediately after his death a sub-scription was set up within the Owenite movement to assist Frances and her girls: with the money raised she purchased a small shop in Finsbury. But apparently the venture proved unsatisfactory, for by the late 1830s she was living in Salford, where she served as official 'hostess' in the Owenite Social Institution, and then became a stipendiary lecturer, travelling on a northern speaking circuit. 'We have had a glorious day today,' came one report (*NMW*, 17 November 1838) from Huddersfield during one of these tours:

> Mrs Morrison lectured in the afternoon on the rights of women, and . . . in the evening on the marriage question. On both occasions the institution was densely crowded, and from 200 to 300 most respectable females attended each lecture . . . some hundreds must have returned, dis-appointed, being unable to obtain admittance.

Frances produced only one major piece of feminist writing during this later period: an essay on marriage which is discussed in Chapter Six.

77 Owen Corres. 476.

78 She eventually married a pastry-cook called Robert Sutton, and had another daughter by him. She died in 1898. Sever claims she retained her Owenite and feminist sympathies to the last, but there is one piece of evidence which throws this in doubt. In the mid-1840s a woman called Frances Morrison began delivering lectures against Socialism in Manchester and other towns, and *The New Moral World* claimed she was 'the widow of the former editor of *The Pioneer*' (*NMW*, 21 December 1844). Since false reports of Socialist recantations circulated constantly, however, this one may easily have been a fiction.

79 For the occupations of Birmingham Owenites, male and female, see the lists of products sold at the Labour Exchange there (*The Birmingham Labour Exchange Gazette*, January-February 1833).

80 *NMW*, 17 August 1839.

81 *ibid.*, 25 November 1838.

82 F. Engels, *The Condition of the Working Class in England*, first ed. 1845; first English trans. 1877 (1969), p. 263.

83 *NMW*, 23 May 1840.

84 A most useful contemporary source for the lives of the upper working class is the series of reports which appeared in *The Morning Chronicle* under the title 'Labour and the Poor' between October 1849 and May 1851, of which Henry Mayhew's four volume *London Labour and the London Poor* (1861) was a part. (Sources which have been used for specific groups of workers are indicated in separate notes.) General secondary sources include: Prothero, *Artisans*; Thompson, *Making*, chapters 8, 10, 12, 16; Sally Alexander, 'Women's Work in Nineteenth Century London', in Mitchell and Oakley, *Rights*, pp. 59–111; M.D. George, *London Life in the Eighteenth Century* (Harmondsworth, 1965); J.F. and L.B. Hammond, *The Skilled Labourer, 1760–1832* (1920).

Unionized male workers in skilled trades in London could expect to earn thirty shillings a week or more. E.P. Thompson has estimated that about five or six per cent of the workforce in most trades were 'society men' with earnings at about this level (*Making*, p. 277n.).

85 For an interesting discussion of these schools see P.J. Miller, 'Women's Education, Self-Improvement, and Social Mobility; a Late Eighteenth Century Debate', *British Journal of Educational Studies*, XX (October 1972). Frances' school, in Bury St Edmunds, was run by two women named Leache (Sever, 'Morrison', p. 12).

86 For an interesting account of women's involvement in friendly societies and other self-help associations, see Elizabeth Nicholson, 'Working Class Women in Nineteenth-Century Nottingham 1815–1850' (B.A. Thesis, University of Birmingham, 1974). Kenneth Corfield's 'Some Social and Radical Organizations among Working-Class Women in Manchester and District, 1790–1820' (B.A. Thesis, University of Birmingham, 1974) has similar information for the South Lancashire area.

87 William Lovett, *Life and Struggles of William Lovett, in his Pursuit of Bread, Knowledge and Freedom*, first ed., 1876 (1967), pp 31–2.

88 *ibid.*, p. 34.

89 G.J. Holyoake, *Sixty Years of an Agitator's Life*, 2 vols. (1893), vol. 1, pp. 10–19.

90 T. Kelly, *Thoughts on the Marriages of the Labouring Poor* (1806), p. 12.

91 See Chapter Four for a discussion of how an incompatibility between waged work and domestic labours developed in many sectors of the working class in this period.

92 For wage-levels of women in all major areas of employment in the early nineteenth century, see Pinchbeck, *Women Workers*. One-half to two-thirds of a male wage level seems to have been a typical level for women's wages in most industries, on·Pinchbeck's evidence.

93 'Labour and the Poor', *The Morning Chronicle*, 25 November 1850, reprinted in P.E. Razzell and R.W. Wainwright, *The Victorian Working Class: Selections from Letters to The Morning Chronicle* (1973), p. 297. See also Pinchbeck, *Women Workers*, p. 312, and Sir F.M. Eden, *The State of the Poor*, 2 vols. (1797) vol. 1, p. 630, for a discussion of working-class women's lack of legal control over their own wages.

94 'Labour and the Poor', *The Morning Chronicle*, 11 July 1850, reprinted in Razzell and Wainwright, *Working Class*, p. 125.
95 *ibid.*, 4 July 1850 and 26 September 1850, reprinted in Razzell and Wainwright, *Working Class*, p. 122, 151.
96 *ibid.*, 11 July 1850, reprinted in Razzell and Wainwright, *Working Class*, p. 125.
97 For the involvement of women in food riots, see E.P. Thompson, 'The Moral Economy of the English Crowd in the Eighteenth Century', *Past and Present*, no. 50 (1971), pp. 115–20. For women and strike action, see below, pp. 90–94. For women's involvement in Luddism, see Samuel Bamford, *Early Days* (1848), p. 304. See also E.J. Hobsbawn and G. Rude, *Captain Swing* (Harmondsworth, 1973), pp. 202–3, 208–9 for women's involvement in the 'Swing' outbreaks in the agricultural districts.
98 Dorothy Thompson, 'Women and Nineteenth Century Radical Politics: a Lost Dimension', in Mitchell and Oakley, *Rights*, pp. 112–38. See also E. and R. Frow, 'Women in the Early Radical and Labour Movement', *Marxism Today* (April 1968) and O'Malley, *Women in Subjection*, ch. 10.
99 Castlereagh, in his speech introducing the Seditious Meetings Prevention Bill in November 1819, reminded the Female Reformers that 'when the French Republicans were carrying on their bloody orgies, they could find no female to join them except by ransacking the bagnios or public brothels . . .' (*Hansard*, 29 November 1819, Vol. XLI, p. 391; quoted in O'Malley, *Women in Subjection*, p. 319). For horrified reports of female involvement in radical politics see, for example, *The British Volunteer*, 10 July 1819.
100 *The Black Dwarf*, 14 July 1819.
101 Quoted in Frow, 'Women', p. 106.
102 *The Black Dwarf*, 14 July 1819.
103 *The Manchester Observer*, 26 June 1819; quoted in Corfield, 'Working Class Women', p. 40. 'Exclusive dealing' (shopping only in those shops whose owners supported reform demands) was a tactic seen to be particularly appropriate for women. 'This is what woman can do . . . without a moment's neglect of our ordinary occupations,' as one woman wrote in support of exclusive dealing in 1831, 'the spending of money (especially in domestic concerns) is the province of women, in it we can act without the risk of being called politicians.' (*The Poor Man's Guardian*, 26 May 1832).
104 Malmgreen, 'Women's Suffrage', p. 25.
105 See, for example, *The Black Dwarf*, 16 September; 7, 14 October 1818. The transmission of feminist ideas into the radical working class was part of a wider process which might best be described as the proletarianization of the Enlightenment. By the early decades of the nineteenth century it was mostly among working people that writers such as Rousseau, Volney, Diderot, Godwin and Wollstonecraft were read. When Engels arrived in Manchester in the early 1840s he was astounded to discover that whereas 'the bourgeoisie . . . trembles, blesses and crosses itself' before the ideas of the French materialists, or Shelley's poetry, or Godwin's philosophy, 'the proletarian has open eyes for it, and studies it with pleasure and success'. (He added that the Owenites were particularly praiseworthy in this respect.) 'The proletariat has formed upon this basis a literature, which . . . is far in advance of the whole bourgeois literature in intrinsic worth' (Engels, *Working Class*, pp. 265–6).

106 See, for example, *The Prompter*, 9 April 1830; *The Gauntlet*, 22 September
     1833; *The Isis*, 22 September, 14 April 1832. Carlile's *Everywoman's Book*
     included an impassioned plea for women's sexual liberation, based on the
     separation of sexual pleasure from reproduction (for its place in the history
     of birth control literature, see Peter Fryer, *The Birth Controllers* [1965],
     pp. 74–8).
107 *The Isis*, 3 March 1832.
108 G.D.H. Cole, *Richard Carlile*, Fabian Society Biographical Series Number
     13 (1943). For a letter to Carlile from 150 Birmingham women who sold his
     illegal newspapers there, see *The Gauntlet*, 25 August 1833 (where the
     women compare themselves to the women of the 1830 Revolution in
     France). For an account of the trial of Susannah Wright, one of Carlile's
     London volunteers (a lacemaker), see Thompson, *Making*, pp. 802–3. She
     was thrown into prison with her infant. In London, several dozen of these
     female 'unstamped' newspaper vendors organized themselves into a group
     called the Friends of the Oppressed; their activities may be traced through
     The Poor Man's Guardian in 1832 and 1833. The only recorded discussion of
     women's position held by the 'Friends' was in November 1832, when they
     decided to 'set an example to females' by refusing to be churched after child-
     birth (*The Poor Man's Guardian*, 1 December 1832). This group was
     probably a predecessor of the London Female Chartist groups of the late
     1830s, although no doubt some of its members were Owenites as well.
109 *The Isis*, 14 April 1832. Eliza Sharples, the daughter of a Bolton merchant,
     first met Carlile when he came to Bolton to lecture in 1829. She began to
     correspond with him, and in 1832 came to London on his urging. They soon
     became lovers, and she remained with him until his death (for his account of
     their 'Moral Marriage' see *The Gauntlet*, 22 September 1833).
110 For an account of the movement of Carlileans (sometimes known as
     'Zetetics') into Owenism, see Edward Royle, *Victorian Infidels* (Manchester,
     1974), p. 50. Among them were men like Alexander Campbell, Rowland
     Detrosier and John Gale Jones, all of whom actively supported women's
     equality; no doubt some of the female supporters of Owenite feminism had
     also been associated with Carlile, although no individuals can be traced.
         After Carlile's death, Eliza Sharples briefly joined the Richmond com-
     munity known as the Ham Common Concordium, where she did
     needlework to earn her living; thereafter she became the manageress of the
     Warner Street Temperance Hall in London, where she befriended the young
     Charles Bradlaugh and converted him to secularism. She corresponded with
     Owen, but despite this and her brief residence at the Concordium, there is no
     evidence that she ever embraced Owenite ideals. For her life (and some of
     her correspondence with Carlile) see T.C. Campbell, *The Battle of the Press,
     as told in the story of the life of Richard Carlile, by his daughter* (1899).
         Another source of working-class feminism within Owenism were the
     followers of Thomas Spence (see Prothero, *Artisans*, pp. 257–8, for an
     account of the Spencean presence within Owenism). George Petrie (who
     wrote under the name 'Agrarius') and another Spencean, Richard Lee, pro-
     duced a very popular periodical in 1833 called *The Man* which carried a
     number of articles advocating women's emancipation. Petrie lectured on
     women's rights at the Institution of the Working Classes in Theobalds Road
     in London in 1832 (I. Prothero, 'London Working-Class Movements,

1823–1848' [Ph D Thesis, Cambridge, 1966], p. 150). There was also a Spencean couple called the Neesoms who promoted feminist ideas and women's trade union organization in London in the 1830s and early 1840s.

111　*The Destructive*, 23 November 1833. Hetherington soon altered his views, however, and became a polemical (if somewhat capricious) proponent of sexual equality. He was one of Emma Martin's closest friends.

IV　'The Men Are As Bad As Their Masters . . .': Working Women And The Owenite Economic Offensive, 1828–34

1　*Co-operative Magazine*, vol. 1 (1826), p. 309, quoted in S. Pollard, 'Nineteenth Century Co-operation: from Community Building to Shopkeeping', in A. Briggs and J. Saville, eds. *Essays in Labour History* (1967), p. 80.

2　*The Lancashire Co-operator*, 11 June 1831.

3　*To Unionists. Abstracts of the Proceedings of a Special Meeting of Trades' Unions Delegates, held in London on the 13th, 14th, 15th, 17th, 18th and 19th of February, 1834 . . . etc . . .* (1834), p. 13.

4　For a recent re-telling, see Harrison, *Owen*, pp. 197–216. Pollard's 'Nineteenth Century Co-operation' is very good for the co-operative societies in general, while A.E. Musson, 'The Ideology of Early Co-operation in Lancashire and Cheshire', *Transactions*, Lancashire and Cheshire Antiquarian Society, vol. LXVII (1958), is an illuminating regional account of co-operative shopkeeping and trading associations. Prothero's *Artisans* contains an interesting account of plebian Owenism in London in the early 1830s (see especially chapters 13–16).

5　Gareth Stedman Jones, 'The Limits of a Proletarian Theory in England before 1850' (unpublished ms. in author's possession), p. 6. I am grateful to the author for letting me see this essay. My own interpretation of class theory in the early 1830s is heavily indebted to it, and also to his 'Class Struggle and the Industrial Revolution', *New Left Review*, no. 90, 1975, pp. 35–69. The most important neo-Ricardian texts, in terms of influence on the radical working class, were Thompson's *Inquiry* and also his *Labour Rewarded* (1827), which was a response to Thomas Hodgskin's enormously influential *Labour Defended Against the Claims of Capital* (1825). See Harrison, *Owen*, pp. 63–78 for a useful summary of Owenite economic doctrine.

6　Add. Ms. 27822, ff. 15–27, reprinted in D.J. Rowe, *London Radicalism, 1830–34* (1970), p. 139.

7　Quoted in Sidney and Beatrice Webb, *The History of Trades Unionism* (1926), 157n.

8　*The Lancashire and Yorkshire Co-operator*, May 1832. The same issue of this periodical (which is a very rich source for working-class Owenism) carried a letter from the secretary of the Sheffield Co-operative Society in which he reported the response of his members to these new ideas. When the executive of his society announced that they had written to London for a bundle of BAPCK tracts, *'many blamed us for this, and thought it money thrown away'* but opinions were soon revised:

> it was the best spent money, we ever laid out in our lives; as by the instruction we received from these publications, we were enabled to discover our real state and condition as a society, to perceive, what it was that hindered our progress, and how to avoid it, we also discovered what it was that made us poor, in the midst of plenty; how the competitive system operated upon us, and how machinery was made to work against us, and also how we might make it work for us.

9 Lovett, *Life*, p. 34. A little poem sent to Owen by 'Fanny, a Female Co-operator' (Owen Corres. 562) captured the spirit of these co-operative enterprises;

> Why should we labour only for those
> Who on our labour live
> For labours [sic] wealth which from us flows
> Then why that labour give
>
> How swett [sic] to labour for ourselves
> And taste the joys of life
> Dispel the gloom that's long prevailed
> Oer Albions [sic] sons of light.

10 Harrison, *Owen*, p. 201. For accounts by participants of this growth, see Lovett to Place, in Rowe, *London Radicalism*, p. 139; Thompson, *Practical Directions*, Introduction; Lloyd Jones, *Life, Times and Labours of Robert Owen*, 2 vols. (1889), vol. 2, p. 8.
11 Lovett, in Rowe, *London Radicalism*, p. 139.
12 Lovett, *Life*, p. 35.
13 Benjamin Warden, *Rewards of Industry* (1832), p. 2. For the Labour Exchanges, see W.H. Oliver, 'The Labour Exchange Phase of the Co-operative Movement', *Oxford Economic Papers*, n.s. X (1958), pp. 355–67.
14 Quoted in R.W. Postgate, *The Builders' History* (1923), p. 97.
15 *The Crisis*, 12 October 1833. The plan was adopted at the Co-operative Congress held in Huddersfield in November.
16 'The consequence of this excitement [over the Reform Bill] was a general persuasion that the whole produce of the labourers' and workers' hands should remain with them,' Francis Place recorded, noting that by the end of 1832 the 'nonsensical doctrines preached by Robert Owen' and other leading Co-operators had 'pushed politics aside among the working people . . .' (Add. Mss. 27, 791, f. 242; Webbs, *Trade Unionism*, p. 156). In fact although disillusionment with the Bill was intense, most Co-operators remained political democrats in the early 1830s, just as many were to become leading Chartists in the later part of the decade. But what the Reform Bill had taught them, as J.F. Bray wrote (*Labour's Wrongs and Labour's Remedy* [Leeds, 1839], p. 6) was that 'the producers have . . . to determine whether it be not possible to change that social whole which keeps them poor, as well as that governmental part which oppresses them because they are poor', and in the early 1830s many workers obviously thought it was. A worker takeover of the economy, men like Morrison, James Smith and John Doherty explained,

would eventually lead to the establishment of what Morrison described as a parliamentary system run 'by LABOURING PEOPLE, in the LABOURERS' INTERESTS' which would wholly supersede the existing State, simply by undermining its class base (see especially the 'Letters on Associated Labour' by 'Senex' – probably Morrison and Smith – to *The Pioneer*, 15 March–28 June 1834).

17 *The Man*, 22 December 1833.

18 *The Poor Man's Guardian*, 4 January 1834.

19 *The Pioneer*, 28 December 1833.

20 For earlier attempts, see G.D.H. Cole, *Attempts at General Union, 1818–1834* (1953).

21 *The Poor Man's Guardian*, 19 October 1833.

22 The most detailed account of the Consolidated Union is to be found in W.H. Oliver, 'Organizations and Ideas Behind the Efforts to Achieve a General Union of the Working Classes in England in the Early 1830s' (Ph D Thesis, Oxford, 1957). The most interesting discussion of its membership is contained in Prothero, 'London Working-Class Movements'. Other sources include Cole, *Attempts*, and Webbs, *Trades Unionism*, although both of these have been superseded by Oliver's work.

23 For women's (mostly needlewomen's) co-operative workshops see *The Crisis*, 27 October 1832, 20 April 1833; *The Pioneer*, 18 January 1834. See G.J. Holyoake, *The History of Co-operation in England*, 2 vols., first ed. 1875–79 (1906). vol. 1, p. 135, for an account of a women's co-operative shop in London, and Prothero, 'Working-Class Movements', p. 408, for a women's co-operative trading association in East London. Female managers for the co-operative shops were suggested by *The Co-operator* magazine; they should be paid a shilling a day, the editor stated, which would add to their income 'without them being too much drawn away from . . . domestic cares' (1 February 1830). A number of societies adopted this suggestion (including the London society which employed Mary Lovett). But if women liked to work in the shops, they often did not like to shop in them. According to Prothero (*Artisans*, p. 248) the no-credit rule which most co-operative shops adopted forced working-class housewives to shop elsewhere, but William Ellis, an Owenite, stated that it was the 'quality and prices' of the goods offered which turned his own wife against the shops (*Reminiscences and Reflections of an Old Operative* [1851] p. 17). Lovett, on the other hand, offered the interesting guess that it was the women's dislike 'that their husbands should be made acquainted with the exact extent of their dealings' which prejudiced them against co-operative shopping (*Life*, p. 35).

24 The Society of Industrious Females was initially formed in April 1833, with the assistance of one Mr Poulter (*The Crisis*, 20 April 1833); its representative to the Fourth Co-operative Congress was a woman called Miss Green, who reported that having begun with only fourteen members and 7s. 6d., they were now able to fully employ sixty women (*ibid.*, 19 October 1833; see also 28 September 1833).

25 For the 'Official Articles' of the Consolidated, see *The Pioneer*, 8 March 1834. For reports of women's unions see, for example, *ibid.*, 15 March, 17 May 1834; *The Poor Man's Guardian*, 16 March 1833; *The Official Gazette of The Trades Unions*, 21 June, 12 July 1834; *The Gauntlet*, 30 March 1834.

26 *The Pioneer*, 26 October 1833.

27 *ibid.*

28 *ibid.*, 14 June 1834; *The Times*, 2 May 1834.

29 *The Leeds Mercury*, 4 May 1833. See *The Times*, 3 May 1834, for a satirical report on the formation of a Grand United Lodge of Operative Ladies' Maids, whose demands supposedly included the right to appropriate all their mistresses' clothes and to have as many 'followers' as they chose. Since so many employers expressed genuine fears about the impact of union propaganda on their domestic servants, this 'joke' was probably a bit too close to the bone for some of *The Times* readership.

30 Harrison, *Owen*, p. 213; Webbs, *Trades Unionism*, p. 134.

31 See above, pp. 76–80, for a discussion of women's wage-earning activities.

32 B.L. Hutchins, *Women in Modern Industry*, first ed. 1915 (Wakefield, West Yorkshire, 1978), p. 95; Barbara Drake, *Women in Trade Unions* (1920), pp. 5–7; Ross Davies, *Women And Work* (1975), pp. 56–7; Sheila Lewenhak, *Women and Trade Unions; an Outline History of Women in the British Trade Union Movement* (1977), pp. 29–43. Lewenhak's account is the most detailed, and does contain a brief discussion of some of the sexual conflicts which emerged in the nascent labour movement at the time.

33 Thompson, *Making*, p. 883.

34 *ibid.*, pp. 258–96; J.F.C. Harrison, *The Early Victorians, 1832–51.* first ed. 1970 (1973), pp. 53–9; Prothero, *Artisans*, chapters 2, 3, 11; Alexander, 'Women's Work', pp. 80–3.

35 Thompson, *Making*, p. 277. See also Henry Mayhew's analysis of the changed condition of the artisan, as discussed in Eileen Yeo, 'Mayhew as a Social Investigator', in E.P. Thompson and Eileen Yeo, *The Unknown Mayhew* (Harmondsworth, 1973), pp. 56–109.

36 *The Pioneer*, 19 April 1834.

37 G.D.H. Cole and Raymond Postgate, *The British Common People*, first ed. 1956 (1961), pp. 168–272; Prothero, *Artisans*, chapters 2, 3, 9, 11; Thompson, *Making*, 277–84, 546–69.

38 Pinchbeck, *Women Workers*, pp. 223–4.

39 Don Manuel Alvarez Espriella [Robert Southey], *Letters from England* (1808), pp. 46–7; quoted in Thompson, 'Women and Politics', pp. 116–7.

40 Pinchbeck, *Women Workers*, p. 225.

41 *The Crisis*, 1 March 1834.

42 *The Pioneer*, 8 February 1834.

43 N.G. Osterud, 'Women's Work in Nineteenth Century Leicester' (1978; unpublished ms. in author's possession), p. 24, n.4. I am grateful to the author for allowing me to read this excellent essay.

44 *The Magazine of Useful Knowledge*, 30 October 1830; *Report of the Select Committee on Artisans and Machinery* (1824), p. 418.

45 *Artisans and Machinery*, p. 418.

46 *The Times*, 19 April 1834. These women were members of the Society for Promoting National Regeneration, an Owenite-influenced body based in the milltowns whose goal was the eight-hour working day (at a time when the mainstream of the Short-Time movement supported a ten-hour day). The Regenerationists did not join the Consolidated Union, probably because the Consolidated was so firmly rooted in the old hand trades, especially the London trades, but many of its members identified with the quasi-syndicalist ideals of the Consolidated, including its leader, John

Doherty. (See D.S. Gadian, 'A Comparative Study of Popular Movements in North West Industrial Towns, 1830–50' [PhD Thesis, Lancaster University, 1976, pp. 53–55], and also John Foster, *Class Struggle and the Industrial Revolution* [1974], pp. 110–14.) The women who were most active in the Society were in two (friendly societies? trades unions? the evidence is unclear) called the 'Female Gardeners' and the 'Ancient Virgins', which were presumably made up either of factory women or the wives of factory operatives.

47 *The People's Conservative*, 8 February 1834.

48 *The Times*, 15 February 1834: 'latterly a considerable number of females have ceased from their usual employment in consequence of refusing to sign the declaration required of them by the manufacturers to the effect that they will not subscribe to the funds for the support of those who are members of Trades Unions and who are consequently destitute of work', it was reported from the Derby area. In fact large numbers of working women subscribed to the Derby relief fund, including one washerwoman who sent in the 'proceeds from the washing of two surplices' and a Barnsley woman called Margaret Parrington who could send only sixpence because although 'rich in principle' she was 'poor in pocket' (*The Pioneer*, 18 January 1834).

49 *The Pioneer*, 22 March 1834.

50 *ibid.*, 22 February 1834.

51 *ibid.*, 22 March 1834. But there were also accounts, early in the lock-out, of women complaining at losing their employment when they did not support the union (*The Poor Man's Guardian*, 12 December 1834) and another of a male unionist being scolded by his wife when he was assuring an interviewer that he did not repent his support for the struggle: 'Aye, you do repent it – you know you do, ever since you did it!' (*The Pioneer*, 18 January 1834).

52 *The Official Gazette of the Trades Unions*, 12 July 1834.

53 *The Pioneer*, 22 February 1834.

54 *ibid.*, 31 May, 26 April 1834. Morrison proposed the establishment of housewives' unions committed to co-operative housekeeping, but this came to nothing (*ibid.*, 22 March 1834).

55 *ibid.*, 22 February 1834.

56 For pre-Owenite trade unionism among women, see Lewenhak, *Women*, pp. 13–34. There were some mixed unions affiliated to the Consolidated, such as the London shoemakers' union, and of course many of the all-female unions were based in all-female trades, such as strawbonnet-making, dressmaking, millinery, and lace-making. It is also worth speculating whether some of these women's unions grew out of female friendly societies.

57 Lewenhak, *Women*, pp. 40–3.

58 'If ever a man is introduced amongst the other sex, they will stick to him like feathers on a tarred seaman, and he will carry the whole union on his back . . . Therefore, we say, let woman look to herself, consult with women on her own affairs; allow no male to enter her meetings, until she has obtained sufficient skill and experience to act in public . . .' (*The Pioneer*, 8 March 1834).

59 Marx and Engels, *Communist Manifesto*, pp. 55–6.

60 In his influential *Labour Rewarded*, William Thompson claimed that the old exclusionist policies operated by the guilds and trades societies were no longer capable of holding back the tide of unapprenticed, unorganized

labour being drawn into the trades, and that such policies served only to set different groups of workers against each other. He urged the formation of a general union on the grounds that it was only when intraclass divisions were overcome that it would be possible for the working class to form a common front against the employer class. His arguments, or variations on them, appeared again and again in the Consolidated. 'The interests of labour, skilled and unskilled, are one and universal, to which the interests of capital under existing arrangements will constantly be opposed . . . they are both sailing in the same vessel, and though the former may have the advantage of being a cabin passenger, one cannot sink without the other, though there may be a little difference in the time. Let the well-paid artisan reflect on this, and let him hesitate no longer to join his brethren in Union' (*The Official Gazette of the Trades Unions*, 2 August 1834). One of the most widely-publicized attacks on the Consolidated included in its list of charges against the Union the fact that it promoted 'levelling' within the working population by discouraging the display of superior ability on the part of skilled workers (E. Tufnell, *Character, Object and Effects of Trades Unions* [1834], p. 93). But in fact there were still many workers involved in the general union mobilization, particularly those who occupied the top rungs of the labour hierarchy in their trades, who clung to the old defensive ways, and the Owenite press carried many exchanges between these 'Exclusives' and their 'Universalist' opponents, which together provide a fascinating glimpse into the changing character and self-consciousness of the 'labour aristocracy' in this period.

61 *The Lancashire and Yorkshire Co-operator*, August 1832.
62 *The Crisis*, 25 August 1832.
63 *ibid.*, 14 December 1833.
64 *ibid.*
65 The 'Page' began on March 8th and had its name changed in the April 26th issue.
66 *The Pioneer*, 8 February 1834. This letter in fact appeared one month before the 'Page' began, when Morrison was already publishing editorials favouring female unionism. It is interesting to speculate whether it was Frances who was actually responsible for the 'Page', rather than James himself.
67 *ibid.*, 12 April 1834.
68 It seems that at Owen's Grays Inn Exchange women workers were initially paid at a lower rate than men, and many women refused to sell their goods there 'unless there was something like a more equitable adjustment in the price fixed upon their labour'. Several male members of the United Trades Association supported the women's demands, arguing that 'female labour should be upon the same par with male and paid the same price, and exchanged upon equal terms' but there is no record of whether the price was eventually adjusted. The women affected appear to have been mostly needlewomen and shoemakers. (See *The Crisis*, 25 May 1833; *The Weekly Free Press*, clipping in William Pare Scrapbook, University of London Library, f. 6.)
69 *The Pioneer*, 17 May 1834.
70 *ibid.*, 15 March 1834.
71 *The Crisis*, 1 March 1834.
72 *The Pioneer*, 12 April 1834.
73 *ibid.*, 22 March 1834.

74   *ibid.*, 29 March 1834.
75   *ibid.*, 12 April 1834.
76   *ibid.*
77   *The Crisis*, 8 March 1834, *The Pioneer*, 12 April 1834.
78   Quoted in Rowbotham, *Women*, p. 23.
79   *The Pioneer*, 12 April 1834.
80   *ibid.*
81   *ibid.*, 22 March 1834.
82   *ibid.*
83   Prothero, 'London Working-Class Movements', p. 119, 155, 157; Oliver, 'Organization', p. 45.
84   Prothero, 'London Working-Class Movements', p. 350.
85   Thompson, *Making*, p. 288–9; Alexander, 'Women's Work', p. 83. A similar process, it should be emphasized, occurred in many skilled women's trades, where merchant capitalists also encouraged the proliferation of small employers who subcontracted work out to women (or children). The straw-bonnet-maker, 'PAS', described in a series of letters to the 'Women's Page' how this process happened in her own trade:

> When the war ceased, in the year 1815, many useful men were thrown out of employment, their wives having to support them. The men, not wishing to be idle, were taught by the women to block; and in a very short time these men went round to all the principal warehouses in London, and offered to take home the work, and finish it for less money than the masters gave in-doors, the latter finding every thing for the girls' use. It was soon discovered by the women that these men were more tyrannical than their former masters . . . This mad competition has sunk the business from one of the best to one of the worst a woman can have . . . (17 May 1834).

A similar process occurred in lacemaking, where small lace 'mistresses' employed women on material supplied by large warehouses, which then paid piece-rates for the finished lace. Fierce competition among the mistresses for the right to supply the warehouses led to constant wage-cutting: the Nottingham lace embroiderers – who joined the Consolidated Union – had had their wages cut by almost one-half between 1831 and 1833 (Pinchbeck, *Women*, pp. 209–15). In 1840 these women mounted a major strike (Lewenhak, *Women*, pp. 48–9, Pinchbeck, *Women*, pp. 213–4; Jo O'Brien, *Women's Liberation in Labour History: A Case Study from Nottingham, Spokesman Pamphlet* no. 24, n.d.).
86   *The Pioneer*, 22 March 1834.
87   The main sources for this account of the tailoring trade are: S. and B. Webb, Trade Union Mss. Collection (London School of Economic and Political Science), Section A:XIV (Clothing trades); Francis Place, 'Minutes of Evidence', *Artisans and Machinery*, pp. 44–6; Henry Mayhew, Letters to *The Morning Chronicle*, Letters VII to XI, and XVI to XVIII (6–23 November and 11–18 December 1849), reprinted in Thompson and Yeo, *Unknown Mayhew*, pp. 137–273; Prothero, 'London Working-Class Movements'; T.M. Parrsinen and I.J. Prothero, 'The London Tailors' Strike of 1834 and the Collapse of the Grand National Consolidated Trades Union: a Police Spy's Report', *International Review of Social History*, no. 22 (Spring 1977),

pp. 119–42; Thomas Carter, *Memoirs of a Working Man* (1845); F.W. Galton, ed. *Select Documents Illustrating the History of Trade Unionism: 1: The Tailoring Trade* (1896); Anon., 'The War of the Purses, or the Tailors of London', *Notes to The People*, vol. 1 (1851), pp. 363–9; Alexander 'Women's Work', pp. 80–8. C.R. Dobson, *Masters and Journeymen: a Prehistory of Industrial Relations, 1717–1800* (1980), contains a good deal of information about earlier conflicts in the trade. Both *The Pioneer* and *The Crisis* also carried articles discussing the conditions in the trade.

88 Place, 'Evidence', pp. 44–6; Webbs, 'Clothing Trade'; Galton, *Select Documents*, Introduction.

89 George, *London Life*, p. 425.

90 Mayhew, Letter XVII, *The Morning Chronicle* (14 December 1849), in Thompson and Yeo, *Unknown Mayhew*, p. 236.

91 Mayhew, Letter VI, *The Morning Chronicle* (6 November 1849), in Thompson and Yeo, *Unknown Mayhew*, pp. 143–4.

92 *The Pioneer*, 15 March 1834.

93 *ibid.*, 19 April, 15 March 1834.

94 Galton's introduction (*Select Documents*, pp. xii–xcviii) gives an excellent account of this decline.

95 Galton, *ibid.*, p. li.; Prothero, *Artisans*, pp. 246–7; Thompson, *Making*, pp. 869–70.

96 *The Times*, 29 April 1834.

97 Oliver, 'Consolidated Trades Union', p. 80.

98 Thompson, *Making*, p. 290.

99 *The Birmingham Co-operative Herald* (June 1829).

100 Marx described this situation as one of 'formal subordination' of labour to capital. 'Real' subordination is attained only when employers acquire direct control over the production process itself, which is achieved either through mechanization or the 'de-skilling' of labour through piecework, reorganization of work processes, etc. (Karl Marx, 'Results of the Immediate Process of Production', Appendix, *Capital*, vol. 1 [Harmondsworth, 1976], pp. 995–1039). The significance of this distinction for working-class theory in the 1830s is discussed in Gareth Stedman Jones, 'Class Struggle', pp. 35–69.

101 *The Co-operator*, December 1828. The analysis of class relations developed in the writings of neo-Ricardian economists reflected this experience of the capitalist as a dispensable 'middleman' rather than a commander of labour within the production process. The Socialists 'do not object to the existence of capital,' as one article in *The New Moral World* explained, 'or to the influence on labour which capital is fitted to exercise. Their objections are directed against the institution of private property' through which the owners of capital derived wealth from the labour of workers through monopolistic possession of tools and raw materials (15 December 1838). 'Betwixt him who produces food and him who produces clothing, betwixt him who makes instruments and him who uses them, in steps the capitalist, who neither makes nor uses them, and appropriates to himself the produce of both . . . He is the *middleman* of all labourers' (Hodgskin, *Labour Defended*, p. 20–1). While corralling all large merchants, like the garment warehousemen, under the category of exploiter, this analysis also managed to exempt the small, working master in the trade, whose income and lifestyle

were usually very similar to that of his journeymen (Stedman Jones, 'Limits'; Prothero, *Artisans*, p. 256).

102 *The Times*, 9 May 1834.
103 *The Pioneer*, 3 May 1834.
104 Thompson, *Appeal*, p. 197.
105 Henry Mayhew, *London Labour and the London Poor*, 4 vols. (1861), vol. 2, p. 314, quoted in Alexander, 'Women's Work', pp. 81–2.
106 *The Gorgon*, 10 October 1818.
107 Pinchbeck, *Women*, p. 179n.
108 Parssinen and Prothero, 'London Tailors' Strike', p. 70.
109 *The Pioneer*, 5 April 1834.
110 Heidi Hartmann, 'Capitalism, Patriarchy, and Job Segregation', in Zillah Eistenstein, ed., *Capitalist Patriarchy and the Case for Socialist-Feminism* (1979), pp. 217–23.
111 *The Pioneer*, 19 March 1834.
112 *ibid.*, 12 April 1834.
113 *ibid.*
114 Mayhew, Letter XVII, *The Morning Chronicle*, 14 December 1849, in Thompson and Yeo, *Unknown Mayhew*, p. 251.
115 *The Pioneer*, 12 April 1834.
116 *ibid.*
117 For an interesting discussion of the relationship between women's role in social production and the sexual division of labour, see F. Edholm, K. Young, and O. Harris, 'Conceptualising Women', *Critique of Anthropology*, vol. 3, no. 9–10 (1977), pp. 101–103. They suggest that it is precisely at the point when women's productive roles no longer coincide with their conventional family role that women begin to question their condition, and to protest their subordinate status (p. 126).
118 *The Pioneer*, 10 May 1834.
119 N.J. Smelser, *Social Change in the Industrial Revolution* (1959); Michael Anderson, *Family Structure in Nineteenth Century Lancashire* (Cambridge, 1971); Margaret Hewitt, *Wives and Mothers in Victorian Industry* (1958). For contemporary accounts of the effects of married women's employment on family life in the textile districts, see P. Gaskell, *The Manufacturing Population of England* (1833); 'Labour and the Poor', *The Morning Chronicle*, 18 October 1849 to 10 March 1851, reprinted in Razzell and Wainwright, *Working Class*, pp. 165–324.
120 Engels, *Working Class*, p. 173.
121 *Report and Resolutions of a Meeting of Deputies from the Handloom Worsted Weavers residing in and near Bradford, Leeds, Halifax, etc.* (1835), quoted in Thompson, *Making*, p. 335; *Manchester and Salford Advertiser*, 8, 15 January 1842, quoted in Pinchbeck, *Women Workers*, p. 200. For an interesting discussion of male opposition to female factory employment which links it to domestic authority relations, see Smelser, *Social Change*, especially pp. 180–312.
122 Nancy Tomes, 'A "Torrent of Abuse": Crimes of Violence Between Working-Class Men and Women in London, 1840–75', *Journal of Social History*, vol. 11, no. 2 (1978), p. 332.
123 Engels, *Working Class*, p. 174. It should also be noted however, that Engels himself was no exponent of housebound, dependent womanhood; indeed,

as far as he was concerned, the 'inhumanity' of the 'reign of the wife over the husband' created by the factory system, simply indicated that 'the pristine rule of the husband over the wife must have been inhuman too',

> if the wife can now base her supremacy upon the fact that she supplies the greater part, nay, the whole of the common possession, the necessary inference is that this community of possession is no true and rational one, since one member of the family boasts offensively of contributing the greater share. If the family of our present society is being thus dissolved, this dissolution merely shows that, at bottom, the binding tie of this family was not family affection, but private interest lurking under the cloak of a pretended community of possessions.

The influence of the Owenites, with whom Engels had previously been closely associated, is clearly audible here.

124   R.J. Richardson, *The Rights of Woman* (1840), pp. 18–19.
125   One way of uncovering women's own attitudes would be to investigate their reaction to the factory reform movement. This has yet to be done, but from some of the evidence which I have encountered, it seems clear that those who were trying to limit or eliminate female employment in the mills occasionally encountered resentment among the women themselves (see, for example, *The Examiner*, 26 February 1832 and *The Pioneer*, 12 April 1834).
126   *The Pioneer*, 12 April 1834.
127   *ibid.*, 26 April 1834. In 1848 the London Statistical Society surveyed 354 'single' individuals in East London, of whom 229 were 'unprotected' women. Of these women, two thirds had families wholly dependent upon their earnings (many were abandoned wives) (cited in Alexander, 'Women's Work' pp. 82–3).
128   *The Pioneer*, 12 April 1834.
129   *The Crisis*, 30 November 1833.
130   *The Man*, 19 November 1833.
131   *ibid.*, 20 October 1833.
132   *The Pioneer*, 5 April 1834.
133   *ibid.*
134   *ibid.*, 12 April 1834.
135. Contemporary sources for the strike include *The Times, The True Sun, The Poor Man's Guardian, The People's Conservative, The Pioneer, The Crisis*, and a series of police spy reports sent to the Home Office, some of which have been reproduced in Prothero and Parssinen, 'London Tailors' Strike'. Secondary sources include the last-mentioned article (which, however, almost entirely ignores the role of women in the strike); Lewenhak, *Women*, pp. 42–3; 'The War of the Purses', pp. 363–9.
136   *The Pioneer*, 5 April 1834.
137   *The Times*, 1, 3 May 1834.
138   *ibid.*, 29 April 1834.
139   *The Crisis*, 17 May 1834.
140   HO 40/32.
141   *The Crisis*, 17 May 1834. The female scab workforce was largely the creation of the large merchant employers; most of the small, working masters supported the strike (*The True Sun*, 27 March 1834). Francis Place actively opposed the unionists, in his capacity as a master tailor.

142 *The Pioneer*, 10 May 1834.

143 *The True Sun*, 20 May 1834.

144 *The Pioneer*, 10 May 1834. John Browne, the union's secretary, mentioned the possibility of a women's union in a letter written to Owen at the time (Owen Corres. 679).

145 *ibid.*, 9 May 1834. There was also a very interesting editorial published in *The Herald of the Rights of Industry* (10 May 1834), comparing the situation in tailoring to sexual competition in the cotton industry, written by the Owenite spinners' leader, John Doherty. Commenting on the 'dastardly strategem' of 'running the labour of the women against the men in the race of tailoring competition', Doherty went on to note that

> this has been successfully done in the cotton manufacture, and the consequence is that there is now very little employment in it which will pay a man living wages. One of our earliest endeavours must be to root out this abominable principle of degrading the labour of females in order to destroy the value of the males' . . . What is the antidote? Why merely for you to acknowledge the natural equality of women; include them in all your schemes of improvement and raise them as high in the scale of sense and independence as yourselves.

This editorial is particularly interesting because five years earlier Doherty had supported a move to exclude women from the National Spinners' Union (although they were urged to form a separate union).

146 *The People's Conservative*, 17 May 1834.

147 Prothero and Parsinnen, 'London Tailors' Strike', pp. 79–80.

148 Mayhew, Letter XVI, *The Morning Chronicle*, 11 December 1849, in Thompson and Yeo, *Unknown Mayhew*, p. 227.

149 *The Pioneer*, 3 May 1834.

150 *ibid.*, 11 January 1834. This was an 'Address to the Trades Union' issued even before the Consolidated was formed, when Owen was already terrified by the militant mood of the general union movement; fears which were only confirmed by subsequent events.

It is worth adding here while the collapse of the Consolidated did not mean the end of trade unionism, it did create a terrible disillusionment with the idea of mass, class-based unionism: 'We were present,' one man wrote in 1841, 'at many of the meetings of the Grand National Consolidated Trade Union, and have a distinct recollection of the excitement that prevailed in them . . . but a little molehill obstructed their onward progress; and rather than commence the labour of removing so puny an obstacle, they chose to turn back, each taking his own path, regardless of the safety or the interests of his neighbour. It was painful to see the deep mortification of the generals and leaders of this quickly inflated army, when left deserted and alone in the field' (quoted in Cole and Postgate, *Common People*, p. 272). To describe the obstacles faced by the Consolidated as 'puny' seems extraordinary, but certainly the mood of disenchantment, and the subsequent retreat to the old sectionalist union organizations, seems to have been widespread.

151 Quoted in F. Podmore, *Robert Owen: a Biography*, 2 vols. (1906), vol. 2, p. 462.

V Eve And The New Jerusalem

1   *NMW*, 14 May 1836.
2   'The breaking up of the various Co-operative Societies, the unfortunate progress and termination of the Labour Exchange, and the dismemberment of the great Trades' Unions . . . have caused such distrust among the working classes that some time must elapse before sufficient confidence will be restored as to induce them once more to return to *co-operation*,' local Owenites reported (*NMW*, 6 May 1837). It should be emphasized, however, that although the 'enthusiastic' early phase of co-operative trading ended in 1834, co-operative trading did not completely die out at this time. (See *The Northern Star*, 6 January 1838 and 5 October 1839 for reports of co-operative shopkeeping in Huddersfield and Hull.)
3   Marx and Engels, *Communist Manifesto*, pp. 89–93. For Engels' more detailed account of the Owenites in 1844, see his *Working Class*, pp. 262–4, and also his *Socialism: Utopian and Scientific*, pp. 398–410.
4   For a detailed assessment of Owenite strength in 1840, see the speeches delivered by the Bishop of Exeter to the House of Lords denouncing Owenism as a blasphemous sect in February of that year (reprinted in *NMW*, 1, 8, 15 February 1840). For a discussion of the problem of estimating the level of Owenite support in this period, see above, p. 300, n.1.
5   *The Liverpool Standard*, 7 September 1839.
6   *NMW*, 22 November 1834.
7   'Now the middle class is the ONLY efficient DIRECTING class in Society, and will, of necessity, remain so, until our system shall create a NEW class of very superior DIRECTORS as well as OPERATORS; a class very superior to any men or women who have ever yet lived,' Owen informed his followers through the pages of *The New Moral World* in 1839, 'The working class never did DIRECT any permanent successful operations' (*NMW*, 11 July 1839).
8   See Owen's speech to the 1840 Congress of the UCSRR, reprinted in *NMW*, 20 June 1840.
9   For a discussion of the relationship between Owenism and Chartism, see Chapter Nine and n.15 below.
10 *The Movement*, 20 January 1844.
11 Opposition to Owen's 'paternal' system was cited by local organizers as one of the main reasons for the slow revival of the movement (*NMW*, 17 October 1835), and when new branches finally began to form, many refused to adopt the system (like the Salford branch, whose executive was fully re-elected every six months by the whole of the membership [*ibid.*, 17 September 1836]). Others who did follow the Central Board's directives soon reverted back to democratic structures. By 1843 one delegate to the Annual Congress was able to sum up the situation by noting that the paternal system had succeeded only when branches had modified it to suit their own inclinations, 'and they had been obliged to return to the old democratic system' (*ibid.*, 20 May 1843). See Eileen Yeo 'Robert Owen and Radical Culture', in Pollard and Salt, *Owen*, pp. 88–9, for a discussion of this conflict.
12 Joseph McCabe, *Life and Letters of George Jacob Holyoake*, 2 vols. (1908), vol. 1, p. 47.

13 *The Northern Star*, 24 October 1840.

14 *ibid.*, 26 June 1841.

15 *NMW*, 8 December 1838. So far as I know, there is no published study which explores the interpenetration of Owenism and Chartism. From my own work, it seems clear that in many towns local Owenites, or at least some of them, functioned as left-wing Chartists, campaigning for the Six Points while at the same time arguing that it was only when working people had control of the economy that they would really achieve the social emancipation which both movements desired. Both *The New Moral World* and *The Northern Star* bristle with reports of debates between local Owenites and Chartists in which the key issue at stake was not the desirability of a new, non-capitalist social order – this generally seems to have been taken for granted by both sides – but whether that order could be achieved through electoral democracy or community-building. The voice of working-class Owenism which is heard in these debates is very far indeed from the caricature presented in the *Communist Manifesto*. For examples of these debates, see *The Northern Star*, 31 July, 14 August, 16 October, 4 December 1841; *NMW*, 15 May, 2 July 1841. See also *NMW*, 15 September 1838, for a very interesting letter from a Socialist defending the Charter, and *The Northern Star*, 4 August 1838, for an editorial by Feargus O'Connor stating his support for 'the *practical* social arrangements recommended by Mr Owen' which he is convinced, however, will only be attained through 'Universal Suffrage' (by which he meant male suffrage). The Home Office also received a number of spy reports on joint Owenite-Chartist meetings, including one where the concluding speaker told the audience that 'if they all stuck true to their cause, and that by taking Chartism in one hand, and Socialism in the other, they would soon carry their cause' (HO 40/59).

I have no direct evidence on the number of Owenite women who were also Chartists. Nearly all the leading Owenite feminists spoke in favour of the Charter's demands at one time or another, and Emma Martin presided over a protest meeting on behalf of John Frost (*The London Social Reformer*, 9 May 1840; *The Northern Star*, 1 February 1840).

16 Thompson, *Inquiry*, p. 427, quoted in Harrison, *Owen*, p. 47n.

17 The admission procedure, as outlined in *NMW*, 22 November 1834, was as follows: when a man or woman desired to join an Owenite branch, they had first to appear before a junior committee of that branch which would examine them in order to ensure 'that they comprehend the cause of moral or social good . . . and . . . are ready to relinquish the practice of moral or social evil . . .' Having satisfied the branch on this score, the candidate was then allowed to attend 'Sunday lectures, weekly discussions and Social festivals' at half the price charged non-members, for a three month period. At the end of this time they were examined by the senior committee of the branch; if they passed this examination they were made full members. How many branches actually adopted such an elaborate procedure is unknown, although occasional letters to the Owenite press signed 'A Prospective Socialist' or 'A Candidate for Admission to the Association of All Classes of All Nations' indicate that some did. Certainly the stringent educative ideal behind it was to be found in every Owenite group, whether they used such formal methods or not.

18 *The Weekly Free Press,* clipping (February 1830) in William Pare Scrapbook, f.61.

19 For a discussion of the revival, see Chapter Five. For the relationship between religious revivalism and working-class radicalism, see E.J. Hobsbawm, 'The Labour Sects' in *Primitive Rebels* (Manchester, 1978), pp. 126-49; Thompson, *Making,* chapters two and eleven; R.F. Wearmouth, *Methodism and the Working-Class Movements of England* (1937).

Evangelicalism was a broad term used to describe all those who became swept up in the religious revival from the Methodists onwards; the Evangelical Party, however, was the revivalist wing of the Anglican church. The difference between the two is indicated by lower-case (for evangelicalism) and upper-case (for the Evangelicals).

20 Richard Mant, D D, *The Female Character, A Sermon preached in the Parish Church of St James, Westminster . . . on behalf of the Burlington Female Charity School* (1821), pp. 10-11; 'Christianity; the Only True Socialism', *The Evangelical Magazine and Missionary Chronicle* (1840), vol. xviii, p. 170.

21 Lewis, *Woman's Mission,* p. 50.

22 'A Philanthropist' [Anon.], *Domestic Tyranny or Woman in Chains* (1841), p. 35, 41.

23 W.L. O'Neill, *Everyone was Brave: The Rise and Fall of Feminism in America* (Chicago, 1969), pp. 11-12.

24 Mant, *Female Character,* p. 24.

25 Nancy F. Cott, 'Passionlessness: an Interpretation of Victorian Sexual Ideology, 1790-1850', *Signs,* vol. 4, no. 2 (Winter 1978), p. 225. See also Hall, 'Domestic Ideology', pp. 15-32.

26 Mrs Sarah Stickney Ellis, *The Women of England* (1838). Mrs Ellis' many books on Female Duty were major classics of early Victorian sexual morality, addressed to an audience which she defined (with admirable precision) as that part of the female population 'who are restricted to the services of from one to four domestics' . . . truly class definition from the female point of view.

27 Lewis, *Woman's Mission,* pp. 62-5.

28 *ibid.,* p. 129.

29 Wilberforce, *Practical View,* p. 453, quoted in Hall, 'Domestic Ideology', p. 26.

30 Ellis, *Women,* p. 37.

31 For the role of women in the charity movement, see F.K. Prochaska, 'Women in English Philanthropy, 1790-1830', *International Review of Social History,* vol. 19 (1974), pp. 426-441. Despite the auxiliary role played by women in these organizations, however, philanthropy soon became an important seedbed of feminist ideas and female career possibilities (see Ray Strachey, *The Cause* [1928] chapters 1 to 13). 'Philanthropist' urged married women's right to own property on the grounds that they would then be able to employ their financial resources in various philanthropic activities (*Domestic Tyranny,* p. 51).

32 L.F. Church. *More About the Early Methodist People* (1949), pp. 40-168; Wesley F. Swift, 'The Women Itinerant Preachers of Early Methodism', *Proceedings of the Wesley Historical Society,* vols. 28 and 29 (1952-1953).

33 George Eliot, *Adam Bede,* first ed. 1859 (New York, 1961) p. 95.

34 Lewis, *Woman's Mission*, p. 22.

35. HO 44/38. Margaret's opponent was a law student who subsequently reported the meeting to the Home Office. In his report he described Margaret as a 'singularly cool, brassfaced, tolerably good looking, hatless and capless, black haired and ringletted, clever eloquent woman, about thirty'. 'She seems a moral mildew,' he added.

36 *The Isis*, 25 February 1832.

37 Church, *Methodist People*, p. 168.

38 Ellis, *Women*, p. 16.

39 E.P. Thompson, 'Outside the Whale', in *The Poverty of Theory and Other Essays* (1978), p. 32.

40 Hypatia Bradlaugh Bonner, *Charles Bradlaugh, A Record of His Life and Work By His Daughter*, 2 vols. (1894), vol. 1, p. 9.

41 Owen Corres. 1239 for a letter from Margaret Chappellsmith to Owen which mentions her conversion. Margaret, whose maiden-name was Reynolds, was born in Aldgate in 1806, probably to an upper working-class family (hostile observers mocked her working-class accent). Like Emma Martin, she spent her early adult years in the Baptist church, but soon became interested in radical politics (first by reading Cobbett, who gave her a permanent interest in the currency issue, then by reading Owen), and also became concerned with the question of women's status. By 1836 she was writing articles for the Owenite press on women's position, currency reform and communitarian plans; she had also disavowed the church and begun lecturing publicly against orthodox religion. By 1839 she was working as a salaried Owenite lecturer. In the same year she married another Owenite, John Chappellsmith, who was very supportive of her political activities; they had no children. In 1842 she opened a bookshop in London. Apparently the shop did not flourish, since around 1850–51 she and John emigrated to America, where she died (at New Harmony) in 1883 (J.M. Wheeler, *Biographical Dictionary of Freethinkers of All Ages and Nations* [1889], pp. 74–5; *The Present Day*, July 1883).

There was a hostile but very interesting portrait of Margaret published by the Tory newspaper, *Old England* in 1839 (12, 26 October). The author was an *Old England* reporter who attended a series of lectures delivered by her at the Lambeth Social Institution to an audience which he described as a 'motley company' including 'soldiers . . . black women . . . ancient dames of other hues . . .' Margaret herself he described as a 'person of diminutive stature, with a Jewish face and very bold withal'. She suffered from a speech defect, he claimed, and also attempted to disguise her working-class accent.

For a brief account of Harriet Law's career, see Chapter Nine.

42 See above, p. 71.

43 *The Glasgow Evening Post*, 19 October 1833.

44 *The Isis*, 11 February 1832.

45 *NMW*, 10 June 1837. See Yeo, 'Radical Culture', pp. 95–103, for a discussion of the Socialist 'religion of brotherliness'.

46. Owenite meetings were often held in Methodist chapels in the early years, particularly in the North; on one occasion a Primitive Methodist congregation turned itself into a co-operative society. (*Lancashire and Yorkshire Co-operator*, June 1832). According to William Carson of Wigan, 'in that part of the country from which he came, people co-operated from Christian

principles. He himself was a Christian co-operator . . .' (quoted in Musson, 'Ideology of early Co-operation', pp. 133–4). Both the Primitive Methodists and the Independents had a reputation for political radicalism dating back to earlier struggles in which chapels had broken away from the parent body over reform issues, and it was undoubtedly from these sects that some Socialists emerged.

47 *NMW*, 11 April 1840.

48 Emma Martin, *God's Gifts and Men's Duties*, (1843), p. 15.

49 Emma Martin, *A Few Reasons for Renouncing Christianity and Professing Infidel Opinions*, (? 1850), p. 4. For the Particular Baptists, see A.C. Underwood, *A History of the English Baptists* (1947), pp. 128–36.

50 Martin, *God's Gifts*, p. 14.

51 *ibid.*, p. 15.

52 For many of these facts relating to Emma's pre-Socialist days I am indebted to her great-great-grand-daughter, Mrs Grace Cowie, who has spent some years researching her ancestor's life. She shared some of the results of her work with me before presenting them in 'Emma Martin : Socialist, Free Thinker and Women's Rights Advocate', co-authored with Edward Royle, to be published in Bellamy and Saville, *Dictionary of Labour Biography*, in the near future. I am grateful to both the authors and the editors for allowing me to see the ms. prior to publication.

53 G.J. Holyoake, *The Last Days of Emma Martin* (1851), p. 4.

54 Martin, *A Few Reasons*, p. 5. Emma continued to lecture on women for the two years she remained in the church.

55 *ibid.*, p. 7.

56 *NMW*, 6 April 1839.

57 *Proceedings of the Fourth Congress of the Universal Community Society of Rational Religionists, held in Birmingham in May 1839* (1839), p. 28.

58 Holyoake, *Last Days*, p. 4.

59 See, for example *First/Second Conversation on the Being of God*, (? 1850).

60 *NMW*, 12 June 1841.

61 Both Emma and Margaret Chappellsmith were employed as salaried lecturers by the Central Board; their wages are not known, but since Social Missionaries received 30s. a week they presumably got about the same (*NMW*, 16 May 1840). For child-care arrangements while she was on tour, see Holyoake's Diary (Bishopsgate Institute) where he notes (sometime in 1843, the exact date is not clear) that his family has been taking care of Emma's youngest daughter for nine weeks at 5s. a week.

62 Two accounts of this tradition are: Edward Royle, *Victorian Infidels* (Manchester, 1974); Gwyn Williams, 'Rowland Detrosier: a working-class infidel, 1800–1834', *Borthwick Papers*, no. 28 (York, 1965). See also Stan Shipley, *Club Life and Socialism in Mid-Victorian London*, History Workshop Pamphlet, no. 5 (Oxford, 1971) for a very interesting account of the persistence of Socialist infidelism in the years after the disappearance of the Owenite movement.

63 Reported in *NMW*, 24 October 1840.

64 *London City Mission Magazine*, vol. IV (June 1839), pp. 108–9; see also pp. 114–5 for an interesting analysis by a missionary of Owenism's popular appeal.

65 Matilda Roalfe, *Law Breaking Justified* (1844), p. 12.

66   Royle, *Infidels*, p. 62.
67   George Pearson, *The Progress and Tendencies of Socialism* (Cambridge, 1839), p. 33.
68   *London City Mission Magazine*, vol. VII (February 1842), p. 31, 44. See also *ibid.*, vol. IV (October 1839), pp. 165–7.
69   F. Meyrick, *The Outcast and Poor of London* (1856), p. 150.
70   *The Christian Lady's Magazine*, vol. 13 (1840), p. 378.
71   *ibid.*, pp. 378–9.
72   *ibid.*, p. 382.
73   Reported in *NMW*, 9 February 1839.
74   *ibid.*, 1, 8, 15 February 1840. See also Hansard, *Parliamentary Debates*, 3rd series, LI (1840), col. 530, 1187; and editorials in *The Times*, 3, 7, 11 February 1840.
75   *ibid.*, 24 October 1840.
76   *ibid.*, 4 January 1840.
77   Owen Corres. 267.
78   Royle, *Infidels*, p. 62.
79   *NMW*, 27 July 1839. For an interesting account of Owenite/Christian controversy in a Yorkshire weaving village (apparently an Owenite stronghold) see Joseph Lawson, *Letters to the Young on Progress in Pudsey* (Stanninglen, 1887), pp. 76–7. Thanks to John Gillis for this reference.
80   *ibid.*, 14 August 1841.
81   *ibid.*, 24 October 1840.
82   Report from *The Hull Packet*, reprinted in *The Movement*, 23 October 1844.
83   *NMW*, 11 November 1843; *NMW*, 31 August 1844.
84   *The London Social Reformer*, 9 May 1840.
85   *The Evangelical Magazine and Missionary Chronicle*, vol. xviii (February 1840), p. 117.
86   Martin, *God's Gifts*, p. 14. For an illuminating discussion of freethought doctrine, see Royle, *Infidels*, chapter 3.
87   Emma Martin, *A Funeral Sermon Occasioned by the Death of Richard Carlile, preached at the Hall of Science, City Road, London* (1843). The persistence of what Patricia Hollis has described as the 'Old Corruption' style of analysis in Emma's thought is very clear in this tract. At one point she lists the enemies of 'the people' as 'the clergy, who draw large revenues from the people, by working upon their fears, and pandering to their hopes, – and the aristocracy, who looked to *'orders'* as a neat provision for the younger members of their family, – and the state, who knew well the value of their spiritual jackals . . .' (p. 6). For Hollis' contrast between this style of analysis and the new anti-capitalist ideology of the 1830s and 1840s, see her *The Pauper Press* (Oxford, 1970), chapters 6 and 7, especially pp. 206–208 for an analysis of the 'anti-priestcraft' rhetoric of Carlile and his supporters.
88   *NMW*, 23 October 1841.
89   Emma Martin, *The Missionary Jubilee Panic and the Hypocrites' Prayer, Addressed to the Supporters of Christian Missions* (1844), p. 5.
90   Martin, *God's Gifts*, p. 6.
91   The concluding summary phrase is pilfered from Royden Harrison (letter, *History Workshop Journal*, no. 5 [1978], p. 216).
92   *NMW*, 8 June 1839.

93   Martin, *A Few Reasons*, p. 9.
94   Quoted in Royle, *Infidels*, p. 108.
95   *The Movement*, 13 January 1844.
96   G.J. Holyoake, *The Logic of Death* (1852), p. 6.
97   For this style of Biblical criticism, see her, *The Bible No Revelation, or the inadequacy of language to convey a message from God to man* (?1845).
98   *NMW*, 31 August 1844.
99   Reported in Bishop of Exeter's speech, *Hansard*, 4 February 1840, reprinted in *NMW*, 15 February 1840.
100 Martin, *God's Gifts*, p. 14.
101 *NMW*, 6 March 1841.
102 Emma Martin, *Baptism a Pagan Rite* (1844), pp. 8–16.
103 *The Movement*, 13 January 1844.
104 *The Isis*, 7 April 1832.
105 *NMW*, 19 July 1845.
106 *NMW*, 17 November 1832. Harriet told the minister that she converted to Owenism because 'it was entirely a system of love, and just such a system as Christ taught'.

   I told him I would no longer entertain the narrow-minded opinion I formerly held, that every man must believe a certain creed before he could be saved; but that I now believed all were right as regarded the safety of their souls. I told him Christ had taught us to love one another: whilst sectarianism taught us to hate one another.

   After this discussion the preacher went on to exemplify Mrs Adam's point by denouncing her from his pulpit and warning the people of Cheltenham to avoid her. 'Some did shun me, indeed, whilst . . . others could see nothing so awful in me. But my own sister . . . has forbid me her house.'

107 *NMW*, 3 October 1840.
108 *The Oracle of Reason*, 14 January 1843.
109 Wright, *Popular Lectures*, p. 38.
110 *NMW*, 10 December 1842.
111 Holyoake, *Last Days*, p. 5.
112 See, for example, her *Religion Superseded, or the Moral Code of Nature Sufficient for the Guidance of Man* (?1844), p. 8.
113 *NMW*, 30 May 1840.
114 'Woman and the Social System', *Fraser's Magazine for Town and Country*, vol. xxi, no. cxxvi (June 1840).
115 *NMW*, 12 June 1841.
116 Holyoake, *Last Days*, p. 7.
117 *NMW*, 25 July 1840.
118 *ibid.*, 30 March 1844.
119 *ibid.*, 13 February 1841.
120 *ibid.*, 12 June 1841.
121 *ibid.*, 11 July 1840.
122 *ibid.*
123 *The London Social Reformer*, 9 May 1840.
124 *The Movement*, 23 October 1844.
125 *ibid.*, 27 November 1844.

126 Descriptions of this confrontation are to be found in: Martin, *Missionary Jubilee Panic*; *The Movement*, 16 October 1844.
127 Martin, *Missionary Jubilee Panic*, p. 11.
128 *NMW*, 19 October 1844.
129 *The Movement*, 27 November 1844.
130 *NMW*, 21 December 1844.
131 *ibid.*, 5 April 1845.
132 *The Movement*, 26 February 1845.
133 Martin, *Missionary Jubilee Panic*, p. 3.
134 *The Movement*, 13 January 1844.
135 Martin, *Missionary Jubilee Panic*, pp. 16–17.
136 *NMW*, 25 January 1845.
137 In 1852 one Heywood cleric delivered a lecture on the 'Life, Character and End of Mrs Martin' in which he suggested that the mere fact that Holyoake had delivered Emma's funeral oration was proof of his own immoral character. One of Emma's supporters rose to defend her against the clergyman's charges of loose living: 'I did my best to show him that it was her duty to herself as well as her children that she should leave [her husband], but was not able to satisfy the Rev . . .' (*The Reasoner*, vol. 13, no. 333 [1852], p. 284).
138 *NMW*, 26 July 1845.
139 Holyoake, *Last Days*, p. 4.
140 'The Death of Mrs Emma Martin', *The Reasoner*, vol. 10, no. 282 (1851), p. 349.
141 Emma Martin, 'A Review and a Prospect', *The Reasoner*, vol. 4, no. 91 (1848), p. 177.
142 *ibid.*, p. 178.
143 *ibid.*, p. 179.
144 *The Movement*, 3 February, 20 April 1844.
145 Martin, 'A Review', pp. 178–9.
146 Ambrose Barker, *Henry Hetherington* (1938), p. 52.
147 Holyoake, *Last Days*, p. 2.
148 *The Reasoner*, vol. 12, no. 286 (1852), p. 4.
149 Holyoake, *Last Days*, p. 7.
150 *The Promethean, or Communitarian Apostle*, vol. 1, no. 1 (January 1842).
151 The major study of popular millenarianism in the late eighteenth and early nineteenth century is J.F.C. Harrison, *The Second Coming: Popular Millenarianism, 1780–1850* (1979), to which I am heavily indebted. Harrison discusses the relationship between millenarianism and radicalism in the last section of his book (pp. 220–8); for other accounts of this relationship, see: Thompson, *Making* (pp. 385–440 and 882–3) and Hobsbawm, 'Labour Sects', pp. 129–42.

In using the term 'millenarian' rather than 'millennialist', I am following Harrison, who makes the useful distinction (*Second Coming*, pp. 5–6) between millennialist theory, as elaborated by sophisticated biblical scholars ('respectable, orthodox, scholarly millennialism') and popular millenarian belief, as it emerged among poorer, self-taught enthusiasts (those usually condemned as 'the lunatic fringe'). The division, as Harrison emphasizes, is not hard and fast, and certainly a number of the men and women we are about to examine straddled both camps (particularly James

Smith and Goodwyn Barmby), although their radical politics pushed them more towards the popular end of the spectrum.

152 Harrison, *Owen*, plate 14 (facing p. 100); p. 133.

153 *ibid.*, p.133; *NMW*, 12 June 1841.

154 Cole and Postgate, *Common People*, p. 270.

155 Harrison, *Owen*, pp. 135–7. Harrison's argument is a nuanced and important one, and deserves a more extended discussion than I can give it here. He is fully aware of the ways in which Owenism differed entirely from the usual type of millenarian sect, but rather than taking these as evidence that it was in fact something else – i.e. the radical movement that the Owenites thought it was – he broadens his definition of millenarian sectarianism to the point where it is conflated with almost any form of revolutionary organization. He states that the Owenites 'emptied the concept of the millennium of all theological content, leaving it simply and essentially a description of a state of society in which the new system prevailed', a state which was to be achieved not through 'withdrawal from the world' (which was typical of most millenarian sects), but through direct 'opposition' to the existing social order, including such 'basic institutions' as 'the family, private property and the churches'. He also points to the Owenites' emphasis on creating a spiritual home for themselves within their movement, where they would attempt to build a new style of loving comradeship based on a shared way of life and thought. If these are, as Harrison suggests, characteristics of millenarian sectarians then it has to be said that there are still many Socialists (particularly many Socialist feminists) today who fit that description. (For a good example of a present-day text espousing a style of socialist organization very similar to that of the Owenites, see Rowbotham, Segal, and Wainwright, *Beyond the Fragments*).

156 Cole and Postgate, *Common People*, pp. 270–1.

157 J. Lacan, *Ecrits: a Selection*, first English ed. (trans. Alan Sheridan), 1977, p. 72.

158 Robert Owen, *Life of Robert Owen* (1857), p. 135, quoted in Harrison, *Owen*, pp. 134–5. 'In taking a calm retrospect of my life from the earliest remembered period of it . . .' Owen wrote in the year before his death, 'there appears to me to have been a succession of extraordinary or out-of-the-usual-way events, forming connecting links of a chain, to compel me to proceed onward to complete a mission, of which I have been an impelled agent.' The ultimate Planner of this mission, as Harrison points out (*Owen*, p. 134), could be dubbed Providence or Nature as well as God, but in any case it was a transcendental force behind human progress, with a Purpose which mankind was intended to recognize and assist.

159 The first number of *The New Moral World* (1 November 1834) opened with an editorial by Owen proclaiming 'the great Advent of the world, the second coming of Christ . . .' with Whose arrival 'the foretold millennium is about to commence'. Owen was a Deist whose interpretation of the millennium was, as Harrison has shown (*Owen*, pp. 92–3, 106, 132–3), heavily influenced by Enlightenment concepts of evolutionary progress; nonetheless, the idea that this progress had a transcendental source was very marked in Owen's thought. For an interesting discussion of Owen-as-millenarian see W.H. Oliver, 'Owen in 1817: the Millennialist Moment' in Pollard and Salt,

Owen, pp. 166–87. Oliver also offers a definition of the millenarian 'mood' which is so sweeping, however, as to pull Edward Irving and the general unionists of 1834 under the same umbrella, thereby implying that the dream of the Second Advent and the plan for 'producer-based socialism' were each as wildly visionary as the other (p. 183).

160 See the section titled 'Disciples and Prophets' in Harrison, *Owen*, pp. 103–32, where he discusses men like John Finch, Abram Combe, James Smith, and the 'Sacred Socialist', James Pierrepont Greaves.

161 See *The Co-operative Magazine* (December 1827) for mention of some early Owenites who treated Owen as the new Messiah; also Harrison, *Owen*, p. 126, for Finch's adulation of his leader. See Oliver, 'Owen in 1817', for a discussion of Owen's ambivalent attitude towards his own possible messianic status.

162 Goodwyn Barmby, 'To All People, Faith, Peace, and Health', in *Some Progress of the Truth As It is In Jesus*, no. 6 (1843), p. 72. This was the newspaper of the White Quakers, who are discussed below (pp. 174–175).

163 M.F. Melcher, *The Shaker Adventure* (Princeton, 1941); Muncy, *Sex*, pp. 17–21, 36–41, 46–9; Harrison, *Second Coming*, pp. 165–77.

164 Harrison, *Second Coming*, pp. 31–8.

165 Letter to *The Shepherd*, quoted in W.H. Armytage, *Heavens Below: Utopian Experiments in England, 1560–1960* (1961), p. 135. For Owen's favourable impression of the Shakers, see above, p. 40.

166 *The Shepherd*, 21 February 1835.

167 This account of Southcott's life and thought is drawn from a selection of her own autobiographical writings, as compiled in Alice Seymour, *The Express: . . . containing the Life and Divine Writings of the Late Joanna Southcott*, 2 vols. (1909) and as found in Joanna Southcott, *Copies and Parts of Copies of Letters and Communications, Written from Joanna Southcott and Transmitted by Miss Towney to Mr W. Sharp in London* (1804). The following secondary sources were also used: G.R. Balleine, *Past Finding Out: The Tragic Story of Joanna Southcott and Her Successors* (1956); J. Evans, *A Sketch of the Various Denominations of the Christian World* (1841); Charles A. Lane, *The Life and Bibliography of Joanna Southcott* (1912); Mary S. Robertson, *The True Story of Joanna Southcott* (Ashford, Middsx., 1923); Thompson, *Making*, pp. 420–6; Harrison, *Second Coming*, pp. 86–134.

168 Joanna Southcott, *The Strange Effects of Faith* (Exeter, 1801–2).

169 Balleine, *Past*, p. 46.

170 Harrison, *Owen*, p. 110.

171 Harrison, *Second Coming*, p. 110.

172 Joanna Southcott, *The Answer of the Lord to the Powers of Darkness* (1802), reprinted in Seymour, *Express*, vol. 1, p. 231.

173 *ibid*. See Harrison's interesting discussion of what he describes as Joanna's 'theological feminism' (*Second Coming*, pp. 108–9).

174 Southcott, *Answer*, reprinted in Seymour, *Express*, vol. 1, p 65.

175 *ibid*., p. 67.

176 For the militant feminism of the Shakers, see Harrison, *Second Coming*, pp. 167–9; Muncy, *Sex*, pp. 17–9. One of the first rules of the Shaker community in Hancock, New York, was that men and women should be treated as equals in all matters, from spiritual ministry to the day-to-day

government of the community (which was governed by an equal number of male and female 'Elders'). The rules still hang in the halls of Hancock to be seen by visitors to the wonderful Shaker museum there.

177 Seymour, *Express*, vol. 2, p. 117.
178 Southcott, *Copies*, pp. 16–21.
179 *ibid.*, pp. 18–20; Joanna Southcott (original text not specified), reprinted in Seymour, *Express*, vol. 1, p. 172.
180 Joanna Southcott, *A Dispute Between the Woman and the Powers of Darkness* (1802), reprinted in Seymour, *Express*, vol. 2, p. 96.
181 Southcott, *Answer*, reprinted in Seymour, *Express*, vol. 1, p. 228.
182 Balleine, *Past*, p. 58.
183 Harrison, *Second Coming*, p. 107.
184 See, for example, Joanna's highly erotic dream about Christ quoted in Harrison, *ibid.*, p. 107, and also her account of her relationship with her father, in *Copies*, pp. 10–14. In her autobiographical writings, Joanna recorded the many suitors who had plagued her for her sexual favours, or even her hand in marriage. Harrison takes these claims at face-value (*ibid.*, pp. 106–7) but it seems likely that some, at least, were fantasies (including possibly the tales of Rigsby and Wills), in the same vein as the Oedipal incest/rape fantasies which dominate her descriptions of her youthful relations with her father.
185 Harrison, *Second Coming*, p. 36.
186 *ibid.*, p. 167.
187 *ibid.*, p. 119.
188 Thompson, *Making*, p. 879: Harrison, *Second Coming*, pp. 152–5.
189 The account of Smith given here is necessarily brief and omits much of the career of this extraordinary man. A useful, but biased, source for his life is the biography written by his nephew, Smith, *'Shepherd' Smith*; for his millenarian thought, see Harrison, *Owen*, pp. 112–21. His political activities and writings are discussed in J. Saville, 'J.E. Smith and the Owenite Movement, 1833–34', in Pollard and Salt, *Owen*, pp. 115–44. Smith's feminism is briefly discussed by Harrison (*Owen*, pp. 120–1) and also in Saville, 'Owen on the Family', pp. 112–3. Smith's own writings are to be found in *The Isis* (1832); *The Crisis* (1832–34); *The Pioneer* (1833–34); *The Shepherd* (1834–38); *The New Moral World* (1834–35) and several books and tracts, some of which are referred to elsewhere in this chapter.
190 Saville, 'Smith', p. 118. Smith described the time he spent among the Christian Israelites in his semi-fictionalized book, *The Coming Man* (1875).
191 Oliver, *Organization*, p. 174.
192 For a summary of his post-Owenite career, see Harrison, *Owen* pp. 114–6.
193 *The Shepherd*, 15 August 1835.
194 *The Crisis*, 31 August 1833.
195 *ibid.*, 4 May 1833.
196 For Smith's relationship with Wheeler, see Smith, *'Shepherd' Smith*, p. 148, 205, 335–7.
197 Fontana and Prati, Chief and Preacher of the St Simonian Religion in England, *St Simonism in London* (1834) pp. 23-4. See Pankhurst, *Saint Simonians*, pp. 107–112, for an account of the doctrine of *La Mère*.
198 Pankhurst, *Saint Simonians*, p. 96.

199 See, for example, a report of a lecture delivered by Smith at the Charlotte Street Institution on Saint Simonianism (*The Crisis*, 28 December 1833).
200 *The Crisis*, 4 January 1834.
201 *The Shepherd*, 21 February 1835.
202 For Smith's support for female trade unionism, see *The Crisis*, 1 March 1834.
203 *The Shepherd*, 16 May 1835.
204 Quoted in Smith, *'Shepherd' Smith*, p. 270.
205 See his exchange of letters with Anna Wheeler's daughter, Lady Lytton, *ibid.*, pp. 325–401.
206 This account of the Communist Church is derived largely from the following contemporary sources: *The New Moral World; The Educational Circular and Communist Apostle* (November 1841–May 1842); *New Tracts for the Times*, (1843); *The Promethean or Communitarian Apostle* (1842); *The Communist Chronicle and Communitarian Apostle* (1843); *The Apostle and Chronicle of the Communist Church* (1848); *Some Account of the Progress of the Truth As It is in Jesus* (1843–44); Thomas Frost, *Forty Years Recollections*, (1880). Goodwyn's life and writings are discussed in: Armytage, *Heavens*, pp. 196–208; Armytage, 'The Journalistic Activities of J. Goodwyn Barmby between 1841 and 1848', *Notes and Queries*, CCI (1956); A.L. Morton, *The English Utopia* (1952). A.L. Morton has also produced an entry for *The Dictionary of Labour Biography* (volume forthcoming) on the life and political work of both Goodwyn and Catherine ('Chartists, Feminists, and Utopian Socialists') which has proved most helpful to me. I am grateful to the author and editors for allowing me to see it prior to publication. Goodwyn's career as a Chartist is discussed in Arthur Brown, 'Suffolk Chartism' (unpublished, 1974), and I am also grateful to him for sharing his findings with me. Catherine's maiden name was Watkins (*The Dictionary of National Biography* incorrectly lists it as Reynolds – Margaret Chappellsmith's maiden name).
207 Quoted in Armytage, *Heavens*, p. 198.
208 *NMW.*, 29 June 1839.
209 See, for example, *ibid.*, 6 April 1839, 19 December 1835.
210 *ibid.*, 6 February 1836.
211 *The Educational Circular*, vol. 1, no. 1 (1841).
212 *NMW*, 20 September 1845.
213 Brown, 'Chartism', p. 6. In 1841 Barmby signed the declaration announcing the formation of the National Association of the United Kingdom for Promoting the Political and Social Improvement of the People – a Chartist body which supported an alliance with middle-class liberals to win an expanded franchise. Whether Barmby remained in this wing of Chartism or later abandoned it, as some of the other declaration signatories did, is unknown. Thanks to Dorothy Thompson for this information.
214 *NMW*, 28 August, 4 September 1841.
215 *Some Account of the Progress*, no. 28 (1843), pp. 22–3.
216 Joshua Jacob was a grocer who abandoned his business and wife on receiving God's Call. He formed a partnership with Abigail Beale, and together they established their sect in a large house in Dublin. In addition to white clothing (Russian duck trousers, to be precise) the men also wore beards; the women had braids and left their heads uncovered. The White Quakers were continually accused of improper sexual conduct, and eventually (according

to one hostile account) their commune was stormed by another group of Quaker men who were trying to retrieve their wives who had been seduced into the White heretics' fold (Sarah Greer, *Quakerism, or the Story of My Life* [Dublin, 1851], p. 79; see also Isabel Grubb, *Quakers in Ireland* [1927], pp. 103–7). In the late 1840s Jacob was arrested for misappropriating the sect's funds and jailed; later he became a Roman Catholic. The White Quakers were in continual contact with the Communist Church in the early 1840s, and their newspaper, *Some Account of the Progress of the Truth As It is in Jesus*, carried many letters from the Barmbys.

217 For the story of the Ham Common Concordium, see Armytage, *Heavens*, pp. 171–83.

218 [Henry Wright], *Man's Appeal to Woman* (1842), no pagination.

219 Their activities in these years can be traced through *Some Account of the Progress* and their many short-lived newspapers, as listed above (n. 206).

220 *The Educational Circular*, vol. 1 no. 1 (November 1841).

221 *Some Account of the Progress*, no. 21 (1843), p. 12.

222 *The Educational Circular*, vol. 1, no. 2 (December 1841). See also J.G. Barmby, *The Outlines of Communism, Associality, and Communisation* (1841).

223 *Some Account of the Progress*, no. 7 (1843), p. 54.

224 *ibid.*, no. 32 (1844), pp. 62–66; Armytage, *Heavens*, p. 199.

225 *ibid.*, no. 32 (1844), p. 7; *The Movement*, 19 February 1845.

226 *Some Account of the Progress*, no. 31 (1844), pp. 40–1. Anne Knight was writing to the Barmbys asking for their support in a campaign for female enfranchisement, which they both willingly offered, although with the proviso that while the vote was necessary for improvements in women's status, only a communist society could truly free women.

227 *NMW*, 1 May 1841.

228 Catherine Isabella Barmby, 'Invocation', *The Educational Circular*, vol. 1, no. 2 (December 1841).

229 Barmby, 'Demand for Emancipation', p. 39.

230 R. Southey, 'Doctrine de Saint Simon', *The Quarterly Review*, no. LXXXIX (April–July 1831), p. 443.

231 *NMW*, 17 July 1841.

232 *ibid.*, 28 August 1841; *The Promethean*, vol. 1, no. 1 (January 1842).

233 Barmby, 'Demand for Emancipation'.

234 *ibid.*, p. 34.

235 Catherine Barmby, 'Women's Industrial Independence', *The Apostle and Chronicle of the Communist Church*, vol. 1, no. 1 (1848).

236 Barmby, 'Demand for Emancipation', p. 38.

237 *ibid.*

238 *ibid.*, p. 37.

239 *ibid.*, p. 34.

240 *ibid.*, p. 36. Catherine attempted to start a feminist journal in the later 1840s, but without success (see undated letter from Goodwyn to Holyoake, probably written in 1846 or 1847, describing Catherine's attempts to initiate such a magazine: Holyoake Corres. 339). She continued to write feminist articles for the Communist Church's journals and also for other progressive periodicals (see, for example, *The Whittington Club Gazette*, 17 November 1849). She had another child, a daughter, in 1846, but then her health

deteriorated and she died in 1854.

The Communist Church disintegrated in 1848. Goodwyn became a Unitarian minister, based in Wakefield from 1858 on. He remained active in various progressive causes, including support for Mazzini and the campaign for the 1867 Reform Bill, until his death in 1881. He re-married, this time to a women called Ada Shepherd, in 1861. Ada was apparently also a feminist, since her name appears alongside Goodwyn's in a list of subscribers to the National Society for Women's Suffrage published in the late 1860s. In 1868 Anne Knight, the early suffragist organizer, received a letter from another leading feminist, Lydia Becker, who told her that the Barmbys had informed her of Anne's interest in the suffrage issue (letter of 31 January 1868, in the uncatalogued collection of Anne Knight correspondence at Friends' House Library).

VI Love And The New Life: The Debate Over Marriage Reform

1 *NMW*, 4 April 1840.
2 'Christianity; the only true Socialism', *The Evangelical Magazine and Missionary Chronicle*, vol. XVIII (May 1840), p. 216.
3 Joseph Barker, *The Overthrow of Infidel Socialism; or the Gospel and Socialism Contrasted* (?1840), p. 26.
4 Edward Hancock, *Robert Owen's Community System, and the Horrid Doings of the Saint Simonians . . . etc . . . Letter Third* (?1837), pp. 34–44.
5 Barker, *Overthrow*, p. 27.
6 Thomas Frost, *Forty Years Recollections: Literary and Political* (1880), p. 19.
7 *ibid.*, p. 16.
8 *What is Socialism and What Would Be Its Practical Effects Upon Society? A Correct Report of the Public Discussion between Robert Owen and Mr John Brindley . . . etc . . .* (1841).
9 *NMW*, 20 July 1839. The fullest reports of Owenite marriage lectures were those published by the Owenites themselves, but their lectures were also recorded by hostile listeners, particularly by their Christian opponents. Some people were so horrified by what they heard that they even sent *verbatim* reports to the Home Office (see HO 45/OS 92 and OS 338 [1841–42] for examples of such reports). A *Times* reporter attended a meeting in London where Charles Southwell spoke on marriage (*The Times*, 23 August 1839) and afterwards printed a report of Southwell's speech in which (according to the report) Southwell argued that

> the people were weighed down by a condition of unhappiness, in consequence of the marriage law. Out of every ten marriages under the present system there was but one which was productive of happiness . . . there was no sincerity – nothing but hypocrisy – nothing but a mutual course of deception carried on – in the married state . . .'

He then, according to the reporter,

poured forth a torrent of words, and at length arrived at the conclusion that the marriage state would by no possibility lead to happiness unless it were arranged on scientific principles. Altogether, the exhibition was calculated to induce a feeling of pity, if not disgust, in the breasts of those who chanced to be in the room. The views of Mr Robert Owen, of course, constituted the basis of the lecture.

It is interesting to note that even progressive periodicals, like *The Sheffield Iris*, although prepared to defend Socialism against the Bishop of Exeter's attack, condemned Owenite marriage doctrine as advocacy of 'promiscuous intercourse' (*The Sheffield Iris*, 11, 25 February 1840).

10 John Wade, *The History of the Middle and Working Classes* (1833), p. 491.
11 Barker, *Overthrow*, p. 59.
12 *What is Socialism . . . ?*, p. 38.
13 *NMW*, 28 November 1840.
14 Frost, *Recollections*, p. 20.
15 Richard Matthews, *Is Marriage Worth Perpetuating? The Ninth of a Series of Lectures against Socialism . . . under the Direction of the Committee of the London City Mission* (1840), p. 51.
16 HO 44/38.
17 *NMW*, 5 October 1839.
18 *The Christian Lady's Magazine*, vol. 13 (1840), pp. 378–80.
19 *NMW*, 22 June 1839; *The Whitehaven Herald*, 15 January 1842.
20 Harriet Jay, *Robert Buchanan* (1903), p. 6.
21 *The Whitehaven Herald*, 15 January 1842.
22 *NMW*, 1 August 1840; 26 June 1841. In 1840 a laundress living in Hulme was picked up by the police who accused her of having stolen goods (she was carrying a bundle of washing at the time). They knocked her about and tore at her clothes, and demanded to know whether she was an Owenite, 'for she looked like one'. Presumably they meant she looked like a prostitute; it is interesting to see how strong was the popular equation between Socialism and sexual immoralism, particularly as applied to women. (For a report of this incident, see *The Manchester and Salford Advertiser*, 20 June 1840.)
23 *ibid.*, 16 March 1839.
24 *ibid.*, 21 March 1840.
25 *ibid.*, 25 August 1838.
26 *The Social Pioneer*, 16 March 1839.
27 *NMW*, 3 April 1841.
28 *ibid.*, 3 November 1838; *The Crisis*, 22 June 1833.
29 A few recent studies provide insights into these developments. See Stone, *Family*, pp. 602–48; Edward Shorter, *The Making of the Modern Family* (1977); Louise Tilly and Joan Scott, *Women, Work and Family* (New York, 1978); J. Weeks, *Sex, Politics and Society: the Regulation of Sexuality since 1800* (1981), ch.4. Tome's essay on wife-battering ('A Torrent of Abuse') contains some very illuminating remarks on changing sexual mores in the London working class at the mid-century, while John Gillis 'Servants, Sexual Relations and the Risks of Illegitimacy in London, 1801–1900' (*Feminist Studies*, vol. 5, no. 1, [1979]) discusses the pressures which economic and social change placed on older modes of sexual behaviour during the same period. In May 1980 I was also able to discuss with John

Gillis the results of some of his current research into plebian marriage patterns (John Gillis, *Resort to Common-Law Marriage in England and Wales, 1700–1850* [unpublished, 1980]). His findings more than confirm my own surmises about the level of 'irregular' sexual behaviour in the working class in the early nineteenth century. I am grateful to him for sharing his ideas with me, and look forward to the publication of his book on working-class marriage.

30　Reprinted from *The Monthly Repository*, in *NMW*, 17 August 1844. For an interesting discussion of the problems of middle-class spinsterhood, see Ian Watt, *The Rise of the Novel* (Harmondsworth, 1977), chapter five. The problem continued to worsen; by 1851, one-quarter of all women of marriageable age were unwed, as compared to one-fifth of all men of equivalent status (McGregor, *Divorce*, p. 85). Suggestions as to what should be done with these 'surplus women' abounded; for some classic contributions to the debate see: Harriet Martineau, 'Female Industry', *Edinburgh Review*, no.109 (1859); W.R. Greg, 'Why are Women Redundant?' *National Review* (April 1862); Jessie Boucherett, 'How to Provide for Superfluous Women', in J. Butler, ed., *Women's Work and Women's Culture* (1869).

31　Mayhew, Letter XI, *The Morning Chronicle*, 23 November 1849, reprinted in Thompson and Yeo, *Unknown Mayhew*, p. 202.

32　*The London City Mission Magazine*. vol. XVI (January 1851), p. 16. Unwillingness to be wed within the Established Church was a barrier to marriage after 1753, when Hardwicke's Marriage Act was passed, which gave the Church a monopoly over the solemnization of marriage. For a discussion of working-class attitudes towards the Hardwicke Act, see Gillis' forthcoming study, *Common-Law Marriage*.

33　Rev J. Ross, *The Parish of St James Pockthorpe with a Statement of its Conditions and Wants . . . etc* (Norwich, 1854). In his parish of 2490 persons there were often less than eleven marriages a year, he reported, while the private diary of another clergyman in the area showed an even lower rate. Both were convinced this was due to the number of couples living together without benefit of the ceremony. I am grateful to Lin Shaw for providing me with these references.

34　Mayhew, Letter VIII and XI, *The Morning Chronicle*, 13 and 23 November 1849, in Thompson and Yeo, *Unknown Mayhew*, pp. 175–81, 200–16; *Report of the Select Committee on Children's Employment*, xiv (1843), pp. 172–3 and pp. A 10–12 and p. 225; 'Labour and the Poor', *The Morning Chronicle*, 29 October 1849, in Razzell and Wainwright, *Working Class*, p. 190; P. Gaskell, *Artisans and Machinery: the Moral and Physical Condition of the Manufacturing Population* (1836), pp. 99–113. See also Jennie Kitteringham, 'Country Work Girls in Nineteenth Century England', in R. Samuel, ed., *Village Life and Labour* (1975), p. 118 and pp. 127–33, and Pinchbeck, *Women Workers*, pp. 310–11.

35　Charles Bray, *The Industrial Employment of Women* (1857), p. 7.

36　*London City Mission Magazine*, vol. XIII (July 1848), p. 148.

37　*ibid.*

38　*ibid.*

39 *ibid.*, vol. IX (August 1844), p. 129.
40 *ibid.*, vol XIII (July 1848), p. 148.
41 'Labour and the Poor', Letter XIII, *The Morning Chronicle*, 1 December 1849, in Razzell and Wainwright, *Working Class*, pp. 33–4.
42 George, *London Life*, p. 199.
43. Place, *Autobiography*, p. 57.
44 Sir Charles Shaw, *Replies to Lord Ashley, MP, Regarding the Educational and Moral and Physical Condition of the Labouring Classes* (1843), p. 28; C. Allen Clarke, *The Effects of the Factory System* first ed. 1899 (1913), p. 18; P. Gaskell, *The Manufacturing Population of England: Its Moral, Social, and Physical Conditions* (1833), pp. 28–9. See also Hewitt, *Wives*, p. 55, and Stone, *Family*, pp. 605–7.
45 PEH Hair, 'Bridal Pregnancy in Rural England in Earlier Centuries', *Population Studies*, 20 (November 1960), pp. 233–43.
46 Samuel Bamford, *Early Days* (1849), p. 229, 291.
47 Gaskell, *Manufacturing Population*, p. 29. For examples of these sanctions, see Michael Anderson, *Family Structure in Nineteenth Century Lancashire* (Cambridge, 1971), p. 88; and (for the European context) Shorter, *Family*, pp. 216–24. John Gillis (*Common-Law Marriage*) documents the rituals surrounding informal sexual contracts in many working-class communities: in South Wales, for example, 'besom weddings' were celebrated up to the mid-nineteenth century. Each partner jumped over a branch of besom birch into the joint home, and they were then considered wed. In other areas an exchange of rings was sufficient, or private vows, or simply the fact of cohabitation itself (Gillis, *Common-Law Marriage*, pp. 2–4). Gillis argues that all these forms of 'irregular' union increased after 1753, when the narrowing and rigidification of the legal definition of marriage (with the Hardwicke Act) forced many couples who would previously have been wed clandestinely (by ordinary but none-too-scrupulous clergymen, who abounded in large towns) to resort to common-law practices. Tilly and Scott (*Women, Work and Family*, pp. 96–8 and 121–3) also suggest that the number of couples living in consensual unions rose in the late eighteenth century, and certainly the anxious vigilantes of the local City Missions seemed to think so. But it is essential to recall that this was also a period when the Evangelical conscience created a heightened sensitivity to plebian 'immoralism' within the upper classes, which may partly account for their reports of this immoralism being on the increase (as well as the fact that urbanization brought working-class customs under their noses for the first time).
48 *The Crisis*, 23 November 1833.
49 For Frances Morrison, see above, p. 75. For cohabiting radicals in London, see *The London City Mission Magazine*, vol. VIII (June 1843), p. 83 and *ibid.*, vol. IX, 'Ninth Annual Report' (May 1844), p. 10–2.
50 *The Gauntlet*, 22 September 1833. Carlile, of course, presented the issue as one of high moral principle: 'As a public man, I will be associated with nothing that is to be concealed from the public. Many, I know, will carp upon my freedom as to divorce and marriage; and to such persons I say . . . that I do so because I hate hypocrisy, because I hate everything that is foul and indecent . . . I have led a miserable wedded life through twenty years, from disparity of mind and temper; and for the next twenty, I have resolved

to have a wife in whom I may find a companion and a helpmate. I have in this lady found such a companion . . .' Sharples was already pregnant when they began to live together, and stayed with him until he died.

51 *The Crisis*, 4 January 1834.
52 Frost, *Forty Years*, p. 16.
53 See below, pp. 253–257.
54 *The London City Mission Magazine*, vol. VIII (June 1834), p. 83.
55 E.P. Thompson, 'Wife-Sales', lecture delivered to the Sussex Society for the Study of Labour History, 1978. For examples of wife-sales, see Ivan Bloch, *A History of English Sexual Morals* (1936), pp. 50–8. Gillis (*Common-Law Marriage*, pp.18–9) records other informal 'divorce' procedures, such as the return of rings, or in the case of besom weddings, jumping backwards over a branch or broomstick.
56 *NMW*, 9 March 1939. Owenite newspapers contained many reports of wife-sales.
57 HO 94/OS 981.
58 *NMW*, 16 November 1839.
59 *NMW*, 25 January 1840.
60 Jay, *Buchanan*, chapters one and two.
61 Charles Southwell, *Confessions of a Freethinker* (?1850). pp. 23–34. Thanks to Jill Liddington for help with this reference.
62 For City Mission efforts, see their *Magazine*. For the role of the Mechanics Institutes in instilling repressive sexual norms, see J.F.C. Harrison, *Learning and Living, 1790–1960* (1961), pp. 84–88. For the evangelical moralizing campaign in general, see Quinlan, *Victorian Prelude*, esp. chapter seven.
63 *The Working Bee*, 31 October 1840.
64 Owen, *Marriages*, p. 75.
65 *NMW*, 5 September 1840.
66 *Report on the Discussion of Marriage as Advocated by Robert Owen between L. Jones and J. Bowes . . . etc . . .* (Liverpool, 1840), p. 8.
67 *The Advocate*, 23 February 1833.
68 Gillis, 'Servants', pp. 162–3.
69 *The Crisis*, 4 January 1834.
70 Mayhew, 'Letter XI', *The Morning Chronicle*, 23 November 1849, in Thompson and Yeo, *Unknown Mayhew*, p. 202. For this interpretation of factors leading to women's greater sexual vulnerability, I am indebted to the work of Louise Tilly and Joan Scott ('Women's Work and the Family in Nineteenth Century Europe', *Comparative Studies in Society and History*, 17 [1975], esp. pp. 56–7; and also *Women, Work and Family*, pp. 96–8 and 121–3).
71 Gillis, 'Servants', p. 162. See Alexander, 'Women's Work', p. 83 for evidence from mid-century London about the large numbers of deserted wives found in East London neighbourhoods. Abandonment of lovers or wives by impoverished journeymen was obviously not a new problem in this period, even if it did intensify then: for an account of its widespread occurrence in London in the late eighteenth century, see George, *London Life*, p. 307.
72 Mayhew, 'Letter XI', *The Morning Chronicle*, 23 November 1849, in Thompson and Yeo, *Unknown Mayhew*, p. 208.
73 *ibid.*, p. 202–4.

74 Mayhew, Letter VIII, *The Morning Chronicle*, 13 November 1849, in Thompson and Yeo, *Unknown Mayhew*, p. 176.
75 *The London City Mission Magazine*, vol. IX (May 1844), p. 79; vol. IX (July 1844), p. 111; vol. IX (August 1844), p. 129.
76 'A Woman' [Mrs Richard Napier?] *Women's Rights and Duties Considered with Relation to Their Influence on Society and On Her Own Condition*, 2 vols. (1840), vol. 1, p. 3.
77 Wade, *History of the Classes*, p. 491.
78 *ibid.*, p. 490.
79 'Women and the Social System', *Fraser's Magazine for Town and Country*, vol. XXI, no. CXXVI (June 1840).
80 *NMW*, 18 August 1838.
81 Morrison, *Influence of the Present Marriage System*, p. 5.
82 *The Crisis*, 22 June 1833.
83 *NMW*, 9 February 1839.
84 *ibid.*, 3 November 1838.
85 *The Crisis*, 23 November 1833.
86 *NMW*, 18 August 1838.
87 Charles Southwell, *An Essay on Marriage; Addressed to the Lord Bishop of Exeter* (?1840), pp. 10–17.
88 *NMW*, 6 February 1841.
89 *Social Hymns, for the Use of the Friends of the Rational System* (Manchester, 1835), Hymn 88.
90 William Pare, the Birmingham Owenite, was the first registrar to be certified under the new Act to perform marriages, and two of his early customers were George and Eleanor Holyoake. Holyoake later recalled:

> I was one of the first persons married in his office, intending to testify in favour of civil marriage, though the prosaicness of the arrangement provided by the Act inspired me with resentment. No bright chamber, hall or temple to give distinction to the ceremony; only the business office of the Registrar of Deaths infusing funeral associations into a wedding. (*Sixty Years of an Agitator's Life*, 2 vols. [1892], vol.1, p. 41.)

The Socialists' decision to start providing their own wedding ceremonies was a response to complaints like these, as well as an attempt to bind members into the movement through emotional associations.
91 *NMW*, 29 March 1845. These British Owenite weddings had been preceded by similar (although less grandiose) ceremonies at New Harmony in the late 1820s, where Owen persuaded his co-residents to wed by simple declaration, without the presence of a clergyman (Muncy, *Sex*, pp. 57–8). In 1832 Robert Dale Owen married Mary Robinson in a ceremony in which both signed a document waiving Robert Dale's 'unjust rights . . . over the person and property' of his wife: a statement which John Stuart Mill may well have used as a model when he penned his own marriage contract for himself and Harriet Taylor in 1851 (*ibid.*, p. 58; J.S. Mill, 'Marriage Pledge', reprinted in Hayek, *Mill and Taylor*, p. 168).
92 *Moral World*, 25 October 1845.
93 *Discussion of Marriage . . . between L. Jones and J. Bowes*, pp. 12–16.
94 *What is Socialism . . .?*, pp. 22–67.
95 *NMW*, 25 April 1840.

96   Morrison, *Marriage System.*
97   *ibid.*, pp. 9–12.
98   *NMW*, 27 October 1838.
99   *ibid.*, 9 May 1840.
100 Southwell, *Marriage* , pp. 5–6.
101 *NMW*, 22 March 1845.
102 *ibid.*, 17 May 1845.
103 *ibid.*, 9 August 1845.
104 *ibid.*, 22 March 1845.
105 See below, p. 257.
106 Morrison, *Marriage System*, p. 14.

VII   Women And Socialist Culture

1   *Brighton Co-operator*, 1 November 1828, quoted in Yeo, 'Owen and Radical Culture', p. 86. This essay is the only systematic examination of Owenism as a radical culture, and my own interpretation of branch life is heavily indebted to it.
2   *NMW*, 12 June 1841.
3   *ibid.*, 25 April 1840.
4   Hancock, *Owen's Community System*, p. 44.
5   *NMW*, 14 April 1838.
6   Alexander Campbell, *An Address on the Progress of the Co-Operative System* (Glasgow, ? 1832), p. 4–5. Campbell campaigned for female enfranchisement during the 1832 Reform Bill agitation.
7   *NMW*, 20 July 1836.
8   *ibid.*, 27 April 1839.
9   *ibid.*, 20 May 1843.
10 *The London Social Reformer*, 10 May 1840. See also *NMW*, 12 June 1841.
11 *NMW*, 22 May 1841.
12 *ibid*, 27 April 1839.
13 Thompson, 'Women and Radical Politics', pp. 131–8.
14 For a discussion of some of these problems in the modern context, see Sheila Rowbotham, *Women's Consciousness, Man's World* (Harmondsworth, 1973), especially chapter six, and Audrey Wise, 'Trying to Stay Human', in *Conditions of Illusion* (Leeds, 1974), pp. 278–88.
15 *NMW*, 8 June 1839.
16 For a good discussion of the radical improving spirit, see Thompson, *Making*, pp. 812–20. See also T.R. Tholfsen, *Working-Class Radicalism in Mid-Victorian England* (1976). pp. 117–9, for a brief discussion of the self-improvement component in Owenite culture. To my mind, Tholfsen places undue emphasis on the integrationist features of Owenite cultural life.
17 R.B. Rose, 'John Finch, 1784–1857', *Transactions of the Historical Society of Lancashire and Cheshire*, vol. 109 (1957), p. 172; Brian Harrison, *Drink and the Victorians* (1971), p. 173.
18 See below, pp. 232–234.
19 Shaw, *Replies to Lord Ashley*, p. 20.

20 Yeo, 'Owen and Radical Culture', p. 87.
21 *The Working Bee*, 2 January 1841. As Gareth Stedman Jones has written, 'if men spent St Monday drinking, women spent it washing', and nearly all the traditional recreations to which moral improvers objected were male. I know of no study which examines this sex-segregation of leisure in the nineteenth century. (G. Stedman Jones, 'Class Expression versus Social Control? A Critique of Recent Trends in the Social History of 'Leisure', *History Workshop*, no. 4 [1977], p. 162).
    For Owenite opposition to rough sports (in this case Derby football), see *The Pioneer*, 22 February 1834; for opposition to the 'gaudy and debasing' pleasures of the fairground, see the report from Salford branch (*NMW*, 16 November 1839). This branch deliberately held a festival on the same day as the local fair as a counter-attraction. Implicit in many of the Socialist attacks on fairs, pubs, etc., was also an attack on centres of prostitution, for which Social events (and Socialist women) were held to be healthy substitutes (see *The Working Bee*, 2 January 1841).
22 *NMW*, 20 July 1839, quoted in Yeo, 'Owen and Radical Culture', p. 92.
23 *ibid.*, 30 October 1840. For an excellent statement of the Hall of Science philosophy and the need to involve women, see *The Working Bee*, 2 January 1841.
24 *NMW*, 4 April 1840. See also *ibid.*, 6 June 1840 and L. Faucher, *A History of Manchester* (1844), p. 25, for descriptions of the Manchester Hall, the biggest built by the Owenites. Others were far less grand, consisting of small, one-room halls or even just converted workshops. In all, fourteen Halls were built capable of holding over 22,000 people, at a total cost of 32,000 pounds. Most branches raised the money themselves, in small shares bought by members and sympathizers, but the poorest branches received assistance from the Central Board (see *NMW*, 25 January 1840, for a letter from the Tunstall branch asking for such financial help). See the *NMW*, 19 May 1838, for a fascinating description of the Birmingham Hall of Science.
25 Reports from the Manchester Hall can be found in many numbers of *The New Moral World* from 1840 to 1844; see, for example, 6 June 1840; 26 November 1842. For the wearing of 'community dress' at Social functions see *ibid.*, 14 July 1838, 3 August 1839.
    Owenite cultural events often involved large numbers of Chartists (see, for example, *NMW*, 9 October 1841, for a report of a tea given by the Manchester Owenites for both the local Owenite and Chartist branches, which was attended by over 1600 people). *The Northern Star* carried many reports of Owenite festivals, tea parties, and picnics (as well as regular reports on Owenite meetings and lectures), and often these reports mentioned the large number of Chartists in attendance. Chartists regularly used Owenite Halls as their own meeting places as well. (For *Northern Star* reporting on Owenite events see, for example, 11, 25 August, 1, 8, 15 September, 10 November 1838; 6 April, 28 September 1839; 13 June 1840; 16 October 1841.)
26 Holyoake, *Sixty Years*, vol. 1, p. 133.
27 Jones, *Life of Owen*; p. 55; *NMW*, 20 July 1836.
28 *NMW*, 5 January 1839.
29 *ibid.*
30 *ibid.*, 24 March 1838.

31   *The Working Bee,* 28 March 1840.

32   *NMW,* 30 March 1844.

33   *ibid.,* 1 December 1838. Even the fireworks at one Social Festival were used to promote the Social message, spelling out against the night sky, 'Each for All, and All for Each' (Frost, *Recollections,* p. 14).

34   Owen, *Moral Physiology,* p. 12.

35   *NMW,* 7 November 1840.

36   *ibid.,* 26 November 1842.

37   Finch addressing the Liverpool Social Festival, *ibid.,* 1 December 1838.

38   *The Co-operator,* 1 June 1829. Chartists like Bronterre O'Brien urged a similar policy on their followers, arguing that tea parties and soirees were preferable to pub meetings because women could attend (see, for example, *The Northern Star,* 14 August 1840).

39   For a very brief but interesting discussion of the effects of male drinking on women's lives, see Harrison, *Drink,* pp. 46–7, where he tries to assess the reality behind the temperance movement's attack on the selfish squandering of family resources by male over-indulgers. His conclusion, however, that 'where . . . masculine selfishness did exist, there were good reasons for it' appears to have no foundation but his own prejudices.

40   *NMW,* 15 May 1841. For the masculine selfishness theme in Owenite temperance thinking, see the report from Hyde branch, *NMW,* 3 August 1839. The level of temperance support in the movement is obvious from all the branch reports; see, for example, one from Salford branch (*NMW,* 8 October 1836) in which it was claimed that there were more temperance supporters in the Socialist ranks there than 'in any church, chapel or meeting house in the area'.

41   *NMW,* 19 January 1839.

42   For women's support for the temperance movement, see Harrison, *Drink,* pp. 174–5, 192; for later feminist campaigns around prostitution, age of consent, etc., see Strachey, *The Cause* and J. Walkowitz, *Prostitution and Victorian Society: Women, Class and the State* (Cambridge, 1980).

43   Thompson, 'Women and Radical Politics', p. 136; J.J. Rowley, 'Drink and the Public House in Urban Nottingham, 1830-60' (unpublished, 1974), p. 23. According to Rowley, the new attitude towards female drinking was the most important effect wrought by the activities of the Nottingham temperance societies: 'by 1860 . . . entrance into even a high-class inn had become damaging to the good name of a respectable lady.'

44   *The Social Pioneer,* 16 March 1839.

45   *NMW,* 24 October 1840.

46   *ibid.,* 21 May 1842. There is a very good account of Owenite educational theory and practice in Brian Simon, *The Two Nations and the Educational Structure, 1780-1870,* first ed. 1960 (1974), pp. 193-243. See also Harold Silver, *The Concept of Popular Education: a Study of Ideas and Social Movements in the Early Nineteenth Century* (1965).

47   For the Dalkeith class, see *NMW,* 16 January 1836. Other Female Classes were recorded in Huddersfield (*NMW,* 14 April 1838); Leeds, (*ibid.*), Birmingham and London (see below, pp. 233–236.). Salford Owenite women had a continuous history of class meetings from the late 1820s on (see reports in *The Lancashire and Yorkshire Co-Operator* for the earlier period).

48 *NMW*, 11 February 1843.

49 *Coventry Standard* report, reprinted in *NMW*, 19 May 1838.

50 There is, so far as I know, no published account of the education of working-class girls in the early nineteenth century. Information is scattered throughout both contemporary and secondary sources on working-class education, including: Sarah Trimmer, *The Oeconomy of Charity* (1787); F. Hertz, 'Mechanics Institutes for Working Women', *Transactions of the National Association for the Promotion of Social Science, 1859* (1860); Rev. J. P. Norris, 'On Girls Industrial Training', *ibid.*; Society for the Diffusion of Useful Knowledge, *Quarterly Journal of Education* (various mentions of girls' education throughout the 1830s); Thelma Tyfield, *The Industrial Revolution, Women and Education* (B Ed Thesis, University of Cape Town, 1935); Simon, *Two Nations*; Thompson, *Making*, (for Sunday Schools), pp. 412–6.

   Socialist Sunday Schools, which were for both children and adults, were usually sexually mixed and highly anti-clerical in tone. Some were taught by women as well as attended by them. The Owenites' refusal to teach the Bible in these schools led to constant attacks from local clergymen, and sometimes threats to parents who sent their children that they would lose their rights to poor-relief. This happened in Wisbech, where the right of parents to send their children to the local Socialist infant school became a major political issue in 1838. This school had equal education for girls as one of its key policies: one visitor there in 1839 reported watching a gymnastic display by the pupils where 'one girl climbed to the top of a rope suspended from a festoon' (*Star in the East*, 20 January, 13 October 1838; 5 January 1839).

51 *The Pioneer*, 28 September 1833.

52 *ibid.*, 8 February 1834.

53 Unsigned article in *Cleave's Gazette*, reprinted in *NMW*, 15 October 1838. The idea of genuine intellectual companionship between husbands and wives loomed large in Owenite hopes for future marital relations, and some of them tried to live that hope in the present. See, for example, a letter received by Holyoake from a Coventry friend congratulating him on his marriage:

   > I can fancy that I see you seated beside your intellectual companion working out a problem in mathematics, or giving or receiving other general instruction. Oh! what a delightful contemplation.
   > (reprinted in McCabe, *Holyoake*, vol. 1, p. 33.

54 For the relationships between working-class radicals and the Mechanics Institutes, see Simon, *Two Nations*, pp. 177–276; M. Tylecote, *The Mechanics Institutes of Lancashire and Yorkshire before 1851* (Manchester, 1957), pp. 110–115; Yeo, 'Owen and Radical Culture', pp. 89–90; John Salt, 'Isaac Ironside and Education in the Sheffield Region in the First Half of the Nineteenth Century' (MA Thesis, University of Sheffield, 1960); Harrison, *Learning*, chapter three. For the role of women in the Institutes, see Tylecote, *Institutes*, pp. 185–8; Hertz, 'Institutes', pp. 347–54; J.W. Hudson, *The History of Adult Education* (1851), pp. 64–5, 81, 88, 100, 135–7, 183; T. Kelly, *George Birkbeck* (Liverpool, 1957), pp. 23–8, 126, 247, 264; James Hole, *An Essay on the History and Management of Literary, Scientific and Mechanics Institutes* (1853), p. 35–7. Thanks to Maxine Berg for supplying me with many of these references.

55 Tylecote, *Institutes*, pp. 110, 113, 115.
56 Salt, 'Ironside', pp. 58–62. See the report of Owenite secessions in *The Coventry Standard*, reprinted in *NMW*, 19 May 1838; also the anxious reports from Institute supporters of their members being drawn towards the Socialist Halls (e.g. Society for the Diffusion of Useful Knowledge [T. Coates], *Report on the State of Literary, Scientific and Mechanics Institutes in England* [1841], p. 30).
57 *The Co-operative Magazine*, January–February, 1826. See also the militantly feminist speech by the Belfast Owenite, Henry McCormac, in which he demanded the open admission of women to the Institutes: *On the Best Means of Improving the Moral and Physical Condition of the Working Classes* (1830), p. 13.
58 For the story of the secession, see Yeo, 'Owen and Radical Culture', pp. 89–90; for the radicals' support for women's classes, see R. Detrosier, *An Address Delivered at the New Mechanics Institution* (Manchester, 1830), pp. 11-12.
59 *NMW*, 6 June 1840.
60 *ibid.*, 28 March 1840.
61 The Society for the Diffusion of Useful Knowledge (B.F. Duppa), *A Manual for Mechanics' Institutes* (1839), p. 143n.
62 Hertz, 'Institutes', p. 348.
63 In a letter to the *NMW*, 1 March 1843.
64 *NMW*, 20 July, 4 May 1839.
65 *ibid.*, 20 June 1840.
66 *ibid.*, 16 March 1844. The Finsbury Branch also established a 'Women's Class', taught by a Miss Thetford (*ibid.*, 10 December 1842).
67 *ibid.*, 13 July 1844.
68 *ibid.*, 5 October 1844.
69 *ibid.*, 20 April 1844.
70 *ibid.*, 2 March 1844.
71 *ibid.*

VIII Paradise Lost: Women And The Communities

1 The most detailed account of the major Owenite communities (with the exception of Manea Fen) is R.G. Garnett, *Co-operation and the Owenite Socialist Communities in Britain, 1825–45* (Manchester, 1972). A livelier account (which includes Manea Fen) is W.H. Armytage, *Heavens Below: Utopian Experiments in England, 1560-1960* (1961), Part II. See also Podmore, *Owen*, vol. 2; Harrison, *Owen*, pp. 163–92.
2 *NMW*, 3 June 1843; 8 June 1844; 24 May 1845.
3 *ibid.*, 8 June 1844.
4 *The Working Bee*, 4 July 1840.
5 Pankhurst, *Thompson*, p. 185.
6 *NMW*, 30 April 1842.
7 *The Crisis*, 4 January 1834.
8 Robert D. Storch, 'Owenite Communitarianism in Britain' (MA Thesis, University of Wisconsin, 1964), pp. 47-8.

9   Manchester branch, for example, had by 1843 paid £1065 into the central community fund, compared with £6760 on its Hall of Science and £7458 on other local activities (Storch, 'Communitarianism,' p. 152).

10 Letter IV (undated) from William Thompson in the William Pare papers, Goldsmiths' Library, quoted in Garnett, *Co-operation*, pp. 26–7.

11 *NMW*, 12 May 1838.

12 Garnett, *Co-operation*, chapter 1; Harrison, *Owen*, pp. 50–51, 56–7; Pollard, 'Co-operation', pp. 102–6.

13 *The Official Gazette of the Trades Unions*, 12 July 1834.

14 *The Crisis*, 8 June 1833.

15 'Where are we going, – into what state are our law-mongers driving us?' ran a *Crisis* editorial at the time of the enactment of the New Poor Law, 'We shall tell you, friends, countrymen, and lovers – they are driving us into pauper communities; large monasteries, where the men and women shall live apart as they did in days of old, and only see each other through the grating . . . If you do not interfere, by doing business for yourselves, and entering into great national and social arrangements – this is your fate. In a short time you will eat, drink and breed, by government allowance' (1 March 1834).

16 *NMW*, 12 July 1845.

17 Smelser, *Social Change*, pp. 253–61; Harrison, *Owen*, pp. 59–62.

18 For the impact of capitalist development on working-class family life, see chapter four.

19 See above, pp. 202–205.

20 Smelser attributes the popularity of Owenite communitarian schemes among certain groups of working people to changes in their familial relationships (*Social Change*, pp. 253–61). He identifies what he describes as 'symptoms of disturbance' within the families of northern textile workers (including increased role differentiation between men, women, and children, and the attenuation of family-based economic bonds), and argues that co-operative communities represented an attempt to overcome these symptoms by restoring an older pattern of sexual/familial relations in which role divisions were not so sharply demarcated and parents were able to exert direct control over their children. The argument has been sharply criticized (see, for example, M.M. Edwards and R. Lloyd-Jones, 'N.J. Smelser and the Cotton Factory Family: a Reassessment', in N.B. Harte and K.G. Ponting, eds., *Textile History and Economic History* [Manchester 1973]), but Smelser's underlying assumption – that changes in family patterns have a determining effect on the forms and content of worker consciousness – remains a challenging and potentially fruitful one. However, the actual account which Smelser provides of changes in working-class family life is neither clear nor well-documented despite, or perhaps because of, the elaborate sociological apparatus in which it is entangled, and differs substantially from my own interpretation.

　　Smelser does point to one factor (*ibid.*, p. 159) which was obviously important to workers contemplating community life, and that was the problem of economic dependants. The isolation of individual family units, coupled with growing dependence on the wage as a sole source of income, had greatly increased the vulnerability of those unable to work for a wage (the old, the sick, the very young, the mother with tiny or ailing children) – and this was definitely a problem which communal life was intended to remedy. What happens in the Old Immoral World when a key family member dies? Owen demanded at one point ('Address Delivered in the City of London Tavern, 21 August 1817', quoted in Garnett, *Co-operation*, p. 10). Usually, he reminded his audience, the entire family is thus driven into poverty, but in a community they would manage as well as before since 'around them on all sides, as far as the eye can reach, or imagination extend, thousands on thousands, in strict, intimate and close union, are ready and willing to offer their aid and consolation'. Thus support of the elderly, the ill and children would become a shared public function: a prospect which was undoubtedly very appealing to many women currently carrying the burden of direct care for these relations, and who had become increasingly vulnerable to loss of the male wage.

21 *NMW*, 18 May 1839. See also *The Working Bee*, 25 April 1840, and letters received by Owen over the years from individuals hoping to set up communal household units, including one from a Charlotte Tight who was torn between setting up house with a couple who had advertised for someone to join them in their mini-community and waiting for the chance to join a larger experiment (Owen Corres. 414; see also Owen Corres. 745).

22 *NMW*, 7 November 1840.

23 *The Lancashire and Yorkshire Co-Operator*, May 1832 (Supplementary Number).

24 *NMW*, 12 May 1838.

25 For a more detailed discussion of this, see chapter four.

26 See Cooper, *Contrast*, for this vision of the Socialist 'domestic economy'.

27 Thompson, *Practical Directions*, p. 138.

28 *NMW*, 12 July 1845.

29 Rev. Marriot, 'Community, a Drama', *ibid.*, 17 June 1837.

30 *ibid.* See also Cooper, *Contrast*, and Harrison's discussion of the pastoral strain in Owenism (*Owen*, pp. 57–9).

31 *NMW*, 14 July 1838. This report is by John Finch, who did not live in the community, but it is confirmed by E.T. Craig ('Socialism in England: Historical Reminiscences', *American Socialist*, August 1877-February 1878), who did. This would at least seem to indicate that conscious attempts at reform were made, although it is difficult to credit the success claimed by Finch and Craig (it would be interesting to know the views of Mary Craig, who taught the women there, as well).

32 *The Economist*, 2 March 1822. The editor of *The Economist* was also the founder of the community, so the newspaper carried detailed reports of its progress.

33 Thompson, *Making*, p. 868.

34 Garnett, *Co-operation*, pp. 100–29; Armytage, *Heavens*, pp. 105–12; *NMW*, 12 May 1838. Women provided one-third of the workforce at Ralahine.

35 Armytage, *Heavens*, pp. 107-10; *NMW*, 12 May 1838.

36 *The Register for the First 'Society of Adherents to Divine Revelation at Orbiston*, 19 August 1826.

37 Although each Socialist who entered Queenwood was supposed to have paid £50 into the Community Fund, since 'at present the most useful and indispensable labourers are the worst paid', it was found necessary to subsidize many would-be entrants, including – it was claimed – those first

chosen for community life because of their strong political principles and 'most useful' skills. (National Community Friendly Society report, *NMW*, 8 July 1837).

38   One early visitor to Queenwood (who saw fit to send his or her observations on the community to the Home Office) gave the following account:

> Their Dining room is a large unfurnished sort of Barn with 8 windows (oiled paper ones) in it and a number of Seats made of rough deal or fir boards nailed to blocks of the same material. The table is of the same description the floor is not boarded . . . but the common earth covered with straw and saw dust. The whole place has the most untidy appearance.

Most of the residents seemed to be staunch Chartists, the report also noted, and many were from Yorkshire (HO 44/38).

39   *NMW*, 29 May 1841.
40   *ibid*. Local women were employed as laundresses, while their husbands were hired to work in the fields. The decision to employ wage-labour was taken only after a furious debate in the movement, in which many Owenites argued that to become employers of labour was antithetical to the democratic spirit of their enterprise, while their opponents derided such purism and pointed out that not to employ local workers would only breed ill-feeling in the neighbourhood. Anyway, they added, these labourers would be invited to attend classes and other social events in the community and thereby become educated to Social principles, perhaps eventually joining as full-fledged residents. The debate raged on in issue after issue of *The New Moral World* (see, for example, 22 December 1838 and 12 January 1839). In August, 1844, the laundresses had to be dismissed due to lack of funds and their work was taken over by the women of the community (*NMW*, 31 August 1844). By the summer of 1845 the burden of domestic tasks had proved too much for the women and finally even the adult men had to lend a hand (*NMW*, 7 June 1845).
41   *NMW*, 29 May 1841.
42   *ibid*.
43   'One Who Has Whistled at the Plough' (Alexander Somerville), *Notes from the Farming Districts, no. XVII, A Journey to Harmony Hall* (1842), p. 6.
44   *NMW*, 27 May 1843.
45   *ibid*.
46   *ibid*.
47   *ibid*., 25 May 1844.
48   *The Working Bee*, 4 July 1840.
49   *The Co-operative Magazine*, February 1827. For similar problems of domestic disarrangement and female discontent at the New Harmony community, see Lockwood, *New Harmony*, p. 192. Owen could not understand why the women found the work at New Harmony so laborious, and suggested that perhaps it was because they spent too much time gossiping (*ibid*.).
50   *NMW*, 31 December 1836.
51   *The Crisis*, 28 December 1833.
52   *ibid*., 4 January 1834.
53   'Rules for Relief Provision', Community Friendly Society (1836), Rule XLXX.

54   *The Crisis*, 4 January 1834.
55   William Thompson, *Weekly Free Press* clippings, William Pare Collection, University of London Library, f.74.
56   *ibid.*
57   For 'family meetings' at Queenwood see *NMW*, 27 May 1843; for Orbiston see *The Co-operative Magazine*, May 1826; for Ralahine, *NMW*, 14 July 1838. Only one community ever had a woman President: the Ham Common Concordium at Richmond, which for a time was led by a wealthy feminist (and patron of James Smith), Sophia Chichester.
58   *The Working Bee*, 7 November 1840.
59   HO 44/38.
60   Hennell, *Outline of the Social Systems*, p. 175.
61   HO 44/38. George Cruikshanks's *Comic Almanac* contained a cartoon of Queenwood accompanied by the following rhyme:

> They've everything in common, so they say:
> Even not uncommon wives, perchance they may;
> And, if the principle they carry through,
> The babies may be sometimes common too;
> Making it puzzling, rather,
> For some to find their father.

(Quoted in Armytage, *Heavens*, p. 166).
62   *NMW*, 14 July 1838.
63   See above, p. 196.
64   For Hodson's pre-Owenite career, see *NMW*, 20 June 1840; *The Working Bee*, 27 July 1839, 8 February 1840; *Star in the East*, 31 March 1838. The major source of information on Manea Fen is its own newspaper, *The Working Bee*. Armytage, *Heavens*, contains a detailed secondary account (see also his 'Manea Fen; an Experiment in Agrarian Communitarianism, 1838-41', *Bulletin of the John Rylands Library*, XXXVIII, no. 2 [1956]). Armytage neglects to use another important source for the community, *The Social Pioneer*, where most of the marriage controversy was aired.
65   For Central Board and branch reactions see (for example): *NMW*, 2, 9, 16 February 1839. Owen was personally opposed to the establishment of the unofficial community, and in an open letter to him Hodson suggested that this was because he feared the democratic policies of Manea Fen. 'The Socialists are the worst of all men to submit to be governed by others, and they themselves be silent. We have found this to be the case here, which induced me to throw the government into the hands of the members' (*The Working Bee*, 3 October 1840). Whether Manea Fen was as democratically run as Hodson claimed is not clear from the evidence available: it had a governing executive (Hodson was President) which was supposed to be guided by the votes of the residents (including the women's votes), but Hodson seems to have exercised arbitrary powers on a number of occasions as well. He also had a bigger house than anyone else (*ibid.*, 21 March 1840).
66   William Hodson, 'To the Working Classes, the Real Producers of Wealth' (circular, 1838), Owen Corres. 1042.
67   *The Working Bee*, 10 August 1839. In a speech delivered in London in May 1840, Emma Martin spoke critically of the 'costly' schemes of the Central Board and favourably of Manea Fen (*The London Social Reformer*, 9 May 1840).

68 *The Working Bee*, 28 September, 30 October 1840. At one point Hodson and some of his supporters even tried to initiate a counter-organization to the Rational Society, with a branch structure. Two or three 'Cambridgeshire Community' branches were formed before the initiative collapsed (see *The Social Pioneer*, 6 April 1839; *The Working Bee*, 28 December 1839).

69 *ibid.*, 30 November 1839.

70 *NMW*, 9 January 1841.

71 *ibid.*, 20 February 1841. Not long after, Hodson wrote a letter to the Home Office in which he denounced Socialism and his former colleagues (HO 45/OS 92).

72 Local newspaper report, quoted in *The Working Bee*, 28 November 1840.

73 *The Working Bee*, 27 July, 3 August, 30 November 1839.

74 *ibid.*, 3 August 1839.

75 Owen Corres. 1094.

76 *The Social Pioneer*, 13 April 1839.

77 *ibid.*, 27 April 1839.

78 *ibid.*, 20 April 1839. At this time E.T. Craig and his wife entered the colony, and wrote back that the marriage procedures adopted there were 'wholly in accordance with the views of Mr Owen'.

79 *The Working Bee*, 27 July 1839. With regard to this, it is interesting to note that the Manchester branch apparently included a large number of female domestic servants. (*ibid.*, 12 December 1841); perhaps it was these women whom Hodson had urged to join the community.

80 *The Social Pioneer*, 27 April 1839.

81 *The Working Bee*, 24 August 1839.

82 *ibid.*, 16 November 1839.

83 *ibid.* The editor who wrote these remarks actually left the community, and his wife in it, not long after (*ibid.*, 23 November 1839).

84 *ibid.*, 14 September 1839. For an interesting discussion of the effects of the legal right to divorce on women's status, see *ibid.*, 31 October 1840.

85 *ibid.*, 14 September 1839.

86 See in particular *ibid.*, 16 November 1839.

87 *What is Socialism . . .?*. pp. 62–3.

88 Jones, *Life of Owen*, pp. 145–6. *The New Moral World* reported regularly on Queenwood's progress. Jones, *Life of Owen*, also gives an interesting first-hand account of the community's development. The most detailed secondary accounts are Garnett, *Co-operation*, chapter six, and Podmore, *Owen*, chapters twelve and thirteen. Harrison, *Owen*, pp. 172–91 has an interesting discussion of the community's problems, as does Armytage, *Heavens*, pp. 145–67.

89 Garnett, *Co-operation*, p. 183.

90 Jones, *Life of Owen*, pp. 145–6.

91 Holyoake, *Co-operation*, vol. 1, p. 301. Podmore has done detailed financial calculations to show how the financial affairs of the community were mismanaged (*Owen*, pp. 538–41).

92 *NMW*, 20 April 1844.

93 Garnett, *Co-operation*, pp. 189–90.

94 Holyoake, *A Visit to Harmony Hall* (1844), pp. 16–17. After all, as one delegate to the 1842 Congress put it, 'in supporting communities . . . [the capitalist] class would be lending itself to the destruction of its own

accumulative tendency and influential power', so why should their help be anticipated? (*NMW*, 13 August 1842). This was, of course, one of the central points at issue between Owen and his class-conscious associates.

95 Podmore, *Owen*, p. 553.
96 *NMW*, 1 June 1844.
97 *ibid.*, 20 May 1843.
98 Garnett, *Co-operation*, p. 195.
99 *NMW*, 8 June 1844.
100 *ibid.*
101 *ibid.*, 5 July 1845.
102 The London A1 Branch became a Literary and Scientific Society; Manchester branch turned into a Friendly Society. A few became emigration societies. The John St Institution in London became a well-known secularist hall.
103 *NMW*, 30 August 1845. Typically, Owen himself appears to have been the least affected by the collapse of the movement. By then a very sprightly seventy-four-year old, he went off on further tours of America and Europe (managing to be in Paris in 1848), writing constantly and occasionally lecturing. His final burst of propagandistic effort was on behalf of the spiritualist faith, which he embraced in his last years. He died in his birthplace – Newtown, in Wales – in 1858.

IX Sex And Class In The Post-Owenite Era

1 Even the Rotunda, a continual centre of ultra-radicalism since 1830, closed down: 'the Socialists, having packed up their traps, have moved off . . .' *The Times* reported gleefully (9 March 1844). Other Socialist halls survived as Secularist halls, Literary Institutes, and so on.
2 Quoted in Pollard, 'Co-operation', p. 106.
3 *ibid.*, pp. 106–7. See also Asa Briggs, *The Age of Improvement, 1783–1867*, first ed. 1959 (1979), pp. 402–12; A.L. Morton and G. Tate, *The British Labour Movement*, first ed. 1956 (1973), p. 95. I should emphasize here that I am not arguing that Owenism disappeared because life got better for those men and women who had swelled its ranks in the preceding decades: indeed, in many cases, life got very much worse (as for the tailors and tailoresses, and many other domestic outworkers). Increased prosperity, when it came, was confined only to certain sectors of the working class, while for others the 'Golden Years' of British capitalism were dim indeed.
4 Thompson, 'Women and Radical Politics', p. 138.
5 Barmby, 'Industrial Independence'.
6 See above, p. 331, n. 240.
7 See above, p. 322, n. 41.
8 Thompson, 'Women and Radical Politics', pp. 118–34.
9 *The Northern Star*, 27 April 1839.
10 This was particularly true during the controversy which erupted over the marriage issue. For an example of a piece of anti-feminist propaganda directed at women Chartists which identified the destruction of patriarchal

values with Socialism see Rev. F. Close, *A Sermon Addressed to the Female Chartists of Cheltenham, Sunday, August 25, 1839* (1839).

11 *The Northern Star*, 9 February 1839, reprinted in D. Thompson, ed., *The Early Chartists* (1971), p. 128.

12 *ibid.*, pp. 128–9.

13 *The Northern Star*, 2 February 1839. I am grateful to Eileen Yeo for assistance with these *Northern Star* references.

14 *The Northern Star*, 12 November 1841.

15 *ibid.*, 22 December 1838.

16 *ibid.*, 11 May 1839.

17 *ibid.*, 29 January 1842.

18 See, for example, *ibid.*, 15 December 1838; *The Morning Star* (January 1840).

19 Shaw, *Replies to Ashley*, p. 32. Shaw noted, however, that the working women themselves were unlikely to agree with this demand.

20 This aspect of Chartism deserves much closer attention than it has thus far received, since it was obviously one crucial factor pointing towards mid-century 'restabilization', as Gareth Stedman Jones points out in his 'Class Struggle', p. 54, 64.

21 William Lovett, *Social and Political Morality* (1853), p. 32.

22 Lovett, *Life*, p.32.

23 Thompson, 'Women and Radical Politics', pp. 120–1. See also *The Union*, August 1842.

24 See, for example, *The Northern Star*, 16 October 1841.

25 Lovett, *Morality*, p. 89. R. J. Richardson argued essentially the same position in his *Rights of Woman*.

26 Lovett, *Life*, p. 141.

27 Carole E. Martin, 'Female Chartism: a Study in Politics' (MA Thesis, University of Wales, 1973), pp. 24-7. In 1846 one man pointed to Emma Martin as an example of the sort of 'highly intelligent' women who were being excluded from the franchise while 'the most stupid men' were able to vote (*ibid.*, p. 24).

28 *ibid.*, p. 24.

29 *The Northern Star*, 16 April 1842.

30 *NMW*, 28 August 1841.

31 *ibid.*, 15 May 1841.

32 *ibid.* Leach went on to add, however, that he personally 'had no objection to women being in possession of the suffrage'.

33 *The Regenerator*, 2 November 1839.

34 *The Northern Star*, 1 July 1843.

35 Even R. J. Richardson, for all his militant pro-women's suffrage sentiments, did not support the vote for married women. 'I *believe*,' Elizabeth Pease wrote in 1842, 'that the Chartists generally hold the doctrine of the equality of woman's rights – but I am not sure whether they do not consider that when she marries, she merges her political rights in those of her husband . . .' (quoted in Thompson, 'Women and Radical Politics', p. 131).

36 *The Regenerator*, 2 November 1839.

37 Martin, 'Female Chartism', p. 85. Ironically, the only woman to hold an official position at a Chartist Convention was Mary Lovett, who in 1839 took over her husband's post of secretary to the Convention when he was imprisoned.

38 *ibid.*
39 *The Northern Star,* 22 June 1839.
40 *ibid.,* 2 February 1839.
41 See *NMW,* 27 November 1841, for an account of a woman Chartist attacking Owenite marriage doctrine at a public meeting. In general the Chartists seem to have had little to say on Owenite marriage reform proposals, or at least little that appeared in print.
42 Sally Alexander, Anna Davin, and Eve Hostettler, 'Labouring Women: a reply to Eric Hobsbawm', *History Workshop,* no. 8 (1979), p. 179.
43 R. Gray, *The Aristocracy of Labour in Nineteenth Century Britain, 1850–1900* (1980), quoted in M. Barrett and M. McIntosh, 'The Family Wage: Some Problems for Socialists and Feminists', *Capital and Class,* no. 11 (1980), p. 55.
44 Alexander et al, 'Labouring Women', pp. 175–82.
45 *ibid.,* pp. 179–80.
46 Henry Broadhurst, quoted in Ramelson, *Petticoat Rebellion,* p. 103.
47 Hilary Land, *The Family Wage* (Eleanor Rathbone Memorial Lecture, Leeds, 1979), p. 9.
48 Hannah Mitchell, *The Hard Way Up: the Autobiography of Hannah Mitchell, Suffragette and Rebel,* first ed. 1968 (1977), p. 126.
49 *ibid.,* p. 130.
50 *ibid.,* p. 126.
51 Morton and Tate, *Labour Movement,* pp. 100–12. See also Royden Harrison, *Before the Socialists: Studies in Labour and Politics, 1861–1881* (1965).
52 Mrs Hugo Reid, *A Plea for Woman* (1843), p. 122, pp. 63–4.
53 Harriet Taylor, *Enfranchisement of Women,* first published in *The Westminster Review* (July 1851), edited and with an introduction by A.S. Rossi (1970), p. 119.
54 Strachey, *Cause,* chapter two; Malmgreen, 'Women's Suffrage', pp. 91–3, 99–101.
55 Gail Malmgreen, 'Anne Knight, 1786–1862' (unpublished ms., 1978), p. 4. I am grateful to the author for letting me see this essay.
56 Strachey, *Cause,* pp. 13–29, 77–88, 187–204; Bauer and Ritt, *Free and Ennobled,* chapter four. See also Walkowitz, *Prostitution,* for an excellent discussion of this form of feminist thought and action.
57 Killham, *Tennyson,* pp. 120–41.
58 Taylor, *Enfranchisement,* p. 105.
59 J.S. Mill, *The Subjection of Women,* first ed., 1869, edited and with an introduction by A.S. Rossi (1970), p. 154.
60 *ibid.*
61 Strachey, *Cause,* chapters four to six. Strachey notes, however, that many lower middle-class women – particularly impoverished governesses, ladies' companions, teachers and other 'genteel' working women – were drawn to the early feminists for advice and support, and it seems likely that some of these became activists as well (*ibid.,* p. 95). For a good analysis of the social background of Victorian feminists, see Walkowitz, *Prostitution,* chapter six, where she examines the membership of the Ladies National Association for Repeal of the Contagious Diseases Acts.

62   Quoted by Sally Alexander in her introduction to M. Pember Reeves, ed., *Round About a Pound a Week*, first ed. 1913 (1979), p.xx.

63   Bauer and Ritt, *Free and Ennobled*, pp. 139-52.

64   Hester Burton, *Barbara Bodichon, 1827-1891* (1949); Strachey, *Cause*, chapters one to six.

65   Burton, *Bodichon*, pp. 112-3. Of course mass meetings, marches and even more militant tactics were yet to come, at the height of the women's suffrage struggle.

66   Millicent Garrett Fawcett, introduction to the 1891 ed. of Wollstonecraft, *Rights of Woman*, pp. 3-4. Thanks to Anne Phillips for help with this reference.

67   Bessie Rayner Parkes, *Essays on Woman's Work* (1865), p. 8.

68   Burton, *Bodichon*, p. 6.

69   Walkowitz, *Prostitution*, p. 123.

70   *ibid.*, p. 123.

71   *ibid.*

72   Mary Smith, *The Autobiography of Mary Smith: Schoolmistress and Nonconformist* (Carlisle, 1892). Thanks to Richard Johnson for this reference.

73   Malmgreen, 'Anne Knight'.

74   Ramelson, *Petticoat Rebellion*, p. 72.

75   *ibid.*, pp. 72-3.

76   Letter to Anne Knight from Lydia Becker, 31 January 1868, in uncatalogued box of Anne Knight papers, Friends House, London.

77   Holyoake Corres. 339; Holyoake, *Sixty Years*, vol. 1, pp. 222-5.

78   Holyoake, *Sixty Years*, vol. 1, p. 225.

79   *ibid.*

80   The story of the Secularist movement is told in Royle, *Infidels*, pp. 171-293. See also E. Royle, ed., *The Infidel Tradition from Paine to Bradlaugh* (1976).

81   Royle, *Infidels*, p. 187.

82   E. Royle, 'Harriet Teresa Law (1831-97): Feminist, Secularist and Radical', in Bellamy and Saville, *Labour Biography*, vol. 5 (1979), p. 134.

83   *ibid.*, p. 135.

84   For examples of articles on feminist themes in *The Secularist Chronicle* see the issues for 20 May 1877; 17 June 1877; 1 July 1877; 9 September 1877 (this article is on the life and work of Emma Martin). See also the issue for 1 January 1979 for a report on the high level of female recruitment into the National Secular Society.

85   Royle, 'Law', p.135.

86   Eleanor Marx, writing in an Austrian women's journal in 1892, quoted in Draper and Liplow, 'Marxist Women', p. 225.

87   For Besant's career as a freethinker and socialist, see A.H. Nethercot, *The First Five Lives of Annie Besant* (1961).

88   Rowbotham, *Hidden*, p. 96.

89   Logie Barrow, 'Socialism in Eternity: The Ideology of Plebian Spiritualists, 1853-1912', *History Workshop*, no. 9 (1980), p. 39.

90   Shipley, *Club Life*.

91   Letter from John Watts to *The Boston Investigator* (1864), reprinted in Royle, *Infidel Tradition*, p. 85.

92   Shipley, *Club Life*, p. 6.

351

93 Barrow, 'Socialism', pp. 60–1.
94 Shipley, *Club Life*, p. 47.
95 The phrase is Engels, who described the Owenite hopes as 'stupendously grand thoughts': *Socialism: Utopian and Scientific*, p. 403.
96 Thompson, *Morris*, pp. 787–8.
97 For an insightful examination of the development of this anti-feminism on the Left, and its implications for working-class women's involvement in feminist struggles, see Liddington and Norris, *One Hand*; for a first-hand experience of it see Mitchell, *Hard Way*. See also Rowbotham, *Hidden*, chapters 13–15. The essay by Draper and Liplow ('Marxist Women') provides a classic example of these attitudes today.
98 Harry Quelch of the SDF, quoted in Liddington and Norris, *One Hand*, p. 186.
99 Eleanor Marx Aveling and Edward Aveling, 'The Woman Question: from a Socialist Point of View', *The Westminster Review*, CXXV (1886).
100 Sheila Rowbotham, 'Edward Carpenter: Prophet of the New Life' in S. Rowbotham and J. Weeks, *Socialism and the New Life: the Personal and Sexual Politics of Edward Carpenter and Havelock Ellis* (1977), pp. 28–138.
101 Mitchell, *Hard Way*, pp. 114–121; see also Liddington and Norris, *One Hand*, p. 118, for an account of the Socialist Ten Commandments of the Labour Church which included looking forward 'to the day when all men and women will . . . live together as equals in peace and righteousness'. See Stephen Yeo, 'A New Life: the Religion of Socialism in Britain, 1883–1896', *History Workshop* no. 4 (1977), for an account of this Socialist religion of brotherhood and sisterhood in the late nineteenth century. It is also interesting to note that in 1898 Thompson's *Appeal* was serialized in a feminist newspaper, *The Woman's Signal* (August 1898 to March 1899).
102 Sheila Rowbotham, *A New World for Women: Stella Browne-Socialist Feminist* (1977). Browne was a pioneer in abortion reform.
103 In this country, Sheila Rowbotham's work has been the most influential in this respect, while in America there have been a number of books published by socialist feminists exploring the contribution of the early socialists to the development of sexual politics: see in particular Linda Gordon, *Woman's Body, Woman's Right* (Harmondsworth 1977), pp. 81–91. In France, the journal *Le Mouvement Social* has over recent years carried a number of essays by socialist feminists examining the feminist ideas and practice of the Saint Simonians.
104 Charlotte Despard, *Woman and the Nation* (1913), p. 7. Thanks to Sally Alexander for help with this reference.

LIST OF SOURCES*

Primary Sources

1. Manuscripts and Collections
2. Rules, Reports and Proceedings
3. Published Works by Owenites and Associated Contemporaries (Including Contemporary Opponents)
4. Newspapers and Periodicals
5. Other Primary Sources

Secondary Sources

1. Published Books and Articles
2. Unpublished Works

Primary Sources

1. Manuscripts and Collections

Association of All Classes of All Nations.
> Minute book of the Central Board, 26 May 1838–13 April 1840 (microfilm, 1978).

George Jacob Holyoake Correspondence.
> 1840–1860 (Co-operative Union Library, Manchester).
> Diary and diary extracts, 1831–52 (George Howell Collection Bishopgate Institute Library, London).

Home Office Papers (Public Record Office).
> For tailors' strike:
> HO 52/24; HO 64/15; HO 64/19; HO 40/32; HO 52/25.
> For Socialism, 1841–45:
> HO 45. OS 92; HO 45. OS 338; HO 45. OS 981.

National Community Friendly Society.
> Minute book of directors, 4 June 1838–29 April 1839 (continued in the AACAN minute book, 16 April 1840–21 July 1842, 2 April 1843–28 September 1843) (microfilm, 1978).

*Place of publication is London, unless otherwise indicated.

Pare, William.
  Collection of broadsides and newspaper cuttings, relating to Owenite cooperation, 1828–42, mostly from the *Weekly Free Press*. University of London Library.
Rational Society.
  Minute book of directors, 1 October 1843–5 March 1845 (microfilm, 1978).
Robert Owen Correspondence.
  1821–1854 (Co-operative Union Library, Manchester).
Webb, S. and B.
  Trade Union Mss. Collection (London School of Economic and Political Science), Section A: XIV (Clothing trades).

2. *Rules, Reports And Proceedings*

Association of All Classes of All Nations.
  Manual of the Association of All Classes of All Nations founded May 1, 1835 (1835–36).
Cooperative Congress – Second.
  Proceedings of . . . held in Birmingham, October 4, 5, and 6, 1831, and composed of Delegates from the Cooperative Societies of Great Britain and Ireland (Birmingham, 1831).
Cooperative Congress – Third.
  Proceedings of . . . held in London, on the 23rd of April, 1832 (1832).
Cooperative Congress – Fourth.
  Proceedings of . . . held in Liverpool on . . . 1st October, 1832, and by Adjournment on Each of the Five following Days (Salford, Manchester, 1832).
Grand National Consolidated Trades' Union.
  Rules and Regulations of . . ., instituted for the Purpose of the more effectually enabling the Working Classes to Secure, Protect, and Establish the Rights of the Industry (1834).
London Co-operative Society.
  Articles of Agreement for the Formation of a Community on the Principles of Mutual Cooperation, within Fifty Miles of London (1825).
National Community Friendly Society.
  Rules, as revised by the Delegates assembled in Congress, May, 1838 (?1838).
Universal Community Society of Rational Religionists.
  Proceedings of the Third Congress of the Association of All Classes of All Nations, and the First of the National Community Friendly Society . . . held in Manchester, in May 1838. (Birmingham, London, 1838).

- *Proceedings of the Fourth Congress . . . held in Birmingham, in May 1839* (Birmingham, 1839).
- *Full Report of the Proceedings of the Fifth Annual Congress . . . Holden in Leeds, 1840* (?1840).
- *Proceedings of the Sixth Congress of the Association of all Classes . . .* (Birmingham, London, 1841).
- *Report of the Proceedings of the Eighth Annual Congress of the Rational Society . . . held in Harmony Hall, Hampshire, May, 1843, and composed of Delegates from Branches of the Society in England and Scotland* (1843).

3. Published Works By Owenites And Associated Contemporaries (Including Contemporary Opponents)

Baines, Edward.
  Mr Owen's Establishment at New Lanark, a Failure!! As proved by Edward Baines . . . and other Gentlemen deputed with him . . . to visit and inspect that Establishment . . . (Leeds, 1838).
- *The Socialists, a Society of Beasts. Important and interesting Proposal addressed to Robert Owen Esq.* (Edinburgh, ?1840).

Barker, Joseph.
  Abominations of Socialism exposed, in Reply to the Gateshead Observer (Newcastle, 1840).
- *The Gospel Triumphant; or, a Defence of Christianity against the Attacks of the Socialists; and an Exposure of the infidel Character and mischievous Tendency of the Social System of Robert Owen* (Newcastle, 1839).
- *The Overthrow of Infidel Socialism* (1840).
- and Lloyd Jones. *Report of a Public Discussion which took place at Oldham on the Evenings of Tuesday and Wednesday, February 19th and 20th, 1839 . . . on the Influence of Christianity* (Manchester, 1839).

Barmby, Catherine.
  'The Demand for the Emancipation of Woman, Politically and Socially', *New Tracts for the Times*, vol. 1, no. 3 (1843).
- 'Invocation', *The Educational Circular*, vol. 1, no. 2 (December 1841).
- 'Women's Industrial Independence', *The Apostle and Chronicle of the Communist Church*, vol. 1, no. 1 (1848).

Barmby, J.G.
  The Outlines of Communism, Associality, and Communization (1841).

Beard, John Relly.
  The Religion of Jesus Christ defended from the Assaults of Owenism, . . . in Nine Lectures (1839).

Bower, Samuel.
> *The Peopling of Utopia; or; the Sufficiency of Socialism for Human Happiness: being a Comparison of the Social and Radical Schemes* (Bradford, 1838).
> – *A Sequel to the Peopling of Utopia . . .* (Bradford, 1838).

Bowes, Rev. John.
> *The Social Beasts; or, an Exposure of the Principles of Robert Owen* (Liverpool, 1840).

Bray, Charles.
> *The Industrial Employment of Women* (1857).
> – *The Philosophy of Necessity*, 2 vols. (1841).

Bray, J.F.
> *Labour's Wrongs and Labour's Remedies* (Leeds, 1839).

Brindley, John.
> *The Immoralittes of Socialism: being an Exposure of Mr Owen's Attack upon Marriage . . .* (Birmingham, 1840).

Buchanan, Robert.
> *A Concise History of Modern Priestcraft . . .* (Manchester, 1840).
> – *Exposure of the Falsehoods, Calumnies and Misrepresentations of a Pamphlet entitled 'The Abominations of Socialism Exposed', being a Refutation of . . . the Rev. Joseph Barker and all Others who have adopted a similar Mode of opposing Socialism* (Manchester, 1840).
> – *A Budget for the Socialists, containing The Female Socialist: a Doggerel worthy of its Burthen: also the Lord's Prayer of the Owenites, and the Gospel according to St Owen* (1840).

Campbell, Alexander.
> *An Address on the Progress of the Co-Operative System* (Glasgow, ?1832).

Carlile, Richard.
> *Everywoman's Book, or What is Love?* (1828).

Concordium.
> *A Brief Account of the First Concordium, or Harmonious Industrial College. A Home for the Affectionate, Skilful, and Industrious* (Ham Common, 1843).

Cooper, Robert.
> *A Contrast Between the New Moral World and the Old Immoral World* (Hulme, 1838).

Craig, E.T.
> 'Socialism in England: Historical Reminiscences', *American Socialist* (August 1877 – February 1878).

Davenport, Allen.
> *The Life, Writings and Principles of Thomas Spence* (1836).

Detrosier, Rowland.
> *An Address delivered at the New Mechanics' Institution, . . . Manchester, . . . December 30, 1829* (Manchester, 1829).

- *Address delivered to Members of the New Mechanics' Institution, Manchester, on March 25, 1831, on the Necessity of an Extension of Moral and Political Instruction among the Working Classes* (Manchester, 1831).

Ellis, William.
Reminiscences and Reflections of an Old Operative (1851).

Engels, F.
The Condition of the Working Class in England. First ed. 1844 (1969).

Finch, John.
Moral Code of the New Moral World . . . corrected, revised and approved by Robert Owen (Liverpool, 1840).

Fontana and Prati, Chief and Preacher of the St Simonian Religion in England.
St Simonism in London (1834).

Fourier, Charles.
The Utopian Vision of Charles Fourier: Selected Texts on Work, Love, and Passionate Attraction, translated and edited by J. Beecher and R. Bienvenu (Boston, 1971).

Frost, Thomas.
Forty Years Recollections: Literary and Political (1880).

Gale Jones, John.
Sketch of a Political Tour (1796).

Grant, Rev. Brewin.
An Apology for Christianity: or, Modern Infidelity examined in a Series of Letters to Robert Owen (1840).

Gray, John.
A Lecture on Human Happiness (Edinburgh, 1825).

Grimstone, Mary Leman.
Cleone (1834).
- *Woman's Love* (1832).

Hancock, Edward.
Robert Owen's Community System, and the Horrid Doings of the Saint Simonians . . . etc . . . Letter Third (?1837).
- *A true Exposure of the noted Robert Owen. Concerning his late Visit to the Queen . . . and showing up his Doctrines. The dark Scenes, and midnight Revels that were carried on, in a Male and Female 'Co-operative Society'. With an Account of the Victims of Seduction and his New Moral Marriage System* (n.d.).

Heath, William.
Paul Pry's Ramble through the 'New Moral World', with 'First Impressions' (Doncaster, 1838).
- *Paul Pry's Second Ramble through the 'New Moral World', with Rhymes and Reflections on 'The Rights of Woman'.* (Doncaster, 1839).

- *Paul Pry's Third Ramble through the 'New Moral World'. With 'Gatherings by the Way'* (Doncaster, 1840).

Hennell, Mary.
: *An Outline of the Various Social Systems and Communities on the Principle of Co-operation.* First ed. 1841 (1844).

Hobson, Joshua.
: *Socialism as It is!* (Leeds, 1838).

Hodgskin, Thomas.
: *Labour Defended Against the Claims of Capital* (1825).

Holyoake, George Jacob.
: *Bygones worth Remembering.* 2 vols. (1905).
- *The History of Co-Operation.* First ed. 1875–79, 2 vols. (1906).
- *The Last Days of Mrs Emma Martin, Advocate of Free Thought* (1851).
- *The Life and Character of Richard Carlile* (1849).
- *Life and Last Days of Robert Owen of New Lanark . . .* (1859).
- *Rationalism; a Treatise for the Times* (1845).
- *Sixty Years in an Agitator's Life* (1893).
- *A Visit to Harmony Hall. (Reprinted from the 'Movement') With Emendations and a new and curious vindicatory Chapter. Dedicated to the Socialists of England and Scotland* (1844).

The Human Eccaleobion; or the New Moral Warren: being a concise but faithful Exposition of Socialism, instituted by Robert Owen . . . (1842).

Hunt, Thomas.
: *Chartism, Trades Unionism, and Socialism; or, which is the best calculated to produce permanent Relief to the Working Classes? A Dialogue* (1840).

Jones, Lloyd.
: *Life, Times and Labours of Robert Owen.* 2 vols. (1889).
- and Reverend J. Bowes. *Report on the Discussion of Marriage as Advocated by Robert Owen Between L. Jones and J. Bowes . . .* (Liverpool, 1840).

Lees, Frederic Richard.
: *Owenism dissected: a calm Examination of the Fundamental Principles of Robert Owen's misnamed Rational System . . .* (Leeds, 1838).

Lovett, William.
: *Life and Struggles of William Lovett, in His Pursuit of Bread, Knowledge and Freedom.* First ed. 1876 (1967).
- *Social and Political Morality* (1853).

McCormac, Henry.
: *On Improving the Moral and Physical Condition of the Working Classes* (Belfast, 1830).

Macauley, Elizabeth Wright.
  Address to the King, Legislature, and Population of the United Kingdom, on the Subject of an improved System of mental Cultivation, claiming the particular Attention of Parents, but most especially of young Mothers: delivered . . . September 30th, 1828 (1828).
- *Autobiographical Memoirs* (1834 and 1835).
- *Facts against Falsehood, Being a Brief Statement of Miss Macauley's Engagements at the Winter Theatre; the Subterfuges by which she has been driven from the regular exercise of her profession and withheld from at least two-thirds of the Public of this Metropolis, etc . . .* (1824).
- *Lecture addressed to the Inhabitants of Surrey and Southwark, delivered at the New Surrey and Southwark Institution . . . July 29th, 1832* (1832).
- *Poetical Effusions* (1812).
Martin, Emma.
  Baptism a Pagan Rite (1844).
- *The Bible No Revelation, or the inadequacy of language to convey a message from God to man* (?1845).
- *A Few Reasons for Renouncing Christianity and Professing Infidel Opinions* (?1850).
- *First/Second Conversation on the Being of God* (?1850).
- *A Funeral Sermon Occasioned by the Death of Richard Carlile, preached at the Hall of Science, City Road, London* (1843).
- *God's Gifts and Man's Duties* (1843).
- *The Missionary Jubilee Panic and the Hypocrites' Prayer, Addressed to the Supporters of Christian Missions* (1844).
- *The Punishment of Death* (1849).
- *Religion Superseded, or the Moral Code of Nature Sufficient for the Guidance of Man* (?1844).
Matthews, Richard.
  Is Marriage Worth Perpetuating? The Ninth of a Series of Lectures against Socialism . . . under the Direction of the Committee of the London City Mission (1840).
Morgan, John Minter.
  Hampden in the Nineteenth Century, 2 vols. (1834).
Morrison, Frances.
  The Influence of the present Marriage System upon the Character and Interests of Females contrasted with that proposed by Robert Owen, Esq., A Lecture delivered in the Social Institution, . . . Manchester, . . . 2nd September, 1838 (Manchester, 1838).
Noyes, J.H.
  Strange Cults and Utopias of Nineteenth Century America (title of first 1870 ed.: *History of American Socialisms*), edited and with an introduction by M. Holloway (New York, 1966).

Owen, Robert.

> *An Address . . . Delivered at the City of London Tavern, April 12th, 1830* (1830).

- *An Address . . . delivered at the great Public Meeting, held at the National Equitable Labour Exchange . . . on lst May, 1833 . . .* (1833).
- *The Book of the New Moral World, containing the Rational System of Society*, Pt.I (1836).
- *The Book of the New Moral World*, Pts. II, III (1842).
- *The Book of the New Moral World*, Pts. IV–VII (1844).
- *The Catechism of the New Moral World* (Manchester, 1838).
- *The Future of the Human Race; Or, a Great Glorious and Peaceful Revolution, Near at Hand, to be Effected Through the Agency of Departed Spirits of Good and Superior Men and Women* (1853).
- *Lectures on an Entire New State of Society: comprehending an Analysis of British Society, relative to the Production and Distribution of Wealth; the Formation of Character; and Government, Domestic and Foreign* (1830).
- *Lectures on the Marriages of the Priesthood of the Old Immoral World, delivered in the Year 1835, before the Passing of the New Marriage Act* (Leeds, 1835).

  (Second and Third Editions, Leeds 1838 and 1839).

  (Fourth Edition): *Lectures on the Marriages of the Priesthood . . . with an Appendix containing the Marriage System of the New Moral World* (Leeds, 1840).

- *Life of Robert Owen, By Himself*. First ed. 1857. Reprinted, with an introduction by M. Beer (1920).
- *Mr Owen's proposed Arrangements for the distressed Working Classes, shown to be Consistent with Sound Principles of Political Economy . . .* (1819).
- *Mr Owen's report to the Committee for the Association for the Relief of the Manufacturing and Labouring Poor . . .* (1817).
- *A New View of Society; or Essays on the Principle of the Formation of Character*. First ed. 1813. Edited and with an introduction by VAC Gattrell (Harmondsworth, 1969).
- *Observations on the Effect of the Manufacturing System: with Hints for the Improvement of those Parts of It which are most injurious to Health and Morals* (1815).
- *Outline of the Rational System of Society*, in *Social Tracts* no. 7 (1838).
- *Report to the County of Lanark of a Plan for relieving Public Distress and removing Discontent . . .* First ed. 1821. Edited and with an introduction by VAC Gattrell (Harmondsworth, 1969).
- and John Brindley. *What is Socialism? . . . a correct Report of the Public Discussion between Robert Owen and Mr J. Brindley . . . January, 1841 . . .* (1841).

– and Rev. J.H. Roebuck. *Public Discussion between Robert Owen . . . and the Rev. J.H. Roebuck, of Manchester . . .* (Manchester, 1837).

Owen, Robert Dale.
Divorce: being a Correspondence between Horace Greeley and Robert Dale Owen (New York, 1960).
– *Moral Physiology; or, a brief and plain Treatise on the Population Question* (New York, 1830).
– *Situations: Lawyers, Clergy, Physicians, Men and Women* (New York, 1830).
– *Threading My Way. Twenty-Seven Years of Autobiography* (1874).

Pearson, George.
The Progress and Tendencies of Socialism (Cambridge, 1839).

Petrie, George.
The Works of George Petrie, comprising Equality, a Poem . . . with a Portrait and Biographical Memoir by R.E. Lee (?1836).

Rational Society.
Full Account of the Farewell Festival given to Robert Owen, on his departure for America (1844).

Reid, James R.
Exposure of Socialism. A Refutation of the Letter on Harmony Hall, by 'One who has whistled at the Plough', which appeared in the Morning Chronicle of the 13th December Last; with an Appendix of Facts regarding Socialism . . . (1843).

Roalfe, Matilda.
Law Breaking Justified (1844).

Saint-Simon, Henri.
New Christianity, translated and introduced by James E. Smith (1834).

Shorter, Thomas.
Confessions of a Truth-Seeker (1859).

Simmons, G.
The Working Classes (1849).

Smith, Rev. James Elishama.
Lecture on a Christian Community, delivered . . . at the Surrey Institution (1833).

Social Hymns, for the Use of the Friends of the Rational System (Manchester, 1835).

Somerville, Alexander.
Notes from the farming Districts. No. XVII. A Jouney to Harmony Hall, in Hampshire, with some Particulars of the Socialist Community, to which the Attention of the Nobility, Gentry, and Clergy, is earnestly requested (1842).

Southey, R.
'Doctrine de Saint Simon', *The Quarterly Review*, no. LXXXIX (April-July 1831).

- *Sir Thomas More; or, Colloquies on the Progress and Prospects of Society.* 2 vols. (1829).

Southwell, Charles.

Confessions of a Freethinker (?1850).
- *An Essay on Marriage; Addressed to the Lord Bishop of Exeter* (?1840).
- *Socialism made easy; or, a plain Exposition of Mr Owen's Views* (1840).

Thompson, William.

Appeal of One-Half the Human Race, Women, against the Pretensions of the other Half, Men, to retain them in political and thence in civil and domestic Slavery; in Reply to a paragraph of Mr Mill's celebrated 'Article on Government' (1825).
- *An Inquiry into the Principles of the Distribution of Wealth most conducive to Human Happiness; applied to the newly proposed system of Voluntary Equality of Wealth* (1824).
- *Labor Rewarded. The Claims of Labor and Capital conciliated: or, how to secure to Labor the whole Products of its Exertions . . .* (1827).
- *Practical Directions for the speedy and economical Establishment of Communities on the Principles of Mutual Cooperation, united Possessions and Equality of Exertions and of the Means of Enjoyments* (1830).

Tristan, Flora.

Promenades dans Londres (Paris, 1840).

Tufnell, Edward.

Character, Object, and Effects of Trades Unions (1834).

Warden, Benjamin.

Rewards of Industry (1832).

Wheeler, Anna.

'Letter from a Pioneer Feminist', reprinted and with an introduction by Stephen Burke, *Studies in Labour History*, vol. 1. no. 1 (1976).

Whitwell, Stedman.

Description of an architectural Model from a Design by ----, for a Community upon a Principle of United Interests as advocated by Robert Owen . . . (1830).

Wright, Frances.

An Address to young Mechanics, as delivered in the Hall of Science, 13th June, 1830 (New York, 1830).
- *Course of Popular Lectures* (New York, 1829).
- *Explanatory Notes, Respecting the Nature and Objects of the Institution of Nashoba, and of the Principles Upon Which it is Founded* (New York, 1830).

Wright, Henry.

Man's Appeal to Woman (1842).
- *Marriage and its Sanctions* (1840).

4. Newspapers And Periodicals

The Anti-Socialist Gazette, and Christian Advocate (Chester, 1841–1842).

The Apostle and Chronicle of the Communist Church (Isle of Man, 1848).

The Associate (1829–1830).

The Birmingham Co-operative Herald (Birmingham, 1829–1830).

The Birmingham Labour Exchange Gazette (Birmingham, 1833).

The British Co-operator; or, Record and Review of Co-operative and Entertaining Knowledge (1830).

The Communist Chronicle and Communitarian Apostle (1843).

Co-operative Magazine and Monthly Herald (1826–29).

The Co-operator (also known as the *Brighton Co-operator*) (Brighton, 1828–1830).

The Crisis; or, the Change from Error and Misery, to Truth and Happiness (1832–1834).

The Christian Lady's Magazine (1840).

The Destructive and Poor Man's Conservative (1833).

The Economist; a Periodical Paper Explanatory of the New System of Society Projected by Robert Owen, . . . and of a Plan of Association for Improving the Condition of the Working Classes, . . . (1821–1822).

The Educational Circular and Communist Apostle (1841–1842).

The Evangelical Magazine and Missionary Chronicle (1838–1841).

The Free Thinker's Information for the People (1840–41).

The Gauntlet (1833–1834).

The Herald of the Rights of Industry (Manchester, 1834).

Herald to the Trades' Advocate and Cooperative Journal (Glasgow, 1830–1831).

The Investigator (1834).

The Lion (1828–1829).

The London City Mission Magazine (1835–1852).

The London Social Reformer (1840).

The Magazine of Useful Knowledge and Co-operative Miscellany (1830).

The Manchester and Salford Advertiser (Manchester, 1838–1841).

Midland Representative and Birmingham Herald (Birmingham, 1830–1832).

The Monthly Repository (1830–35).

The Movement : Anti-Persecution Gazette and Register of Progress (1834–45).

The New Age, Concordium Gazette and Temperance Advocate (1843–1844).

The New Harmony Gazette (New Harmony, Ind., 1825–1828); continued as *The New Harmony and Nashoba Gazette or the Free*

Enquirer (1828–1829); continued as *The Free Thinker* (New York, 1829–1835).

The New Moral World . . . developing the Principles of the Rational System of Society (November 1834 – October 1835); continued as *The New Moral World Or Millennium* (October 1835 – October 1836); continued as *The New Moral World and Manual of Science* (October 1836 – June 1837; Manchester June 1837 – June 1838; Birmingham June – October 1838); continued as *The New Moral World* (Birmingham, October 1838 – July 1839); continued as *The New Moral World, or Gazette of the Universal Community Society of Rational Religionists* (Leeds, July 1839 – June 1842; London, July 1842 – February 1845; Harmony, Hants., February – August 1845; London, August – September 1845); continued as *The Moral World and Advocate of the Rational System of Society* (August – November 1845).

The Northern Star (Leeds, 1837–1844).

The Oracle of Reason (1841).

The Pioneer: or, Trades' Union Magazine (Birmingham, London, September 1833 – July 1834); continued as *The Pioneer; or Grand National Consolidated Trades' Union Magazine* (July–August 1834); continued as *The Pioneer and Official Gazette of the Associated Trades' Union* (September, 1834).

The Poor Man's Advocate, and People's Library (Manchester, 1832–1833).

The Poor Man's Guardian (1831–1835).

The Promethean; or Communitarian Apostle (1842).

The Prompter (1830–1831).

The Rational Religionist, and Independent Inquirer into Social and Political Economy, Religion, Science and Literature (Manchester, 1841).

The Reasoner (1846–1853).

The Register for the First Society of Adherents to Divine Revelation at Orbiston (Edinburgh, Orbiston, 1825–1827).

The Republican (1819–1820).

The Sheffield Iris (Sheffield, January 1838 – December 1841).

The Shepherd, a London Weekly Periodical, illustrating the Principles of Universal Science (1834–1835).

The Social Pioneer; or, Record of the Progress of Socialism (Manchester, 1839).

Some Account of the Progress of the Truth As It is In Jesus (Mountmelick, 1843–1844).

Star in the East (Wisbech, 1836–1840).

The Times (1820–1846).

Trades Newspaper and Mechanics' Weekly Journal (1825–1827).

The Union: a Monthly Record of Moral, Social and Educational Progress (1842–1843).

The Union Exchange Gazette. By the Union Exchange Society . . . (1829).

The United Trades' Co-operative Journal (Manchester, 1830).

The Voice of the People. By an Association of Working Men (Manchester, 1831).

The Voice of the West Riding (Huddersfield 1833–1834).

The Westminster Review (1825–1840).

The Working Bee and Herald of the Hodsonian Community Society (Manea Fen, 1839–1841).

5. Other Primary Sources

Astell, Mary.
   Reflections on Marriage (1700).
Balfour, C.L.
   Women and the Temperance Reformation (1849).
   – *A Whisper to a Newly-Married Pair* (1850).
Bamford, Samuel.
   Early Days (1848).
Bauer, C. and L. Ritt. eds.,
   Free and Ennobled : Source Readings in the Development of Victorian Feminism (Oxford, 1979).
Bodichon, B.
   The Most Important Laws Concerning Women (1854).
Bradlaugh, Charles.
   Five Dead Men Whom I Knew (1884).
Bradlaugh Bonner, Hypatia.
   Charles Bradlaugh, A Record Of His Life and Work by His Daughter, 2 vols. (1894).
Burke, E.
   A Letter from the Right Honourable Edmund Burke to a Noble Lord (1796).
Butler, Josephine, ed.,
   Women's Work and Women's Culture (1869).
Can Women Regenerate Society? (1844).
Cappe, Catherine.
   Observations on Female Friendly Societies.
Campbell, T.C.
   The Battle of the Press, as Told in the Story of the Life of Richard Carlile, By His Daughter (1899).
Carter, Thomas.
   Memoirs of a Working Man (1845).
Checkland, S.G. and E.O.A., eds.,
   The Poor Law Report of 1834 (Harmondsworth, 1974).
Clarke, C. Allen.
   The Effects of the Factory System. First ed. 1899 (1913).

Cobbett, William.
  Advice to Young Men and (Incidentally) to Young Women in the Middle and Higher Ranks of Life (1830).
Dall, Caroline H.
  Woman's Rights under the Law (1861).
Eden, Sir F.M.
  The State of the Poor, 2 vols. (1797).
Eliot, George.
  Adam Bede. First ed. 1859 (New York, 1961).
Ellis, J.B.
  Free Love and Its Votaries (San Francisco, 1870).
Ellis, Mrs Sarah Stickney.
  The Women of England (1838).
Engels, F.
  Socialism : Utopian and Scientific. First English ed. 1880, in K. Marx and F. Engels, *Selected Works* (New York, 1969).
Evans, J.
  A Sketch of the Various Denominations of the Christian World (1841).
Faucher, L.
  Manchester in 1844 : Present Condition and Future Prospects (1844).
Galton, F.W.
  Select Documents Illustrating the History of Trade Unionism : 1: The Tailoring Trade (1896).
Gaskell, P.
  Artisans and Machinery : the Moral and Physical Condition of the Manufacturing Population (1836).
  – *The Manufacturing Population of England : Its Moral, Social, and Physical Conditions* (1833).
Gisborne, Thomas, M.A.
  An Enquiry into the Duties of the Female Sex (1813).
Godwin, William.
  Enquiry into Political Justice (1793).
  – *Memoirs of the Author of 'A Vindication of the Rights of Woman'* (1798).
Greeley, Horace.
  Recollections of a Busy Life (New York, 1868).
Greer, Sarah.
  Quakerism, or the Story of My life (Dublin, 1851).
Hertz, F.
  'Mechanics Institutes for Working Women', *Transactions of the National Association for the Promotion of Social Science, 1859* (1860).

Hole, James.
    An Essay on the History and Management of Literary, Scientific and
    Mechanics Institutes (1853).
Jameson, Anna.
    Winter Studies and Summer Rambles, 3 vols. (1838).
Kelly, Thomas.
    Thoughts on the Marriages of the Labouring Poor (1806).
Lawson, Joseph.
    Letters to the Young on Progress in Pudsey (Stanninglen, 1887).
Lewis, Sarah.
    Woman's Mission (1839).
Malthus, Thomas.
    An Essay on the Principle of Population (1798).
Mant, Richard.
    The Female Character, A Sermon preached in the Parish Church of
    St James, Westminster . . . on behalf of the Burlington Female
    Charity School (1821).
Martineau, Harriet.
    Autobiography (1877).
  - Biographical Sketches (1869).
  - 'Female Industry', Edinburgh Review, vol. CCXXII (1859).
  - Society in America. 3 vols. (1837).
Marx, K. and F. Engels.
    The Manifesto of the Communist Party. First ed. 1848 (Moscow,
    1977).
Mayhew, Henry.
    London Labour and the London Poor, 4 vols. (1861).
Meyrick, F.
    The Outcast and Poor of London (1858).
Mill, James.
    An Essay on Government. First ed. (in the Supplement to the
    Encyclopedia Brittanica) 1821, edited and with an introduction by
    Ernest Barker (Cambridge, 1937).
Millar, John.
    The Origin of the Distinction of Ranks (1777).
Milne, J.D.
    Industrial and Social Employment of Women in the Middle and
    Lower Ranks (1870).
More, Hannah ('Will Chip').
    Village Politics (1792).
Morgan, Lady.
    Woman and Her Master (1844).
Paine, Thomas.
    Rights of Man (1791–92).

'A Philanthropist'.
  Domestic Tyranny or Woman in Chains (1841).
Place, Francis.
  Autobiography, edited by Mary Thale (Cambridge, 1972).
Polwhele, Richard.
  The Unsex'd Females. First ed. 1793 (New York, 1800).
Radcliffe, Mary Anne.
  The Female Advocate (1810).
Razzell, P.E. and R.W. Wainwright, eds.
  The Victorian Working Class : Selections from Letters to 'The Morning Chronicle' (1973).
Report of Select Committee on Artisans and Machinery. Parliamentary Papers (1824).
Richardson, R.J.
  The Rights of Woman (1840).
Ross, Rev. J.
  The Parish of St James Pockthorpe with a Statement of its Conditions and Wants . . . etc (Norwich, 1854).
Seymour, Alice.
  The Express . . . containing the Life and Divine Writings of the Late Joanna Southcott, 2 vols. (1909).
Shaw, Sir Charles.
  Replies to Lord Ashley, M.P., Regarding the Educational and Moral and Physical Condition of the Labouring Classes (1843).
Shaw, William.
  An Affectionate Pleading for England's Oppressed Women Workers (1850).
Shelley, P.B.
  Queen Mab, A Philosophical Poem, with Notes (1813).
Smith, Mary.
  The Autobiography of Mary Smith : Schoolmistress and Nonconformist (Carlisle, 1892).
Southcott, Joanna.
  The Answer of the Lord to the Powers of Darkness (1802).
  – *Copies and Parts of Copies of Letters and Communications, Written from Joanna Southcott and Transmitted by Miss Townley to Mr W. Sharp in London* (1804).
  – *A Dispute Between the Woman and the Powers of Darkness* (1802).
Spence, Thomas.
  The Right of Infants; or, the Imprescriptable RIGHT of MOTHERS to such share of the Elements as is sufficient to enable them to suckle and bring up their Young (1797).
Storey Farrar, A.
  A Critical History of Freethought in Reference to the Christian Religion (1862).

Tonna, Charlotte Elizabeth.
   The Wrongs of Woman (1843).
Thompson, E.P. and E. Yeo, eds.
   The Unknown Mayhew (Harmondsworth, 1973).
Trimmer, Sarah.
   The Oeconomy of Charity (1787).
Vaughan, Robert.
   The Age of Great Cities (1843).
Wakefield, Priscilla.
   Reflections on the Present Condition of the Female Sex with Suggestions for its Improvement (1798).
Wilberforce, William.
   A Practical View of the Prevailing Religious System of Professed Christians in the Higher and Middle Classes in this Country, Contrasted with Real Christianity (1797).
Wollstonecraft, Mary.
   An Historical and Moral View of the Origins and Progress of the French Revolution (1795).
   – *Letters Written During a Short Residence in Sweden, Norway and Denmark* (1796).
   – *Maria or the Wrongs of Woman.* First ed. 1798 (New York, 1975).
   – *A Vindication of the Rights of Man in a letter to the Right Honourable Edmund Burke* (1790).
   – *A Vindication of the Rights of Woman* (1792).
'A Woman' (Mrs Richard Napier?).
   Women's Rights and Duties Considered with Relation to Their Influence on Society and on Her Own Condition, 2 vols. (1840).
Young, Arthur.
   An Enquiry into the State of the Public Mind (1798).

Secondary Sources

1.   Published Books And Articles

Adburgham, A.
   Women in Print (1972).
Alexander, Sally.
   and Anna Davin. 'Feminist History' (Editorial), *History Workshop*, no. 1 (1976).
   – and Anna Davin and Eve Hostettler. 'Labouring Women: a Reply to Eric Hobsbawm', *History Workshop*, no. 8 (1979).
   – 'Women's Work in Nineteenth Century London', in Juliet Mitchell and Ann Oakley, eds., *The Rights and Wrongs of Women* (Harmondsworth, 1976).

Anderson, Michael.
  Family Structure in Nineteenth Century Lancashire (Cambridge, 1971).
Anderson, O.
  'The Incidence of Civil Marriage in Victorian England and Wales', *Past and Present*, no. 96 (1975).
Anderson-Smith, W.
  'Shepherd' Smith the Universalist: the Story of a Mind (1892).
Aries, P.
  Centuries of Childhood (Harmondsworth, 1973).
Armytage, W.H.
  Heavens Below: Utopian Experiments in England, 1560–1960 (1961).
  – 'The Journalistic Activities of J. Goodwyn Barmby between 1841 and 1848', *Notes and Queries*, CCI (1956).
  – 'Manea Fen; an Experiment in Agrarian Communitarianism, 1838–1841', *Bulletin of the John Rylands Library*, XXXVIII, no. 2 (1956).
Balleine, G.R.
  Past Finding Out: The Tragic Story of Joanna Southcott and Her Successors (1956).
Banks, J.A.
  Prosperity and Parenthood, a Study of Family Planning Among the Victorian Middle Classes (1954)
  and O. *Feminism and Family Planning in Victorian England* (Liverpool, 1964).
Barker, Ambrose.
  Henry Hetherington (1938).
Barrett, M. and M. McIntosh.
  'The "Family Wage": Some Problems for Socialists and Feminists', *Capital and Class*, no. 11 (1980).
Barrow, Logie.
  'Socialism in Eternity: Plebian Spiritualists, 1835–1913', *History Workshop*, no. 9 (1980).
Basch, F.
  Relative Creatures (1974).
Beales. H.L.
  The Early English Socialists (1933).
Beer, Max.
  A History of British Socialism 2 vols. (1919).
Bestor, A.E.
  Backwoods Utopias: the Sectarian and Owenite phases of Communitarian Socialism in America: 1663–1829 (Philadelphia, 1950).
  – 'The Evolution of the Socialist Vocabulary', *Journal of the History of Ideas*, vol. 9, no. 3 (1948).

List of Sources

Black, A.
'Education before Rochdale: (2) the Owenites and the Halls of Science', *Cooperative Review*, XXIX, no. 2 (February 1955).

Bloch, Ivan.
A History of English Sexual Morals (1936).

Brailsford, H.N.
Shelley, Godwin and Their Circle (1913).

Bridenthal, R. and C. Koonz.
Becoming Visible: Women in European History (1977).

Briggs, Asa.
The Age of Improvement, 1783–1867 (1959).

– ed., *Chartist Studies* (1959).

– 'The Language of Class in Nineteenth Century England', in A. Briggs and J. Saville, eds., *Essays in Labour History* (1960).

Burnett, J., ed.,
Useful Toil: Autobiographies of Working People from the 1820s to the 1920s (1975).

Burstyn, J.N.
'Religious Arguments Against the Higher Education of Women in England, 1840–1890', *Women's Studies*, vol. 1, no. 1 (1972).

Burton, Hester.
Barbara Bodichon, 1827–1891 (1949).

Bury, J.B.
A History of Freedom of Thought (1913).

Butt, J. ed.,
Robert Owen, Prince of Cotton Spinners (Newton Abbot, 1971).

Checkland, S.G.
The Rise of Industrial Society in England (1964).

Church, L.F.
More About the Early Methodist People (1949).

Clark, Alice.
The Working Life of Women in the Seventeenth Century. First ed. 1919 (1968).

Cole, G.D.H.
Attempts at General Union, 1818–1834 (1953).

– and R. Postgate. *The British Common People* (1961).

– *A Century of Co-operation* (Manchester, 1945).

– *Richard Carlile*, Fabian Society Biographical Series Number 13 (1943).

– *A History of Socialist Thought: Vol.1: The Forerunners, 1789–1850* (1953).

– *Robert Owen* (1925).

Cole, Margaret.
Robert Owen of New Lanark, 1771–1858 (1953).

Collier, Frances.
The Family Economy of the Working Classes in the Cotton Industry, 1784–1833 (Manchester, 1964).
Cone, B.
The English Jacobins (New York, 1968).
Cott, Nancy F.
'Passionlessness: an Interpretation of Victorian Sexual Ideology, 1790–1850', *Signs*, vol. 4, no. 2 (Winter 1978).
Courtney, J.E.
The Adventurous Thirties (1933).
Cowie, Grace and E. Royle.
'Emma Martin: Socialist, Free Thinker and Women's Rights Advocate' in J. Bellamy and J. Saville, eds., *The Dictionary of Labour Biography*, vol. 6, 1982.
Crossick, G.
An Artisan Elite in Victorian Society: Kentish London 1840–1880 (1978).
Crow, Duncan.
The Victorian Woman (1971).
Davies, Ross.
Women and Work (1975).
Devey, Louisa.
Life of Rosina, Lady Lytton (1887).
Dobson, C.R.
Masters and Journeymen: a Prehistory of Industrial Relations, 1717–1800 (1980).
Drake, Barbara.
Women in Trade Unions (1920).
Draper, Hal and Anne G. Lipow.
'Marxist Women Versus Bourgeois Feminism', *The Socialist Register* (1976).
Edholm, F., K. Young and O. Harris.
'Conceptualising Women', *Critique of Anthropology*, vol. 3, no. 9–10 (1977).
Edwards, M.M. and R. Lloyd-Jones.
'N.J. Smelser and the Cotton Factory: a Reassessment', in N.B. Harte and K.G. Ponting, eds., *Textile History and Economic History* (Manchester, 1973).
Fabian Society.
The Economic Foundations of the Women's Movement (1914).
Field, John.
'Private Schools in Portsmouth and Southampton 1850–1870', *Journal of Educational Administration and History*, vol. X, no. 2. (July, 1978).
Flexner, Eleanor.
Mary Wollstonecraft (New York, 1972).
Flinn, M.W. and T.C. Smout.
Essays in Social History (Oxford, 1974).

Foster, John.
  Class Struggle and the Industrial Revolution (1974).
Fox-Genovese, Elizabeth.
  'Property and Patriarchy in Classical Bourgeois Political Theory',
  Radical History Review, vol. 4, no. 2-3 (1977).
Frow, Edmund and Ruth.
  'Women in the Early Radical and Labour Movement', *Marxism
  Today* (April, 1968).
Fryer, Peter.
  The Birth Controllers (1965).
Gammage, R.G.
  History of the Chartist Movement, 1837-1854 (1854).
Gans, J.
  'Les Relations entre Socialistes de France et d'Angleterre au debut du
  XIX Siecle', *Le Mouvement Social*, no. 46 (1964).
Garnett, R.G.
  *Co-operation and the Owenite Socialist Communities in Britain,
  1825-45* (Manchester, 1972).
Gattey, C.N.
  Gaugin's Astonishing Grandmother: a Biography of Flora Tristan
  (1970).
George, M.D.
  London Life in the Eighteenth Century (Harmondsworth, 1965).
George, Margaret.
  One Woman's Situation (Illinois, 1970).
Gillis, John.
  'Servants, Sexual Relations and the Risks of Illegitimacy in London,
  1801-1900', *Feminist Studies*, vol. 5, no. 1 (1979).
Gordon, Linda.
  *Woman's Body, Woman's Right: A Social History of Birth Control
  in America*. First ed. 1976 (Harmondsworth, 1977).
Gray, Robert Q.
  The Labour Aristocracy in Victorian Edinburgh (Oxford, 1976).
Grisewood, H., ed.,
  Ideas and Beliefs of the Victorians (1949).
Haller, W. and M.
  'The Puritan Art of Love', *Huntingdon Library Quarterly*, vol. 5
  (1942).
Hair, P.E.H.
  'Bridal Pregnancy in Rural England in Earlier Centuries', *Population
  Studies*, 20 (November 1960).
Hall, Catherine.
  'The Early Formation of Victorian Domestic Ideology', in S.
  Burman, ed., *Fit Work for Women* (1979).

Hammond, J.F. and L.B.
   The Skilled Labourer, 1760–1832 (1920).
   – *The Age of the Chartists, 1832–1854: A Study of Discontent* (1930).
Hampson, Norman.
   The Enlightenment (Harmondsworth, 1968).
Harrison, B.
   Drink and the Victorians: the Temperance Question in England, 1815–1872 (1971).
Harrison, J.F.C.
   The Early Victorians, 1832–51 (1971).
   – *Learning and Living, 1790–1960* (1961).
   – 'A New View of Mr Owen', in S. Pollard and J. Salt, eds. *Robert Owen, Prophet of the Poor* (1971).
   – *Robert Owen and the Owenites in Britain and America: The Quest for the New Moral World* (1969).
   – *The Second Coming: Popular Millenarianism, 1780–1850* (1979).
   – ed., *Utopianism and Education: Robert Owen and the Owenites* (New York, 1968).
Hartmann, Heidi.
   'Capitalism, Patriarchy, and Job Segregation', in Z. Eisenstein, ed., *Capitalist Patriarchy and the Case for Socialist-Feminism* (1979).
Hayek, F.A.
   John Stuart Mill and Harriet Taylor: Their Friendship and Subsequent Marriage (1951).
Henriques, U.R.Q.
   'Bastardy and the New Poor Law', *Past and Present*, no. 37 (1967).
Hewitt, Margaret.
   Wives and Mothers in Victorian Industry (1958).
Hill, Christopher.
   Puritanism and Revolution (1958).
   – *The World Turned Upside Down* (1972).
Himes, Norman E.
   'The Place of J.S. Mill and Robert Owen in the History of English Neo-Malthusianism', *Quarterly Journal of Economics* (Spring 1928).
Hobsbawm, E.J.
   The Age of Revolution: Europe 1789–1848 (1962).
   – and G. Rudé. *Captain Swing* (Harmondsworth, 1973).
   – *Industry and Empire* (1968).
   – *Labouring Men: Studies in the History of Labour* (1964).
   – 'Man and Woman in Socialist Iconography', *History Workshop*, no. 6 (1978).
   – 'The Labour Sects', in *Primitive Rebels* (Manchester, 1978).
Holcombe, Lee.
   Victorian Ladies at Work (Newton Abbot, 1973).

Hollis, Patricia.
    Class and Conflict in Nineteenth Century England, 1815–1850 (1973).
    – *The Pauper Press, a Study in Working Class Radicalism of the 1830s* (1970).
    – *Women in Public: the Women's Movement, 1850–1900* (1979).
Houghton, W.E.
    The Victorian Frame of Mind, 1830–70 (Princeton, 1957).
Hufton, Olwen.
    'Women in Revolution, 1789–1796', *Past and Present*, no. 53 (1971).
Hutchins, B.L.
    – and A. Harrison. *A History of Factory Legislation* (1903).
    – *Women in Modern Industry*. First ed. 1915 (Wakefield, West Yorkshire, 1978).
Inglis, K.S.
    'Patterns of Worship in 1851', *Journal of Ecclesiastical History*, XI (1960).
James, Louis.
    Fiction for the Working Man, 1830–1850 (1963).
Janes, R.M.
    'On the reception of Mary Wollstonecraft's *A Vindication of the Rights of Woman*', *Journal of the History of Ideas*, vol. 39, no. 2 (1978).
Harriet, Jay.
    Robert Buchanan (1903).
Johnson, J.T.
    'The Covenant Idea and the Puritan View of Marriage', *Journal of the History of Ideas*, vol. xxxii, no. 2 (1971).
Johnson, Richard.
    ' "Really Useful Knowledge": radical education and working-class culture, 1790–1848', in J. Clarke, C. Critcher and R. Johnson, eds., *Working-Class Culture: Studies in History and Theory* (1979).
Kelly, T.
    George Birkbeck (Liverpool, 1957).
Kent, C.
    'The Whittington Club: a Bohemian Experiment in Middle-Class Social Reform', *Victorian Studies*, vol. XVIII, no. 1 (September 1974).
Kiernan, V.
    'Evangelicalism and the French Revolution', *Past and Present*, no. 1 (1952).
Killham, John.
    Tennyson and 'The Princess': Reflections of an Age (1958).
Kitson Clark, G.
    The Making of Victorian England (1962).

Kitteringham, J.
>'Country Work Girls in Nineteenth Century England', in R. Samuel, ed., *Village Life and Labour* (1975).

Knox, R.A.
>*Enthusiasm, A Chapter in the History of Religion* (Oxford, 1950).

Land, Hilary.
>*The Family Wage* (Eleanor Rathbone Memorial Lecture, Leeds, 1979).

Lane, Charles A.
>*The Life and Bibliography of Joanna Southcott* (1912).

Lane, M.
>*Frances Wright and the 'Great Experiment'* (Manchester, 1972).

Laquer, T.W.
>*Religion and Respectability: Sunday Schools and Working-Class Culture, 1780–1850* (New Haven, 1976).

Laslett, Peter.
>*The World We Have Lost* (1965).

Lewenhak, Sheila.
>*Women and Trade Unions: an Outline History of Women in the British Trade Union Movement* (1977).

Lichtheim, George.
>*The Origins of Socialism* (1968).

Liddington, J. and J. Norris.
>*One Hand Tied Behind Us: the Rise of the Women's Suffrage Movement* (1978).

Lockwood, G.
>*The New Harmony Movement*. First ed. 1905 (New York, 1971).

McCabe, Joseph.
>*Life and Letters of George Jacob Holyoake*, 2 vols. (1908).

McGregor, O.R.
>*Divorce in England* (1957).

McLaren, Angus.
>'Contraception and the Working Classes: the Social Ideology of the English Birth Control Movement in its Early Years', *Comparative Studies in Society and History*, vol. 18, no. 2 (April 1976).
>– 'Phrenology : Medium and Message', *The Journal of Modern History*, vol. 46. no. 1 (1974).

Malmgreen, Gail.
>*Neither Bread Nor Roses: Utopian Feminists and the English Working Class, 1800–1850* (Brighton, 1978).

Marcus, Steven.
>*The Other Victorians* (1966).

Mayne, E.G.
>*The Life and Letters of Anne Isabella, Lady Noel Byron* (1929).

Medick, Hans.
'The Proto-industrial Family Economy: the Structural Function of Household and Family During the Transition from Peasant Society to Industrial Capitalism', *Social History*, no. 3 (1976).

Melcher, M.F.
The Shaker Adventure (Princeton, 1941).

Menger, Anton.
The Right to the Whole Produce of Labour, translated by M.E. Tanner (1899).

Miliband, Ralph.
'The Politics of Robert Owen', *Journal of the History of Ideas*, vol. XV, no. 2 (April 1954).

Miller, P.J.
'Women's Education, Self-Improvement, and Social Mobility; a Late Eighteenth Century Debate', *British Journal of Educational Studies*, no. 20 (October 1972).

Mineka, F.E.
The Dissidence of Dissent: 'The Monthly Repository', 1806–1838 (Chapel Hill, 1944).

Mitchell, Juliet.
Woman's Estate (Harmondsworth, 1971).
– 'Women and Equality' in J. Mitchell and A. Oakley, eds., *The Rights and Wrongs of Women* (Harmondsworth, 1976).

Morris, R.J.
Class and Class Consciousness in the Industrial Revolution, 1780-1850 (1969).

Morton, A.L. and J. Saville.
'John Goodwyn and Catherine Isabella Barmby: Chartists, Feminists, and Utopian Socialists' in J. Bellamy and J. Saville, eds., *The Dictionary of Labour Biography*, vol. 6, 1982.

Morton, A.L. and G. Tate.
The British Labour Movement (1956).

Morton, Arthur L.
The English Utopia (1952).
– *The Life and Ideas of Robert Owen* (1962).

Muncy, R.L.
Sex and Marriage in Utopian Communities : Nineteenth Century America (Bloomington, 1973).

Musson, A.E.
British Trade Unions, 1800–1875 (1972).
– 'The Ideology of Early Co-operation in Lancashire and Cheshire', *Transactions, Lancashire and Cheshire Antiquarian Society*, LXVIII (1958).
– and R.G. Kirkby. *The Voice of the People: John Doherty, 1798–1854: Trade Unionist, Radical and Factory Reformer* (Manchester, 1975).

Nairn, Tom.
'The English Working Class' in Robin Blackburn, ed., *Ideology in Social Science* (1972).

Nesbitt, G.L.
Benthamite Reviewing: the First Twelve Years of the Westminster Review (1934).

O'Brien, Jo.
Women's Liberation in Labour History: A Case Study from Nottingham, Spokesman Pamphlet no. 24 (n.d.).

O'Malley, I.B.
Women in Subjection: A Study of the Lives of Englishwomen before 1832 (1933).

O'Neill, W.L.
Everyone was Brave: The Rise and Fall of Feminism in America (Chicago, 1969).

Oliver, W.H.
'The Consolidated Trades' Union of 1834', *Economic History Review*, 2nd series, XVII, no. 1 (August 1964).
– 'The Labour Exchange Phase of the Co-operative Movement', *Oxford Economics Papers*, n.s. X (1958).
– 'Robert Owen and the English Working Class Movements', *History Today* (November 1958).

Oren, Laura.
'The Welfare of Women in Labouring Families: England, 1860–1950', in M.S. Hartmann and L. Banner, eds., *Clio's Consciousness Raised* (New York, 1974).

Pankhurst, R.K.P.
'Anna Wheeler: a Pioneer Socialist and Feminist', *Political Quarterly*, vol. 25., no. 2 (1954).
– *The Saint-Simonians, Mill and Carlyle* (1957).
– *William Thompson, 1775–1833, Britain's Pioneer Socialist, Feminist and Co-operator* (1954).

Pearsall, Ronald.
The Worm in the Bud: the World of Victorian Sexuality (1969).

Peel, John.
'Birth Control and the Working Class Movement', *Bulletin of the Society for the Study of Labour History*, no. 7 (1963).

Perkin, H.J.
The Origin of Modern English Society, 1780–1880 (1969).

Perkins, A.J.G. and T. Wolfson.
Frances Wright, Free Enquirer (New York, 1924).

Peterson, M. Jeanne.
'The Victorian Governess', in M. Vicinus, ed., *Suffer and Be Still: Women in the Victorian Age* (Bloomington, 1973).

Phillips, M. and W.S. Tomkinson.
English Women in Life and Letters (1926).

Pinchbeck, Ivy.
   Women Workers and the Industrial Revolution, 1750–1850. First
   ed. 1930 (1969).
Plummer, Alfred.
   Bronterre: a Political Biography of Bronterre O'Brien, 1804–1864
   (1971).
Podmore, F.
   Robert Owen: a Biography, 2 vols. (1906).
Pollard, S.
   *The Genesis of Modern Management: A Study in the Industrial
   Revolution* (1965).
   – 'Nineteenth Century Co-operation: from Community Building to
   Shopkeeping', in A. Briggs and J. Saville, eds., *Essays in Labour
   History* (1967).
   – and J. Salt, eds.,
   Robert Owen, Prophet of the Poor (1971).
Postgate, R.W.
   The Builders' History (1923).
Pratt, E.A.
   Pioneer Women in Victoria's Reign (1897).
Prochaska, F.K.
   'Women in English Philanthropy, 1790–1830', *International Review
   of Social History,* vol. 19 (1974).
Prothero, I.
   *Artisans and Politics in Early Nineteenth Century London: John
   Gast and his Times* (Folkestone, 1979).
   – 'Chartism in London', *Past and Present,* no. 44 (1969).
   – and T.M. Parrsinen. 'The London Tailors' Strike of 1834 and the
   Collapse of the Grand National Consolidated Trades Union: a
   Police Spy's Report', *International Review of Social History,* no. 22
   (1977).
   – 'William Benbow and the Concept of the "General Strike" ' *Past and
   Present,* no. 63 (1974).
Quinlan, M.J.
   Victorian Prelude (New York, 1941).
Racz, Elizabeth.
   'The Women's Rights Movement in the ˙French Revolution',
   Women: a Journal of Liberation, vol. 2, no. 1 (1970).
Ramelson, Marion.
   The Petticoat Rebellion: a Century of Struggle for Women's Rights
   (1967).
Ranum, O. and P. eds.,
   *Popular Attitudes Toward Birth Control in Pre-Industrial France
   and England* (New York, 1972).
Rattray Taylor, Gordon.
   The Angel-Makers (1973).

Reiss, Erna.
>   *The Rights and Duties of Englishwomen* (Manchester, 1934).
Robertson, J.M.
>   *A History of Freethought in the Nineteenth Century*, 2 vols. (1929).
Robertson, Mary S.
>   *The True Story of Joanna Southcott* (Ashford, Middsx., 1923).
Rose, R.B.
>   'John Finch, 1784–1857', *Transactions of the Historical Society of Lancashire and Cheshire*, vol. 109 (1957).
Rover, Constance.
>   *Love, Morals and the Feminists* (1970).
Rowbotham, Sheila.
>   'Feminism and Labour History', in R. Samuel, ed., *People's History and Socialist Theory* (1981).
>   – *Hidden from History: Three Hundred Years of Women's Oppression and the Fight Against It* (1973).
>   – *Women, Resistance and Revolution* (1973).
>   – and Jeffrey Weeks. *Socialism and the New Life: The Personal and Sexual Politics of Edward Carpenter and Havelock Ellis* (1977).
>   – *Woman's Consciousness, Man's World* (Harmondsworth, 1973).
Rowe, D.J.
>   *London Radicalism, 1830–34* (1970).
Royle, E.
>   'Harriet Teresa Law (1831–97): Feminist, Secularist and Radical', in J. Bellamy and J. Saville, eds., *Dictionary of Labour Biography*, vol. 5 (1979).
>   – ed., *The Infidel Tradition from Paine to Bradlaugh* (1976).
>   – *Radical Politics 1790–1900: Religion and Unbelief* (1971).
>   – *Victorian Infidels* (Manchester, 1974).
Rudé, George.
>   *The Crowd in History, 1730–1848* (New York, 1964).
Rudkin, O.D.
>   *Thomas Spence and his Connections* (1927).
Sadlier, M.
>   *Bulwer Lytton and his Wife* (1933).
Saville, J.
>   'J.E. Smith and the Owenite Movement, 1833–34' in S. Pollard and J. Salt, eds., *Robert Owen, Prophet of the Poor* (1971).
>   – 'Robert Owen on the Family', in M. Cornforth, ed., *Rebels and Their Causes* (1978).
Scott, Joan and Louise Tilly.
>   *Women, Work and Family* (New York, 1978).
>   – 'Women's Work and the Family in Nineteenth Century Europe', *Comparative Studies in Society and History*, 17 (1975).
Scott, W.S.
>   *The Bluestocking Ladies* (1947).

Shipley, Stan.
    Club Life and Socialism in Mid-Victorian London, History Workshop Pamphlet, no. 5 (Oxford, 1971).
Shorter, E.
    'Female Emancipation, Birth Control and Fertility in European History', *American History Review*, no. 18 (1973).
    – *The Making of the Modern Family* (1977).
Silver, Harold.
    The Concept of Popular Education : a Study of Ideas and Social Movements in the Early Nineteenth Century (1965).
Simon, Brian.
    The Two Nations and the Educational Structure, 1780–1870. First ed.1960 (1974).
Smelser, N.J.
    Social Change in the Industrial Revolution (1959).
Stedman Jones, G.
    'Class Expression versus Social Control? A Critique of Recent Trends in the Social History of "Leisure" ', *History Workshop*, no. 4 (1977).
    – 'Class Struggle and the Industrial Revolution', *New Left Review*, no. 90 (1975).
    – 'Working-Class Culture and Working-Class Politics in London, 1870–1900; Notes on the Remaking of a Working Class', *Journal of Social History*, vol. 7. no. 4 (1974).
Stenton, D.M.
    The English Woman in History (1957).
Strachey, Ray.
    The Cause (1928).
Stone, L.
    The Family, Sex and Marriage in England, 1500–1800 (1977).
Storr, M.S.
    Mary Wollstonecraft et le Mouvement Féministe dans la Litterature Anglaise (Paris, 1932).
Tawney, R.H.
    The Radical Tradition (1964).
Taylor, Barbara.
    'The Men are as Bad as Their Masters . . .': Socialism, Feminism and Sexual Antagonism in the London Tailoring Trade in the Early 1830s', *Feminist Studies*, vol. 5, no. 1 (1979).
    – 'The Woman-Power: Religious Heresy and Feminism in Early English Socialism', in S. Lipshitz, ed., *Tearing the Veil* (1978).
Thibert, M.
    Le Féminisme dans le Socialisme Français (Paris, 1929).
Tholfsen, T.R.
    Working-Class Radicalism in Mid-Victorian England (1976).

Thomas, Clara.
    Love and Work Enough: the Life of Anna Jameson (1967).
Thomas, Keith.
    'The Double Standard', *Journal of the History of Ideas*, vol. xx.
    no. 2 (1959).
    – 'Women in the Civil War Sects', *Past and Present*, no. 13 (1958).
Thompson, David.
    Nonconformity in the Nineteenth Century (1972).
Thompson, Dorothy.
    The Early Chartists (1971).
    – 'Women and Nineteenth Century Radical Politics: a Lost Dimen-
    sion', in J. Mitchell and A. Oakley, eds., *The Rights and Wrongs of
    Women* (Harmondsworth, 1976).
Thompson, E.P.
    The Making of the English Working Class (Harmondsworth, 1972).
    – 'Romanticism, Utopianism and Moralism: the Case of William
    Morris', *New Left Review*, no. 99 (1976).
    – 'The Moral Economy of the English Crowd in the Eighteenth
    Century', *Past and Present*, no. 50 (1971).
    – *The Poverty of Theory and Other Essays* (1978).
Thompson, Patricia.
    The Victorian Heroine, A Changing Ideal, 1837–1873 (1956).
Thrupp, S.L.
    Millennial Dreams in Action: essays in comparative study (The
    Hague, 1962).
Tillotson, Kathleen.
    Novels of the Eighteen-Forties (Oxford, 1954).
Tomes, Nancy.
    'A "Torrent of Abuse": Crimes of Violence Between Working-Class
    Men and Women in London, 1840–75', *Journal of Social History*,
    vol. 11, no. 2 (1978).
Tylecote, M.
    The Mechanics Institutes of Lancashire and Yorkshire before 1851
    (Manchester, 1957).
Underwood, A.C.
    A History of the English Baptists (1947).
Utter, R.P. and G.B. Needham.
    Pamela's Daughters (1937).
Vicinus, Martha, ed.,
    Suffer and Be Still: Women in the Victorian Age (Bloomington,
    1973).
    – *A Widening Sphere* (Bloomington, 1977).
Walkowitz, J.
    Prostitution and Victorian Society: Women, Class and the State
    (Cambridge, 1980).

Ward, J.T.
   Popular Movements, 1830–1850 (1978).
Wardle, Ralph.
   Mary Wollstonecraft (Kansas, 1951).
Waterman, W.R.
   Frances Wright (New York, 1924).
Watt, Ian.
   The Rise of the Novel (Harmondsworth, 1977).
Wearmouth, R.F.
   Methodism and the Struggle of the Working Classes, 1850–1900 (Leicester, 1954).
   – *Methodism and the Working-Class Movements of England, 1800–50* (1937).
Webb, Beatrice.
   The Co-operative Movement in Great Britain (1891).
Webb, Catherine.
   ed. *Industrial Cooperation: the Story of a Peaceful Revolution. Being an Account of the History, Theory, and practice of the Co-operative Movement in Great Britain and Ireland* (Manchester, 1904).
   – *The Woman with the Basket* (1927).
Webb, R.K.
   The British Working Class Reader, 1780–1848 (1955).
   – *Harriet Martineau: a Radical Victorian* (1960).
Webb S. and B.
   The History of Trades Unionism (1926).
Weeks, J.
   Sex, Politics and Society: the Regulation of Sexuality since 1800 (1981).
Weiner, J.H.
   The War of the Unstamped: The Movement to Repeal the British Newspaper Tax, 1830–1836 (1969).
Swift, Wesley F.
   'The Women Itinerant Preachers of Early Methodism', *Proceedings of the Wesley Historical Society*, vols. 28 and 29 (1952–1953).
Wheeler, J.M.
   Biographical Dictionary of Freethinkers of All Ages and Nations (1889).
Wickwar, W.H.
   The Struggle for the Freedom of the Press (1928).
Williams, Gwyn.
   Artisans and Sans Culottes (1968).
   – 'Rowland Detrosier: a working-class infidel, 1800–1834', *Borthwick Papers*, no. 28 (York, 1965).

Williams Raymond.
    Culture and Society, 1780-1950 (1958).
Williford, Miriam.
    'Bentham on the Rights of Women', *Journal of the History of Ideas*,
    vol. 26, no. 2 (1975).
Yeo, Eileen.
    'Robert Owen and Radical Culture', in S. Pollard and J. Salt, eds.,
    Robert Owen, Prophet of the Poor (1971).
Yeo, Stephen.
    'A New Life: the Religion of Socialism in Britain, 1883-1896',
    History Workshop, no. 4 (1977).
Zaretsky, Eli.
    Capitalism, the Family and Personal Life (1976).

2. Unpublished Works

Brown, Arthur.
    'Suffolk Chartism' (essay, 1974).
Corfield, Kenneth.
    'Some Social and Radical Organizations among Working-Class
    Women in Manchester and District, 1790-1820' (BA Thesis, Univer-
    sity of Birmingham, 1974).
Gadian, D.S.
    'A Comparative Study of Popular Movements in North West
    Industrial Towns, 1830-50' (Ph D Thesis, Lancaster University,
    1976).
Gillis, John.
    'Resort to Common-Law Marriage in England and Wales,
    1700-1850' (1980, chapter from a forthcoming book on plebian
    marriage in Britain).
Malmgreen, G.K.
    'Anne Knight, 1786-1862' (essay, 1978).
    – 'Women's Suffrage in England: Origins and Alternatives,
    1792-1851' (M A Thesis, Hull University, 1975).
Martin, C.E.
    'Female Chartism: A Study in Politics' (M A Thesis, University of
    Wales, 1973).
Morris, D.C.
    'The History of the Labour Movement in England, 1825-1852' (Ph D
    Thesis, University of London, 1952).
Nicholson, Elizabeth.
    'Working Class Women in Nineteenth Century Nottingham,
    1815-1850' (B A Thesis, University of Birmingham, 1974).
Oliver, W.H.
    'Organizations and Ideas Behind the Efforts to Achieve a General

Union of the Working Classes in England in the Early 1830s' (Ph D Thesis, Oxford, 1957).

Osterud, N.G.
'Women's Work in Nineteenth Century Leicester: A Case Study in the Sexual Division of Labour' (1978).

Prothero, Iorwerth.
'London Working-Class Movements, 1823–1848' (Ph D Thesis, Cambridge, 1966).

Rowley, J.J.
'Drink and the Public House in Urban Nottingham' (paper presented to the Society for the Study of Labour History Annual Conference, November 1977).

Salt, John.
'Isaac Ironside and Education in the Sheffield Region in the First Half of the Nineteenth Century' (M A Thesis, University of Sheffield, 1960).

Saywell, Ruby.
'The Feminist Idea in England, 1789–1833' (M A Thesis, University of London, 1936).

Sever, John.
'James Morrison of the Pioneer' (typed manuscript in the British Museum, 1963).

Stedman Jones, Gareth.
'The Limits of a Proletarian Theory in England before 1850' (1978).
  – 'Utopian Socialism Reconsidered – Science and Religion in the Early Socialist Movement' (forthcoming, *History Workshop*).

Tyfield, Thelma.
'The Industrial Revolution, Women and Education' (B Ed Thesis, University of Cape Town, 1935).

Wolfe, Stephen F.
'The Rhetoric of English Radicalism' (Ph D Thesis, York University, 1976).

Yeo, Eileen.
'Quest for the New Moral World' (M A Thesis, University of Wisconsin, 1963).
  – 'Social Science and Social Change: A Social History of some Aspects of Social Science and Social Investigation in Britain, 1830–1890' (PhD Thesis, University of Sussex, 1972).

[No. 3. Vol. I.]   [Price 1d.]

NEW TRACTS FOR THE TIMES:

OR,

WARMTH, LIGHT, AND FOOD FOR THE MASSES.

THE DEMAND

FOR

THE EMANCIPATION OF WOMAN,

POLITICALLY AND SOCIALLY.

BY CATHERINE BARMBY.

" Never will peace and human nature meet
Till, free and equal, man and woman greet
Domestic peace ; and ere this power can make
In human hearts its calm and holy seat,
This slavery must be broken."—SHELLEY.

THE emancipation of the woman, the man, and the child, is now demanded. By the prophets of the future, and the advanced minds of the present, is the demand made. To the emancipation of woman, neither forgetting the man nor the child, is this tract dedicated. By it I would assist to raise woman from her political serfdom to the freedom of the electoral vote. By it I would assist to raise woman from her ecclesiastic slavery to the liberty of the teacher and the priestess. And by it I would assist in raising woman from the domestic drudge and helot to being with her husband the sharer of equal rights, and the possessor of the noble independence of her own industry. Woman requires this elevation ; she is at present degraded by society, her destiny is unacknowledged. To this elevation she has a right, for she possesses both desires and capacities, which are, in fact, the power and the strength to obtain, and to preserve it : and this elevation she shall enjoy, without a good hope, is a falsehood, and an ardent industry in her great behalf, is, contrary to every law of the universe, an unproductive thing.

Who is not aware of the unhappy condition of society ? By whom are its evils not felt ? In this country of class distinctions above all others, where are they exempt from its Lazarus sores, its Promethean rock and chain ? Where are they, we repeat, who in the veritableness of their humanity, can lift up their heads and say, " society thou hast done me no wrong."

If, then, all suffer—if genius, talent, skill, and industry—if integrity of motive, and purity of sentiment can have no abiding place; if, in short, society beholds no glory in the grass, or splendour in the flower, are we not just in saying that the root of societarian condition, whether it be its religion, its politics, its institutions, or whatever else it may, is founded in error. And if, on examination, all are discovered to be suffering from this mighty error, how great the regeneration that has to be effected—which, in its reckoning, leaves not one untold!

Society suffers, that is, man and woman suffers; this we repeat, because this truth, like all other truths, is valuable to know. To some it appears that others are exempt from suffering; that while clouds ever attend them, the sun shines unceasingly upon others; so do the poor recognise the destinies of the rich. Why, why am I so persecuted, and wherefore dost thou escape? But may there not be putrid sores under the robe of purple and fine linen? may not the vulture be within, where all is fair without?

I believe that, in dissecting the anatomy of society, woman's sufferings, from its evil construction, are found to be the greatest; the sphere of man's action is larger, and, therefore, were the amount similar, the suffering in the case of woman, must exceed that endured by him. There is, too, a reverberation, if I may so express myself, of man's sufferings upon woman, and hence is created for her intense misery: I would only enumerate that, is there depression of trade, or loss and bankruptcy, she is deeply affected; are drunkenness and profligacy the vices of her husband, they are visited upon her with a fearful retribution. To her ills so many smaller streams contribute, that an ocean of magnitude indeed is ever rolling its waves against her.

Woman does not enjoy the common rights, which, as an influential portion capable of adding to, or detracting from this world's greatness, she has the positive capacity of possessing and exercising. Her ecclesiastic, her domestic, her political rights, where are they? in what code of laws are they written?

WE DEMAND THE TOTAL EMANCIPATION OF THE WOMAN.
We demand the emancipation of woman,

1st. *Politically*.
2nd *Ecclesiastically*.
3rd. *Domestically*.

1st. We demand the political emancipation of woman, because it is her right, possessing as she does with man, a three-fold being, sentimental, intellectual, and physical, because she is subject to like wants, expected to pay the same taxes, taxation without representation being tyranny, and because all other laws act as severely, many more severely upon her than upon man. We demand, therefore, that the mind of woman be acknowledged in the electoral and administrative departments of legislation, with which she is compelled to act in accordance, or to suffer the penalty.

2nd. We demand the ecclesiastical emancipation of woman, because from her strong percipient power she has the ability to educate, and thus to benefit society; because the rights of the child demand the ecclesiastical freedom of woman, and because the heart of woman is destined to illumine and hallow the feelings of goodness when addressing itself to the assembly, as the mind or intellect of man is destined to strengthen the being, and to impart to it wisdom. We have the priest, we therefore demand the priestess, the woman teacher of the word, the woman apostle of God's Law!

3rd. We demand the domestic emancipation of woman, that is to say, we claim her freedom at the hearth and the board. We demand for her independence in the pursuit of those labors for which she is most particularly adapted, and which alone can be her security from the tyranny of her husband, and her preservation from the oppressions of society. In fine, we demand the emancipation of the hand of woman from mere household drudgery, so that her sentiment and intellect be protected, and with them her ministerings of good be insured. Who, in the face of day, will object to the demand we have made for the political, ecclesiastical, and domestic emancipation of woman ? What arguments can they bring which would even afford a shadow of defence ? In so false a view none can be urged ? That woman is not the equal of man, who can assert ? Her mind, sentiment, and feeling, are fully acknowledged ; and present enlightenment must prevent any denial to her equality. What have not women done in the political world ? What are they not capable of doing ? Can all men act as a Roland, or a Charlotte Corday have done ? Or at this epoch, when selfishness, ignorant selfishness is the prevailing evil, how many men would act with the pure nobility of our Harriet Martineau ? Plato, in his Commonwealth, has thought it reasonable to admit woman into an equal share of the dignities and offices with man. And what has been said by Cato of his countrymen, may be said of the men of all countries. " The Romans," spoke he, " govern the world ; but it is the women that govern the Romans." " All the great revolutions," wrote Rousseau, " were owing to woman." For proof of woman's political ability, much testimony can be found were it necessary. Even the great man, Bonaparte, was afraid of the great woman, De Stael. Is it said that sanction, full sanction cannot be given to woman's possessing the franchise ; I would ask on what basis is the right of voting established ? Is it to oppose the attainment of happiness, or is it to promote the great societarian good—the good of man and woman ? Who will presume to say, that woman, with her fine sensibilities, is not to the utmost as capable of comprehending and appreciating what is necessary and desirable for her particular happiness as man can possibly be ? And if, as I have sometimes heard, there is a distinction between them, how can man pronounce what is good for woman, when he claims no identity with her ? But this is too ridiculous, and as monstrous as is the spirit of the laws from which she suffers. The sun is shining, its influence is felt, its power known, and yet, at the same time, a denial is given to its capacity of diffusing light and warmth : thus Solon-like does man act in withholding his assent to the political independence of woman. Give her the vote, nor forget that her influence has directed many to bestow it, wisely and unwisely, but as her wish decided. That woman was not admitted to the senate of Rome, or to the assemblies of ancient Greece, is no reason why she should be deprived of her attendance at our Courts of Legislature. Where is our enlightenment if it be not shown in accordant action ? The carriage moves steadily when its wheels roll together ; so will society's progression be uniform in its course, when its interests co-operate.

Why, in the name of that holiness which it professes to teach, are women excluded from the priesthood ? Energy and faith, grace and eloquence, courage and devotion, are the well-proved attributes of woman. And shall these, the finest elements of inspired teaching, be forbid to do their ministry ? When every thing around proclaims the gross and the material, why is not woman working on her mission in the pulpit and the lecture-room ? We ask it, and would, if in our power, obtain a reply from those who should give it to us—from the Pope and the archbishop, from the preacher of whatever sectarian creed, we would know it ? The society of Freemasons, with many others which adopt its example, why do not they admit women ? they declare their object to be good, universal in its tendency, and elevating in its comprehension. If good, and if universal, why are not women accepted by them ? It is the same as saying that they belong not to the universal, and that the knowledge of good they are better without. Every society that so acts, must, in so swerving from their written law, as well as the grand law of the Universe, fail in the true object—the elevation of society in its human individuality, as manifested in a two-fold manner by man and woman in union. In early times the most refined religion, the Pagan, admitted women as its priestesses ; and the Roman church has admitted women to saintship ; they have their Saint Martha as well as their Saint Peter, their Saint Theresa as well as their Saint John, their Holy Mother of God as well as God their Father ! How few clergymen can be found so conscientiously devoted to the performance of their duties, in whatever danger it might cast them, as were these women so chosen for saintship and patronship. The courageous and good Sisters of Charity, what a light through their pure deeds is shed upon Roman Catholicism! Oh, believe it, a religion to interpenetrate, to be known and felt even as it were the circulation which is our life's-blood—a religion so sacred, and yet so sensible, and actual, can never be ours till woman is chosen the priestess, and man is rendered the true priest. Woman the priestess and man the priest. The grand call is to establish this holy order, this new priesthood! Let man assist for the cause is his, let woman assist for the cause is her's and her children's.

How much of woman's time is spent in household drudgery. No short period of remitment can the day afford to her, in which to worship the Lares, the household gods or goods, the pleasances and the delights of domestic life! How poor the education she can impart to her children, how limited the companionship she can afford to her husband. Thus, the man and the child suffer because the domestic existence of woman is so cramped and confined; and the women, the poor women of the working class, with their intelligence undeveloped, toiling, ever toiling on, are told by men who know all the wretchedness of their condition, that home and the fire-side, duty to their children, and love to their husbands, must be the never-failing spring, the bright star to yield them light in the darkest darkness! Oh, it is sad to think of the helotage which women suffer, more sad to think of the startling doom which every moment of the passing hour condemns the mind, the beautiful, entire affection, which society contains, to lingering or to sudden death!

To effect the domestic emancipation of woman, the present organization of society is inefficient. The proper divisions of industry cannot be established, while the barriers of commerciality are so thickly planted. It is in a new order of societary destiny that we place our faith, in the redemption of woman from slavery: and it is the knowledge which has been acquired of the just application of labor, skill, and property, which is the basis of our faith.

The world has shamefully used woman; well does Mrs. Grimstone write :—

> " Shame on the world! In madness, or in pride,
> Has woman's mental birthright been denied.
> Be she the weaker, kindly give her might;
> Be she man's equal, then it is her right :
> Whether or not, 'tis policy to dower
> Woman with wisdom since she must have power—
> The power to sear or soothe, to blight or bless,
> To mar or make all moral happiness."

Whether or not 'tis policy in man to emancipate woman, we stay not to inquire. She demands her own emancipation, politically, ecclesiastically, and domestically. And now we proceed to suggest those means which we deem to be the most efficient for feminine emancipation.

The political emancipation of woman first demands our attention. This can only be acquired by her possession of the suffrage equally with man. The means for obtaining this are similar to the means adopted by the men. There is now being agitated an electoral document, entitled the PEOPLES' CHARTER, advocating a general masculine suffrage. Women must, before they give it their support, insist upon the insertion of clauses advocating general feminine suffrage as well; so that the document becomes a requirement for the universal adult franchise; and thus advocates the electoral rights of the man and the woman together.

To the ecclesiastical emancipation of woman, secondly, our thought is called. The means for effecting this, the most important, appear to us to consist in the formation of a "woman's society" in every city, town, and village possible. In this society women might converse, discuss, and speak upon their rights, their wrongs, and their destiny; they might consult upon their own welfare, and that of the great human family, and thus prepare each other for the mission of the apostle in society at large, and for the right use of that influence which they must ever exercise.

Lastly, the domestic emancipation of woman requires our attention. The means for this are to be found only in that communitive state of society of which these tracts are the advocate. In the present state of competition, man will ever deprive woman, bereft of common advantages with him, of a fair chance of success in industry, while in a community of goods and labors properly organised, woman as well as man would have the liberty of working in those functions which Nature has assigned her ; and possessing, in virtue of her common works, a share in the common property, she will become independent as man in all the relations of domestic life.

Thus, then, it will be seen we deem the means for the complete emancipation of women to be—

Politically—the obtaining the addition of the demand for woman suffrage to the Peoples' Charter.

Ecclesiastically—the institution of woman societies wherever possible ; and

Domestically—the establishment of communization.

Finally, we would recommend the publication of " The Woman's Magazine," for the diffusion and organization of these means for obtaining woman's just emancipation.

I would add, that what is here written has been written in earnestness. Harsh I have long known the destinies of woman to be; and that is a knowledge which creates sympathy, and causes inquiry. There is a time when the light breaks in upon us, shewing the darkness in which we are enveloped ; there is another period shining yet more brightly, when we perceive that the darkness needs not an eternal but a limited endurance—that the gloominess may be dispersed, and the light be made perfect unto salvation. Love and Wisdom are the lights of the world; the masculine and feminine principles which blent in the man, the woman, and the child, should rule over the society. Who can describe the action continued under these influences ? The individual mind must fail, even under the most powerful will, in the attempt ; society, viewed as one mind in its mental wholeness, cannot compass the embodiment of that actualization which the union of the spiritual and the material will evolve, in language of any kind. It is beyond the reach of human eloquence. Woman, I trust, will bestow her attention on the subject of this paper. It demands the fullest consideration. With feelings deeply centered in her behalf, I intreat of her not to let time flee without the demonstration of the minor attempts which must precede the great measures that will follow. There are no words, however strong, could they be written upon the living heart in characters enduring as their life, that I would hesitate to give to call forth in the mind of woman the knowledge of her wrongs, and the power she possesses in herself to procure their redression, and her own and her childrens' salvation.

I have made the demand for the emancipation of woman, let her hear it and work out her own redemption. Against any manifestations of decision of a unitive character on her part, the strongest obstacles are most certain to be raised. Man has hitherto possessed all direct power in the regulation of societary destiny. He has been taught to consider that he alone is capable of moving its vast machinery.

Thus then it must be remembered that custom and prejudice are prepared to oppose and combat with any demonstrations in favor of woman's emancipation. But knowing this, let the shield of defence be proportionately strong, and all apprehension will be removed. Cowardice is the opposite of courage ; and courage is the defence of the good and the wise in all ages. And here it must be stated, that there is no cowardice so mean and base as that betrayed towards woman in the journals of this country, whenever the written expression or spoken word admits an opportunity. The conductors of all the leading papers in this land, know that woman's feelings are susceptible of the slightest assailment. Hence, whenever woman has made any, the slightest attempt to secure feminine emancipation, to offend her delicacy becomes their peculiar care. And how greatly does this spirit of cowardice pervade the literature of the day, and destroy the efficacy which belongs to it? As to woman, the law assists the journalists and literatures in their unrighteous attacks; for by the law, the equitable temporal law of this country, woman is left fully exposed to the slanders of malignity and falsehood!

Custom and prejudice are the tyrants that must be overcome. Man is their slave, and woman is so likewise. To exemplify the state and position of the women of all classes, the men of the working class will serve me, as the men of the upper and wealthiest classes are opposed to their progression, to their obtaining a knowledge of their injuries, and a desire for the redression of them, so are the men in all conditions whatever, equally as strongly influenced in crushing every thought, and every hope that may spring from it, of amelioration and good in the heart of woman; any expression of her wrongs, or any question as to their amendment. But as I have said before, *from prejudice* this misconstruction of good arises; and this same prejudice, which prevents the looking with an equal share of regard upon the interests of one set of men, and another set of men, is reigning in the mind of woman at this moment, and blinding her to the light of the most righteous truths. Of the women of this country, how few may be thought upon as willing to endure the price that reformation or revolution of any kind must involve. To the labourers their work and exertion will bring increase, and increase will establish power, which is the mighty agent for all societies and all worlds.

Only a short time, comparatively speaking, it is only a short time since the working men came forward to declare their own grievances, and to appeal in their own voices for the reformation of these grievances. They met with persecutions, but they were then and still are capable of supporting themselves through them; since that time much power has increased to their ranks. If they are not more loved by those above them in rank and wealth, they certainly are more feared by them. And fear may by some of the varied changes that are ever on the wing in time and space produce love, brotherly love—the grand desideratum—between the men of all classes, the brethren of every creed.

What we hope and desire is that woman should set a new example in the demonstration of her rising intelligence, and for this end that she makes truth or justice—justice for the man, the woman, and the child, the basis of every demand she seeks permanently to establish. Filled with this determination, earnest in its success as the sole hope of her reward, how pure would be her eloquence, because how truthful; how sacred her advocacy, when her preachings were directed not to gain victory for a party, but to win all mankind to love the one great family of all the dwellers upon earth.

The demand for woman's religious and social emancipation cannot be brought forward until primarily the right of the suffrage has been claimed by her. And this demand my faith is that she will soon make. In this important declaration who will be her supporters beyond herself? The working men, or great will be their dereliction; for should they not at once perceive the justice of her demand, it will prove indeed that evil example worketh much mischief: as the Tories have evilly acted towards them, so would they in thus proceeding be acting evilly towards woman.

Not only is woman in the present state the slave of political institutions, she is also the serf of social regulations. Custom, even in her dress, tyrannises over her throughout all countries. Custom forces the Japanese women to gild their teeth, it makes those of some Indian tribes paint them red or black; custom compels the women in Greenland to color their faces with blue and yellow; it plaisters the face of the Russian women with paint; it cramps the feet of the Chinese females; and it makes the Turkish women tinge their finger nails and dye their eye-brows. In Venice the Council of Ten forced the signoras of their republic into wearing any costume they decided upon ; and in the present civilized countries caprice and fashion habit our sex in robes as many as they are frequently ridiculous. This must not be in the future. The free woman must be adorned with a new dress ; uniting freedom and delicacy, utility and grace. The emancipation of woman from the garb of her slavery will be the outward sign of her liberty.

The equality of woman and man must be our rallying cry. Woman's slavery under Muhummedism, and her subaltern situation under Christianity, must be repealed, and her equality with man be acknowledged under Communism. But although we would equalize, we would not identify the sexes. Such identification would be unnatural, unbeautiful, and accordant with the miserable state of the sexes among the lowest of the low orders. Woman and man are two in variety and one in equality. Their physical frames are as various as are the stems of the poplar and of the oak, but yet should the sun of equal right be alike shining upon them. In woman, sentiment ; in man, intellect, variously prevail ; but society should equally provide, through its institutions, that the sentiment of the woman should be strengthened by intellect, and the intellect of the man refined by sentiment; in fine, society should be so organised that without identifying the sexes, it should give to them equal educational opportunities and equal general advantages in every sphere.

In conclusion, we sum up the subject of this tract.

1st. We have shown the inequality between man and woman, and the injustice practised upon woman in consequence of that inequality in the present state of society, not only politically, but also ecclesiastically and domestically.

2nd. We have demanded the political, ecclesiastic, and domestic emancipation of woman, and shown her right to, and the justice of, this demand.

3rd. We have suggested, as the means for her political emancipation, the addition of the demand for woman-suffrage to the People's Charter.

4th. We have proposed, as the means of her ecclesiastic emancipation, the formation of woman societies in every town and village possible.

5th. We have noticed, as the means of her domestic emancipation, the necessity for her entry into the communitive life.

And, lastly, we have pointed out the establishment of a Woman's Magazine, as a requisite step for the advocacy and formation of these political, ecclesiastic, and domestic means for her complete emancipation.

We appeal now to all who can aid us in the enfranchisement of woman. We appeal to woman especially, as it is her own absolute cause. We appeal also to man, as it is relatively his cause, for without woman is free, man cannot obtain his own liberation. By the yellow buddings of the primrose we know it is ready to burst into flower. By the bud like indications of woman's progress we know she is ready for emancipation. We demand, therefore, the *complete emancipation* of woman.

QUESTIONS TO WOMAN.

TO THE EDITOR OF LVERY LIBERAL PAPER.

Sir,—The succeeding questions, important as they are, will, I trust, have insertion in your truly liberal journal. I address them to the woman class :—

1. Is not the present distribution of labor most severe and unjust as regards woman ; and should there not be demanded a totally new arrangement in its mode ?

2. Is not a union of interests in the industrial department necessary for the correct organization of industry ?

3. Would not the principles of Communization best insure this union of interests ?

4. Would not woman's happiness be increased and rendered permanent by an attention individually paid to her industrial taste and ability?

5. Would not the removal of the Societarian prejudice existing against the exercise of labor by woman, contribute to their sentimental, intellectual, and physical welfare?

6. Has not woman as a component part of society, with interests *at present* individually her own, a claim to the right of the franchise?

7. Has not woman, as a part of humanity, with relations essentially her own, a right to a share in the administration over these relations?

8. Should not the institutions of society be so ordered as to prevent the consideration of money from entering into the important state of marriage?

9. Should not the law of marriage which is love, admit where it is broken, the gospel of love, which is divorce?

10. Should not woman in her relations of maternity and parentage possess a freedom of action?

11. Should not the influence of woman be exerted against the selfishness, cruelty and grossness of the present state of individualization?

12. Should not the influence of woman be directed in favor of the state of Communization, and the immense benefit it will confer upon herself and others?

These questions are made, Sir, with the fullest confidence in woman's high destiny and the capacity she possesses to insure in her varied relations of daughter, wife, and mother, the actualization of that divinest sentiment—"Love ye one another."

I am, Sir, your's respectfully,
CATHERINE BARMBY.

6, *Whittlebury Street, Euston Square, London.*

"While the People's Charter asks but for general male suffrage, the Communitarian requires Universal Adult Suffrage. He recognizes as well, a common right to the franchise, as a common right to property."—*Communist Declaration in favor of Electoral Reform,* published in the PROMETHEAN, No. 1.

"He could not agree with the quibbles of Daniel O'Connell, as they were merely nominal, but in reality he saw nothing but general masculine suffrage in the Chartist demand, while he thought that universal adult suffrage, the franchise for man and woman, was the Electoral Reform wanting."—*Speech of* GOODWYN BARMBY.

"It is Pantheism which teaches or reveals to us that God is the Common Entity, the Universal Being—that his habitation is in the hearts of all human beings—that all are in his image, and that he is all in all; and moreover, that in virtue of this common or universal divine presence in Humanity, all have a communal nature to require, a communal power to exercise, and a communal right to use, the divine boon of the function of the suffrage, universally, both man and woman."—*Address by Goodwyn Barmby in the Cheltenham Free Press.*

"I look with an assured confidence in the reign of social harmony in proportion, as I behold the 'woman power' acknowledged, and its influence provided for as well as that of the 'man power.'"—*Catherine Barmby,* 1841.

"Woman has her distinct wants inseparable from her nature as woman; and those of *accoucheurship* will be best performed by her own sex."—*Societarian Views on the Medical and Surgical Professions, Chap.* 3, *by Goodwyn Barmby.*

"Although Communism asserts the equality of man and woman, and negatives both the slavery of woman under Muhummedanism and her subalternity under Christianism, still it does not pretend to the identifying of the sexes."—*Ibid.*

B. D. COUSINS, PRINTER, 18, DUKE STREET, LINCOLN'S INN FIELDS.

INDEX

Dear E,

As a woman and feminist, I just want to say that I am deeply sorry for whatever stress, pain or anxiety my involvement w/ Na. earlier in the summer may have caused you.

I only began to realize the full significance of N's duplicitous and deceptive personal life in late August, my friend Jane told me that while he was trying to seduce her back in May, he was at the same time telling her of his plans

to break up with
you — and this was
about 3 weeks before
he showed up w/you
at a party on his
birthday. In addition
I discovered that ~~my~~ his
'personal' email account
~~email to him~~ was
~~actually~~ ~~it~~ attached
to an internet dating
service,
(see enclosure). which means he was
he was ~~hypothetically~~ common colma via
While I'm sorry the same
mail box
that he turned out was
to be so deceptive willing
to receive
towards women, I mail
from
want you to know that you.
I hope you are okay
and that, at least in my
opinion, his

ostensible departure
from you was really
his loss. At first I
believed he was mistrusted
his story about
being excluded from
your family, but in the
end I came to
think that he had
really take
you for granted.